Fifty-five Years
in Five Acts

Advisor in music to Northeastern University Press

GUNTHER SCHULLER

Fifty-five Years in Five Acts

My Life in Opera

ASTRID VARNAY

with Donald Arthur

foreword by LAWRENCE LUECK

preface by WOLFGANG WAGNER

Northeastern University Press
BOSTON

Northeastern University Press

Library of Congress Cataloging-in-Publication Data
Varnay, Astrid.
    [Hab mir's gelobt. English]
    Fifty-five years in five acts : my life in opera /
       Astrid Varnay with Donald Arthur.
       p.   cm.
    Translation of: Hab mir's gelobt.
    Includes index.
    ISBN 1-55553-455-4 (cloth : alk. paper)
    1. Varnay, Astrid.   2. Sopranos (Singers)—
Biography.   I. Title: 55 years in 5 acts.
II. Title.

ML420.V29 A3   2000
782.1′092—dc21
[B]   00-042728

Designed by Diane F. Levy

Composed in Electra by Coghill Composition Co.,
Richmond, Virginia. Printed and bound by Maple Press, York,
Pennsylvania. The paper is Sebago Antique, an acid-free stock.

MANUFACTURED IN THE UNITED STATES OF AMERICA
04 03 02 01 00   5 4 3 2 1

To my parents and my husband

CONTENTS

ACKNOWLEDGEMENTS

THIS BOOK CAME ABOUT on the suggestion of our two publisher friends Roland Astor and Claus Obalski, and a number of other friends, new and old, offered their kind assistance in researching the text. Valerie Glazer and Virginia Ahrens refreshed memories of my début, as seen from the standing room area I once haunted as a youngster, and Maestro Erich Leinsdorf shared his memories of the first days of my professional career. András Kürthy, Director of the Hungarian State Opera, helped us contact the theatre archivist Nóra Wellmann, who sent us invaluable information on my parents' early career. When Oliver Golloch subsequently visited Budapest, Ms. Wellmann put him in touch with Agnes Gádor at the Franz Liszt Conservatory of Music, who supplied us with my mother's school records. Later, in Berlin, Oliver unearthed a complete list of performances conducted by Hermann Weigert in that city.

Our research in the Scandinavian countries was initiated by Helena Jungwirth and Clæs-Håkon Ahnsjö and their sons, Fredrik and Matthias Ahnsjö, Kjellaug Tesaker, Ingrid Bjoner, Carsten Hopstock, and Bergljot Kron Bucht. Berit Holth, head of the music library at Oslo University, and Torstein Gunnarsson, Kirsten Flagstad's official biographer, supplied us with enormous quantities of invaluable firsthand information on both my parents' lives in Norway and the true story of Mme Flagstad. Fredrik Ahnsjö, along with Birgit and David Kehoe, kindly translated much of the material we received from up north.

Cesar Arturo Dillón helped us reconstruct my family's stay in Buenos Aires, while John Pennino of the Metropolitan Opera Archives provided us with a wealth of information and photographs from that theatre, starting with my mother's first audition and concluding with my final performance. He also kindly verified everything we wrote about the Metropolitan. Francesca Franchi and Dr. Stephen Ash were most generous with their records of performances at the Royal Opera House, Covent Garden, in London. At the Bayreuth Festival, Gabriele Taut and Erna Pitz in the front office, Peter Emmerich and Sebastian Tiller in the press department, Ana Haffter and Matthias von Stegmann on the stage staff, and, of course, Wolfgang and Gudrun Wagner kindly supplied us with the information we needed from that august establishment. Helga and Hans Hotter generously shared their recollections on a wide variety of subjects—operatic, historical, and personal.

At the Bavarian State Opera, Professor August Everding, Heinrich Bender, Evelyne Harder, Inge Hippmann, Rita Loving, Christine Reif, Ursula Schleuning, David Thaw, and the theatre's archivist, Franz Hajek, all shared both memories and factual information with us, while Claudia and Stefan Biffar gave us factual material on Claudia's father, Professor Joseph Keilberth. Dr. and Mrs. Christian Strauss aided us with recollections of Dr. Strauss's grandfather, Richard Strauss, while Professor and Mrs. Hans Maier and Dr. Wolfgang Doering gave us the material we needed on the *Maximiliansorden*. Sabine Toepffer and Siegfried Lauterwasser shared their magnificent photographs of my performances in Munich and Bayreuth. Daniel F. Tritter in New York and Dr. Benno Keim and Reiner Walch in Munich gave us invaluable legal advice, while Dr. Siegfried Hiemstra and Dr. Fritz Tiller checked all the medical references in the book. Daniel Spiess, John Hunt, and Werner Will provided us with pertinent information on recorded performances, and my dear friends Lys, Randolph, and Victor Symonette shared memories of Düsseldorf and valuable information on Kurt Weill and Lotte Lenya.

Other devoted friends and colleagues without whose help this book of memories would not have been possible include Götz Aumüller, Magdalena Barth, Florian Bender, David Chapman, Richard Dyer, Andrew Farkas, Bruni Hagen-Löbel and Holger Hagen, Elizabeth and Franklin Heller, Helga Hösl-Thaw, Barbara Korn, James and Thomas Levine, Martha Mödl, Marianne Seibel-Neumann and Wolfgang Neumann, Birgit Nilsson, Kit and Ulf Raeder, Estelle and Robert Roth, Annette Rudolf, Toon Schets, Svetlana and Alexander von Schlippe, Rita Shane, Eleanor Steber, Risë Stevens, Bernhard Struckmeyer, Lilian Sukis, Marina de Tiews, Alan Titus, Horst Wandrey, Felicia Weathers, Rita and Kurt Wilhelm, Lotte Zahn, and Bill Zakariasen.

Our German translator, Maurus Pacher, was the conscience of this book from the start of his participation, assiduously re-researching every detail before committing it to paper and seeing to it that no stone had been left unturned to make this volume—in all languages!—a reliable primary source as well as entertaining reading in a style that is anything but ponderous thanks to his adroit pen, his inborn Viennese lightness, and his inexhaustible vocabulary. We translated much of his input for this original English edition. The finishing touches were expertly applied by our ultraproficient editors, Mechthild Frick in Berlin and Ann Twombly in Boston. Many thanks, too, to the books other New England godparents, William Frohlich, Sarah Rowley, and Jill Bahcall.

These memoirs could not have happened without the generosity of Mr. and Mrs. Laurence Lueck and the Wagner Societies that offered us their support. Finally, our everlasting gratitude to A. D. Schwarz, who gave Donald Arthur his first writing lessons, and Noah Webster, who was never at a loss for words.

THERE SHE WAS, Astrid Varnay herself, at a table in the Café Roma in Munich, awaiting our arrival. Although we had never met before, I felt I had known her for years, and indeed I had, if only through the many sound recordings and videos I owned of operas in which she had sung. But seeing her in person and spending several hours in her company that August day in 1999 was one of the great thrills of my life! And it resulted in a decision to make her autobiography available in the original English-language version.

The publication of this book is actually the result of a curious—indeed amazing—chain of events, which I think merits comment here. It all began one day in late 1997 in Honolulu, Hawaii, where I live and serve as president of the local Wagner Society. I received a call from Evelyn Lance, one of our members and an avid Wagner enthusiast. "You won't believe what I just purchased!" she exclaimed. "Sight-unseen, I bought a box of old clippings at a flea market book sale, and when I opened it, I couldn't believe my eyes. The box is jam-full of photo albums and loose clippings, all relating to the career of Astrid Varnay. I'm turning over this collection to you in the hope you can get everything sorted out, as the contents are in rather poor condition."

When I received the box of documents from Ms. Lance, I, too, couldn't believe my eyes. Here were reviews of almost every performance she had ever given, from her Met début on December 6, 1941, as Sieglinde in *Die Walküre*, to her successes at Bayreuth in the fifties and sixties, and on and on until nearly 1970. There were many, many photos and a faded copy of *Der Spiegel* magazine with Astrid Varnay on the cover, not only reviewing her performance as Brünnhilde, but also detailing the entire resumption of the Bayreuth Festival in 1951. There were other magazines, too, with articles about her in half a dozen languages and clippings of many related musical events in which she had taken part.

I soon discovered that this amazing collection had been assembled by Mária Jávor, Astrid Varnay's mother, who had spent her final years living in Honolulu. When she passed away, the albums containing her daughter's clippings, along with many photos, magazines, and personal letters, were all stuffed together by someone into a big cardboard box, which was then stored in the attic of the house where Mme Jávor had lived. It remained there, apparently ignored and forgotten, for twenty-some years until it was finally removed along with unrelated books and other paraphernalia and sent to the flea market to raise money for a local charity. By some wondrous stroke of luck, or perhaps divine providence, a Wagnerian opera lover chanced upon the box and bought it.

It took me over a year to sort through all the documents, removing the very sticky Scotch tape, which had been used to paste many of the reviews into the albums, and cleaning everything to the point that each document could be easily handled, read, and catalogued. What an education I received reading this wonderful collection of reviews, letters, and magazine articles!

It was apparent from the beginning that the entire collection, once made presentable, should be given to Astrid Varnay. Since I had no idea where to send it, I contacted Liese Bauer, the president of the Wagner Society of Northern California, who told me she was reasonably certain Ms. Varnay lived in Munich, but she did not have the address. This was subsequently obtained from Gudrun Wagner in Bayreuth, and the entire collection, carefully packaged, was sent off to Astrid Varnay in early 1999 along with a letter explaining how everything had come into my possession.

Not long after the package was sent, I received a call from her. As you can easily imagine, she was surprised and thrilled to receive this collection and heartily thanked me for sending it. We talked for more than half an hour and finally agreed that my wife and I would visit her the next time we were in Germany. Our get-together took place on August 8, 1999, concurring with another historical event—the total eclipse of the sun, which we all witnessed from Munich's Maximilianstrasse.

I knew that her autobiography had been published in German, but I was surprised to learn from Donald Arthur, her friend and co-author, that, both of them being New Yorkers, they had originally written the book in English. Mr. Arthur then sent me a diskette containing the original English text, and after reading just the prologue, I resolved that the book would have to be published in English as soon as possible. It was simply too good a story, and Astrid Varnay too important an artist, for it not to be available in its original English version.

But first we had to find a willing publisher. Donald Arthur put us in contact with Northeastern University Press. We explained to William Frohlich, the director, that our Wagner Society of Hawaii, along with several other Wagner Societies in the United States, would be willing to underwrite some of the publishing costs. Mr. Frohlich was immediately interested. In fact, this book owes its existence to his fine cooperation and complete support. It would also never have been published without contributions from several Wagner Societies in the United States and a sizable number of individuals within those societies. The names of those societies and individuals appear below.

All of us who helped in the publication of this book are pleased that Astrid Varnay's story, told in her own words in the language in which she wrote it, and unmodified by translation, is finally available to everyone who honors her as one of the greatest Wagnerian sopranos of the twentieth century. It has been a privilege and pleasure to participate in this undertaking.

A majority of the contributions made in support of this book's publication came from the Wagner Society of Hawaii as a group, as well as from the following members who made individual contributions: Mrs. Ruth Ballard, Ms. Nancy Bannick, Mr. and Mrs. Robert Bunn, Mrs. June Chambers, Dr. Julia Cherry, Mr. and Mrs. Herbert Dauber, Ms. Suzanne Engel, Drs. Peter and Mary Kim, Mr. and Mrs. Laurence Lueck, Mr. and Mrs. James McCoy, Mr. and Mrs. Ronald Nagy, Ms. Jean Rolles, Mr. and Mrs. Robert Trankle, and Mrs. Norma "Poni" Watson. In addition, the Wagner Society of Northern California and the Wagner Society of Southern California each made contributions, as did both Dr. Sheldon Huffman and an anonymous donor. We are grateful for their cooperation and thank them for their contributions.

Laurence B. Lueck, President
The Wagner Society of Hawaii
August 15, 2000

PREFACE

IT IS AN HONOR and, of course, a great pleasure to provide a few words of introduction to Astrid Varnay's autobiography. Needless to say, it is completely superfluous to explain her book in any way at this point: you simply have to read it! This is the only way to discover, bit by bit, the rich, many-faceted personality of Astrid Varnay, who with her incomparable artistry has given not only Bayreuth but also the world far more than can be stated in just a few sentences. I am fairly certain she would find any attempt to wax rhapsodic about her a bit much, and it would inevitably prompt a smile or one of her contagious, eternally young outbursts of laughter. Humor is perhaps one of the most outstanding characteristics in this account of her life—indeed a healthy, earthbound, and unpretentious humor, which fits in perfectly with greatness and dignity. She has assembled living memories, which attest to her powerful vitality: nothing seems distant, even if it happened far in the past. In each line we can sense the whole person of Astrid Varnay; each story appears three-dimensionally before the mind's eye of the reader. From beginning to end, the book is an exact mirror image of her character: honest, full of kindness, with justified pride in her accomplishments, raging at the mediocre and half-hearted, loving art, her art, as much as she loves people.

From 1951 on, Astrid Varnay was a key figure in the Bayreuth my brother and I re-established. In the roles she delineated, she set permanent standards of valid interpretation, which still continue to have a profound and lasting effect. For New Bayreuth she was, so to speak, one of the artists "present at the creation" and made a major contribution to returning the Bayreuth Festival in a new way to international recognition after the terrible horrors of the Second World War. She decisively helped shape the image of the Festival, and left behind traces that are still visible to this day, because, then as now, she remains a role model for many participants. In all of this, she never played the diva, never put on airs, but rather comprehended the task she had to fulfill as an ongoing "service to the work," a truly noble attitude in both human and artistic terms. I wish the book many readers. They will be able to draw informative pleasure and pleasurable information from it. "In colorful reflection here we have life"—this quote from Goethe's *Faust* perhaps most distinctly characterizes Astrid Varnay's book.

Wolfgang Wagner
July 10, 2000

Translated from the German by Donald Arthur.

From the Subway to the Stage

To SEE ME RIDING the BMT subway from Greenwich Village to midtown Manhattan around nine o'clock on that cold December morning, anyone might have thought I was just another local New York girl on her way to work. In fact, I was. The only difference was that I was off to a day's work at the Metropolitan Opera House, where I had recently been contracted as a dramatic soprano. Yet, as far as I was concerned, I was going to work the same as the shop girl or the secretary sitting across the aisle from me. After all, opera was the family business.

From earliest childhood, I had become used to tiptoeing around the house on performance days, communicating with my parents in sign language and hushed whispers, to spare their preperformance nerves and make sure they wouldn't have to use their precious voices before they needed them onstage. "Conversation on a performance day," my mother used to say, "is like having to sing an extra act," and Mother was too much of a professional to give away a whole act gratis. My own first stage appearance had been scheduled for shortly after the New Year, on January 9, 1942, as Elsa in Richard Wagner's *Lohengrin*, and I was already in the final stages of intensive preparation, which was why I was going to the opera house this cold Friday morning. At least, that's what I thought.

I stepped out of the south end of the Broadway train and emerged from the station at the Fortieth Street exit. As I came out on the street, I noticed that quite a few friends from my standing room days were already lined up waiting

1

to buy their tickets, despite the early hour. One of the standees indicated that they didn't want to miss the very special matinée scheduled for that Friday afternoon. It was *Don Giovanni* with Bruno Walter's "dream cast": Rose Bampton, Jarmila Novotná, Bidù Sayão, Ezio Pinza, Salvatore Baccaloni, Charles Kullmann, Norman Cordon, and Arthur Kent, in a production staged by Herbert Graf. I made a mental note to slip into the wings and catch a bit of the performance after my *Lohengrin* rehearsal. I was twenty-three years old at the time, and just a glimpse of the captivating Pinza could set a girl up for the rest of the day.

Rounding the corner of Seventh Avenue, I stopped for a moment to watch the sets being unloaded for the coming day, a daily delivery service very few repertory theatres need. This was just one of the many annoyances and inconveniences resulting from the peculiar design of the building. The old Metropolitan Opera House, with its ugly duckling exterior and its golden swan auditorium, had been designed by an architect named Josiah Cleaveland Cady, who specialized in office buildings and churches. The "Met" was his one and only theatre, and while it might have been the most lavish interior structure the city had ever seen, as a working opera house it was a disaster.

The glittering Golden Horseshoe was largely set up so that the more affluent members of the audience could see one another, even if their view of the stage might be impeded by the curvature of the five sweeping balconies or the massive, decorative pillars Cady used to hold the place up. It was even more irksome that the architect had omitted the usual backstage storage space so crucial to operations in a repertory house with at least seven changes of opera a week. It meant the sets had to be kept in a warehouse up in the Bronx and carted to and from the theatre by Erie Transport Company truck convoys running up and down Broadway like camel caravans.

As I passed the back of the building, the stagehands were taking delivery on the rough-hewn Teutonic décor for the following afternoon's *Walküre* performance. When they started unloading the massive ash tree that grows in the middle of Hunding's hut in act 1, a stray dog came over and checked it out. He had probably never seen a real tree in this stone and brick city, but blood will tell, and from the look in his eye, it was clear he considered this piece of scenery a more than adequate alternative to his accustomed fire hydrant. Fortunately for the next day's cast, one of the stagehands shooed the mutt away.

I entered the building through the official Thirty-ninth Street stage door and moved into the heart of the theatre. An elevator that sounded like it

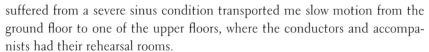

suffered from a severe sinus condition transported me slow motion from the ground floor to one of the upper floors, where the conductors and accompanists had their rehearsal rooms.

Before keeping my appointment with Maestro Erich Leinsdorf, I found an empty room and slipped in there with my pitch pipe to get my voice warmed up. Vocalizing at home in December would have been counterproductive. Even though my mother kept the steam heat down to an acceptable minimum, she still made certain I never stepped out into a cold day with a warmed-up voice, which would have been just asking for a cold. The dearth of rooms available backstage often had me using the ladies' room for my daily vocalizing routine, but I knew I couldn't afford not to be vocally ready for a Met rehearsal. With that ritual out of the way, I was off to see the maestro.

In contrast to the ornate gold leaf and glitter in the auditorium, the rehearsal rooms were stark and functional: a couple of music stands, a piano (usually an upright), and a chair or two. Erich Leinsdorf was only a few years older than I, but he was already in a top position at the Met. The great Artur Bodanzky, doyen of the German wing conductors, had died in November 1939, shortly before opening night of the 1939–40 season. This catapulted the young Viennese conductor into the forefront of activities, but he was well prepared for his tasks, having served as a piano accompanist for both Bruno Walter and Arturo Toscanini at the Salzburg Festival. He then got out of Austria by the skin of his teeth, just in time to escape the consequences of Hitler's *Anschluss*. Vienna's loss was New York's gain. Leinsdorf was beginning to attract a lot of positive attention, with audiences and press alike looking forward eagerly to more of the brisk, youthful style that marked his Wagnerian interpretations.

As I stepped into the room, he greeted me rather cryptically with the question: "What are we rehearsing today?" At first, I didn't catch on that Leinsdorf might have been trying to tell me something, and simply said, "I suppose we'll continue working on Elsa." The conductor replied that he wanted to check through the role of Sieglinde in *Die Walküre*. There was no need, Leinsdorf told me, to sing out. I was welcome to "mark"—that is to say, sing half-voice or take the top notes an octave lower—something all professional singers do to spare their voices and keep them in trim for the big rehearsals and the performances. I still wasn't quite sure why he didn't want to hear the Sieglinde full voice, with no performances scheduled for me until after the New Year, but he was the boss.

After I had softly warbled through Sieglinde from start to finish, the maestro nonchalantly told me to report to the make-up and costume department.

Then the penny dropped. I later discovered that Mme Lotte Lehmann had a cold, which had forced her to cancel the Saturday matinée. Somebody else would have to take over for her.

There were five of us in all: with Mme Lehmann out of the picture, Helen Traubel scheduled for the first Brünnhilde of her career, and Rose Bampton justifiably unwilling to follow up a Donna Anna in *Don Giovanni* on one day with what would have been her first Met Sieglinde in the New York house the next, somebody checked with Irene Jessner, who was on a concert tour in the Middle West and would be unable to make it back to New York in time for the performance. There was only one Sieglinde left—yours truly. And nobody knew whether or not I could make it through the role. That was what Leinsdorf had been asked to find out.

And so I would be making my début in one of the most prestigious opera houses in the world, in a difficult principal role in one of the longest operas in the repertoire, with one of the biggest orchestras, sharing the stage with a virtual *Almanach de Gotha* of Wagnerian singers, each one twice my age and more, despite the fact that I had never once set foot onstage or even rehearsed this work with any of the people involved. If somebody had put this story in a movie, I would probably have questioned his sanity, but here I was, living the quintessential show business cliché, but much too busy getting ready to worry about it.

After my session with the costume department and a visit to "Papa" Adolf Senz, the great grey eminence of the theatre, who supplied us with our wigs, make-up and plenty of TLC before, during, and after performances, I had the presence of mind to stop on the way back home to buy a bunch of roses for my mother, whose diligent instruction had brought me to the threshold of my operatic career. When I got back to the Village, Mother's response to the flowers completely bowled me over. Silently placing the roses in water, she put on her coat and announced she was going out to get me a steak to serve as a kind of cowboy breakfast the next morning. I would need an extra shot of protein, she insisted, to make it safely through the Sieglinde.

What goes through the mind of a twenty-three-year-old soprano in a situation like this? Well, as I said before, opera was the family business, and I simply remembered I had been taking care of business for the last three years. How? First of all, by preparing myself, vocally and musically, to top form, guided by my mother, who gave me my vocal training, and my mentor, Maestro Hermann Weigert, who taught me most of my repertoire.

Sleep that night was sparse. I kept trying to recall all the things I'd seen

"Papa" Adolf Senz was the ultimate make-up and wig artist and the founder of a Hollywood make-up dynasty. *Metropolitan Opera Archives.*

Sieglinde do, watching performances back in my standing room days. My mother, however, had a remedy for the kind of insomnia which afflicts any performer before a big day. She suggested that, rather than tossing and turning, counting sheep, or indulging in any other rituals, I should just lie there and relax. Sooner or later, repose would come in one form or another. I finally managed to get some sleep, and what did I dream about? You guessed it—Sieglinde.

The following morning, that breakfast steak tasted like filet of straw, but my mind was everywhere else but on my appetite. Calmly I gathered together the necessities I would need backstage at the theatre: a bar of soap, a box of tissues to remove the make-up, and a towel. Just before I left for the Met, I also packed up my good luck charm, a double frame with two pictures of Kirsten Flagstad, who had been a close friend of our family since my infancy. I would need a friend in the dressing room, and Mme Flagstad was a more-than-appropriate choice. In fact, our dear family friend was my Wagnerian idol and has remained so from that day to this. I then bundled up against the December cold and went off to the BMT station. I remember mumbling a little prayer as I rode uptown.

Back at the theatre, I saw a long queue of my standing room chums braving the winter wind for today's matinée. As Virginia Ahrens, one of my standee friends from those days, recently reported, nobody really registered my presence as I walked by. Later, somebody told the standees that Lehmann was out, and a groan went right down the line. Lotte Lehmann had a special significance for music lovers in New York. In addition to her eminence as an artist, Madame Lehmann's immense popularity was also based on her enormous personal integrity. Although not Jewish herself, she had renounced her German citizenship and moved to Austria when Hitler came to power, continuing on to the United States after the *Anschluss*.

When my standing room friends recovered from their initial disappointment, one of them went inside the theatre to find out who had been selected to replace Mme Lehmann. The others heard my name, and a resounding "Whozat?" went through the crowd. Finally somebody mentioned a girl named Varnay, who occasionally stood with them, and who had told them she was studying singing. But her name wasn't Astrid; it was Violet. Eventually another standee went into the Thirty-ninth Street outer lobby to check the photos of the ensemble on the wall and see if any of the portrait shots there matched the person they knew. Sure enough, the Astrid Varnay who was about

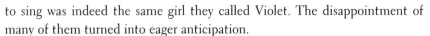

to sing was indeed the same girl they called Violet. The disappointment of many of them turned into eager anticipation.

Although I couldn't know it that early in the game, I actually began setting certain patterns that afternoon which have remained with me throughout the fifty-five years and more of my career. First of all, my early arrival. I always try to be in the theatre at least two hours before the performance. As with rehearsal days, warming up the voice comes first. Then I like to take time doing my make-up and checking to make sure my costume is right. From the first day on, I was one of the very few singers at the Met who always did her own make-up. I had learned this craft from one of my mother's pupils, who was a portrait painter and studied singing as a hobby.

About the time those preparations are completed, the "visits" usually begin. Sometimes the director stops in for a last-minute reminder of some bit of stage business, and the conductor always comes by for a moment, checking on a musical fine point or to ask if there is anything he ought to know before we encounter one another across the chasm of the pit.

After that I went onstage. The executive stage manager, Désiré Defrère, met me there and took me through the paces of a staging I had watched from standing room ever since 1935, when this *Walküre* production first premièred.

At the time, that staging was created to patch up a previous *Ring* production dating back to 1914. The reason for this repair job was that the Metropolitan, like most other theatres, often performed *Walküre* separate from the rest of the *Ring*. As a result, the sets were in such frayed condition, it was decided to replace the shopworn 1914 production with a new staging by Leopold Sachse, designed by Jonel Jorgulesco. Interestingly enough, this ancient *Ring* production, including the Sachse-Jorgulesco patch job, remained in the repertoire until 1948!

Even though I had theoretically absorbed Dr. Sachse's fairly uncomplicated staging, it was still good to trace the route with my own feet and then check to make sure all my props were in the right place. Over on the other side of the stage, I saw a mountain of a man doing the same thing—checking props. I smiled over at my partner for the afternoon, Lauritz Melchior, impressed that somebody with his long years of stage experience still took the time and trouble to make sure everything was where it belonged before he stepped out in front of an audience. Melchior walked over, gave me a reassuring smile and an affectionate slap on the shoulder, then simply said, "Verlass dich auf mich." What a beautiful thing to tell a newcomer. This great artist and gracious gentleman was telling the new kid on the block to leave things to him, and he would take care of me.

It was time. Two o'clock. Announcer Milton Cross, who presented all the matinée performances to an audience of millions all over North America, entered his broadcast booth, put on his headphones, waited for the ON AIR sign on the wall to light up, and started his preperformance presentation. Backstage, the radio on the stage manager's desk was turned on, and I heard Mr. Cross's inimitable pear-shaped tones pronouncing my name wrong. I made a mental note that I would have to give him the right pronunciation later. Now I had a show to do.

The signal came. Maestro Leinsdorf entered the pit, acknowledged the welcoming applause, and the orchestra began the agitated music leading to Siegmund's entrance. Right from the beginning, I noticed, there would be no pussyfooting in this performance. Leinsdorf kept the music moving at a good clip and kept the audience keenly aware of just how many musicians were in the pit with him. But a lot of those musicians were Italians, and Italians love voices and singing. Hundreds of times in the intervening years, I noticed the way, no matter how powerfully a maestro may want to take a piece, an Italian orchestra, or an orchestra with a fair proportion of Italian players, will stubbornly, automatically adjust to the voices on the stage. No adjustment, however, would be called for in the case of the first singer in the opera.

The curtain parted, and Lauritz Melchior hurtled onto the stage as Siegmund. The New York papers used to refer to this enormous Scandinavian tenor as "the great Dane" in reference not only to his nationality, but also to his incredible size, well over six feet, as well as the equally gigantic dimensions of his warm-hued voice, which no tenor before or since has ever matched. As Siegmund collapsed in front of the hearth like an exhausted grizzly bear, he touched the hearthstone to establish his right of shelter. As I made my own entrance, I could sense that Melchior was looking through the corner of his eye to check out the newcomer he would be sharing the next couple of hours with. He seemed satisfied, but I had no time to think about that. He had just gasped for a drink of water, and Sieglinde is the water bearer in this show.

I returned to the stage and handed him the drinking horn. He looked back at me with a little twinkle in his eye, indicating that he meant what he said about leaving things to him. At that point, I understood why that insurance company uses the Rock of Gibraltar as its symbol. For the next two hours, Lauritz Melchior was going to be my insurance policy.

Act 1 of *Die Walküre* is a trio. In addition to Siegmund and Sieglinde, we have Sieglinde's rough-hewn husband, Hunding, whose fateful encounter with Siegmund sets much of the story in motion. The Hunding in this performance was another titan—the Ukrainian basso Alexander Kipnis, with a burnished ebony voice easily as large as Melchior's and a fondness for theatrics that occasionally put the two of us at friendly loggerheads. In his adversarial position as my abusive husband, Kipnis made no concessions to my operatic innocence, for which I am grateful to this day. He—in his character, of course—menaced me. I—in my character—defied him.

Down in the pit, Mr. Leinsdorf was not giving any of us an inch as far as volume was concerned. After all, he also had Melchior and Kipnis to accompany, and their voices could soar over any orchestra. But the really big singing was yet to come. Finally, Kipnis roared his challenge to Melchior and retired for the night. After a parting glance at Siegmund, I preceded Hunding out of the main room to slip him his mediaeval Mickey Finn, and Melchior came downstage for Siegmund's heartrending monologue with its desperate cries of "Wälse, Wälse!"

When people talk of special experiences in the opera house, certainly Melchior's "Wälse" cries number among them. Even today, over fifty years later, I can't think back on this huge man pouring all his considerable passion into that enormous voice without feeling a chill of excitement down my spine. Recently, as a matter of fact, I timed that part of the performance with a stopwatch. Melchior's "Wälse"'s were twelve seconds each—what tenor has ever matched that? Maybe Melchior himself—he has been timed at eighteen! But even if a present-day tenor could match it, what present-day conductor would let him?

There is a kind of singing so great that every other singer who hears it is humbled into silence. And there is an even greater level of vocalism that in fact inspires any colleague who has the honor of sharing the experience. That was my feeling about Melchior. It was as if he was giving me the strength to do my best.

The rest of the first act passed like a thrilling dream. While I kept my singing under careful control, I was so emotionally involved in what I was doing theatrically, I wasn't really aware of how this kind of emotional involvement, and the way I expressed it, was relatively new to the operatic scene, certainly to the German repertoire in the United States. Watching my two eminent colleagues begin act 2, I realized that, even at this very early stage, the "something new" I was doing would become something I would do to the fullest when the time came.

Leading off act 2 were two of the finest Wagnerian singers ever to grace the stage of the Metropolitan. Singing in the same performance with the Hungarian-born *Heldenbariton*, Friedrich Schorr, even though we had nothing in this opera to sing together, made me feel a little like one of those runners in a relay race, receiving the baton from one of the top men in the business. It was my first public appearance—and one of the last Schorr would sing in a long and distinguished career.

That afternoon, Mr. Schorr was suffering from the stress of a terribly heavy schedule, and the wear and tear was beginning to tell on his noble voice. This was anything but the case with his Brünnhilde, the burgundy-voiced Helen Traubel, essaying this huge role for the first time at the age of forty-two. Traubel's career development could not have been more different from mine. Offered a Met contract in 1926, she politely declined, because she felt she simply wasn't ready. More than ten years later, in 1937, she finally joined the Met at the age of thirty-eight to sing the soprano lead in Walter Damrosch's *The Man without a Country*. Wagner came even later, but this was the usual development pattern for Wagnerian singers. In short, Traubel was the rule, I the exception.

It is impossible for me to think about Helen Traubel without smiling at that generous voice and the generous spirit of its owner, who had the most infectious laugh I ever heard. Anyone who saw her on television a few years later with Jimmy Durante knows what I'm talking about.

Act 3 of *Walküre* gives the audience an opportunity to compare the intensity and volume of two big soprano voices. Listening to Traubel's radiant "Hojotoho!" at the beginning of the second act, I knew I would have yet another major hurdle to surmount before I could take off my make-up.

Act 3 arrived. Suddenly I realized Traubel's singing and mine wouldn't be competing at all. This has something to do with the way the music is constructed, but even more to do with the musical intelligence of my colleague. If both sopranos simply follow Wagner's instructions, there is no competition possible, and both sopranos that afternoon were disciplined professionals. As was the case in my collaboration with Melchior, Traubel's voice and mine dovetailed. She would begin a grand phrase; I would meet it and take the phrase through to its conclusion. Very seldom have I experienced this kind of exchange, but on this occasion, with Traubel in her first Brünnhilde and me in my first performance anywhere, the atmosphere was vocally electric.

And yet, anyone looking at Traubel and me could not help but notice the difference in our dramatic approach: Traubel was a mighty oak with her feet planted like solid roots on the stage, her hands either clasped in front of her or raised for one of her occasional gestures, while I was totally involved in the complicated character of Sieglinde. It would be unfair to fault Traubel on this—most of her generation had learned to perform according to the "stand and deliver" rules, which were traditional at that time. My generation was still open to further development when it came to drama.

There were also eight authentic *prime donne* performing the roles of the other Valkyries in act 3. Much has been said about the quality of every voice on the Metropolitan stage in those days. This *Walküre* featured Anna Kaskas, Maria van Delden, Helen Olheim, Lucielle Browning, Maxine Stellman, Doris Doe, Mary van Kirk, and Thelma Votipka as Brünnhilde's sisters. A few years later, when I became ill during a *Lohengrin* performance on tour, Maxine Stellman came over from a nearby hotel and completed the performance for me. I can't help wondering how many *Walküre* sisters could rise to that challenge today.

The *Walküre* performance concluded in a burst of glory for all parties. The generous audience showered us with applause, and all my colleagues welcomed me to the pack. Back in my dressing room, I was swamped by friends from standing room days. When Ginny Ahrens finally realized to whom she had been listening for several hours, the shock struck her speechless. All she could do was stand there and point at me open-mouthed.

Another friendship with a standee was formed that day. Valerie Wagner was a secretary whose duties included taking cash to the bank on Saturday morning. One Saturday, she happened to notice the opera house across the street from the bank and decided to find out what all the people in the line were waiting for. From moment one she was hooked. She later shared her enthusiasm with her husband, Si Glazer. On this particular occasion, as she puts it in her no-nonsense Manhattan style, she "lined up for Lehmann and got Varnay." As I signed an autograph for this stranger, I had no way of knowing how important Valerie and Si's friendship would figure at a crucial moment in my life.

The Metropolitan Opera House on a Saturday is a busy place. Hardly had the *Walküre* performance come down, when the crew went into action setting up the *Nozze di Figaro* for that evening. Jenny Cervini, the head wardrobe mistress and an institution like Papa Senz in the wig department, discreetly asked me to finish up, so that she could prepare the dressing room for one of the ladies in the distinguished *Figaro* cast. That "distinguished cast" included Elisabeth Rethberg and Risë Stevens! With the realization of the kind of company I had begun keeping, all the potential perils of the tightrope I had just traversed were driven graphically home to me. A shudder suddenly went through my whole body. But then I gathered up my composure, along with my remaining tissues, soap, and towel, as well as the pictures of Mme Flagstad.

As I started to put on my coat, Edward Johnson, the General Manager of the company, came to give me a hug of commendation. He explained to me that, having satisfied himself that my voice could handle the role, he had asked Leinsdorf simply to check whether I knew it musically. But as far as lasting through the performance was concerned, he had no way of predicting that. Having no other choice, he said, since the show had to go on, he decided he would have to let me sink or swim. Then he congratulated me for a good swim.

When Mother joined me at the stage door, we decided the occasion was sufficiently auspicious to justify a taxi ride back to the Village. The following day was Sunday, and I enjoyed a well-earned rest with my mother and brother in our apartment, wondering what the reaction had been to my début. In those days, you could get the reviews of your performances around midnight, even after an evening show, but the music and theatre pages of the Sunday papers always went to press before any of the critics had had a chance to report on a Saturday matinée. This meant we always had to wait for Sunday night, when the Monday editions came out, to find out what the press had thought of our work.

On that particular Sunday, my brother, "Lucky" (his real name was Fortunato, but everybody in New York is in a hurry, so they preferred the two-syllable English translation), volunteered to scout for the next day's editions. Lucky himself was a rather enthusiastic musician for his young years. A regular member of the renowned Trinity Church Boys' Choir and a great music lover, he could hardly wait for his big sister's reviews to come out. All the more reason for our concern when it took him several hours to come back. When he finally did return, with an agitated look on his face, he simply slapped the papers down on the table and said, "There's a war on!"

Each of us grabbed a paper and started reading furiously. The glaring headlines told us the world was about to go through a cataclysmic upheaval. That morning, at 7:55 A.M. local Mid-Pacific time, a Japanese dive bomber had appeared on the horizon over the Pacific Ocean west of the naval port of Pearl Harbor in Hawaii, followed by over two hundred other warplanes in a sneak attack on the United States Navy, despite the fact that the Japanese had a delegation in Washington involved in peace talks with our country. It took us a while to digest this news, and when we finally came to our senses, one of us—I can't remember who—said, "What about the write-ups? We could do with some good news."

The good news could not have been better. The *New York Times'* critic, Noël Straus, said, "Sieglinde, in Miss Varnay's hands, was one of the most satisfying and convincing portrayals the season has brought forth." Louis Biancolli flattered my ego in the *World Telegram* by commenting, "An addition to this troupe's pulchritude wing is always cause for jubilation, especially when accompanied by a flock of fresh high notes." In the *Herald Tribune*, Jerome D. Bohm took notice of the new era my generation was about to usher in. After complimenting my singing, he added, "Her portrayal brought with it not only comeliness and a sympathetic personality, but an extraordinarily sure feeling for the right gesture and apposite facial play."

Edward O'Gorman in the *New York Post* summed things up: "It was not so much the combination of the time and the place, and the various other fortuitous details, that made Miss Varnay's appearance so spectacular, but the fact that Miss Varnay, despite her inexperience, had the voice, the dramatic ability, and the confidence and the training to carry it off with honors. Miss Varnay can make a graceful and significant dramatic gesture of sitting still."

Interestingly enough, the historical events in the Pacific and the successful début on Thirty-ninth Street were both to have a tremendous impact on my future. The next morning, President Roosevelt gave his famous "day that will live in infamy" speech to a joint session of Congress, in which he asked for, and got, a declaration of war against the Empire of Japan. As expected, shortly afterward, Japan's ally, Germany, declared war on the United States, plunging even our operatic world into a special kind of predicament. With a war on the European front, the many international artists and other personnel on the staff of the Metropolitan were forced to make some very hard decisions. Nobody knew how long the war would last, but everyone knew they had to choose between returning to Europe immediately or perhaps never going home again.

Lotte Lehmann and Friedrich Schorr had already made their moves, not that the outspoken Mme Lehmann or Cantor Schorr had much choice. Ezio Pinza, Lily Pons, Jarmila Novotná, Lauritz Melchior, and many others would soon find themselves isolated from native lands they revered, forced to take citizenship in another country. Of course, the famous European singers who had decided to remain at home would not be available to the Metropolitan. This was a special problem for the German wing, which drew most of its casts from the locked-in nations of Central Europe and Scandinavia.

Six days later, on December 12, Helen Traubel was forced to cancel her

Hardly had I finished one role in *Walküre* when I had to add wings for another. They called me "The Seven-Month Brünnhilde." *Metropolitan Opera Archives.*

second Brünnhilde, and I had to take over that daunting task on equally short notice. With a great sigh of relief, I finally managed to make my "official" début, singing Elsa in *Lohengrin* the first month of the New Year, and my career was off and running (at $75 a week!). Traubel and I became friends, and

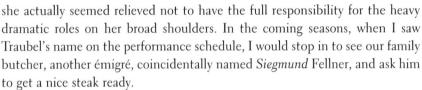

she actually seemed relieved not to have the full responsibility for the heavy dramatic roles on her broad shoulders. In the coming seasons, when I saw Traubel's name on the performance schedule, I would stop in to see our family butcher, another émigré, coincidentally named *Siegmund* Fellner, and ask him to get a nice steak ready.

A year or so after that fateful Saturday in December, a critic by the name of Irving Kolodin wrote a piece in which he paid me a couple of compliments and then suddenly hit me with a backhand I've never forgotten. Giving one of such tender years, Kolodin wrote, so much vocal and musical responsibility was pure folly on the part of the Metropolitan management. Surely, another season or two, and my career would fall victim to an excess of wear and tear. In an era yet to come, where the management of many theatres couldn't care less about the vocal health of the artists on their rosters, that prediction might have come true, but the Met in those days was a different story.

Edward Johnson, the General Manager who fathered my career, was an experienced tenor in his own right, and he made sure I never had to do more than about a dozen performances a season. These included all the evenings I took over from other sopranos. At the time, I was convinced I could handle a much heavier schedule than he gave me, but maturity and experience have shown me how right he was. The most important factor for both me and the theatre was that, even then, I knew how to marshal my resources. In a conversation I had with Erich Leinsdorf shortly before his death in 1993, he remarked that my début was one of many events in his musical career that proved his theory that age is not the ultimate arbiter of musical competence.

Be all of this as it may, here we are, by the grace of the Muses, over fifty-five years later, and I am still active, sharing what I've learned with one generation of colleagues and listeners after another. Even more important than that, the style of "total performance," bringing vocal, musical, and theatrical values together to form a whole which is far greater than the mere sum of its individual parts, has taken hold on the operatic stage, even if some stage directors nowadays tend to go overboard.

For myself, I think the time has come to share my story. I hope my reading audience enjoys it as much as my many theatre audiences over the years have enjoyed my performances.

—

＝＞ *Act I*

THE FAMILY BUSINESS

A Gleam in His Eye

As WE REREAD the write-ups of those first performances, my mother and I could not help being amused at some of the reviewers' attempts to pinpoint where I came from. Since I had been sprung on them so unexpectedly, without any advance publicity, they were not sure what "national characteristics" to attribute to me. Some of the critics thought my origins were Scandinavian. Others claimed me as Hungarian. Both theories are right and wrong. So what is the story?

When I first started to work with Maestro Fritz Reiner around 1948, he told me he had known me when I was still just a "gleam" in my father's eye. As a matter of fact, he said, if it hadn't been for him, I wouldn't have existed at all. It seems that, early in his career, when he was still called by his Hungarian name of Frigyes, Reiner had been engaged to conduct and rehearse performances at a brand-new theatre in Budapest called the Népopera (People's Opera). It was scheduled to open on December 7, 1911, with a work entitled *Quo Vadis* by the French composer Jean Nouguès.

One day, as Reiner told me, a young tenor by the name of Alexander Várnay arrived to start rehearsals for the role of the Emperor Nero. When he stepped into the darkened auditorium for the first time, there was an attractive coloratura soprano rehearsing on stage. Várnay asked Reiner who the beautiful woman was. The conductor told him her name was Mária Jávor, and that she would be singing the principal soprano role of the slave girl Eunice with him in the Nouguès opera. He suddenly looked very solemnly back at Reiner and said prophetically: "That woman is going to be my wife."

For his tender twenty-two years, Alexander Várnay already had the kind of self-assurance which is often born of success. His life thus far had been carefree and adventurous, starting with a blissful childhood as the son of a popular local composer in one of those fascinating corners of the Austro-Hungarian Empire that frequently changed hands in the course of a long and tempestuous history. At the time he was born, on September 11, 1889, his birthplace had been assigned by the Habsburg monarchy to the Hungarian part of the Empire. The period of Hungarian sovereignty lasted from 1867 until 1918, during which period the place was known to the Germans as Kaschau and to the Hungarians as Kassa. In 1918, the region voluntarily joined the Czechoslovak Republic and is today the city of Košice in the eastern part of the new Republic of Slovakia.

My grandparents produced a sizable number of children. My father was the eldest of ten—five boys and five girls—and the whole family enjoyed making music together. As a matter of fact, my grandfather even started a little family chorus when the first children were able to read music, and this activity continued until well after many of them were grown up.

But music was only one aspect of my father's fervent intellectual curiosity. He was fascinated by every aspect of the theatre, he had a profound interest in the natural sciences, and he loved languages. Living in a region that straddled the geographical fence dividing different nationalities provided fertile soil for young Alexander's inquisitive mind. Like most children in multicultural societies, he soon mastered both of the languages spoken at that time in Kassa. Hungarian, the local language, was taught in primary school parallel with German, the lingua franca of the Austro-Hungarian Empire. When he was in his teens, his parents sent him to two German-speaking boarding schools in today's Czech Republic. The point of this was to prepare him for what both he and his parents hoped would be a medical career. There he learned more languages. His academic education included Greek and Latin as a matter of course. He was fluent in both, along with some Hebrew and Aramaic, which he hoped would help him intensify his understanding of biblical texts.

Then he settled in Vienna to study medicine. After three semesters at medical school, his urge to do something professional with his love for music and theatre took hold of his life. He switched from the university to the conservatory operated by the renowned Gesellschaft der Musikfreunde, where he began his vocal studies under the tutelage of Professor Franz Haböck. When the composer Karl Goldmark met him, he was so impressed with the musical and theatrical abilities of the aspiring young tenor that he took my father under his wing, subsidized his musical education, and used his not inconsiderable influence to help the young artist any way he could. Not satisfied with simply studying voice, my father also registered for a course in operatic production, taught by Professor Eduard Gärtner, one of the top experts on the craft. He later amplified these studies under Professor Meisner, a regular member of the production staff at the Vienna Volksoper. At the same time, he continued his vocal studies with the legendary heroic tenor Hermann Winkelmann, who had created the title role in *Parsifal* in Bayreuth, an opera that would mean a great deal to me in future years.

The conductor Felix von Weingartner suggested that my father further his operatic knowledge in France and Italy and even arranged for the Wiener Hof-oper (Vienna Court Opera) to give him a scholarship to study in those places. In Paris, he studied voice with Jean de Reszke, one of the leading members of the "Golden Age of Singing" at the turn of the century. Recently retired from the stage, de Reszke was about to embark on a career as one of Europe's pre-eminent vocal teachers.

In Italy, my father added Italian to his collection of languages, while study-ing singing privately with Maestro Leonetti and staging at the local theatres of Milan and Florence. He also auditioned for Ruggiero Leoncavallo, who pro-nounced him an authentic tenor discovery and immediately wrote a letter of recommendation to that effect in French, so it could be more easily read by the various theatres to which Leoncavallo said he should present it. When I look at the progress of my father's career, I cannot help being amazed at the number of selfless persons in high places and august institutions who not only wished him well but also did something to further his professional advance-ment.

Alexander Várnay returned from Italy to begin a career which covered the far-flung Austro-Hungarian Empire and neighboring countries as well. He sang an extensive repertoire that ran the gamut from such lyric roles as the Duke in *Rigoletto* and the title role in *Faust* to the more dramatic Turiddu in *Cavalleria Rusticana*, Canio in *Pagliacci*, Eléazar in *La Juive*, Don José in *Carmen*, and Manrico in *Il Trovatore*, all the way to the heroic title roles in *Tannhäuser* and *Lohengrin*.

The soprano whom Alexander Várnay had sworn a solemn oath to marry was a local girl. Mária Junghans was born in the town of Perjámos, only a little more than a month later than my father, on October 15, 1889, to be specific. Her father was a prominent judge named József Junghans, and her mother,

Anna (née Partenschlager), had once entertained operatic ambitions, but was never to take them beyond participation in the local church choir, because of parental objections to a "respectable" woman having any other kind of career than wife and mother.

Mária grew up in Rákosliget, some eight miles outside the cosmopolitan capital of Budapest, where she was sent to a convent school. She was so taken with the life of the sisters, she initially wanted to become a nun herself, but the Mother Superior dissuaded her from embarking on a religious vocation, claiming the young girl was simply too "vivacious." But the sisters did encourage her to make full use of her musical talents, which she displayed by singing solos at a very early age. She also took piano lessons as a non-matriculated student at the Royal Academy of Music.

While Judge Junghans was fond of music and theatre, and heartily approved of his wife's interest in both, he agreed with his parents-in-law that the only contact a proper family needed with those art forms could be acquired from attendance at performances or making music at home. This approach was similar to Alexander Várnay's family's. The thought of a member of his own family actually practicing a profession he considered perilously insecure, or consorting with what he regarded as its highly disreputable members, was anathema to him. In short, his views were in line with the general opinion the respectable bourgeoisie have had of theatre people dating back to the Roman Empire, when the profession was looked upon as nothing more than a hotbed of prostitution.

This was why my grandmother had to keep the "cherry tree incident" a secret from him. This is what happened. The family had a cherry tree in the garden, and young Mária enjoyed sitting in the branches and chirping little vocal calisthenics for her own amusement. One afternoon, the music director of Budapest Cathedral, who also served as a professor at the Franz Liszt Academy of Music in the capital, was taking a stroll in Rákosliget and happened to overhear the girl singing. He immediately asked her if he might speak to one of her parents.

The Hungarians are very decorous people, and so I can imagine he began his visit to my grandmother with the usual litany of extravagant courtesies and compliments before getting down to business. The reason for coming to see her, the professor told my grandmother, was that he was enormously impressed with the sound of the girl's voice. He felt she had a future as a singer and should receive some professional vocal instruction as soon as possible,

suggesting further that she apply for acceptance at the academy where he taught.

My grandmother regarded this as a golden opportunity to see her own theatrical ambitions realized by a surrogate in the person of her daughter, but she would have to come up with some kind of ruse to convince her husband of the propriety of this move. Explaining to the culture-loving judge that a music-oriented study program was an appropriate way for the teenaged daughter of one of the better families to round off her education, she delicately maneuvered him into agreeing to send Mária to live with two aunts, who served as ladies-in-waiting at the Hungarian Royal Court. These aunts would then watch over her to make sure she behaved with the proper etiquette and decorum expected of a young lady of her position during the period of her education at the conservatory.

This supervision, as Mother later told me, included some rather stern ideas about audience behavior, all of which I agree with completely. For example, people often came to concerts or the opera sporting handsome walking sticks, which would then clatter noisily to the ground as these dandies dozed off during the performance. If my great-aunts were anywhere near them, they could look forward to a rude awakening. This also applied to the program rustlers and audible chatterers.

But my great-aunts were not always as severe with themselves as they were with others. Their caprice was horse racing, which is to say, attending the races and placing bets, almost invariably on the losers. Every time they returned home from one of these escapades, they would rant and rave over their losses and solemnly swear never to return to the scene of their obsession. This oath usually held until the next race was announced. As my mother reported this, she had all she could do to keep from laughing out loud.

These relatives welcomed seventeen-year-old Mária to Budapest in 1906. She must have taken to the Liszt Academy like a duck to water, because she soon became one of its star pupils. Shortly after entering the academy, she was switched from probation status to a full academic program, at which she excelled—with one ironic exception. Looking over her report cards, I note with pride that she got straight A's in just about every subject but Italian, which puts a smile on my face to this day, when I think about what would happen to Mother's life just a few years down the road.

Quite a number of honors were accorded her in the course of her education. One of them was being assigned to study singing with Mme Abranyi, considered the top voice teacher on the Liszt faculty at the time. In Hungary, it was traditional for married women to teach under their husbands' names, as they might in America, which is why my mother's report card was signed by Abranyi Emilné (Mrs. Emil Abranyi), but she had previously had a singing career under her given name, which was, much to my surprise, Rózsa Várnay.

Another special honor accorded the gifted undergraduate was an invitation to sing in public in March 1907, only a few months after being admitted to the school. Attending the graduation ceremonies in 1910, Judge Junghans was amazed to hear that his daughter had not only passed her courses with flying colors, but had also been awarded the coveted plum of a début in Budapest as Leonora in *Il Trovatore* under the direction of that same Frigyes Reiner, her vocal coach at the theatre. (Reiner, of course, is the one who subsequently introduced her to her husband.) This was followed in short order by Gilda in a *Rigoletto* performance starring no less a celebrity than the great Italian baritone Titta Ruffo. She then appeared with such well-known guest stars as Selma Kurz and Alessandro Bonci.

With that level of success conferred upon his daughter, Judge Junghans finally relented and allowed her to pursue a musical career. But before they gave her their blessing to start at the theatre, taking the more Hungarian-sounding name of Jávor as her stage name, Mária's parents gave her a motto, which served her as a watchword throughout her life, one she would pass down to me, and I would in turn convey to many others. "Künstler sein ist kein Vorwand für Unarten," they told her. Loosely translated, this means: "Being an artist is no excuse for bad behavior."

Years after Mother's début, when I was singing Lady Macbeth at the Maggio Musicale in Florence in May 1951, I contacted Titta Ruffo, who had retired to that city of cities. He told me he remembered that *Rigoletto* with great affection and also accorded me the privilege of his presence at one of my *Macbeth* performances, sending his kind regards to his erstwhile Hungarian Gilda afterward.

By the time Alexander Várnay arrived in Budapest, Mária Jávor was already an established young prima donna. In addition to Gilda, she had sung such principal roles as Philine in *Mignon* and Olympia in *Les Contes d'Hoffmann*, to which she subsequently added the other three leading ladies, Giulietta, Antonia, and Stella. The following season, she was again heard as Leonora in *Il Trovatore*—one of the two roles, by the way, which my coloratura mother and my dramatic soprano self actually shared. The other was Desdemona in Verdi's *Otello*. As a stalwart member of a repertory company, of course, the young soprano also lent her leading-role qualities to a number of secondary parts, including Stella in *I Gioielli della Madonna* and a definitive Frasquita in *Carmen*, incidentally one of the toughest *comprimaria* parts in the entire repertoire, with lots of exposed upper-register singing.

As rehearsals on *Quo Vadis* proceeded apace, Alexander Várnay wasted no time starting to pay court to his leading lady. In those days, this ritual largely consisted of very proper, well-chaperoned visits to tea and the like. Impeccable behavior and correct attire were the order of the day. Needless to say, the major topic of their conversation was music and singing. While Mária listened admiringly, Alexander would pace up and down, orating about opera, discussing and demonstrating the various breathing techniques different singers used, and describing how he felt one should support a tone properly on a column of air.

At one of these visits, it became a source of considerable embarrassment when Alexander took a particularly deep breath, filling his lungs to such a point that one of his vest buttons popped right off the garment, precipitously rendering him improperly dressed for calling on an unattached young lady. Being the resourceful creature he was, Alexander Várnay soon sought out the services of a local tailor, whom he ordered to reattach the vest buttons, this time with sturdy metal wire to avoid having to truncate future visits to his lady love.

For all his self-confidence, Alexander did not find the object of his affection an easy lady to conquer. She had been taught all the tricks of the courting trade by her aunts, and she was not about to relent until she had a chance to use them. Many years later, in the United States, when I had reached the courting age, my mother told me it was about time I learned how to flirt. I didn't have the foggiest notion what she was talking about, but it drove home a significant difference between the highly structured rituals of Central Europe in the early days of this century and the informality of America in the so-called "Age of Sincerity." When I came of age, all of my mother's urgings to be both tempting and coy fell on the deaf ears of a young girl who was determined to tell it like it was.

Over and above enjoying the game of wooing with my future father, there was another significant reason for my mother's coyness. As she later told the story, my mother was an advocate of long courtships. Without the kind of freedoms young people have today, prospective brides and grooms had to be absolutely certain they were making the right decision, and that meant taking plenty of time to get to know their vis-à-vis.

Obviously Mother's studied coyness was more than the passionate Alexander could take, because after his courtship had reached the serious stage, with no apparent binding results forthcoming, his mother decided to pay a call on Mrs. Junghans. Her son, she said, had a huge picture of his beloved on the wall and spent hours every day staring at it with a heartbreaking look of longing in his eyes. She then gave my mother's mother the shocking news that Alexander Várnay had sworn to take his life if Mária did not agree to become his lawfully wedded wife forthwith. Their wedding on February 20, 1914, was also the beginning of an artistic collaboration, which took both husband and wife through the vast reaches of their wide and diverse repertoires and halfway around the world.

A Crib Full of Violets

THE YEAR 1914 marked both the beginning of Alexander Várnay's union with Mária Jávor and the conclusion of their association with the Budapest theatre as regular members of the ensemble. On June 28 of the same year, in Sarajevo, a city that came in for more than its share of tragedy in the twentieth century, a Bosnian Serb assassinated the heir to the Austro-Hungarian imperial throne and his morganatic wife. This triggered the First World War, which had an effect on my parents' lives similar to the one Pearl Harbor had on mine.

With the war soon raging on all fronts, the two singers were recruited by the Red Cross to go on a kind of double tour. In the cities, they sang to raise funds for the charitable organization. They next went on to the army camps, where they sang for wounded soldiers, then visited with them after their performances. These voluntary appearances, for which my parents received only expense money, brought them two medals from the Red Cross, the Cross of Honor from Austria-Hungary, and an unusual series of bouquets as the tour moved on. With produce rationed during the war, my practical mother asked the Red Cross if they wouldn't mind replacing the usual postperformance floral tribute with a bouquet of fruits and vegetables, and the organization was more than happy to comply, thus keeping the two young singers well supplied with natural vitamins during a time of general sacrifice.

It was all a little like the U.S.O., the United Service Organization, which provides entertainment for the American armed forces to this day. I sang for them several times during the Second World War. This encounter with mili-

Some people get married to settle down. My parents wed to go on the road. *Personal photo.*

tary life gave me a vague idea of what things must have been like for my parents on those extended tours. On one occasion, I sang for a large group of soldiers and was deeply moved by their enthusiasm for the kind of music I had to present. Before the concert, I asked one of the officials if he could give me any attendance figures. Knowing how many people I will be entertaining helps me gauge my volume for the performance. He replied, with a straight face, that this was privileged information and could not be divulged "for security reasons." I have yet to figure that one out.

When my parents were not singing for the Red Cross, they appeared in a number of theatres throughout the European continent. Mother added performances in Frankfurt and Cologne to her list of triumphs, while Father began gradually leaving his mark on the operatic world with his all-encompassing tenor repertoire and the fervor he invested in everything he ventured. At one point, he shared the role of Manrico in *Il Trovatore* with the great Leo Slezak. They were good friends, both of whom came from the outskirts of the Empire, my father from Slovakia and Slezak from Moravia. They also shared an enormous lust for great music, thrilling drama, good humor, and good food, which would later bring them together again. In pursuit of this good humor, Slezak wrote three captivatingly irreverent books of memoirs, in one of which he described my father's onstage enthusiasm with the following words:

> Good old, fiery Várnay Alex often enough identified himself so completely with his characterizations that his partners had every reason to fear they might get it in the neck. As Manrico, they say, he once used the tip of his sword to tickle a particularly arrogant Luna in some rather questionable zones. He had real gold in his throat, and, in Italian roles, he would send it pouring out in an endless golden stream. It flowed, flowed and glowed, to the point where many a conductor would love to have picked up a pair of scissors to cut it short. And when his role really took hold of his personality, he could wax so enthusiastic that I wouldn't have put it past him to attach a whole triumphant finale, willy-nilly, to that passionate *stretta!*

Slezak wasn't exaggerating much. My father was obviously an operatic swashbuckler of the first order, who was never at a loss for a dramatic gesture—or a smart answer. That very fastidious, severe maestro Fritz Reiner once told me he had felt honor-bound to remonstrate with my father for refusing to recognize an unmistakable sign from the pit, ordering him to cut off an extended high note. When Reiner sternly asked him, "Why did you hold that note so long, Várnay?" my father nonchalantly replied, "It felt so good up there, I thought I'd stick around for summer vacation."

Long before television was invented, Alexander Várnay had already developed an interesting precursor to the cue card. It happened at a performance of *Rigoletto*. Apparently, he hadn't sung the role of the Duke for so long, he had forgotten most of the words to—of all things—"La Donna è mobile," possibly the most famous piece of music Verdi ever wrote, and certainly the most familiar tenor aria in the repertoire. Rather than have a conniption fit backstage waiting for the grim reality of a memory slip in the fourth act, Papa simply got himself a pack of playing cards and wrote the words to the aria on them. In the performance, while the Duke is waiting to get a little more than friendly with the tavern girl, Maddalena, Father simply whipped out the cards and interpolated a game of solitaire into the action, casually cuing himself from the cards, without anyone in the audience catching on to his cunning little ploy.

As the war continued, my parents began wondering why they went on living and working, at least figuratively, in a perilous war zone. This state of affairs was made all the more hazardous by the fact that my father was still of legal draft age. Why, they thought to themselves, should they endanger their lives and futures for what they perceived as the gratuitous imperialistic claims of a Habsburg monarchy that had already divested their own nations and their neighbors of much of their identity?

Aware that they practiced one of the most internationally marketable professions, they felt the time had come to take themselves and their talents out of the line of fire. They put out some feelers to faraway places. Buenos Aires expressed interest in their services. Until that interest could be put in contractual form, they decided to settle temporarily in one of the neutral Scandinavian countries, where my father opened a vocal studio, while Mother immediately got in touch with the local theatres to arrange for some guest performances. In September 1916, my mother appeared as a special guest artist at the Royal Opera House in Stockholm in the presence of His Majesty, King Gustaf V, and several members of the royal family and the government. Her Swedish début was Gilda in *Rigoletto*, with an all-Scandinavian cast, including, as Maddalena, the Swedish mezzo-soprano Karin Branzell, with whom I would later have the pleasure of singing at the Met.

The press welcomed Mária Jávor to Scandinavia by suggesting that she was one of the spoils of war Sweden was enjoying by simply staying neutral. To be quite candid, the Scandinavian reviews were not as enthusiastic as the ones Mother had received in Central Europe. Some of the write-ups are what one might call "mixed," if not downright negative. Her approach was not the kind of coloratura singing people in those days were used to. They saw Gilda as a poor innocent waif and expected her to sing in that bird-like warble they related to ingenuousness. Few of them recognized that Gilda is also a resolute young woman who has taken it upon herself to disobey her domineering father and fall in love with a virtual stranger. Moreover, her love is so great and her courage so indomitable that she then goes boldly, if somewhat naïvely, to her death to save her lover's life, even though she now knows him to be a philanderer.

A few decades later, when dramatic coloraturas like Maria Callas and Joan

Sutherland began taking over these roles, my mother's approach to coloratura singing was finally hailed as the genuine article. Fortunately, she was still around to see that approach vindicated.

The Scandinavian critics may have carped, but the audience took Mária Jávor to its collective heart. A month later, she made another guest appearance as Queen Marguerite in *Les Huguenots*, and once again the royal family graced the theatre with their presence.

A year and a half after these triumphs on the Stockholm stage, Mother took a little time off from her busy performance schedule to present an enthusiastic Father with a blessed event. The date was April 25, 1918, and the blessed event in question, their only child, was yours truly. If we are to believe their reports, I apparently made the kind of vocal noises that prompt operatic parents to suggest these might be harbingers of another singer in the family.

But my father was not half as captivated with what my parents called my staccato squalling as he was with the fact that his long-cherished dream of becoming father to a daughter had finally come true. Gazing deeply into my purplish eyes, he suddenly expostulated, "Ibolyka," the Hungarian word for "little violet." The baby girl with the violet eyes, in fact, had thrilled her proud father to such a degree that, being the theatrical fellow he was, he immediately staged another grand gesture. Hurrying out to the nearest cut-rate sidewalk flower stand, he returned with an armload of purple flowers, which he proceeded to strew all over my crib, much to the annoyance of the baby nurse. My parents also immortalized Father's first sight of me by giving me the name Ibolyka, which I later shortened to "Bonka," because I had trouble pronouncing it. Mother then shortened the nickname even more to "Bonx."

"Astrid" was an afterthought. Having been blessed with progeny in Scandinavia, my parents felt they should pay their respects to their host country by giving their daughter at least one Scandinavian name. The teenaged Princess Astrid of Sweden was so popular that my courtly Hungarian parents decided to pay tribute to her and her country by also naming me after her. The rules of the Catholic Church, however, required my parents to supply me with the name of a Christian saint as well, and neither Ibolyka nor Astrid qualified. My parents then decided to add my mother's Christian name to the list, which is how I became Ibolyka Astrid Mária Várnay.

Pleased to meet you.

Later on, in America, my first-grade teacher in Brooklyn had as much trouble as I did pronouncing my given first name and summarily anglicized it to

Violet, which explains the confusion in the ranks of the standees when I decided to use my middle name professionally. That combination of a Scandinavian first name and a Hungarian surname also accounts for the fact that people cannot seem to figure out where I come from. The answer, of course, is that I'm like the art I've been practicing well over a half-century: international.

A Nation Reborn

Shortly after i was born, the offer from Buenos Aires began taking on more palpable form. My father went from Sweden to Norway to inquire about the possibility of sailing from a neutral Norwegian port to his proffered engagement in the Western Hemisphere, but the Norwegians told him it was just too risky. The sinking of a number of civilian ships by German submarines had brought the war onto the high seas. The South American journey would have to be indefinitely postponed.

While in Norway, my father picked up an engagement singing a couple of arias in a program at a variety theatre called the Théâtre Moderne. For all I know, he may have made his appearance between a juggling number and a trained seal act, but Papa had to pay for the round trip from Stockholm, and he was in no position to be fastidious about the venue. On top of that, he had a baby to feed. He would soon have another. The director of the Théâtre Moderne was a fellow Hungarian (with a British passport) by the name of Benno Singer. At the time of my father's performance there, the theatre was enjoying enormous popularity, and Mr. Singer had both some money to play with and a dream he wanted to make come true.

A day or so after my father sang in the variety hall, Benno Singer asked to meet with him. Singer confided to Alexander Várnay that he was eager to expand his theatrical empire to include a musical theatre. He had come up with the innovative idea of a Norwegian Opéra Comique, more or less along the lines of the theatre of the same name in Paris. Singer's concept was to stage more popular musical presentations, operettas and the like, to make a profit, and then use that profit to cover the possible deficits of more ambitious, serious operatic productions. The resident company, he felt, should be assigned roles in both the light operas and the serious ones, which he thought would bring a better level of vocal excellence and musicianship to the operettas while supplying the operatic casts with more experienced, adroit acting performers. These proposals for a musical theatre with equal stress on both factors, theatre and music, were right up my father's alley, and so he decided to defer his South American plans for the time being and help Benno Singer put together his new opera and operetta company, the first of its kind in Norwegian history. This theatre would be Papa's other "baby."

The establishment of a new music theatre was just one of many ways the recently reborn nation was manifesting its identity. Norway had emerged from a series of alliances with both Denmark and Sweden in 1905, re-establishing itself as a separate nation for the first time since the end of the fourteenth century. In keeping with this rise of nationalism, the new opera company Mr. Singer planned to found would be performing the great operatic works and a long list of classical operettas largely in Norwegian translations with casts made up almost exclusively of Norwegian artists, plus a few non-Norwegian ensemble members, most of them from other parts of Scandinavia. Mother would be one of the foreign singers asked to join the ensemble as leading coloratura.

Before the young Várnay family moved to Kristiania, my parents made one final appearance in Stockholm. It was a gala performance of Beethoven's monumental Ninth Symphony that included Mária Jávor and the American contralto Mme Charles Cahier. Mme Cahier later sang Azucena in Copenhagen, where she encouraged Lauritz Melchior to switch from baritone to tenor, even persuading her wealthy husband to join with the English author Hugh Walpole in supplementing Melchior's theatre salary so he could put the finishing touches on his studies in Berlin.

Back in Norway, Papa ended his singing career at age twenty-nine and began the arduous work of establishing a new company, complete with soloists, orchestra, chorus, and all the other people needed to make musical theatre come alive onstage. While Mr. Singer handled the business administration and contributed to the artistic decision-making process, Alexander Várnay, under the title of Head Stage Director, would also be the artistic director of the new company. The musical direction was placed under the joint control of a local conductor, Leif Halvorsen, who had studied music in Paris and Berlin and served briefly as first violinist in the renowned Berlin Philharmonic, and the

Milanese composer-conductor Piero Coppola, who had learned the operatic ropes as an assistant conductor at La Scala. Coppola received his first major podium assignment from no less a personage than Giacomo Puccini, who had selected him to conduct performances of *La Fanciulla del West* in Florence, Modena, Bologna, and Brussels. Maestro Coppola's wife, Lina, would join the company as lyric soprano.

In addition to the performing company, the new directors also planned to establish an opera school under the direction of Arne van Erpekum Sem, a former heroic tenor who had recently returned to Norway after a series of performances in Bremen, Vienna, Stuttgart, and Munich. Many years later, in 1987, in the same city of Munich, I joined the faculty of the Opera Studio at the Bayerische Staatsoper, coming full circle with my parents yet another time.

A shipping magnate named Christoffer Hannevig, who was enjoying enormous prosperity as a result of Norway's neutral position on the high seas, had promised to place a sizable amount of capital at the disposal of the company, following the expiration of an eighteen-month government-imposed quarantine on repatriating funds he had earned in the United States during the war years. He also purchased a large plot of land, where he proposed to construct a mammoth office complex, which would house the new opera company on its ground floor.

All of this represented an enormous turning point in my father's life. He had always been a bundle of energy, but this additional set of professional responsibilities turned him into a virtual dynamo. Drawing from his vast wealth of intelligence, his linguistic and musical skills, his education and experience, plus a long list of personal contacts amongst the operatic celebrities of the day, he fabricated this new opera company out of whole cloth.

One of the singers in the company, Erling Krogh, recalled those days on a local Oslo radio talk show in the late 1960s, commemorating the fiftieth anniversary of the company's founding. The talk show also featured several other former members of the company. "Alexander Várnay," Mr. Krogh said, "was the moving force, the soul of the whole enterprise, to be sure. The man who made all the final decisions." In a newspaper interview, my father was quoted as describing those early days of the company as "very hard work, especially the first year. We had to do everything ourselves, sew every single costume, cobble every shoe. It was impossible to order anything from workshops abroad, and it wasn't all that easy here in Norway, either. I spent two hours a day in the sewing atelier, half an hour at the shoemaker's shop, another half hour in the carpentry shop, and so on."

As the newly formed ensemble went into rehearsal, the theatre building was still not ready for use, so the members of the ensemble had to rehearse in whatever large rooms could be made available to them. For a while they practiced in a mineral water factory, and then, in a manner of speaking, moved on to "stronger stuff" by transferring the venue of rehearsals to Frydelund's brewery. In addition, there were solo rehearsals in private homes and practice sessions at the Hals Brothers' piano showroom.

On top of the actual preparation of performances, Papa bore the full responsibility for negotiating and drafting the contracts, having meanwhile acquired native fluency in Norwegian. He also auditioned the singers, corresponded directly with all the guest artists, booked their travel and hotel arrangements, and probably even cleaned the place up. But he loved his job. In his own words: "I have worked as many hours of the day and night as I possibly could. But I have received so much pleasure in return for all my efforts—first and foremost, the pleasure of seeing the artistic success of this company repeated so many times over."

He worked the company almost as hard as he worked himself. As one of the singers, Karl Johansen, reported many years later, my father would urge the singers after performances: "Don't go out drinking. Go home and get some sleep. Don't forget, tomorrow's rehearsal is called for ten o'clock!" Johansen then went on to say: "So we did go home—very often!"

My father was a very superstitious man. Like tennis players Boris Becker and André Agassi, he would stop shaving the minute a production went into rehearsal. As the rehearsal weeks went by, he would arrive at the theatre sporting a mane of hair and an ever-lengthening beard, which he would then promptly have cut off the morning after each première. Perhaps the subject matter of the first opera in the company's repertoire had something to do with this superstition. It was Camille Saint-Saëns's *Samson et Dalila*. Amazingly enough, the one thing he never did throughout his whole activity in Norway was sing. Many of the company members knew of his reputation as a performing artist, but on that same talk show in the 1960s, not one of the company veterans could remember ever hearing him sing a single note.

On November 29, 1918, the big day arrived. At a gala performance of *Samson et Dalila*, in a production by Alexander Várnay, with Maestro Piero Coppola in the pit and an all-Scandinavian cast performing in settings by the prominent Norwegian designer Jens Waldemar Wang, the theatre was officially opened. King Haakon VII, a close relative of King Gustav V of Sweden (who had attended my mother's performances in Stockholm), was in the royal box with his wife, Queen Maud, the sister of England's King George V. The ministers of state were also in attendance, along with a full complement of distinguished guests. The ladies wore their finest gowns and jewels. The gentlemen wore white tie and tails with flowers in their buttonholes. Many of them also sported monocles. The presence of a number of men whose chests were festooned with medals was the final proof that this was, indeed, the apex of Kristiania's social season.

My mother's first performance was as Frau Fluth, the German equivalent of Alice Ford in Otto Nicolai's musical version of Shakespeare's *Merry Wives of Windsor*. Shortly after that she sang her first Gilda in Norway, then Leonora in *Trovatore*, Violetta in *La Traviata*, and the page, Oscar, in *Un Ballo in Maschera*. After life on the road, Mme Jávor was pleased to be settling down with her family in Kristiania, rejoicing in the double delight of stardom and motherhood.

This double delight often became a double dilemma, because she soon found herself faced with the problem of what to do with the baby during performances. One day, she suddenly came up with a brainstorm: why not make a little crib away from home in one of the lower drawers of the make-up table in her dressing room? Unfortunately the lowest drawer in her own table was still a little too high for safety, and so, shortly before a *Ballo in Maschera* performance, mother bundled up the baby, and the two of us went over to the next dressing room, where the soprano who had been cast as Amelia was preparing to go onstage.

Sure enough, the other lady had a drawer close enough to the floor so that I would not do any damage to myself if I happened to fall out of it, and the two sopranos proceeded to bed me down for the duration of the opera. I was only a toddler at the time. It was my first encounter with Kirsten Flagstad.

From Strength to Strength

THAT GALA PERFORMANCE of *Samson et Dalila*, which opened the theatre on November 29, 1918, was sung in a Norwegian translation done by a parliamentary stenographer and amateur violinist who wrote poetry in his spare time. His name was Michael Flagstad, and he was only one member of a large family, all of whom figured importantly in the life of the Opéra Comique. Michael's wife, née Marie Nielsen Johnsrud, was a farm girl who had developed early in life into a keyboard prodigy.

When the Opéra Comique was founded, Mr. and Mrs. Flagstad joined the company, along with their son Ole, who played the cello in the orchestra, and their daughter Karen Marie, who sang small parts in opera and some slightly larger ones in operetta performances. Another son, Lasse, was a pianist and recital accompanist, who occasionally provided the piano accompaniments for the rehearsals at the theatre. The Flagstads even made their home available for those ad hoc rehearsals that were going on all over town. Their older daughter, Kirsten, born in 1895, couldn't join the company at the beginning, because she was away in Stockholm studying with an eminent voice teacher and otolaryngologist by the name of Gillis Bratt. She had already made her operatic début in Norway, singing the soubrette role of Nuri in Eugen d'Albert's opera *Tiefland*, but then returned to Sweden to continue her vocal studies with Dr. Bratt. When she came home for Christmas vacation in 1918, she discovered the Opéra Comique had become a kind of Flagstad family cottage industry.

At the urging of both her parents, Kirsten auditioned for my father and the staff at the opera house. She was immediately engaged as a kind of "utility soprano," starting in 1919 with a small part in the last act of Wilhelm Kienzl's tear-jerker, *Der Evangelimann*. Shortly afterward, she graduated to Anna Reich, the German equivalent of Nan Page, in *Die lustigen Weiber von Windsor*. Kirsten went on to sing a number of Micaëla-sized operatic roles, plus making regular appearances in operettas, at which she excelled. She was a mere slip of a thing, with huge eyes, a natural dramatic gift, and rock-solid musicianship, crowned by perfect pitch and an encyclopedic memory. Right from the beginning, Kirsten used to say she was never afflicted with stage fright, because she always knew what she was doing, and she was never happier than when she was onstage. This combination of technical proficiency and the joy of performing appealed enormously to my father, who said of her simply, "Die Kirsten kann alles!" (Kirsten can do everything!)

In May 1919, shortly after singing her first principal role, Nedda in *Pagliacci*, Kirsten entered into her first marriage, with Sigurd Hall, but, with traditional "show must go on" dedication, she and Sigurd agreed to postpone their honeymoon until the season ended in June. The following year, she took a little time off from her operatic chores, just as my mother had done a couple of years earlier, to give birth to a daughter. She was apparently so happy with her new role as a mother, she wasn't all that eager to go back to the theatre. But her mother would hear none of that! In their family and ours, music was the family business. So, one day, when Marie felt her daughter had recovered sufficiently from childbed to resume her operatic chores, she clamped a couple of scores under one arm and marched over to Kirsten's house to start getting her back in vocal shape for the coming season.

When Marie Flagstad heard what had happened to her daughter's voice, she was completely flabbergasted. "Kirsten's voice," she later said, "had virtually doubled in size." The voice had, in fact, undergone an extraordinary metamorphosis, having developed quite unexpectedly from the pleasant lyric soprano of her previous career into the lustrous silver sound that would soon make operatic history. Fortunately for posterity, Kirsten did not approach this felicitous transformation with the smug attitude of a lottery winner. On the contrary, she had the humility of someone who has just been granted a magnificent gift and realizes instantly that every such blessing entails an enormous amount of responsibility. I cannot help surmising that the fact that she came from professional musical stock, as I did, may have had something to do with the way she marshaled her vocal resources from those early days right through her matchless career, still sounding fresh and wonderful all the way to her final recordings, which she made just before she died in 1962 of bone cancer.

On November 11, 1918, about three weeks before the grand opening of the Opéra Comique, the Great War had finally come to an end. Not very long after that, a number of distinguished Central European singers contacted Benno Singer and Alexander Várnay to advise them that they would be available to join this relatively small company in Kristiania as guest artists. I was once chatting with my friend the late Holger Hagen, a renowned actor and man of music, and I mentioned to him that his aunt Emmi Leisner, a famous contralto from the Berlin Opera, had come to Kristiana to sing Azucena in *Il Trovatore*. When I asked Holger what prompted so many well-known people to make this arduous journey, he explained many of them did it to have a brief respite from the draconian food rationing in post–World War I Germany. Several other artists in that *Trovatore* cast were the real crème de la crème of Central European operatic life. Alongside my mother and Mme Leisner, the great opera and *Lieder* singer Heinrich Schlusnus appeared as Count di Luna, with two international celebrities, Leo Slezak and Hermann Jadlowker, alternating with local tenors as Manrico. Some of the other Berlin vocal imports to Norway included Melanie Kurt and Claire Dux. It was the kind of company both my parents always enjoyed keeping.

Rehearsals for these performances often got pretty heated, with my temperamental Hungarian father and the equally irascible Italian Maestro Coppola vying for position. On one occasion, my father was dissatisfied with Maestro Coppola's tempo, and nonchalantly took up a position behind the conductor where he proceeded to beat his own time in contravention of what was coming from the podium. The minute the maestro realized that his authority was being usurped, he turned around and let loose with a flow of colorful Italian invective, which ultimately had the two men coming to blows. It must have made a change in the otherwise reserved Scandinavian atmosphere.

Incidentally, my father was no slouch in the Italian invective department himself. On one occasion, he discovered that the reputable Italian publishing house of G. Ricordi was dragging its feet in providing him with the performance rights for one of its publications. He promptly sat down and, drawing from the comprehensive knowledge of Italian he had acquired during his years in Milan and Florence, wrote Ricordi a scathing letter in what one commentator referred to as "street urchin language." The certificate of performance rights arrived by return mail.

Among my souvenirs, there is a silver cigarette case, which had been pre-

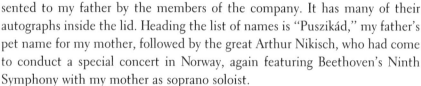

sented to my father by the members of the company. It has many of their autographs inside the lid. Heading the list of names is "Puszikád," my father's pet name for my mother, followed by the great Arthur Nikisch, who had come to conduct a special concert in Norway, again featuring Beethoven's Ninth Symphony with my mother as soprano soloist.

Certainly the most famous name inside the lid was my father's old friend Leo Slezak, who came to Kristiania several times to perform on the stage and tie on the ample Scandinavian feed bag. Once, Slezak and my father were invited to a traditional Scandinavian feast, in which great quantities of one- to one-and-a-half-pound lobsters were served to the guests, accompanied by equally ample quantities of Akvavit. On more than one occasion, those feasts left a few of the guests under the table, oblivious of their surroundings until the following morning. At this particular event, both my father and Slezak noticed that the others' appetites were beginning to flag, and as the waiters were about to remove the basins of lobster, both men, in their most resonant tenor tones, cried out something to the effect of "Stay your hand!" They themselves didn't stay their hands, or their jaws for that matter, and proceeded to finish off the crustaceans, much to the shocked amazement of the others present, except Mrs. Slezak, who had been at her husband's side for so many years, she had gradually (though reluctantly) become resigned to the mischievous side of his personality. After all, she had to live with it on a twenty-four-hour basis.

For all the beauty of his singing, Leo Slezak is best known for his uninterrupted series of stage pranks. You might call him the Till Eulenspiegel of grand opera. To this day, wherever you go in the operatic world, the tales of Slezak's high-jinks are still making the rounds. The most popular Slezak anecdote came about from his using his quick wit to respond to a blunder the stage crew had made. He was standing backstage waiting to make his first entrance as Lohengrin, riding in a swan boat. Suddenly, several bars too early, he saw the stagehands pull the swan boat onstage—without him on board. The audience sat there in stunned bewilderment, wondering how the people onstage were going to get out of this one. While they were still pondering this dilemma, Slezak simply called from his position in the wings, "What time does the next swan leave?"

I adored Leo Slezak and always looked forward to his visits. It was such fun for me, as a tiny kid, to be bounced up and down on the tenor's mammoth knee while he sang silly songs that left me giggling uncontrollably. He really was one of a kind, even if his zany shenanigans could sometimes be a little

Trees have always been my friends—August 1921. *Personal photo.*

trying for the people who had to work with him. This was certainly the case with his final appearance at the Opéra Comique.

By this point in the company's history, the management had apparently overextended itself and felt obligated to call in Mr. Hannevig's promise of working capital. As is so often the case with theatrical "angels," Hannevig's financial wings turned out to be pure papier-mâché. The fortune he said was quarantined for eighteen months had been confiscated by the United States government. It would not be available to the Opéra Comique now or at any other predictable point in time. So, the fickle fortunes of a shipping magnate had turned our palace of song into a castle in the air, but while the company still existed, my father and Mr. Singer did what they could to shore up its resources. While everybody hoped for a miracle, the ensemble continued to put on the finest performances they considered themselves capable of mounting. When these operas failed to meet their own expenses, Mr. Singer quickly scheduled a series of operettas in an attempt to restore the company's finances sufficiently to make history with a production of *Otello*, to headline the company's two biggest drawing cards, Leo Slezak in the title role and the now-established Kirsten Flagstad as Desdemona.

As my mother's services would not be required in this piece, she accepted an offer from the Vox Company in Berlin to go over there and immortalize her voice on wax discs in a series of aria recordings, which were later released in technically improved form on the newer LP. At this point in my narrative I'd like to pay an affectionate tribute to a friend who made possible the re-release of my mother's recording, as well as hundreds of great operatic documents. The late Jürgen Grundheber was an avid collector of operatic memorabilia who circumnavigated the globe to unearth vocal rarities. Not content to enjoy them in his own recording library, Jürgen took it upon himself to find ways of improving the recordings technically and then releasing them to the general public.

While Mother was lighting up the grooves with her vocal pyrotechnics, my father was back in Norway contending with the artillery charges flying back and forth between Kirsten Flagstad and Leo Slezak. Their voices blended magnificently, but Slezak's constant tomfoolery soon got on Mme Flagstad's nerves. Although still young in years, not quite thirty in fact, Kirsten Flagstad was not one to suffer foolishness gladly. At one *Otello* rehearsal, she responded to Slezak at the top of his nonsensical form by turning on her heels and heading for the nearest exit. It took a deputation of one in the person of Mrs. Slezak, armed with a bouquet of flowers and a box of the soprano's favorite chocolates, to lure Kirsten Flagstad back onto the stage of the Comique. Before agreeing to return, however, she exacted a solemn pledge from Mrs. Slezak to read her husband the riot act if he didn't get down to serious business. *Otello*, after all, is a tragic opera, and Flagstad wasn't interested in being strangled by Bozo the Clown.

The *Otello* production was a huge success, but it was still not enough to rescue the theatre. For three glorious years, the Opéra Comique of Kristiania had gone from strength to strength, producing a remarkable total of twenty-six operas, every one of them a new production! On September 1, 1921, the moment had come to ring down the curtain for the last time. The occasion was a performance of Mozart's *Die Zauberflöte*. When the performance ended, there was a torrent of applause. Apparently nobody had to catch the last conveyance to the suburbs. The audience cheered the cast and the conductor, and then somebody set up a chant demanding that Director Várnay come out onstage. When he finally appeared, carried onstage on the shoulders of his colleagues, the basso Magnus Andersen, who had sung Sarastro in the performance, walked over and ceremoniously crowned his head with a laurel wreath. Floral tributes were also given to Leif Halvorsen, the conductor, Jens Wang, the set designer, and Mrs. Marie Flagstad, each accompanied with a rousing salvo of three cheers. Finally, the audience gave my father three times three cheers.

Possibly for the first time in his life, this multilingual gentleman was totally at a loss for words. He stepped to the footlights and simply said, "På gjensyn," the Norwegian equivalent of "See you again," a promise he would be unable to keep. Then everybody went down the street for a farewell party.

In a final joint interview shortly after the theatre closed, Benno Singer expressed his doubts that opera and operetta ever really had a chance in Norway, while my father bitterly commented that perhaps the Norwegians were still not ready for this level of sophistication. The Casino Theatre (as it was later called) on Stortingsgaten, where all that history was made, is now a movie house.

At any rate, my father and mother would now be free to accept the invitation to Buenos Aires that had brought them to Scandinavia in the first place. As we prepared to leave, my parents remembered a historical quote from the great nineteenth-century Norwegian violin virtuoso, Ole Bull, the "Paganini of the North": "The function of art," he once wrote, "is not to divide but rather to bring together." In his short tenure in Kristiania, my father had certainly done that!

Years later, reflecting on those early days, Kirsten Flagstad wrote: "My collaboration with Alexander Várnay was very important to me personally. I have profited from what he taught me throughout my entire singing career." She also made a quiet vow to express her gratitude for both her hometown audience's reception and my father's friendship and tutelage in some palpable form. She kept both promises. In 1959–60, she assumed the leadership of the Norwegian National Opera, which more or less picked up where the Opéra Comique had left off, giving first-rate performances for Norwegian audiences, featuring local artists. As to her gratitude to my father, a few years after we left Norway, I was the member of the Várnay family who had the great good fortune to be the beneficiary of Mme Flagstad's gesture of grateful remembrance.

New Worlds to Conquer

SOME YEARS AGO, in the late summer of 1947, I was singing the *Ring* under the baton of Erich Kleiber at the Teatro Colón in Buenos Aires. Two elderly ladies came backstage after the final *Götterdämmerung* performance, dressed in a quaint old-fashioned style, a little like Josephine Hull and Jean Adair in that wonderful movie version of *Arsenic and Old Lace*. The ladies wanted to know if I was related to the Alexander Várnay who had been invited to produce the very first local performance of *The Magic Flute*, which premièred at the Teatro Nuevo in May 1923, featuring his wife as the Queen of the Night. They then proudly informed me that they had been members of the chorus in that highly successful production and had nothing but the fondest memories of my parents. This Italian-language *Zauberflöte* performance had been preceded by several appearances my mother made in Buenos Aires. Her Argentine début took place in *La Traviata* during the short pre-carnival season at the Teatro Nuevo, which ran from January 1 to February 22, 1923.

Describing her as a "Norwegian soprano," the January 24 edition of *La Prensa* went on to say: "She possesses a very beautiful voice, which she handles artistically, clear diction and expressive stage action; she was a Violetta worthy of a more important stage. She had an instant, well-deserved success, receiving warm applause from the audience." The same newspaper described her performance in *Il Barbiere di Siviglia* with the comment: "Señora Maria Jávor-Várnay had a brilliant personal success as Rosina."

It was at one of those *Barbiere* performances that my voice was heard resounding through a theatre for the first time, albeit unplanned. In those days, I was a docile five-year-old, and my parents saw no reason why they shouldn't let me take an afternoon siesta and then bring me to watch the performance from a box seat with someone to look after me. Up to then, the operas my mother sang resembled the fairy tales that had been read to me, but the Rossini opera is so realistic at points, a child has a hard time differentiating between illusion and reality. In the lesson scene, where Dr. Bartolo flails the air, threatening to hit the Count and Rosina, I was so upset that I vociferously called out from the box, in the smattering of Spanish I had rapidly acquired, "¡No tocar mi madre!" much to the delight of the audience and the dismay of my mother. That was the end of my theatrical career—for the time being.

Maestro Feruccio Cattelani held Mother in such esteem that he went so far as to list his company on programs as "*La Compañia Lirica Italiana*, featuring the famous soprano Maria Jávor-Várnay," even printing her name in large letters above the casts of operas in which she did not participate. Following the carnival period, the company moved to the Teatro de la Opera for a one-month season, which my mother opened with the title role of *Lucia di Lammermoor*, followed by Gilda in *Rigoletto*. She was also scheduled to repeat her triumph as Lucia on March 24, but on March 23, my parents realized they had been tricked into signing a questionable contract, which they promptly abrogated, much to the dismay of the public and the press, which suggested she had been "poorly advised" to cancel her performances. From this vantage point, it would be impossible for me to weigh the issues that caused my parents to break their contract with the company, but it might be worth mentioning an interesting sidelight involving another foreign guest artist, the Italian dramatic tenor Fortunato De Angelis, who also canceled several performances of *Otello* and *Andrea Chénier* during the same season, claiming illness as his reason for not performing. Who knows what the real reason was?

In the spring, another company, this time headed by conductor Bruno Mari, put on another season at the Teatro Nuevo, during which my father's aforementioned first-ever production of *Zauberflöte* was also premièred. In addition to her Queen of the Night, my mother repeated her successes as Lucia, Violetta, and Rosina, while adding a seldom-heard Elvira in Bellini's *I Puritani*. She also appeared in a benefit concert at the renowned Teatro Colón.

When the season closed on May 27 of that year, my parents' successes in South America prompted my father to take full advantage of what he thought would be his temporary position on the western side of the Atlantic to make a detour via New York on our return journey to Europe. The family arrived in the Empire City on November 15, 1923, and checked into a hotel. Hardly had we settled in when my father took a job directing productions at the Manhattan Opera House. It began to look like we might be staying for a while, so my parents left the hotel and moved into a furnished walk-up apartment on the fourth floor of a building at 76 West End Avenue in the Manhattan Beach section of Brooklyn. With the family ensconced in more permanent quarters, my father thought it was time to visit the Metropolitan Opera management with some recordings of my mother's voice as a kind of pre-audition. Those primitive 78 rpm recordings piqued their curiosity so much that they invited my mother for an in-person audition. After she sang, they regretfully admitted that my mother had selected an inopportune time to apply for an engagement at the Metropolitan and suggested she re-apply somewhat later.

In the early to middle 1920s, the company was more than adequately supplied with excellent coloratura and lyric sopranos. Amelita Galli-Curci was at the top of her form at the time, dominating the Italian repertoire together with Lucrezia Bori and Queena Mario, while Mother's role of Leonora in *Il Trovatore* was already shared by Rosa Ponselle, Elisabeth Rethberg, and Florence Easton.

Shortly after this disappointment, my parents began discussing the possibility of returning to Europe, but fate tragically intervened. Father suddenly began feeling ill. Under the circumstances, starting a long ocean journey to Europe would have been impossible. For the time being, at least, we would be in Brooklyn to stay. It was in that Brooklyn apartment that the final tragedy struck. My first memory of the terrible events to come began when I went into the bathroom one day and found the tub spattered with blood.

Recently I asked my physician friend Dr. Siegfried Hiemstra his opinion on what might have happened, and based on what little information I can remember from my childhood, this was his evaluation: In his boyhood, my father had suffered from a form of diphtheria complicated by a hemolytic streptococcal infection, which then turned into glomerule nephritis. The symptoms lay dormant for years and then violently erupted as uremia, a form of kidney poisoning, which, back before the widespread use of penicillin (which was not discovered until 1928), dialysis, or renal transplants, invariably proved fatal.

My father's condition deteriorated so rapidly, in fact, that he had to be admitted to the hospital, but he was determined to get out of that institution, come what may. One afternoon our doorbell rang. My mother and I leaned over the railing to see who was there. Suddenly we saw my father's hands clutching the bannister as he struggled to climb up the stairs. He had left the impersonal surroundings of the hospital, preferring to come back home to take his chances with fate in a more familiar atmosphere. This time, his fate was not as kind as it had been in the past.

Thousands of miles away from home, this remarkable man, who had performed so thrillingly on the stage and made such a telling contribution to the artistic life of every place he touched, even helping one country restore a major portion of its national identity, this gifted linguist, brilliant scholar, and theatrical innovator, whose productions were lauded by kings and queens, this caring, loving husband and father, this inspiring teacher and director, brought down the curtain on a life full of achievements most people would have needed several lifetimes to accomplish. He passed away in our temporary home on June 13, 1924, not quite thirty-five years of age. In his final delirium, they told me, just before he died, he was singing again.

He was laid out in an open casket at the funeral home. I was only six years old at the time, but I distinctly remember how comforting it was to look on his face, smiling serenely as he had in life. My mother took a rose and told me to put it on his chest. To this day, whenever I think back on those sorrowful times, I remember that smile, which appeared to me shortly afterward in a kind of vision. With his head surrounded by an aura of light, my father smiled over at me and, without uttering a word, reassured me things would work out just fine, and so they did.

A few months after my father's death, Mother reapplied to the Metropolitan Opera for a second audition. On November 28, 1924, Mother sang a couple of arias from *La Traviata*, and the gentlemen who listened wrote "beautiful voice" on her audition card. They said they recognized her quality and suggested Mme Jávor get in touch with them, possibly for some smaller parts, such as Rhine Maidens, *Parsifal* Flower Girls, and the like, a little later in the season. Had this suggestion been made to me, with my enterprising American attitude toward things, I would doubtless have stayed in touch, but Mother never knocked on that door again, even though it might have changed her life. Like many another European artist, she felt if they wanted her, they would contact her. She regarded it as a form of bad manners to force this kind of issue. This is one of the differences between an American approach and a European one.

I never did find out what happened to the concert contract my mother signed for the 1924 Buenos Aires season. She was probably unable to organize the trip with a small child without the support of her husband. In fact, I have often wondered why Mother didn't simply return to her well-to-do family in

Looks like I deserved those posies. *Personal photo.*

Europe. Then, many years later in London, I came upon Michael Korda's book *Charmed Lives*, relating the story of his Hungarian film-making family. In the book, the author describes the precipitous departure of many Hungarian intellectuals from their native land following the 1919 takeover of the country by a short-lived Communist revolutionary dictatorship. Perhaps my mother was afraid this régime might subsequently return to power and decided to stay out of Hungary for the time being. But beyond this, she was a lady with a cast-iron will, as resourceful in her own way as her late husband had been, and she derived an enormous satisfaction from facing and conquering challenges, retaining the full measure of her dignity in the process. Never, no matter what the circumstances, would she consider giving up.

I was too young at the time to understand the seriousness of the situation and tried to comfort her as best I could, that is, when I wasn't out playing in one of the many trees that really *do* grow in Brooklyn. My fondness for climbing those trees brought back memories to my mother of the cherry tree which had figured so importantly in her own youth. Trees have always played a significant role in my life as well, and I suppose some day I may even be buried under one, but I'm in no hurry for that. I'd rather sit under a spreading chestnut tree in my present condition, making sure it isn't the season when chestnuts fall on people's heads.

Back then, when my playmates and I weren't scampering around in the trees, we were busy finding holes in the fences at Sheepshead Bay so we could go for a dip in the ocean without paying an admission charge, while my mother set about making a new life for herself in her new country. If she couldn't sing at the Met, she presumed there were plenty of other audiences eager to hear operatic performances. This was a classic European misconception. In Europe, a singer with authentic talent who discovers there are no vacancies in the ensemble of a big theatre like Munich, for example, goes up one road to Augsburg or another one to Nuremberg and auditions there. Sooner or later, that person is likely to find an artistic home much the way water finds its own level.

This was anything but the case in the United States in the 1920s. Apart from short seasons in very distant places such as Chicago and San Francisco, opera was the Metropolitan and little else. There were a couple of ad hoc places that put on some fairly improvised performances in various parts of the city. Sometimes, in these performances, the quality of the singing saved the show. On other occasions, some of these companies had to be seen and heard to be believed. But Mother couldn't afford to be choosy with a child to support, and so she started making contact with the various smaller companies that brought this opulent art form to less well-heeled audiences.

The most formidable impresario on the cut-rate opera circuit in those days was an august gentleman by the name of Alfredo Salmaggi, a self-styled Italian *grand seigneur*, who presided over a company that performed in places like the Brooklyn Academy of Music and at Downing Stadium on Randall's Island in the East River. Whatever else Salmaggi might or might not have been, he was a consummate businessman. He knew the city was full of Italo-Americans yearning for a sound of home, and he saw to it that, wherever they lived, wherever they worked, be it cutting veal in a meat-packing plant, manning a fruit and vegetable stand on Bleecker Street, sweating in a steam-fitting plant, or stitching in a tailor shop in the garment district, they were always visited personally by his ticket sellers to make sure they had a chance to attend the performances. Mr. Salmaggi even did a healthy business with the chorus members, who always received one complimentary ticket and generally augmented this increment with a couple of paid tickets for the rest of the family.

Salmaggi's performances may have been rather hastily slapped together, but what they lacked in theatrical polish they certainly made up in musical enthusiasm, and when people like Mária Jávor were on the stage, drawing from her rich European training and experience, especially if she was singing with some of the other highly competent artists Salmaggi frequently imported from Italy, the audience got a pretty good show for their money. In short, were it not for one unusual incident, I would say my hat was off to Mr. Salmaggi. The incident involved a performance in which my mother was on the stage, and I was sitting in the audience wearing a rather large, floppy hat, in keeping with the style in those days. Suddenly I noticed a gentleman glaring over at me from beneath another big hat—it was Salmaggi, who invariably crowned his very long, handsomely coiffed hair with either a Borsalino or a Panama of gargantuan proportions. My mother said later he was probably jealous because my headgear was even larger than his, so for all my admiration, I'll keep my hat on for Mr. Salmaggi.

He always regaled the audiences with his flamboyant curtain speeches, in which he proudly swooped onto the apron of the stage to announce coming attractions in a blend of Italian and English the largely immigrant audiences probably understood better than if he had stuck obstinately to one language or the other. His sense of showmanship and hyperbole were exceptional, as witness the time when he proudly announced that a coming performance of some opera or other would be featuring a special guest performance by the

"Great Caruso." When a heckler called out from the cheap seats to remind the *Sovrintendente* that the great Enrico Caruso had unfortunately passed away back in 1921, Salmaggi made a grand gesture with his flowing cape and replied, "Not *that* Caruso! *Giuseppe* Caruso, his-a cousin . . . joost as-a good!"

It was during one of those Salmaggi seasons that my mother found herself singing performances with Fortunato De Angelis, the same guest artist who had canceled the remainder of the Teatro San Martín season at the time my mother dropped out of the company. Although he had never had occasion to perform under my father's stage direction in Argentina, he told my mother he had enjoyed knowing my father there and had also been a great admirer of his artistry. Commendatore De Angelis described himself as a "Romano da Roma" in contrast to all the pseudo-Romani who came from somewhere beyond the seven hills. Soon the stage partnership between my mother and her tenor began to deepen into something more, and one day Mr. De Angelis proposed marriage to my mother in a way that touches me to this day, reminding her that her little girl would grow up so much more normally and happily if she had two parents instead of just one. After all, he was no stranger to me.

Back in Buenos Aires, my mother would often park me in my father's office, where Mr. De Angelis sometimes came by to pay a call. On a few of these occasions, when my father was up to his ears in work, he used to ask De Angelis if he would mind taking "la piccola bambina" for a walk. For Mr. De Angelis, a widower with four grown children back in Italy, it was like a godsend to have a little tyke to look after from time to time. Italians and Latins are renowned for being great family men. He would need all of his paternal inclinations with me. As my mother later reported, starting in Norway and continuing in Argentina and North America, I had turned into something akin to a high-grade parrot, chattering away with everybody in his or her own language and chirping every note my mother had ever sung onstage, having apparently memorized her entire repertoire. Mind you, these are facts I have no way of verifying, and proud mothers will be proud mothers, so please take this information with several grains of salt.

Mother's awareness of my fondness for her tenor partner clinched the deal, and she became Mrs. Fortunato De Angelis on May 6, 1926. A little less than a year later, on March 7, 1927, my beloved half brother, Fortunato Anthony ("Lucky") De Angelis, was born. Shortly afterward, the family moved across the Hudson to an Italian neighborhood in Jersey City. The establishment of this enlarged family in new quarters had a powerful effect on all of us.

My stepfather was a very kind and gentle person, but he had as strong a will as his wife, and one of the points on which he was unbending was his insistence on everyone speaking Italian in his home. While his English was adequate for day-to-day communication, his home was his castle, and he had no desire to speak anything but his native language inside it. This meant my mother, whose achievements in the Italian language were the only indifferent grades she had earned in the conservatory, suddenly found herself faced with having to run her home in this added language, while continuing to communicate with her children in either German or English.

My brother was somewhat resentful of this stricture, but he had no choice. His Pappa did much of the cooking, supplying some grandiose Italian dinners, while our mother did equally well with Hungarian recipes. Whenever dinner time came around, Mr. De Angelis recited his inviolable rule: "Chi vuol mangiare in questa casa deve parlare Italiano" (Whoever wants to eat in this house has to speak Italian). My brother liked good food as much as the next kid. If he didn't feel like speaking Italian at meals, he'd simply shut up and help himself to another serving of some heavenly pasta that had just emerged steaming aromatically from the kitchen. Looking back on this period, I often wondered what might have happened had any of us been so rebellious as to speak some other language in the house—but we never did. This proves how healthy our appetites were back then.

Years later, during the Second World War, Lucky came home on furlough from the U.S. Marines and announced that he had eaten magnificently during a port call in Naples because he was able to speak Italian fluently to the waiters in the restaurants. My mother and I just looked at each other!

In contrast to my brother, the idea of *my* adding another language to my quiver of accomplishments was a real delight, plus becoming a skill that would hold me in good stead both onstage and off for years to come. This knowledge of Italian and my increasing interest in the work my mother and stepfather were doing onstage came in handy for the whole family a few years later as I entered my middle teens.

It seems my parents were being threatened with the cancellation of a *Trovatore* performance because the management of the company couldn't find anyone to accept a fee of $20 to sing the tiny role of Leonora's confidante, Ines, whose contribution to the opera largely involves feeding the prima donna a few cues and then singing in the ensembles. In those days, when eggs were literally a dime a dozen and less, twenty dollars looked like a lot of money to a teenager. What's more, I had practically memorized the short part just by listening to my parents practicing the leads, and so I volunteered to take over the role and save the two performances, thus guaranteeing not only the pin money for my own pocket but also the higher fees for my parents. I chose to sing this role under the rather hokey pseudonym of "Ines Milani." In view of the fact that I hadn't even given a thought to vocal training at that time, I regarded this one-timer more as a lark than as a début.

Another offstage benefit from my linguistic skill came about several years later, in September 1946, when I made my first appearance at the San Francisco Opera, certainly second only to the Met in quality and prestige.

The General Manager of the San Francisco Opera at the time was a conductor by the name of Gaetano Merola, whose command of the English language was more or less in keeping with some of the other Italian opera company directors of the day. When I came to his office and answered his English greeting in Neapolitan dialect, he almost fell off the chair. He couldn't believe a soprano he had hired primarily for Wagnerian roles had responded to his "interesting" English in his own native dialect. From there on in, he referred to me affectionately as *scugnizz'*, Neapolitan slang for "street urchin," the same word once applied to describe my father's use of the Italian language when he got mad at Ricordi. Calling the diva who sings Brünnhilde and Isolde an urchin may have been regarded as demeaning by some of the grander ladies in the business, but I was flattered by this familiarity. It also came in very handy when I discovered that friendly relations certainly lubricated the engines of fee negotiation.

Life for us kids in New York and New Jersey was a pretty carefree existence, despite the many privations my mother and stepfather were facing. Twice a year, once just before Easter and once before Christmas, we would be aroused from our slumbers at the crack of dawn and rushed over to the Lower East Side of Manhattan just as the merchants were opening the doors of their clothing stores. My mother remembered from her European days that many Jewish merchants considered it bad luck to lose a sale to the first customer of the day. This knowledge gave her plenty of leverage as she haggled over the price of our garments, much to my embarrassment. Lucky couldn't have cared less.

If life was difficult in those early years, we soon found ourselves on the brink of ruin in the wake of the stock market crash in October 1929, which definitely had a disastrous effect on opera singers. The reason is simple enough—when times are hard, people look to meeting the basic needs of food and shelter. Items like culture and entertainment are among the first things that get stricken from the budget. Rather than jump out the windows, as so many of the stockbrokers were doing in those dismal days, my suddenly impoverished

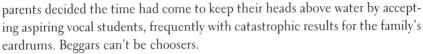

parents decided the time had come to keep their heads above water by accepting aspiring vocal students, frequently with catastrophic results for the family's eardrums. Beggars can't be choosers.

But as long as there was music in our home, whatever it sounded like, there was also plenty of happiness, enhanced by the status of being the daughter of an authentic *primo tenore* and *prima donna* in an Italo-American part of town, where opera singers were looked upon with nothing short of adulation. In the early thirties, Lucky and I saw a newfangled device called a radio. We began badgering our parents to put one in our home to soften the rigors of doing homework. At first reluctant, they finally relented when I mentioned that, as of Christmas 1931, the Metropolitan Opera was broadcasting matinée performances. If we had a radio, we could listen to the Met every Saturday afternoon. Once we got used to even more sound in our musical household, this piece of equipment made a healthy contribution to domestic tranquility.

One of my regular household chores was grocery shopping. As I made my rounds, it was fun to see how the mere mention of an upcoming performance to the neighborhood Italian butcher in Jersey City would get his thumb off the scale and add a couple of free slices of delectable homemade salami to the purchase, plus a little supplemental sausage for yours truly to eat in the store. While the butcher was trying to negotiate a couple of house seats from me for the next *Rigoletto* or *Trovatore*, he often chirped "Questa o quella," or some other aria, the knife whizzing back and forth in his ultra-professional hand, as he cut off one paper-thin slice of salami after another.

That butcher wasn't the only opera lover our family did business with. In the 1920s, before popularly priced refrigerators were available, it was more than convenient to have an ice man who loved to sing and saw to it *i signori cantanti* got an extra-large piece of ice in the box in return for a voice lesson. Mr. Giuseppe Cicciarelli, the ice man in question, had an enormous tenor voice, which was sufficiently serviceable to be featured subsequently on October 25, 1931, in a recital of what Mr. and Mrs. De Angelis referred to as "the most advanced students of their vocal studio." I was thirteen years old at the time, and I also appeared on that program, albeit without opening my yap. I started the second part of the program by playing one movement of Beethoven's "Pathétique" Piano Sonata.

Another momentous event occurred in my fourteenth year as well. A friend of the family, the distinguished concert organist and composer Pietro Yon, who had once been music director at St. Peter's in the Vatican, came to visit one afternoon. Noticing my interest in opera, he invited me to join him in his box at the Metropolitan for a performance of *Simon Boccanegra*, featuring Lawrence Tibbett in the title role and a wonderful Czech soprano named Maria Müller as Maria Boccanegra. Mme Müller had made her Metropolitan début in 1925 in the same role that later launched my career, Sieglinde in *Die Walküre*. She was twenty-six years old on that occasion. By the time the *Boccanegra* production was presented, she was already thirty-three, a captivatingly beautiful woman with a voice to match.

Seeing opera for the first time in these lavish surroundings was thrilling enough, but the great voices of the two protagonists made it even more exciting. As I leaned over the railing of the gilded box to admire this unusually attractive young singer, I felt the same sensation other American kids my age might have experienced in those days watching Greta Garbo in the movies. It was very glamorous, and I was glad to be a part of it, if only vicariously.

With all that music in the air, I soon made up my mind that performing was going to figure in my life as well—but I wasn't all that interested in singing. I had set my heart on becoming a concert pianist. After checking the area to find a piano teacher who could be talked to on the subject of money, my mother found a man named Ralph Ganci in Jersey City. Since we were unable to pay for every lesson, I earned some of them by doing after-school secretarial work for him. When I entered my mid-teens, my fate seemed decided, but destiny had other cards up its sleeve for me, as I would soon find out.

Amonasro's Arrogance

IT ALL STARTED with an argument. I had gone with my family to a performance of *Aida* (not at the Met), and I was annoyed at something I had seen on
the stage. In the middle of the triumphal scene in act 2, the prisoners of war
are led before the King of Egypt. Suddenly Aida recognizes her father, the
Ethiopian King Amonasro, among the prisoners, and, in a moment of injudi-
cious excitement, she blurts out, "Mio padre!" (My father!). To avoid being
discovered as the king and possibly put to death, Amonasro whispers to her
not to give him away. But the Egyptians have heard her outburst, and the King
of Egypt wants a little more information about this particular captive. Looking
him in the eye, he asks him, "Dunque tu sei?" (Who are you?). With great
presence of mind, Amonasro replies simply, "suo padre" (her father) and then
proceeds to tell the Egyptian king a cunningly fabricated story to keep his
identity concealed. That moment when Amonasro replies to the king's question is one of the most suspenseful moments in operatic literature, but a
spasm of vanity took all the tension out of the situation. Obviously the baritone was feeling his vocal oats that evening, so, rather than reply directly to
the king's question, he decided to make a little mini-aria out of a three-note
phrase, holding the penultimate note of this unaccompanied passage for an
unconscionably long time, while he strutted vaingloriously across the apron of
the stage, every inch the self-centered opera singer and not one iota the clever
Ethiopian king.

All the way home, I complained about that bit of gratuitous grandstanding, much to the shocked amazement of both my mother and my stepfather. Both of them tried to explain that as long as the man sang well, his posturing was a secondary consideration not worth further discussion. I begged to differ. There was no justification, as I saw it, either musically or dramatically, for that baritone's proscenium promenade that evening. As the argument went back and forth, my mother finally tossed me a look of total exasperation and asked bluntly, "Well, how would *you* have done it?" Back then, that question had me stumped. I had no specific suggestions, and the subject was promptly tabled for future, *very* future reference. I could not have known then that an unrelated event would set in motion a series of developments that would ultimately find me having to answer this kind of question for years and years to come.

It was the mid-1930s. The family had survived the worst of the Depression and moved back into New York City, taking up residence in a spacious, handsome apartment on West Tenth Street, one of the nicest parts of Greenwich Village. For a while, it seemed like our family had finally found a permanent nest, but this was not to be the case. My stepfather, like many other tenors, both on- and offstage, was a terribly jealous man, and his constant suspicions were becoming a source of friction between him and my mother. Finally the combined pressures of earning a living while keeping a needlessly watchful eye on his entirely faithful wife became too much for him, and he decided to part company with us and return to his native Italy. We never heard from him again.

It was at this point in our lives that my mother took my brother and me and moved into a smaller Manhattan apartment, at 25 Charles Street, another one of the many way stations in the meandering course of my youth. All these occurrences represented a terrific upheaval for a growing youngster like me. The domestic strife and the precarious situation following my stepfather's sudden departure took their toll on both of us children. However, while we were in that Charles Street apartment, a stroke of luck occurred that proved an omen of our future life. I was leafing through one of the many daily newspapers available in New York City in those days, and I came upon a promotional crossword puzzle contest. Anyone solving the puzzle in that day's edition could participate in a lottery with a number of valuable prizes for the winners. A week or so later, we received a letter advising us that I had become the proud owner of an upright piano. Being professionals, we couldn't help wondering if the tone would be up to our standards. We were pleasantly surprised.

In those rough times, owning that piano meant my mother would no longer have to rent an instrument to teach with, and I would have my own piano to practice. The arrival of that little piano in our lives strengthened my own belief in a kind of divine providence, pointing out that music was one of the paths my life could take, and then leaving it to me to get there. The joy of winning that handsome piano, however, did little to solve another problem in my personal life. Over the last few years, I had become comfortably settled in William L. Dickinson High School in Jersey City, and I desperately wanted to graduate there with my classmates. The school authorities said they would be willing to make an exception and allow me to continue there, despite the fact that it would involve crossing a state line. For me, this meant getting up at the crack of dawn, or even before dawn in the winter, taking the Hudson Tube (today's PATH train) from Greenwich Village to Jersey City, and then riding on the streetcar to school, but in view of what happened in the final weeks of my senior year, it was a sacrifice well made.

In the weeks just before graduation, I experienced the "unrelated event" mentioned earlier in this chapter. With graduation time drawing closer and closer, my friends and I all wanted to have as many mentions as possible in the yearbook. For some reason, we believed it always looked better to future employers if, for instance, we could show the world we had spent two terms in the Delta Lambda Law Club, of which I was an enthusiastic member, or had served for a year monitoring the hall leading down to the cafeteria, along with similar contributions to our own development and the well-being of the school community.

The school had a glee club, and I thought it might be fun to sing along with the others and earn a yearbook credit in the bargain. When I completed my audition for Mr. Moritz E. Schwarz, the school's music director, Mr. Schwarz looked at me pensively for a moment and then asked me if I would please bring my mother to school. I was frankly scared. Normally, when a teacher asked a parent to take the time and trouble to come to school, it usually meant a disciplinary matter, and I couldn't figure out why I needed to be reprimanded. My mother was fairly puzzled by this request as well, but nevertheless off we went to Jersey City the next morning. When we arrived, Mr. Schwarz wasted no time explaining to my mother that he had asked her to come see him because he thought I had a voice worth training, and he wanted her to find me a voice teacher. With a smile, she replied that she was a singer and vocal teacher herself, adding that a good mother always strives to teach her child whatever she knows. She simply felt that my voice was not sufficiently mature for professional training. She would rather wait, she said, until

I was eighteen or nineteen, but, even then, she suspected that I had a fairly strong voice, and she didn't believe in starting to train strong voices too early. Mr. Schwarz countered that he felt the time was indeed ripe. I have often reflected that had it not been for Moritz E. Schwarz, I might be practicing law today.

Mother was a demanding teacher. Of the many gifts she gave me in this early stage, possibly the greatest one was the most astute set of ears I have ever encountered in a lifetime of making music. She realized both instinctively and intellectually that every human voice has its own personality, its own dynamic, and its own destiny. As we started to work together, it became increasingly clear to both of us that my voice was already larger, darker, and heavier than hers was. She made no effort to train me, as perhaps other musician parents might have done, as a carbon copy of her coloratura self.

On Saturday, June 29, 1935, at 8:15 P.M., the big moment came: commencement exercises in the auditorium of William L. Dickinson High School. Sitting on the stage with the other members of the graduating class, I watched my friend Melita Patrosio walk away with all the academic prizes. We were very proud, and just a little envious, of her. Then it was time for the first musical portion of the program, in which I was represented both by a little song I had composed for the occasion and by my appearance as soloist. Suddenly I got so nervous, I began staring straight at my mother in the tenth row, as if asking for help. Her encouraging smile still didn't rescue me from repeating the first stanza of the solo rather than moving on to the second verse. As if that weren't enough, what I had always thought was a large voice suddenly wasn't there. Somehow or other, I got through my solo part with what I perceived as a rather inadequate sound; then, as the chorus joined in, I inadvertently began using the sound my mother had helped me put in my throat, and I could actually hear that sound soaring above everyone else's. It was an interesting example of how nerves affect performance, a phenomenon I must have registered for future reference, because I somehow learned to cope with uneasiness and bring the self-assurance of hard work and technical preparation with me to the stage.

One of the great imponderabilia of vocal art is the fact that, while relaxation is necessary to developing the fullness of anyone's tones, *too much* relaxation can be fatal. This is why it is of such paramount importance to take that tension we have naturally and transmute it into the tension of the stage situation. Nothing communicates more graphically and negatively than a blasé ap-

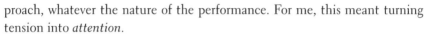

proach, whatever the nature of the performance. For me, this meant turning tension into *attention*.

With commencement over, I put my voice on "hold" for a while and went back to the keyboard. It wasn't always easy to sacrifice the social life many of my friends were enjoying and continue practicing the long hours I would need to achieve my goals. Somewhere along the way I became dissatisfied with the fact that my left hand was not as flexible as it should have been. This made the chance of meeting my own standards as a concert pianist a rather large question mark. My concern about the quality of my piano work was regrettably confirmed by my honest teacher, Mr. Ganci. Whatever my future might turn out to be, I had to start thinking seriously about the present. With school over, I would have to find some kind of employment to supplement the family income and to compensate my mother for her contributions to my musical studies.

The first job I had was doing stenographic work for a firm of denim jobbers on Franklin Street in Lower Manhattan. They imported fabrics from South America and marketed them to retail outlets in the U.S. The pay there was the princely sum of $10 a week, but at a time when everything cost a fraction of what it does today, that constituted a perfectly reasonable salary. At least that's what my employers contended. I had to pay my own carfare, which left me with a pittance for my expenses. Thank goodness I didn't have to pay taxes. Shortly after I started work there, my bosses discovered I could handle the telephone in Spanish and Italian and complimented me on my ability to get whatever they wanted out of their customers just by using my voice cleverly in those various languages. Another little spark had been kindled.

Because this full-time job took too much time away from my piano studies, I decided to quit at Christmas of 1937 and apply for a part-time position at the Kamin Book Shop just south of Central Park. Kamin's was a small, exclusive shop that specialized in first-edition volumes on ballet. Mrs. Kamin said she had selected me over the other applicants because of my intellectual sophistication—I could spell Diaghilev. She was so impressed, in fact, that she added the subway fare to my weekly salary.

On my way to and from work every day, I had to walk behind Steinway Hall, a large office building on Fifty-seventh Street owned by the famous piano company. Several of the upstairs floors above the company's showrooms contained practice studios that aspiring musicians and singers could rent by the hour. That short walk past the building could be a terror. Some of the sounds that emanated from that place sounded more like cattle being slaughtered than singers practicing. I often remember cringing as I walked by. One day I was so disgusted with the noises from that musical abbatoir that when I got home I told my mother I would like to go back to working vocally, just to prove to myself that I really could sing better than many of the people I had heard as I walked up Fifty-eighth Street.

That sealed my fate. Slowly, I switched from piano to voice and began thinking seriously about making singing my career. I never forgot the arrogant baritone who started it all.

Years later, I heard about another baritone, who was singing at the arena in Verona, and who got what was coming to him after repeating the same attention-grabbing trick in *Aida*. Wandering ostentatiously from one side of the giant Verona stage to the other, this prime exponent of the peacock school of declamation bellowed out "Suo padre" at the top of his lungs. When he finally came to the end of his expostulation, somebody up in the bleachers simply called back, "Chi?" (Who?).

Served him right!

The Basics

I<small>T WAS THE LATE</small> 1930<small>S</small>. I had been absorbing my mother's vocal instruction like a sponge. From exercises I moved slowly on to simple songs, and from those I finally progressed to operatic arias. Mother's vocal approach, as she had learned it from Mme Abranyi, was basic and natural, and she was customizing it especially to the nature of my voice.

The development of high-quality vocal production is not an easy subject to write about. In fact, I have never met a singer who learned his craft exclusively from a book. Nevertheless, we may find it interesting to read about our predecessors' or contemporaries' approach. The reason singing is so hard to discuss in words is that it all happens inside a human being. A musical instrument is a palpable object. When we play the piano or violin, we can see and feel what we're doing. When we learn how to sing, however, we train a number of voluntary but invisible muscles to do our bidding.

The task of directing our breath into the hard skeletal areas in the *masque* of our faces, where it has the best chance of reverberating, is not all that far from wrapping a piece of tissue paper around a comb and humming little ditties into it. The aesthetics may be a little more sublime, but the principle is the same. The important thing in developing resonance is to make sure it is evenly distributed throughout the range. I learned this by having to start with simple exercises on one tone, then two and three tones, finally five tones, working steadily through all the vowel sounds (A, E, I, O, U) until I was able to sing a full octave. Once the voice "sits," which is another way of saying, "once we have placed our voices so that we can work with the sound we have developed," we then have to begin using this proper vocal approach in different kinds of compositions—exercises, songs, and arias.

Of course, it all rests on the teacher's ability to communicate the principles and the pupil's ability to turn the teacher's explanations and illustrations into vocal reality. In the final analysis, it is the teacher's acoustical perception of the pupil's singing that makes all the difference. This is an area where charlatans with a glib tongue and a tin ear have a field day, to the eternal detriment of their students. However, the invention of the audio cassette has provided the pupil with an opportunity to hear his or her voice just as the teacher does, then discuss what has been heard and implement the good advice received more rapidly. Fortunately for me, the people who trained me not only knew what they were talking about; they knew what they were listening to!

Working with Mother was no easy task. She insisted on a minimum of one hour's vocal instruction every day, and she was a stickler for detail who would not let me move from one assignment to another until she was satisfied I had mastered whatever had gone before. In my youthful eagerness to keep going forward, this policy often impressed me as downright sluggish. I didn't realize then that she was in fact *saving* time. Had she allowed me to take a quicker pace, she would ultimately have had to clean up those mistakes that become ingrained if they are not dealt with in the first place; but that was not the way she worked.

To prove the omniscience I thought I had garnered from listening to singers from the time I was born, I decided to take advantage of her brief absence on a shopping spree to sing the entire role of Tosca without a break. I was trying to prove that I had the durability to handle this task. When mother returned, I glowingly told her of this feat. Imagine my chagrin when, instead of praising me, she prophesied that I would be hoarse for the next few days. Needless to say, her prophesy came true. Inexperienced as I was, I had failed to take into consideration that I was not yet physically or vocally ready for this taxing exercise. Sadder but wiser after this realization, I knew the time had come to defer to Mother's superior knowledge.

The more I learned about singing and opera, the more eager I was to hear and see it for myself at the highest available level, a special privilege for us New Yorkers, who at that time needed only a 5¢ fare to get to one of the greatest opera houses in the world, the Metropolitan, and only one dollar to be admitted to its auditorium. I became one of the regulars in the standing room area. I made it my business to get to the theatre as early as possible, so I could find a place in the front row of standees with a clear view of the stage. This got to be habit-forming. I still like to get to the theatre as early as possible. It's all a question of overview, whatever side of the curtain I might be occupying. Back then it meant hours of waiting in line, but once the curtain had risen on those performances, all inconveniences were forgotten, as I thrilled (or—once in a while—cringed) over the artistry on stage.

On one occasion, however, I was so involved with other things that I didn't get to the theatre until the last minute for what I thought would be a performance of *Il Trovatore*, a production I was very eager to see. Quickly paying my dollar for the ticket, I rushed into the auditorium. The curtain had already gone up. The sight of the soldiers onstage was somewhat reminiscent of the *Trovatore* opening, and just as I was remarking to myself on the departure I believed had prompted the set design, the music started. I became instantly aware that not only had I arrived at the last minute, I had actually come to the wrong opera, but a dollar is a dollar, and I decided to stay. When I got home after the performance, Mother inquired how I had enjoyed the *Trovatore*. I replied disconsolately that after all my eager anticipation, I found myself confronted with a shocking opera called *Salome*, which almost turned my stomach when the soprano sang an aria to a severed head. I must have looked so utterly devastated that Mother promptly offered to treat me to a ticket for a subsequent *Trovatore* performance. I later saw the Strauss opera through different eyes.

While the level of singing in those days at the Met was as high as I ever remember it anywhere, the quality of the acting varied, although nobody strutted and fretted like that Amonasro baritone. On the distaff side, there were great actresses like Marjorie Lawrence, Lotte Lehmann, Jarmila Novotná, Bidù Sayão, and Risë Stevens, whose perception of musical-dramatic unity served as an inspiration to me. These ladies were so involved in the high drama of what they were doing, we often completely forgot they were singing. To me, however, the strongest acting came from the men in the ensemble. Baritone Lawrence Tibbett had a striking stage personality, and when he sang Jago to the electrifying Otello of Giovanni Martinelli, sparks flew on that stage. Add to that the vocal and physical sex appeal of Ezio Pinza and the pure delight of his regular comic foil, Salvatore Baccaloni, in the buffo roles, and all the ingredients for thrilling musical theatre were there. On top of that, the supporting roles were invariably filled with first-rate, imaginative artists like Alessio de

Paolis, George Cehanovsky, and Gerhard Pechner, whose vocal and dramatic excellence never flagged throughout the many years of their careers. I learned an enormous amount from the acting skills of these artists; yet, instinctively, I felt there was still something missing, though I couldn't quite explain what it was at the time.

A Meaningful Encounter

THE TENSIONS OF THE EARLY DEPRESSION YEARS were beginning to relax under the benevolent administration of Franklin D. Roosevelt. For us, this meant more people were in a financial position to come for singing lessons. One of my mother's pupils invited us to a birthday party at her home, where I had the pleasure of meeting a basso from California named Douglas Beattie. He had just returned from an extended period of singing in Italy to begin his first engagement at the Metropolitan Opera, where he would soon be making his début as the King in *Aida*. I told him I would love a chance to hear him sing, and he was kind enough to supply me with a ticket. The only one available was way to the side of the orchestra seats, but my impression of that performance was still exciting, even at that angle. Being a well-mannered young lady, after the final curtain, I went backstage to thank Mr. Beattie. When I told him how impressed I was with his work, he replied, "I'm doing something much more interesting next week—I'm singing Fafner, one of the giants in *Das Rheingold*."

I had never seen *Rheingold*, and to be perfectly honest, I didn't know what in the world *Rheingold* was, apart from the name of a local New York brewery. But if he thought it was worth seeing, I definitely wanted to go. It was my very first encounter with Richard Wagner. If I thought I had seen good acting in some of the Italian performances, *Rheingold* came as a real revelation. Unlike many Italian operas, with their arias and other formal set pieces, the main stress in *Rheingold* is placed on believable give-and-take amongst the characters in the drama, a factor I found totally captivating.

Rheingold is essentially a men's opera, and the gentlemen on the stage that night were a real operatic élite who kept me so involved in the intensity of the story that I completely lost track of time as this single long act moved majestically past me. The quality of that performance, and especially Mr. Beattie's contribution to it, prompted me to ask him who had helped him in his preparation for the roles he sang. Could he perhaps recommend someone to teach me the kind of interpretive approach he had to the operatic literature? Mr. Beattie told me he worked with a man named Hermann Weigert, who was head assistant conductor for the German wing at the Met. I went home to my mother and said, "I think I may have found somebody," and we noted the name for future reference.

Shortly afterward, Kirsten Flagstad came to New York to begin her 1939–40 season. Mother called her up, as she did every year, to welcome her to the city and arrange one of their regular get-togethers. In the course of this particular conversation, my mother confided to her friend that the baby from the dressing room drawer was now being groomed for an operatic career herself. My mother wanted Kirsten's ideas on where to go from here, because she simply didn't trust herself to be objective about her own daughter. Mme Flagstad invited us to come visit her. She said she would be happy to listen to my singing and give us whatever advice she could.

When we arrived for the visit, the ladies first brought one another up to date on the time since their last meeting. Then Mother broached the subject of my singing. She thought I had the makings of a *jugendlich-dramatische*, the soprano who does the lighter leading Wagnerian soprano roles. We used to call them the three E's: Elsa in *Lohengrin*, Elisabeth in *Tannhäuser*, and Eva in *Meistersinger*. Mother had already taught me the roles of Aida, Leonora in *Trovatore*, and Desdemona, but she felt my repertoire study needed to be supplemented by work with someone with a stronger hand, someone who was also an authentic Wagner expert. Without needing to think it over, Mme Flagstad spontaneously recommended we contact Maestro Hermann Weigert, coincidentally the same man Mr. Beattie was working with. Mr. Weigert, she told us, had made such an impression on her when he played for her Metropolitan audition in Europe, she was sure he was the right choice for us. Then the ladies continued reminiscing about the "good old days" at the Opéra Comique. With all the conversation going on, I never did get to sing for Mme Flagstad.

A week or so later, my mother ran across a conductor of her acquaintance. She asked him the same question she had put to Kirsten Flagstad, and he offered her the same suggestion. It was beginning to look like all roads led to Weigert. Mother then sat down and wrote him a letter, telling him that Mme Flagstad had recommended him to us and asking if he could spare the time to listen to me sing. In her precise European fashion, she then went to the post office and dispatched her letter by registered mail, to make sure he would receive it.

Unlike many of the coaches in places such as the Steinway Building, who pound out accompaniments for anyone with the price of their time, Hermann Weigert was an established operatic pedagogue. He accepted only students who either were actually working in the profession or had sufficient promise to become professional artists in the foreseeable future. It took a while before we received a letter from Maestro Weigert inviting us to his studio. As we found out later, before extending us this invitation, he had first checked back with Mme Flagstad to see if we were "legitimate." She assured him that we were.

Determined to impress the maestro with the size of my voice, I selected "Dich, teure Halle," Elisabeth's jubilant first aria from *Tannhäuser*, to start the audition. He accompanied me at the piano himself. When I finished, he looked up and asked if I also knew a piece with extended delicate, soft passages. Apparently my rendering of Elsa's song to the breezes from act 2 of *Lohengrin* convinced him that I wasn't fixed exclusively on creating sufficient volume to blow his windows out, and so he agreed to accept me as a student— under one non-negotiable condition. For the period of our work together, which he approximated at a minimum of three years, I was to concentrate all my activities on learning repertoire. This meant I was not to sing for anyone during this study period apart from my mother and himself. This automatically eliminated a lot of pickup jobs many vocal students were doing, earning the odd dollar by singing here, there, and everywhere. Weigert was adamant—he felt that I had a valuable instrument, but that I also had a great deal to learn before I could make full use of it. My mother agreed with him wholeheartedly.

Who was this kind but stern musician, who was to play such a dominant role in my life? Hermann O. Weigert's middle name will not be divulged in this book, because he disliked it intensely, so intensely, in fact, that he would often announce to overly inquisitive Americans that he was part Irish, and the name was actually Hermann O'Weigert. He was born into a German-Jewish

The most meaningful encounter in my life: Maestro Hermann Weigert. *Metropolitan Opera Archives.*

family on October 20, 1890, in Breslau, the capital of the Province of Silesia in what was then the eastern part of Germany. After the Second World War, Silesia was ceded to Poland, and the city took its present name of Wrocław. While he was still a teenager, he used to accompany his sister, who studied singing as a hobby. The quality of his pianistic accomplishments advanced so

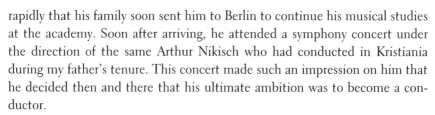

rapidly that his family soon sent him to Berlin to continue his musical studies at the academy. Soon after arriving, he attended a symphony concert under the direction of the same Arthur Nikisch who had conducted in Kristiania during my father's tenure. This concert made such an impression on him that he decided then and there that his ultimate ambition was to become a conductor.

The road to the podium in those days was clearly laid out. Unlike many modern conductors, who rely on what we would have to call "book-learning," conducting students at the turn of the century invariably had to learn piano and then serve an apprenticeship, which involved accompanying vocal and instrumental lessons and rehearsals in the conservatory. In addition, they were urged to take vocal lessons themselves to become acquainted with the principles of breathing and tone production. The result was that conductors trained in this exacting school were not only fine keyboard artists, they were also steeped in all the problems of vocal and instrumental performance.

Just as he was about to embark upon his musical career, the First World War intervened, and Weigert found himself conscripted into military service. The combination of his youth and the remarkable digital dexterity he had learned in all his years at the keyboard got him out of combat duty and into a unit of paramedics. On one cold day, during the Russian campaign, he happened to wander into a church, hoping to see some little work of art, which might take his mind off the terrors of the war. When he saw a horribly destroyed piano in a small ante-room off the sanctuary, he just stood there and wept. He later said war was one of the most dreadful things imaginable, with people destroying both human life and the redeeming possibility of making music.

The first stages of his career following the war consisted of engagements as a young coach at the theatres in Magdeburg and Lübeck in northern Germany. Subsequently he joined the musical staff at the Berlin State Opera under the aegis of such legendary musicians as Max von Schillings, Leo Blech, and Erich Kleiber. Kleiber's administration introduced Heinz Tietjen, an influential stage director who also conducted from time to time. Tietjen later became the forbidding General Manager of the company.

The members of the blue-ribbon roster of opera coaches Weigert had just joined at the Berlin State Opera would ultimately be regarded amongst the great conducting geniuses of the subsequent generation. One of these budding maestri was a Greek musician named Dimitri Mitropoulos. Kurt Adler, who served for many years as chorus master of the Metropolitan Opera, was another member of that crew, as was their Hungarian colleague George Szell, whose major career had already begun.

During Hermann Weigert's early years at the Staatsoper, he was listed as *Korrepetitor*, basically a pianist who coaches singers in their repertoire and accompanies staging rehearsals. Later, he was advanced to the status of *Leiter der Studienklasse*—in other words, the head coach of the theatre—while continuing in his *Korrepetitor* status. Finally, he advanced to the position of *Kapellmeister*, or staff conductor. In addition to his accompanying and conducting duties at the opera house, Hermann Weigert was later appointed to a professorship at the Berlin Music Academy.

During this period, Berlin was becoming a center for a number of new approaches to artistic thinking and activity. Probably the most prominent of these was the Bauhaus movement. The operatic equivalent of the Bauhaus might be said to have been the Krolloper, established in 1924 as an adjunct of the State Opera, and continuing as an autonomous company starting in 1927. When the workload at the Kroll became too heavy for the three conductors on the regular staff, they would borrow the services of colleagues from the Staatsoper. Hermann Weigert was one of those colleagues, and his activities at the Kroll left an indelible impression on his own approach to musical drama. Being the realistic professional he was, he quickly turned these impressions into attitudes and work methods that eventually had a significant impact on his contribution to my musical career.

Like the Opéra Comique in Kristiania, the Kroll was regrettably short-lived. After the conflagration of the Reichstag in 1933, the Kroll was commandeered as a makeshift headquarters for the German Parliament under the newly elected Chancellor Adolf Hitler. Hitler's ideological rigidity and "racial laws" left no doubt as to his political agenda. He meant to stamp out all "alien" (especially Jewish) influences on every area of German society, force the intellectual community into his *Reichskulturkammer*, and turn Europe's large Jewish population into second-class citizens with no rights or privileges. As we know, he didn't stop there, but even this beginning was enough to send hundreds of prominent Germans, not all of them Jewish, in quest of safer terrain. On reflection, it is more than strange that the city of Berlin, which had recently been the spawning ground of many new and important ideas in virtually every field of scientific and artistic endeavor, ultimately became the capital of the most primitive political criminals of modern times.

For Hermann Weigert, the handwriting was on the wall in letters of fire! He would have to get out of the country of his birth while the getting was still

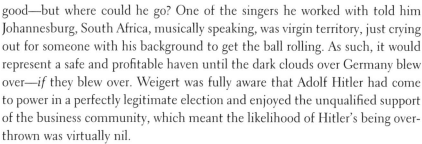

good—but where could he go? One of the singers he worked with told him Johannesburg, South Africa, musically speaking, was virgin territory, just crying out for someone with his background to get the ball rolling. As such, it would represent a safe and profitable haven until the dark clouds over Germany blew over—*if* they blew over. Weigert was fully aware that Adolf Hitler had come to power in a perfectly legitimate election and enjoyed the unqualified support of the business community, which meant the likelihood of Hitler's being overthrown was virtually nil.

In 1934, together with his ballet dancer wife and their two children, Weigert left for South Africa. However, the "virgin operatic territory" he found there was more barren than fertile. In fact, he was forced to make ends meet by giving piano lessons, while his wife taught ballet. In due time, this marriage came to an end, and Hermann Weigert knew he would have to seek his fortune elsewhere alone. He decided to return to a safer part of Europe than Germany, but before he was able to implement this plan, he had to do whatever day labor he could find in South Africa to continue providing support for his family and still save enough to pay for his passage to Italy. When he finally got there, his first stop was at La Scala in Milan, where he was told there were no openings for him at the time, although the management would be happy to use him on occasional musical odd jobs and take messages for him while he was getting settled. Downhearted, he went back to his hotel, and while he was ruminating over where life would lead him, the telephone rang. The secretary from the opera house told him his Berlin colleague George Szell had called to ask if there was someone free to come to Switzerland to accompany auditions for the management of the Metropolitan Opera.

Weigert immediately took the train to St. Moritz and proceeded to Silvretta Haus, an elegant hotel where the Metropolitan often held European auditions. The beautiful, tranquil atmosphere up in the mountains appealed to the visitors from New York, and the political neutrality of the country made it possible to invite artists from any part of the troubled continent. There Mr. Weigert accompanied auditions for two sopranos, both of whom were singing for Giulio Gatti-Casazza, General Manager of the Metropolitan Opera, and Dr. Artur Bodanzky, the head conductor of the Metropolitan's German wing. It seemed that Wagnerian soprano Frida Leider had returned to Berlin to stand by her Jewish husband, and her Viennese counterpart, Anny Konetzni, would be available for only part of the coming season, so the management needed another artist to sing the remaining productions. The first soprano to be heard was the well-known Elisabeth Delius. The other one was an obscure Norwegian singer recommended to Mr. Gatti-Casazza by Alexander Kipnis, who had sung with her during a guest appearance in Oslo. Her name was Kirsten Flagstad. For a while Mr. Gatti-Casazza and Dr. Bodanzky were not sure which of the two excellent sopranos to engage, until Mrs. Gatti-Casazza—Rosina Galli, the Metropolitan's star ballerina—told her husband in no uncertain terms he would be a fool if he didn't hire that Flagstad woman.

Meanwhile, Maestro Bodanzky stepped over to the piano to chat with Weigert. After inquiring rather cryptically if he played a German card game called *Skat*, he invited him to join the opera company as soon as they had a vacancy. Weigert registered this friendly proposal in the "Don't-call-us-we'll-call-you" file of his memory, and, after telling Bodanzky he could be reached at La Scala, took the next railroad connection back to Milan. As the train rolled across the Alps to the south, Weigert had no way of knowing that a member of the Metropolitan's musical staff had fallen ill, and Bodanzky had been serious about wanting to engage him. The only impediment was that the theatre would not be allowed to hire a new staff member until the indisposed man formally withdrew from his contract.

A few days later, the secretary at La Scala called and asked Weigert to come to the theatre immediately. When he got there, he told him, "Congratulations, you've been engaged," to which he incredulously inquired, "Where?" As it turned out, the musician in New York had finally canceled his contract, and the Metropolitan management had wired Milan asking Weigert to come to New York to join the company at once.

Arriving in Manhattan, he went straight to the Opera House. Parking his single valise by the switchboard operator at the Thirty-ninth Street entrance, he asked her to advise the management of his arrival. He was immediately ushered into the General Manager's office. While the welcoming formalities were in progress, the telephone rang on Mr. Gatti's desk, and the General Manager of the Metropolitan Opera casually offered him the phone. This was certainly a far cry from his experiences in Germany, where the members of the staff hardly ever saw Tietjen. Here in New York, he was not only sitting in the boss's office just moments after his arrival, the boss was actually inviting him to use his own telephone!

Dr. Bodanzky was on the other end of the line. He needed to see Weigert immediately at his apartment. Something urgent, he said, had arisen. Weigert countered that he hadn't even had time to check into his hotel. "We'll notify the hotel," was the answer. "Just take a taxi and come up here at once!" Weigert did as he was told. After a brief request for Mr. Weigert to reorches-

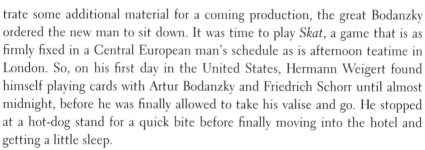

trate some additional material for a coming production, the great Bodanzky ordered the new man to sit down. It was time to play *Skat*, a game that is as firmly fixed in a Central European man's schedule as is afternoon teatime in London. So, on his first day in the United States, Hermann Weigert found himself playing cards with Artur Bodanzky and Friedrich Schorr until almost midnight, before he was finally allowed to take his valise and go. He stopped at a hot-dog stand for a quick bite before finally moving into the hotel and getting a little sleep.

Weigert was appointed the head *Korrepetitor* for the German wing at the Metropolitan, responsible directly to Bodanzky for the musical rehearsals and whatever preparation might be necessary for the world-famous singers performing in the German operas in New York at that time. Very shortly afterward, the name Hermann Weigert became a household name in the operatic world. Anyone who needed to polish up his or her skills, especially in Wagnerian opera, knew there was no better mentor than Weigert, *if* Mr. Weigert accepted you as a student and could find some time in his busy schedule to take you on! He was hardly at a loss for students on the highest level. In fact, when Kirsten Flagstad arrived in New York to begin her first Metropolitan season in 1935, Hermann Weigert went out to the pier to welcome her.

All of these parts of my life converging was a little like the rays of the sun coming together at the apex of the Metropolitan Opera, which at the time represented the ultimate clearinghouse for everything vocal all over the world. In the middle of this operatic ferment, one of the top musical mentors had somehow found the time to instruct a twenty-one-year-old girl from Greenwich Village who worked part-time up the street at a bookstore.

These were my feelings as this distinguished, imposing gentleman welcomed me to my first lesson at his home. Without any further ado, we went to work.

The Story behind the Story

M<small>Y FIRST LESSON</small> with Maestro Weigert began with a surprise. He had as-signed me two roles to prepare: Elsa in *Lohengrin* and Sieglinde in *Die Wal-küre*. I expected he would want to hear me sing. To my amazement, after greeting me at the door and escorting me into the studio, he politely asked me to take a seat. I wasn't used to singing sitting down at a lesson, but I did as I was told. He looked over at me with a pleasant smile and said: "Now then, Miss Varnay, what can you tell me about Sieglinde? Who is she? Where does she come from? Who are the people in her life and what is her relationship to them?"

I soon came to realize that this Socratic method was the way I would be learning all my operatic material. First we would delve into the details of the character and the other people in the story, as they are expressed both verbally and musically. Once I had a clear mental picture of who I was, what I was feeling and doing, and why, I would finally be asked to express my knowledge in singing. We would then continue in even greater detail. Instruments in the orchestra—for example, a horn call—would indicate to Sieglinde that her despised husband, Hunding, had arrived at the house and was stabling his horse. Her onstage reaction and vocal expression would of course be deter-mined by the unseen action she had heard in the orchestral accompaniment.

Mr. Weigert's incisive questions would continue on and on. I worked to find the answers with him, and I gradually found myself developing the skill of taking on another personality and building my own actions and reactions on

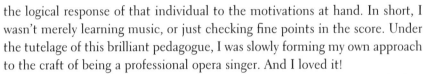

the logical response of that individual to the motivations at hand. In short, I wasn't merely learning music, or just checking fine points in the score. Under the tutelage of this brilliant pedagogue, I was slowly forming my own approach to the craft of being a professional opera singer. And I loved it!

That first lesson at Hermann Weigert's studio represented a watershed in my development. Having become aware of what I wanted to do with my life, I discontinued my piano lessons, put my sparse social life on the back burner for the time being, and set about obsessively redirecting every facet of my existence toward the accomplishment of the objective I had chosen for myself. From then on, my days were carpeted with opera to the exclusion of virtually everything but the obvious basic necessities like eating, sleeping, and getting from one place to another. Since I had to make some kind of contribution to the household budget to supplement my mother's modest income, I remained in my part-time job at Kamin's bookstore, where I worked every evening, five days a week.

Mr. Weigert saw me for two one-hour lessons a week, and the remaining days were devoted either to continuing my work on vocal technique and the Italian repertoire with my mother, or to preparing the material I had been assigned to bring Mr. Weigert at our next lesson. Weekends existed only on the calendar and were invariably set aside for further memorization and study. When all this got to be too much, I would just go out for a little intermission in the fresh air before getting back to work. Mother was a great believer in preparing as much material as possible in advance, without any specific view toward performing it anywhere. In her words, "There's no point opening a shop without merchandise."

I always kept at least one act ahead of wherever I was in my lessons with Mr. Weigert. This meant not merely learning the words and notes of the character I was singing, but also the rest of the opera as well, in order to understand every moment I was either on- or offstage. Only in this way would I ever be able to realize the fullness of the dramatic structure and my participation in it. This preparation particularly helped me at the beginning of my career. Isolde was a good case in point—I worked on that role off and on for five years before I actually had to perform it. How fortunate it was that I did, because my very first Isolde was again a last-minute substitution for Helen Traubel.

Many singers go to a coaching lesson unprepared, expecting the lady or gentleman at the keyboard to pound the words and notes into their heads. They also expect the accompanist to translate the texts of operas they should have researched themselves. This was certainly not my policy, nor would Hermann Weigert have sanctioned it for one minute. He expected his students to follow the letter of the law and do their homework *at home!* Luckily, I had received a solid foundation in theory and harmony from my piano teacher, Mr. Ganci, and I had sufficient keyboard skill to pick out the themes and harmonies I needed as I memorized the music.

To supplement my work at home, I would buy extra piano scores and then divide one of them into three sections. This way, I could take whatever act I was working on with me on the subway to work or on a walk in the park without having to carry a whole bulky volume. Then, whenever I wasn't a hundred percent certain about a given point—a note value or a grammatical point in the libretto—I could always take out my one-third of the score and check it. Fortunately for my purposes, Wagner composed almost all his operas in three acts.

I made it my business to be at Mr. Weigert's studio on the dot, not wanting to miss one precious moment of his knowledge, wisdom, and inspiration. In 1939, when I began my lessons with him, it would have been impossible for any American to acquire a musical education on a European continent that had just been plunged into a new and devastating war. Nor was I in a financial position to attend a full-time training program at one of the few American musical academies or universities that offered operatic preparation programs. This meant that my mother and Maestro Weigert would have to be my conservatory.

At my lessons, once we had the character and the immediate surroundings effectively pinpointed, we would invariably move on to the larger picture. In the case of Elsa in *Lohengrin*, one significant factor is the historical background of the plot, set in the early Middle Ages, when Christianity was still a relatively young religion vying against more established beliefs for primacy. When Elsa makes her first appearance, she is marked for a terrible death— probably on the block or at the stake, following a period of agonizing torture, certainly psychological if not actual physical torment. The realization that this fate awaits her for a crime she knows she never committed almost paralyzes her with anxiety. With no family, friends, or political allies to come to her aid, she desperately turns to the last recourse of prayer, in which she is vouchsafed a vision of a knight in shining armor, who will do glorious battle to redeem both her life and her reputation.

This is the mental and emotional background Elsa brings with her onstage before she utters her first poignant statement, "Mein armer Bruder" (My poor brother), referring to her younger brother, Duke Gottfried, whose mysterious disappearance has set in motion the succession of accusations now directed against her. The prevalent beliefs of those days figure significantly in any characterization of this role. The simple trust in a miraculous answer to a sincere prayer plays an important role in the customs and literature of that period, as does the gnawing quandary that ultimately proves Elsa's undoing: can we be sure that what seems to be a miracle is not really a pernicious form of black magic destined to plunge everyone and everything into irredeemable perdition?

Once we had dealt with these historical issues, Mr. Weigert would then draw from his knowledge of the situation in Wagner's own life as the composer conceived the words and music of his elaborate fable. He inferred that Wagner may have used *Lohengrin* as a kind of veiled reference to an interactive crisis in both his creative work and his marriage. When, at the time of *Tannhäuser*, Wagner's wife, Minna, urged him to continue with the proven formula of German opera in Italian musical style à la *Rienzi*, Wagner most probably felt totally demoralized. He was nurturing visions of charting still-unknown horizons, and the last thing he needed from his own wife was doubt or disapproval. Yet she kept on nagging that he was going out on an artistic limb, and this could mean disaster for the financial rewards she expected from his work. In a sense, Weigert hypothesized, Wagner may have been trying to warn her that she would simply have to have blind faith in his fulfillment of the revelation growing in his imagination, or else he might find himself forced to leave her, just as Lohengrin admonishes Elsa to acknowledge him as her redeemer without inquiring any further into the secret of his background.

The more I learned from Hermann Weigert, the more I thirsted to know even more, until, after about a year of study with him, I abruptly hit a snag. My teacher had assigned me the role of Senta in *Der fliegende Holländer*, and I had a great deal of difficulty memorizing the music. I suppose all of us have ups and downs when it comes to memorization. I have often noticed that when I could animate my emotional and intellectual curiosity, my mind was a steel trap. When that process failed to function, it could turn into a sieve. I discovered that I had a quirk of responding rather spontaneously to roles with complex musical structures while having real problems with repetitious, simple ones. The music allotted to Senta is a good example of the latter case.

Mr. Weigert's reaction to my dilemma baffled me. Instead of heaping me with the wisdom I had become accustomed to hearing from him, he just drily announced that he was about to take his annual summer break. He would first be working at the San Francisco Opera and then taking a month off to rest and relax. When he came back to New York in late autumn, he said, he expected the role of Senta to be completely learned—no excuses—otherwise he would not be willing to move on to the next opera. It was that simple.

As if his reprimand was not enough, that summer was one of the worst scorchers anyone in New York could remember. It found me preparing lemonade by the bucketful to keep me cool as I sat out on the fire escape, trudging laboriously through Senta's repetitive utterances. Often my mother would cue me both verbally and musically as I learned the part. I gradually began to sense a logical pattern in the musical repetitions. I perceived a definite intention in Wagner's composition and in the way it expressed Senta's inner thoughts. Her gnawing obsession manifests itself in the music over and over again as a constant, recurring thread, symbolizing her total involvement with the unknown Dutchman. Having discovered this (hurrah!), I no longer had any difficulty memorizing her repetitive music.

If I had been a trifle perplexed over Mr. Weigert's sudden manifestation of discipline at that point in time, later years have shown me how right he was. He evidently knew that if I didn't find Senta's inner logic for myself, I could never make it my own. In a way, even in his absence, he continued to teach me by putting me on my mettle to do my own research. By the time the summer was over, I heaved a great sigh of relief knowing that both Senta and I were ready for Mr. Weigert's return. Judge of my delight when I rendered the problem role letter-perfect and witnessed my teacher's smile of satisfaction.

Shortly after this event, Mme Flagstad was scheduled for a musical rehearsal with Mr. Weigert at her home preparatory to an upcoming *Holländer* performance. She asked my teacher to bring me along so she could finally hear me sing and suggested I remain while she ran through the role of Senta. My teacher suggested, as *Holländer* was on the day's menu, that I sing Senta's aria for her. After I concluded, she congratulated me on my work and then started her own session. When she got to the aria, as a kind of sign of her recognition, she simply skipped it and went on to the following scene. Years later, she would graciously offer me her place in the limelight on another, more public occasion.

Slowly, meticulously, Mr. Weigert took me from the more lyrical roles to the more vocally demanding music of characters like Brünnhilde and Isolde, and I found myself memorizing not only words and music, but also the tempi at which various conductors were likely to take specific sections of the operas. One of the many mnemonic devices I used for committing these different conductorial approaches to memory involved putting a roast in the oven and then singing through Brünnhilde's Immolation Scene from *Götterdämmerung*. A rapid tempo gave me rare roast beef, while another conductor's more leisurely reading was more ideally suited for a medium leg of lamb. I should perhaps add that at this point, I had yet to meet Hans Knappertsbusch.

As work progressed, I found myself asking more questions of Mr. Weigert than he did of me. By the time we got to Kundry in *Parsifal*, he had to confess I was asking too many questions; he would be forced to refresh his own memory in his reference library.

A few months later, we found ourselves faced with a new complication. The course of study that he had estimated at three years was basically completed after only half that time. In the short span of eighteen months, my unflagging zeal to learn had placed almost the entire Wagnerian repertoire solidly in my head; so solidly, in fact, that even my pedagogue, Mr. Weigert, was somewhat at odds as to where to go from there. A lesser man might possibly have plodded on from that point, filling the remaining eighteen months with some rarefied form of occupational therapy before decisions fell due. Hermann Weigert, however, was far too much of a practical professional to waste his time and mine. He knew that he and I had mined a rich lode, but he still wanted to make sure he hadn't lost the objectivity so crucial in making career decisions. Fortunately for all parties concerned, Hermann Weigert had both the humility and the good sense to ask one of his most distinguished peers and oldest friends for an honest evaluation.

Good for a Laugh

MR. WEIGERT CHOSE one of the colleagues from his Berlin days to give him the objective opinion he wanted. By that time an established conductor in the United States, his choice was a man of impeccable musicianship, albeit a little short on heart. "So don't expect him to understand too much about the expression," Mr. Weigert explained. The conductor turned out to be George Szell, who had been influential in bringing Hermann Weigert to Switzerland to play the Flagstad audition, which ultimately resulted in Mr. Weigert's New York engagement. Mr. Szell had recently made his American début conducting a concert at the Hollywood Bowl and had since moved to New York, where he would soon be conducting at the Met.

Mr. Weigert contacted him, and Mr. Szell said he would be very happy to do a good friend a favor and listen to me sing. For the life of me, I cannot recall what I sang for him. In any case, when my audition was over, the two gentlemen conferred in a corner. Mr. Szell liked my voice and thought a great deal of my musicianship. He then went on to say: "Why don't you have her sing for Edward Johnson? She ought to be heard by another expert on voice. Certainly, Mr. Johnson would have a thought or two on the roles she should learn from here on."

My reaction to Mr. Szell's suggestion was: Would someone in Mr. Johnson's exalted position really take the time to hear a rank beginner *for information purposes only!?* Mr. Weigert countered, "Why not?" and added that he had an enormously high opinion of Mr. Johnson's judgment of singers and singing, just as he regarded George Szell as an unimpeachable expert on musical matters. Of course, Mr. Johnson had a very heavy schedule, but there would be no harm in asking.

At that point in the company's history, the American contingent of singers at the Metropolitan was fairly skimpy and getting skimpier. Mr. Johnson hoped to change that. Perhaps, Mr. Weigert thought, if he liked what he heard, he might find some modest position in the company for Miss Varnay. I was invited to come to the theatre on July 10, 1940, to sing in the "Ladies' Parlor," a small room where preliminary auditions to separate the vocal wheat from the chaff were normally held.

I appeared at the appointed time, and, after catching my breath at the sight of the General Manager, I proceeded to sing one or two arias for him. I don't remember exactly what they were, but obviously I made a good impression on him. Mr. Johnson took out a card the Metropolitan uses to record impressions of every audition and wrote the words: "good material, excellent German and Italian, musical, worthy of attention. (E.J.)." He then asked me to send his office a brief letter, giving him the basic facts on who I was and what I had to offer. My letter read:

Dear Mr. Johnson;

Herewith, please accept the following data for which you so kindly requested after the audition on Wednesday, July 10, 1940.

Name: Violet Varnay
Age: 22
Born: Stockholm, Sweden (Hungarian descent)
Education: Elementary and High School (completed), Private Musical College (8 yrs. pianoforte)
Languages: English, German, Italian, French, Hungarian
Vocal Training received from my Mother.
Repertoire studied with Maestro Hermann Weigert.

Repertoire
GERMAN:

Holländer	Senta
Lohengrin	Elsa
Tannhäuser	Elisabeth
Meistersinger	Eva

Walküre	Sieglinde
Walküre	Brünnhilde
Siegfried	Brünnhilde
Götterdämmerung	Brünnhilde
Tristan & Isolde	Isolde (in preparation)
Götterdämmerung	3rd Norn and Gutrune

ITALIAN:

Aida	Aida
Otello	Desdemona
Cavalleria Rusticana	Santuzza
Forza del Destino	Leonora

Other parts in preparation.
With sincere appreciation and gratitude.

Respectfully yours,
Violet Varnay

When this letter hit Mr. Johnson's desk, the immediate reaction was unbridled hilarity. The General Manager thought he was being subjected to some kind of hoax on the part of Weigert, who had a bit of a reputation as a quick-witted scamp when it came to wisecracks, but never, never, ever in musical matters. Could this pupil of Weigert's really have put thirteen of the toughest soprano roles in her brain and throat at the tender age of twenty-two? And what other "parts" were left for preparation? The whole idea was most inconceivable, but, as Mr. Johnson confessed many years later, he thought this audition might be good for a laugh, to pass the time away on an otherwise dismal November afternoon. It would be most interesting, he thought, to put the claims in the letter to the test.

I was invited to sing a second audition a few months later, on November 8, 1940, in a large rehearsal room known as the "roof stage" on the top floor of the building. In the meantime, my letter had made the rounds of the management office. Two of Mr. Johnson's closest associates, Frank St. Leger, an assistant conductor who also collaborated with the General Manager on artistic matters, and Earl E. Lewis, the Assistant General Manager, who had been around since the early Gatti era, both said they did not want to miss this one. As the great majority of roles listed in my letter were Wagnerian, the new head of the German wing, Erich Leinsdorf, would, of course, also have to be present.

Normally, a minor staff member would be delegated to hear a pre-audition for the theatre, but this was too good to be true, and everyone from the front office wanted to be there to share the fun.

Mr. Johnson and the lieutenants he had corralled thought they would soon be making short work of a presumptuous young woman claiming to have all those difficult roles memorized. Maestro Weigert sat down at the upright piano, and we both looked over at the gentlemen of the managerial staff for initial instructions. Mr. Johnson suggested we start with Brünnhilde's Immolation Scene from *Götterdämmerung*. If that didn't test everything I claimed I knew, nothing would. We then moved on to just about everything else I had learned from my mother and Mr. Weigert combined. I was asked to do bits and pieces from many of the various operas I had listed in my letter.

Somewhere along the way, the faces of my distinguished auditors transformed from "show me" to something vaguely approximating unexpected and somewhat bewildered pleasure. For two hours, I was put through my paces, albeit with an occasional break for relaxation. The gentlemen who had come to scorn were still there listening attentively. Their skepticism had been transformed into sincere admiration, as I could read from the smiles on their faces.

After a short conclave, all the members of the panel but Mr. Johnson went back to their respective offices. Then the General Manager smiled warmly over at me and said he was satisfied I had musically mastered all the roles I had claimed I knew. He was pleased with the quality of my singing; however, he still had to know if my voice would carry clearly from the main stage in a house with 3,465 seats.

If the second audition seemed interminable, the final one on May 22 the following year, 1941, was brevity itself. I sang two arias, including Isolde's "Liebestod" from *Tristan und Isolde*, and then finished off with Brünnhilde's battle cry from the second act of *Walküre*. As I started to sing "Hojotoho," an enormous clap of thunder resounded throughout the theatre. One of those classic New York City thunderstorms started rattling all the windows. I thought to myself, "I feel just like Wotan's daughter," and proceeded to sing the battle cry with great joy, accompanied by celestial percussion.

Mr. Johnson said that was all he needed to hear. He took out his pen and wrote the words "ought to engage" on my audition card. As he later admitted to Mr. Weigert, "I don't know what in blazes to do with the girl, but I've got to have her in the house." Mr. Johnson met me in the wings and asked me courteously, "Whom does one talk to now?" I didn't have the foggiest notion what he meant. Fortunately, Mr. Weigert informed me in a stage whisper,

"He's offering you a contract." I felt like a hole in the surface of the earth was about to swallow me. After all, we had originally come just for a professional opinion.

Once I had taken in this monumental development, I heard Mr. Johnson tell me he would arrange for one of the top agents in the music business in New York to negotiate contracts for me: André Mertens, a charming and elegant gentleman, of European origin, from the notable Columbia Artists Management. At our first meeting, Mr. Mertens told me he always needed information on the background of every artist he added to his roster. He said he was not very happy with my name. "Violet Varnay" sounded a little too contrived to him. I explained my various names and their origins. Mr. Mertens said we should forget all of them. "How do you like the idea of another alliterative name such as 'Virginia Varnay?'" I thought for a minute and said it just didn't jibe. I had become keenly aware of the penchant New York critics have for plays on words. Were I to put some of my dramatic ideas into action, they might just wind up calling me "Virginia Ham." We finally agreed to use my middle name, Astrid.

So much has been said about the venality of agents, much of it regrettably true, I think I had better pause briefly to pay a compliment to Mr. Mertens's generosity. Shortly after my début, Mr. Mertens informed me that a Manhattan night club called the Starlight Room had found out about me and was eager to hire me to sing selections like "Dark Eyes" to the patrons of that swanky establishment. The Metropolitan management would hear none of that. Either grand opera or popular music, but, in their eyes, never the twain could meet! Mr. Mertens had no alternative but to bow to the will of the opera company's management. This left us with a three-year contract with the Met, at a starting wage of $75.00 a week for the first year, $98.00 for the second, and $122.50 for the third. Under these circumstances, he said, he felt honorbound to waive the commission charges for his services in negotiating the Metropolitan contract. In the first three years of my career, one of the most prestigious agents in the business accepted commissions only for the concerts he booked for me!

Even with a signed Metropolitan contract and the joy that went with it, I was still fully aware of the responsibilities that lay ahead. Of course, my mother and Mr. Weigert were overjoyed, but the work with both of them went right on just as intensively, if not more so, as it had before the contract. After all, IT WAS THE FAMILY BUSINESS!!

When the season began that autumn, I virtually lived in the theatre. I made it my business to attend every single rehearsal I could, whether I was directly involved or not. I also got permission to watch performances in the wings in order to hear what the orchestra sounded like on that side of the footlights. Of course, I went right on watching the operas from the standing room section. Meanwhile, I had made friends with a few fellow standees, but I saw no reason to mention that they would some day be looking at me up on the stage, which explains Ginny Ahrens's amazement after that first *Walküre* performance.

Mother did have occasion to tell a friend the good news, whereupon that friend immediately wrote the following letter of congratulation, which began with a reminiscence of my father.

> I will always be grateful to him. Among the wishes I have for your future is the wish that you would find one to help you as your father helped me.
>
> With the inheritance you have from both your mother and father, I knew that you would have a lot to show me both as a personality and as a singer.
>
> Well, Violet, I can only say that the institution that has signed you up now will never regret doing so.
>
> Yours is an exceptional voice; your great musicianship and hard work will carry you very far. That you are in such good hands as your mother's and Hermann Weigert's is an assurance herefore, too. I know what I have to thank Weigert for. Without him, I could never have accomplished what I have done in this country.

The letter was signed "Kirsten Flagstad."

On Saturday, February 3, 1951, I had the golden opportunity of singing Sieglinde in a broadcast matinée to the Brünnhilde of Mme Flagstad at the Metropolitan. It was the first of only two performances in which we appeared together. In the long years of my career, I have sung with a virtual "Who's Who" of operatic greats, from Lauritz Melchior to Risë Stevens to George London to Birgit Nilsson to Hans Hotter to Martha Mödl and finally to Plácido Domingo, to mention only a few. Yet, because of all the sentimental attachment, and more specifically because of the Olympian supremacy of everything she did, our dear family friend really represented the apex of my list of colleagues.

While I was happily amassing practical operatic knowledge, some very serious problems were concerning Mr. Johnson and his managerial staff. News of the war in Europe was becoming more disquieting with every passing day. Although the likelihood of an American involvement in the conflict still seemed remote, Mr. Johnson had nevertheless been placed in the awkward position of planning a season of performances without access to the many artists the company had previously contracted from Europe. With this in mind, Mr. Johnson asked his associate Edward Ziegler to write to Mr. Weigert. In his letter, dated July 2, 1941, he asked, "Can you tell me whether she is ready with the 'Ring' Brünnhilde, and whether you think the voice has enough body to 'resist' these operas in performance?"

My teacher replied on the following day: "Miss Varnay is ready *musically* and vocally with all the parts of her repertory. In my personal opinion, she will have the resistance for performances in spite of her youth." I was then told I would be making my Metropolitan début in the early part of 1942, not in one of the supporting parts we had expected, but in the principal role of Elsa in *Lohengrin*. Our cup ranneth over!

As I transferred my base of operations from the bookshop to the opera house, I couldn't help noticing some similarities between the one job and the other. Just as I had done with Kamin's books, I kept regular hours going to my coaching lessons and my sessions at the *Laboratorium*, where Dr. Lothar Wallerstein introduced us young singers to the technical intricacies of the lyric theatre. And as with the bookshop job, I also continued to go to work on the subway, although I was able to get off the express train one stop earlier—at the Times Square station rather than the Fifty-seventh Street stop. And so it happened that, one frosty morning in early December, I packed up my *Lohengrin* score, bundled up against the cold, and went off to what I thought would be a routine coaching session with Maestro Leinsdorf.

THE EARLY CAREER

Walhalla on the Hudson

IN THE YEARS of World War II, the Metropolitan had the luck of the draw with some of the greatest European singers and conductors living in the United States because of the perverse racial laws in Germany and its occupied countries at the time. With the likes of my début cast—Melchior, Schorr, Traubel, Thorborg, and Kipnis—plus Karin Branzell, Irene Jessner, Lotte Lehmann, Elisabeth Rethberg, Emanuel List, and Herbert Janssen, and such gifted Americans as Rose Bampton, Margaret Harshaw, Emery Darcy, and Julius Huehn onstage, to mention just a few, New York was replete with gods and goddesses, heroes and heroines, who made it a real "Walhalla on the Hudson" for years to come.

We also boasted a truly celestial lineup of Wagnerian conductors. Small wonder they were in America, as most of them were Jewish, and they had been forced to get out of Europe like thieves in the night to save their lives. But there were others, like Fritz Busch, who simply wanted no truck with the "culture" of Hitler and Goebbels. Only a handful of truly great conductors, such as Clemens Krauss, Hans Knappertsbusch, and Wilhelm Furtwängler, had remained in Central Europe. On the other hand, in New York City, in addition to Fritz Busch, we had Paul Breisach, Erich Leinsdorf, Fritz Reiner, William Steinberg, Fritz Stiedry, George Szell, and Bruno Walter gracing the podium *in the Met's German wing alone!*

I had the privilege of singing with all but one of these conductors—Bruno Walter, who had approached me very early in my career, asking me to audition

Leonore's aria "Abscheulicher, wo eilst du hin?" from *Fidelio*. I was flattered that he wanted to hear me, and when I evidently acquitted myself creditably, he commented, "The time has come for you to sing this role." I respectfully begged to differ. While I had no trouble with the aria, I explained, I knew I was still not vocally sure of myself in the big quartet in act 2 after Leonore has threatened Pizarro with a pistol. The last part of the quartet was just too unabatingly difficult for my voice to negotiate at that point in its development. He said he was disappointed with me, and that was that. I much later acquired the facility and security to handle those precarious passages and subsequently sang Leonore many times throughout my career, but never with Dr. Walter.

One other titan of that age also expressed interest in possibly engaging me to perform another Beethoven work. The conductor was Arturo Toscanini, and the composition was the Ninth Symphony. An audition had been arranged for the maestro to hear several sopranos who were under consideration for the solo in the final movement. When I sang for him, he listened attentively, but after I completed the audition, the maestro simply sat there in the auditorium, conversing with Bruno Zirato, one of the managers of the New York Philharmonic Symphony Society. When a quiet "thank you" from Mr. Zirato emanated from the auditorium, I left the stage. Later, Mr. Zirato rather apologetically informed me that Maestro Toscanini was terribly sorry, but he felt my voice was too large for the music. I could not help wondering why the maestro hadn't tried out some dynamics with me. The quality of my pianissimo at that time was an established fact. He later recorded the Ninth Symphony with the immense voice of Eileen Farrell.

No comment.

The musical staff of the Metropolitan's German wing, under the leadership of Hermann Weigert, included at least a half-dozen people who subsequently became fine conductors in their own right. Even at the time, many of them held their own on musical matters with their superiors. In one such incident, Hermann Weigert revealed the scamp qualities that had led Edward Johnson to wonder whether he had been kidding when he introduced me to the management. After the first act of a *Siegfried* rehearsal, the rather autocratic Dr. Fritz Stiedry emerged from the orchestra pit with a smile of deep self-satisfaction on his face, and said, preening: "Weigert, did you hear them? They followed me to the letter!" "Why shouldn't they?" answered Mr. Weigert laconically. "That's what they get paid for."

Stage direction, as I remember it in those days, was fairly rudimentary, consisting mainly of traffic management. This was anything but conducive to ensemble acting. The few singers with a theatrical flair would be permitted to "do their own thing," while the great majority simply went wherever they were placed by the stage director, where they stood with dignity and sang well. Helen Traubel was probably the foremost exponent of this statuesque school of operatic presentation, but when she let loose that incomparably beautiful voice of hers, the audience was amply compensated for whatever might have been missing histrionically.

Among my other colleagues, Kerstin Thorborg and Karin Branzell, who shared the Wagnerian mezzo roles, were a Swedish study in contrasts. Thorborg once said she had married her director husband, Gustav Bergmann, because he was such a good cook. She may have been a ravenous eater, but she certainly wasn't overweight. When standing next to her, one had the feeling of being beside a slender, sturdy pillar. Her musicianship was more than sturdy. In the middle of her career, she had over seventy performed roles, large and small, in her repertoire.

Karin Branzell had sung Maddalena to my mother's Gilda in *Rigoletto* in Stockholm on September 29, 1916, before I was even born. She shared the stage with me quite often at the Metropolitan before her retirement in 1944. Branzell was a very serious artist, but in rehearsals she often delighted us with her surprisingly scatological sense of humor, which often helped enrich the perilously thin air generated by the interaction of all those Central European doctors and professors who presided over our rehearsals. Once, a couple of these overeducated academics were debating some aesthetic fine point or other in terms that next to nobody could understand (least of all themselves), when Mme Branzell returned to the scene from the ladies room, and, without losing one iota of her innate decorum, serenely proclaimed to nobody in particular: "A good number two when you need it can be even more satisfying than indifferent intercourse."

Karin Branzell's sense of humor, however, did not carry over to taking critical reviews lightly. In fact, she became overwrought at times, even when one of her colleagues undeservedly received an unfavorable write-up. Her husband solved the problem by gathering together all the reviews of a given season, rolling them, tying them up, and then placing them in a special drawer until summer. By that time, she could give full vent to her rage over the reviews without any danger to her precious vocal cords.

The circumstances of Karin Branzell's retirement were overshadowed by an act of bad taste on the part of the management. She was informed, in a casual statement at a party, that she would not be scheduled for any further appearances. You can imagine her chagrin, not so much at the dismissal, but that it had been announced to her publicly. However, she enjoyed a small measure of vindication on March 15, 1945, when I first assumed the role of Ortrud in *Lohengrin*. At a fitting in the wardrobe department, I realized that the Metropolitan's Ortrud costumes were out of the question for me, so I called Mother's longtime friend to ask if she would lend me *her* personal costumes. She gladly agreed on condition that she be given a front-row seat for the performance. If she was not singing, she said, she could at least have the enjoyment of seeing her costumes parading across the stage.

The ladies with whom I shared the lighter dramatic roles seemed to be either on the way up or on the way out. Rose Bampton had been with the company since 1932, débuting at the age of twenty-three. She had spent her first four or five years with the company singing mezzo roles. She then moved into the soprano repertoire shortly before I came to the Metropolitan and actually did her first New York Sieglinde a few days after I sang mine. I was the Brünnhilde, substituting for Helen Traubel that evening, on Friday, December 12, 1941. She went on to sing for several more seasons, until she retired from the company in 1950. I had the pleasure of sharing quite a few performances with her in the Brünnhilde-Sieglinde and Elsa-Ortrud configurations, both at the Metropolitan and on the road. She was an all-around artist, a very beautiful woman with a gorgeous voice, who acted magnificently.

An equally first-rate actress was Regina Resnik, who joined the company, aged twenty-two, as Leonora in *Trovatore* on the third anniversary of my own début—December 6, 1944, to be exact. After adding real format to the interpretation of a number of soprano roles, including the Bruno Walter *Fidelio* I felt I was not ready for, Regina finally decided to move down the scale a couple of notes to become one of the finest mezzo-sopranos of our time.

Lotte Lehmann, whose indisposition in 1941 catapulted me onto the stage, had already been singing for forty years. She would remain at the Met for another four seasons until her retirement from opera in 1945. She was a wonderfully warmhearted lady whose intelligence and musicality were legendary. She had been a very successful Leonore in *Fidelio* under the baton of Bruno Walter, in both Europe and the United States, but had recently given up the part. When she heard that I was under consideration for Dr. Walter's *Fidelio*, Mme Lehmann offered to help me prepare it. I remember saying to myself then, should I ever enjoy a long career like hers, I would offer experienced counsel to my younger colleagues with the graciousness that she extended to me on that occasion. I have kept that promise.

For all Mme Lehmann's down-to-earth human qualities, she had a publicity agent who reveled in vicarious snobbery. In the spring of 1942, I found myself face-to-face with this austere woman, who evidently thought it her duty to remind me of the circumstances surrounding my initial substitution for Mme Lehmann, adding with a supercilious grin that Madame was feeling exceptionally well and would be singing her own Sieglinde at the next *Walküre* performance in Boston. I quietly replied that this news was a great relief to me, as I would be enjoying singing Brünnhilde in the same performance. The silence that followed that revelation was deafening.

Irene Jessner recently passed away in her adopted home of Toronto. Her sixteen-season stint at the Metropolitan, from 1936 to 1952, was the end of a career Mme Jessner had started years before in Europe. Her move to Canada came as the result of an invitation to teach at the Edward Johnson Conservatory, where she turned out some of the best singers that country ever produced, including my dear friends Teresa Stratas, Lilian Sukis, and Jeannette Zarou. Her teaching was clearly based on her own excellent vocalism, but as for stage portrayal, she was forever the *very* distinguished Irene Jessner in honorable middle age. One evening, as she came out on the turret to sing her song of gratitude to the breezes as Elsa in *Lohengrin*, I was seated beneath the tower as Ortrud beside Herbert Janssen, the Telramund. Janssen was a bit of a scalawag, and when he looked up at the dignified Mme Jessner, he couldn't resist whispering to me, "Ach, die Frau Kommerzienrat," an untranslatable German title meaning the wife of a captain of industry. In Central Europe in those days, everybody sported a title.

Herbert Janssen and his wife, Erna, became good friends of mine and ultimately turned out to be friends in need when things got arduous a few years later. If anyone's career had been victimized by the need to get out of Europe, it was certainly Herbert Janssen, who could not bring himself to remain in Hitler-infested Germany. He was a fine lyric baritone, but at the Metropolitan he was forced to sing *Heldenbariton* roles, for which he had neither the vocal color nor the temperament. The reason for this was the dearth of other qualified German baritones. Whenever he was allowed to sing one of the truly lyrical baritone roles in the Wagner repertoire, there was nobody better. His meltingly lovely song to the evening star in the third act of *Tannhäuser* could steal the show almost completely from any tenor but Melchior.

A critic once described Lauritz Melchior as the second-finest tenor of the twentieth century, reserving the top honors for the immortal Enrico Caruso. Frankly, I think this is an Americanism, comparing apples and oranges in quest of a superfluous first. Let's just say Melchior was the greatest tenor ever to sing Wagner, and Caruso was the greatest Italian tenor.

Melchior's heart was as big as his voice. From my very first performance with him, he took me under his wing, but not in any romantic way. His affections were very much spoken for. In fact, everywhere that Melchior went, his petite wife, "Kleinchen," was sure to go. Kleinchen Melchior was born Maria Anna Katharina Hacker and acted in motion pictures under the name of Anny Hacker. They met in the garden of Melchior's hunting lodge in Chossenwitz, Germany, under the most bizarre circumstances of any operatic couple I ever knew, or any other couple for that matter.

One afternoon, while Melchior was relaxing in his garden, Kleinchen was a few thousand feet above him in a plane, about to take a parachute jump as part of a role she was playing in a movie. She was a very hardy actress who always did her own stunt work. Apparently the jump was not as precisely calculated as the producers had thought, because Kleinchen wound up landing not at the appointed place, but rather right in the middle of Melchior's backyard. The tenor and the actress took the celestial hint and were married shortly afterward. They were inseparable from that day on.

If the decision to give up first her acting career to be a full-time wife and later her nationality to remain in America after Germany had overrun Denmark and declared war on the United States was a painful one for Kleinchen, she never so much as hinted at it. Lauritz Melchior was her whole life. Kleinchen negotiated all his contracts, handled his correspondence, and took care of all his business details. She even had the unenviable task of making sure her husband stayed on his daily diet. She was a good businesswoman, and she augmented her husband's Metropolitan salary considerably by arranging regular appearances for him in motion pictures, on the radio, and on the concert stage. She also enhanced my much-lower salary by inviting me to perform in joint concerts with her husband.

Once, when a lucrative previous engagement prevented Melchior from singing a Metropolitan *Parsifal* performance, he was replaced by a younger colleague named Emery Darcy, who generally sang such smaller roles as Froh in *Das Rheingold* or Melot to Melchior's Tristan. I was the Kundry in that performance, and I remember how startled I was when I saw the imposing figure of Melchior step onstage during one of the rehearsals to walk Darcy patiently through the entire role, carefully pointing out all the pitfalls he might have to face. It takes a big artist, in more ways than one, for that kind of magnanimity.

From the very first *Walküre* performance, every time Melchior saw my Sieglinde costume, a burlap garment partially covered with a leopard skin, he would shake his head sadly. "Where," Melchior would ask nobody in particular, "would anybody in legendary Germany find a leopard?" I agreed, but there wasn't much I could do about it—at least that's what I thought, because "beginners" can hardly make demands.

On February 20, 1947, I was scheduled for my first New York Brünnhilde in *Siegfried*. A day or so before, the Melchiors said they would like to invite me to join them after the show at their apartment in the Ansonia Hotel. The *Siegfried* was a resounding success, and so was the party. In typical Scandinavian fashion, the "little snack" to which we had been invited looked like it had been delivered in a ten-ton truck, but Wagner makes one hungry, and we went at it wholeheartedly. After sampling the buffet, Mr. Melchior formally asked me to raise a small glass to toast the evening. He instructed me that this drink was traditionally downed in a single swallow. I did as I was told and knocked back the contents of the little glass, which suddenly set my entire bloodstream on fire. It was Akvavit, known to the initiated as Danish dynamite. While I was waiting for my throat to return to normal, Melchior came over with an impish grin on his face like a Cheshire cat and slapped me gently on the shoulder with the words, "Jetzt kannst du mich duzen!" This was an invitation to use the familiar form of the word for "you," equivalent to going onto a first-name basis in English-speaking society—incidentally, not the matter-of-fact thing it is today. Having welcomed me into his circle of intimates, Lauritz handed me a gift, a magnificent sandy beige doeskin to wear over my Sieglinde costume. Lauritz was an enthusiastic hunter, and he had shot the doe himself. Our friendship flourished.

Melchior often used to slip me bits of healthy advice, which invariably worked like a charm. One significant case in point was the time I had to replace Mme Traubel on short notice as Isolde. It was my very first Isolde. He must have sensed something, because he made it his business to come out onstage before the curtain went up on act 1 to wish me well. Without any preamble, he said to me: "Handle your voice as you would a little horse. Keep a firm hand on the reins. When you have a clear track, let him run, and if he starts to get away from you, just rein him in." Then, with a little twinkle in his eye, he added, "I'll take care of the rest." Suddenly he looked down at my hands, and I could tell by the look in his eye that he was annoyed about something. Without telling me the source of his irritation, he turned around and yelled for Kleinchen. When she hurried over, he told her the costume department had forgotten to supply me with rings. "Isolde is a princess," he roared! "A princess *always* wears rings!" He then sent Kleinchen off to his dressing room to fetch the box in which he kept his stage jewelry. I couldn't figure out what he was up to. A ring that fit around his massive finger would probably accommodate two of my fingers with room to spare, or maybe serve as a substitute bracelet. Fortunately these were adjustable stage rings, and so I went onstage decked out with my leading man's jewelry. Without wishing to attribute any magical powers to those rings, the thoughtfulness that came with supplying them certainly served to boost my confidence in my most difficult role to date.

Sensing Isolde would be a watershed characterization for me, I wanted to postpone it until I felt I had fully prepared myself to grapple with its special complexities. The role had always been in the back of my mind. It even figured significantly in many of the interviews that followed my début at the end of 1941. The dramatic circumstances surrounding that début brought out newspaper reporters from every nook and cranny of the city, and my management, Columbia Artists, had a brilliant young publicity woman by the name of Alix Williamson, who knew how to make journalistic hay while the sun shone on my career.

In a few short weeks, the readers of New York's many newspapers were treated to everything from a picture of me leaning over a Greenwich Village fruit stand to an elegant photo portrait of me as Elisabeth in *Tannhäuser* on a full page of the fashion magazine *Mademoiselle*, all the way to a shot of me standing at the upright piano I had won in that crossword puzzle competition, being primed on some vocal fine point by my attentive mother, who frankly was having as good a time with her re-entry into the limelight as I was at my first taste of it. Another picture showed me at my dressing room table at the Metropolitan with the double-framed photos of Kirsten Flagstad, which served as my good luck charms, in a prominent position.

In many of the interviews, reporters would mention the colossal good fortune of a successful Met début at such a tender age and would then ask if there was anything left for me to hope for. I always pinpointed two roles: Kundry and, especially, Isolde. In fact, I was so interested in these roles that I would always take advantage of whatever opportunity presented itself to attend rehearsals of these operas, no matter who was scheduled to sing. I saw on the weekly plan that the awesome Sir Thomas Beecham would be rehearsing the orchestra on the roof stage for a performance of *Tristan*. I formally requested permission to attend his rehearsal, in order to get a feel for the orches-

Début photo: with my talisman in my dressing room. *New York Times.*

tral structure. I was told that I might, if I thought I could withstand the tempest of Sir Thomas's ire, should he be inadvertently rubbed the wrong way.

The stories of Beecham's vitriolic wit have become legendary over the years. I for one witnessed a few of them firsthand. On one occasion, Beecham stopped the orchestra and embarrassed one of the virtuoso wind players, whose work he considered a bit lackluster, by addressing the man at the adjacent stand: "I believe your colleague has fallen asleep. I think if you prod him a bit, it might resuscitate him." Another time, a well-known tenor was having some rather severe pitch problems during a rehearsal of the aria "Celeste Aida." His flat singing got on the orchestra's nerves, and when they started fidgeting, the concertmaster politely suggested he might give the hapless singer the correct pitch. "No need to," Beecham countered, "shortly he'll be an octave lower, and we'll *all* be together again."

The *Tristan* rehearsal started with a burst of Beecham pyrotechnics that set the management back on its heels. In those days, it was customary for the

General Manager to escort a prominent conductor personally to his first orchestra rehearsal. When Mr. Johnson announced Sir Thomas's willingness to replace a stricken colleague, the orchestra greeted the conductor with applause. Hardly had Sir Thomas opened the score when he noticed a couple of massive cuts perpetrated by a previous conductor, probably Dr. Bodanzky, who was notorious for cutting whole scenes out of Wagnerian pieces. Beecham made absolutely no secret of his displeasure at these excisions, which he referred to, in his most resonant Lancashire blare, as "Vandalism!" As he opened one cut after another, I could envision Mr. Johnson cringing at the thought of the overtime charges he might find himself called upon to pay the stagehands, electricians, and other technical personnel if the performance ran past midnight, but who was to argue with as devastating an opponent as Sir Thomas?

As the rehearsal progressed, I followed the music with the piano score on my lap and my eye on Sir Thomas's baton. Almost without noticing it myself, I began marking Isolde's part softly to the orchestral accompaniment, thinking that nobody would hear me, but I was wrong. I hadn't counted on Sir Thomas's keen ears. When the orchestra took its first break, Sir Thomas turned and smiled at me, with the words, "My dear, you certainly do know your role." At first, I thought this might be a kind of calm statement before the storm of a classic Beecham tirade, but it was nothing more than what it seemed, a pleasant vote of approval from a distinguished elder statesman.

The experience brought out two important facts: first, that my pianissimo had carrying power, and second, if I treated Beecham with courtesy and respect, he would return the compliment. As time went by, I ignored all the things other people were saying about him and greeted him cordially whenever the two of us passed in the hall. He always acknowledged the greeting with a pleasant nod.

A few months after the *Tristan* rehearsal, I was offered the solo part in a classical Mass and couldn't find anyone who knew the piece well enough to advise me on the wisdom of accepting the engagement. Not even Mr. Weigert had ever had any contact with the composition, something unusual for him. Somebody knew that Beecham had conducted the work in England, but suggested I keep my distance because he was in the midst of rehearsals and was not amenable to distractions. Disregarding this advice, I proceeded into the dark of the auditorium during Sir Thomas's rehearsal break and quietly asked if he could spare a moment of his time. I had ventured into the lion's den and found myself confronted with a gentle and knowledgeable lamb.

When I broached the subject of the Mass, he said he didn't regard it as appropriate for my voice. It was a friendly exchange and totally devoid of vitriol. It was not the first or the last time I found myself confronted with a forbidding individual, and I continued meeting that sort of person courteously but decisively head-on. I discovered this graphically when I sang my first Gutrune in *Götterdämmerung* to the redoubtable Hagen of Alexander Kipnis. Unlike many of our other colleagues, Mr. Kipnis coupled his gargantuan bass voice with a formidable acting talent, which sometimes had him going a little over the top, voluntarily or involuntarily pushing some of the other people onstage into the operatic equivalent of a neutral corner.

In this *Götterdämmerung* production, Gutrune sat at a table listening to Hagen extol the exploits of a hero by the name of Siegfried, who was wending his way down the Rhine in a barge toward their castle even as he spoke. It is this Siegfried he has in mind for Gutrune's husband. Understandably, fascination gets the better of Gutrune, and she leans forward across the table toward Hagen to ask him what valiant exploits had made this Siegfried such a great hero. Kipnis saw that I was resting my hands on the table, leaning toward him as I had been told to do by the stage director. As he went on singing about the greatness of Siegfried, he clamped his own downstage hand on top of both of mine, gesturing flamboyantly with his free hand, while freezing my captive hands. The next time we sang *Götterdämmerung*, I checkmated him by placing only one hand on the table. When he covered my hand with his, I simply clamped *my* free hand on top of his, cutting his freedom to gesture considerably. The look in his eye told me all I had to know. "You're learning," he seemed to say. He never pulled any more nonsense with me.

The case of Friedrich Schorr was a little more complex. Colleagues had warned me that he was an extremely nervous and difficult man with no patience whatsoever for what he perceived as the inadequacies of beginners. Years after the incident I am about to relate, I met him at a party and, after recounting my side of the event to him, was delighted to hear that the rumor of his impatience with beginners was nothing but the usual irresponsible gossip perpetrated in far too many opera houses. On the contrary, Mr. Schorr assured me, he had a great affection for younger colleagues and did whatever he could to encourage them, but as he was a fairly taciturn individual, this characteristic had often been misunderstood as aloofness.

The performance in question was my very first Brünnhilde. Having been warned about Schorr, I was on the qui vive not to do anything that might irritate the great baritone. In the final act of *Walküre*, there is a long exchange between Wotan and Brünnhilde, in which the latter finally convinces her initially irate father that, although she may have disobeyed his orders, she had indeed acted in his spirit. Wotan's own law demands that he punish his daughter, but he does agree to her plea not to dishonor her by forcing her to accept the first man who finds her. Instead, he mitigates the severity of her punishment by protecting her with a ring of magic fire until a hero worthy of her comes to claim her. In a beautifully touching moment, Wotan knows he is parting from a daughter who is in essence his better self, and holds out his arms to bid her a poignant farewell before surrounding her with this fire.

On this occasion, my eagerness to avoid any acting mistakes got the better of me, and I ran toward Wotan's outstretched arms a couple of musical measures before I was supposed to. When I arrived for the traditional embrace, Mr. Schorr muttered under his breath: "Zu früh" (too soon). I had the presence of mind to fall on my knees before him, and while the audience admiringly gasped, Schorr took advantage of the emotion by raising me slowly to my feet and drawing me gently into his arms. It became a moving scene. Before launching into his "Abschied," he looked down at me with an expression of warm commendation and whispered almost inaudibly: "Du wirst was!" (You'll make the grade!).

As the evidence of his imminent vocal decline became clear to Schorr, he asked that his name be discreetly withdrawn from the roster for the coming season. Mr. Johnson felt that such a distinguished artist should not retire without an appropriate farewell and proposed casting him in one final *Ring* cycle to mark the termination of his career. Mr. Schorr reluctantly agreed, and an almost metaphysical event in the *Siegfried* performance, at which Wotan makes his final exit from the action, possibly confirmed his reluctance.

Wotan, the god, disguised as a wanderer, finds himself face-to-face with his grandson, who will wield the sword given to his father to destroy the mystical spear bearing the runes that confirm much of the god's power. Of course, Schorr was provided with a breakaway prop spear, set to divide in two on a musical cue when Siegfried strikes it with the sword. Unfortunately, however, the spear fell apart of its own volition long before it was supposed to, forcing Mr. Schorr to continue singing several pages of music, then gather up the two halves and make an inauspicious exit, which witnesses say he did mumbling to himself. This left the audience shocked and saddened, silently bidding a most respected and honored man adieu. To his credit, Mr. Schorr saved the emotional situation with a gracious curtain speech, quoting from Hans Sachs's wise words to the burghers of Nuremberg on the village green in act 3 of *Die Meistersinger*, followed by a tribute from an earlier role to the country that had adopted him and saved his life, in the two words ("America forever!") Consul Sharpless sings in *Madama Butterfly*.

This event made me keenly aware of one very important fact: careers that start auspiciously may end with more than a note of sorrow. Still, at the very start of my own career, I was nevertheless determined it would not end like that.

Alliances

IN HER AUTOBIOGRAPHY, *The Flagstad Manuscript*, Kirsten Flagstad tells a revealing story about finding herself alone in an elevator with Charlie Chaplin. Out of deference to his right to privacy, she says, she immediately turned her back, even though she would have enjoyed exchanging a few words with him. Flagstad goes on to say she would like her own personal life treated the same way. So would I. One chapter on private matters, however, sheds a great deal of light on my work as a performer, which is why I would like to take a little pause to share the story of two significant alliances with my readers.

When I started working at the Metropolitan, my mother and I decided we each wanted our own terrain. I needed peace and quiet to prepare for my performances, and she needed a place where she could continue to give her singing lessons without having to worry about disturbing anyone. So we split up our household on Charles Street into two separate apartments, not very far away from one another, on Christopher Street. Mother and Lucky moved into a slightly smaller apartment, and I took a furnished one-room flat for myself. Of course, we saw one another at regular intervals for both family togetherness and vocal lessons, and while I continued to contribute to my mother's budget, Mother continued to give me the benefit of her vocal and musical wisdom.

My beginner's salary at the opera house minus my personal expenses and my contribution to my mother's household left me in such modest circumstances that it was difficult for me to pay for my lessons with Mr. Weigert. I told him about my predicament and explained that I could afford only one lesson a week. He then generously offered to teach me the second weekly lesson on credit, payable whenever my financial situation improved.

A few months later, I arrived for a lesson, and he commented that I seemed to look particularly happy about something. I replied that I felt just wonderful. I was then, and am still, a great lover of motion pictures, especially comedies, and on that particular day I had spent the early afternoon, prior to the lesson, seeing a Danny Kaye picture, which still had me laughing inwardly. Mr. Weigert admitted he was also a great fan of American comedians like Danny Kaye, Will Rogers, and the Marx Brothers, but he felt somewhat disadvantaged in his enjoyment by the fact that he hadn't grown up speaking English, as I had. Beyond this, most of the German wing at the Metropolitan communicated in the German language, and so he had little opportunity to learn American colloquialisms at work.

The thought came to me that I might compensate him for his generosity with a little quid pro quo. I suggested we go to the movies together. This way I could fill him in on any of the linguistic points he might have missed, and I could have the pleasure of discussing with him what we had both just seen. Several movies later, we began to realize that we enjoyed one another's company privately as much as we did professionally, but it was still strictly a professional relationship with the pleasant sideline of an occasional visit to the cinema, where we spent most of our time laughing our heads off.

One afternoon, when, as always, he had the European courtesy to ask me how I was feeling, I confessed that an irritating phone call had upset me that morning, and I just couldn't get it out of my system. Mr. Weigert asked me to tell him about it. I was annoyed, I said, because a young man I had been seeing socially for a while had called me up with the suggestion that he take me away from "all this," and I could cook him ham and eggs every morning. With all respect to the American institution of ham and eggs, I was insulted by this gentleman's suggestion that his affections should be rewarded by my sacrifice of everything I had been working toward for years. Besides this, there was a certain manipulative implication that I frankly disliked.

Mr. Weigert thought about this for a minute, then said: "It sounds like a marriage proposal to me." Of course he was right. Then he looked very intently over at me and said, "You wouldn't do that to *me*, would you?" It was the first time I became truly aware of what a personal involvement Mr. Weigert had in my life.

The attitude of the ham-and-eggs man was the prevalent point of view in those days. All the "career girl" movies and countless popular songs suggested that every woman in the world wanted to abandon her own personality and aspirations for the sake of being subservient to "her man." Naturally, I had thought about married life with home and children, but I saw no reason why I couldn't combine this with my profession, as many of my colleagues were successfully doing. Mr. Weigert agreed. His gentle understanding of my feelings marked the beginning of a closer friendship that, in time, led us both to the realization that there are certain relationships you just don't sever. Our "marriage of true minds," to quote that magnificent Shakespeare sonnet, was one of those relationships, and so, in the fullness of time, we decided to make it a marriage in the legal sense as well.

Not everybody thought this was such a good idea. The suggestion was made that one or both of us would be exploiting the other in a Pygmalion-Galatea combination, hoping to ride to operatic success on one another's coattails. Nothing could have been further from the truth, because both of us were having excellent careers at the time. Others felt that our age difference would doom our marriage to failure. It was a chance we were both more than willing to take. Neither of us ever regretted it.

My turbulent childhood, being jolted around from one country to another, my father's death, my mother's widowhood and the problems that followed, had forced a lot of responsibility on me at a very early age. In addition to the normal chores of shopping and running other errands, one of my more onerous duties involved going around to people to whom we owed money, such as the telephone company, and asking them to wait a little while for payment. All this had made me mature before my time, as a consequence of which I found kindred spirits largely amongst persons older than myself. I didn't feel the least bit awkward about marrying a man almost three decades older than I, nor was Hermann hesitant to enter into this new phase of our lives together. We complemented one another, we enjoyed one another's company, and our senses of humor blended perfectly.

As Hermann was Jewish and I a Roman Catholic, we had to waive the religious ceremony and were married by a justice of the peace in nearby Connecticut. It was in the Nutmeg State, on a beautiful spring day, May 19, 1944, to be specific, that I became Mrs. Hermann O. Weigert. One thing, however, was missing from the wedding. Just as Douglas Beattie had brought me together professionally with Mr. Weigert, our affection for one another had been kindled by our love for the artistry of Danny Kaye. If it had been possible, like a Hollywood dream, he would have been the best man at the ceremony.

We began looking for a place to live. When we inquired if anyone in the theatre knew of a Manhattan apartment we might rent, Nicola Moscona mentioned to Hermann that he was in the process of giving up his flat on West 110th Street. When he told us the place had three good-sized rooms with a view of the Hudson River and a kitchen with a spacious refrigerator and generously proportioned pantries, we both spontaneously knew that was where we wanted to live! Our home on the corner of Riverside Drive became a gathering place for our friends. Most of these friends were Hermann's, Central European immigrants like himself, doctors and lawyers, as well as singers, musicians, and their families, such as Herbert and Erna Janssen. As all of them were highly cultured with wonderful senses of humor, the apartment often rocked with the sounds of heated discussion or unrestrained merriment. These get-togethers were very important in my life, because they increased my German vocabulary, and the old-world sophisticates broadened my horizons beyond the confines of the opera house.

This expansion of my own consciousness was also a major contributing factor in my attitude toward role preparation, either for myself or for the people I teach today. I have always endeavored to return to the source, or the many sources, in my quest for the truth of any character I am portraying. These adventurous quests have taken me to the library, to art galleries, to the hills of Mycenae, to the big cities and hinterlands of many countries, and, in one instance, to the kitchen of an Italian restaurant, but those stories will have to wait for their rightful place in the chronology.

Our own kitchen, which we had taken over from the Athenian basso Moscona, represented a special attraction to another friend of both Hermann's and mine, who also originally hailed from Athens. Whenever Dimitri Mitropoulos came to visit, he would invariably greet us perfunctorily at the door and then make a beeline for the stove to see what was on the bill of fare. Checking the pots is an old Hellenic tradition, but the clatter of Maestro Mitropoulos being "traditional" often made me grateful I never cooked a soufflé. Fortunately our guest was an epicure whose food preferences were as eclectic as his musical tastes. He derived as much pleasure from a well-cooked pot of kidney beans as he did from a plate of oysters. It all depended on his mood. Maestro Mitropoulos was one of the distinguished guests who was always accorded the place of honor at the little table in our kitchen. Many were the evenings when we chatted with him over dinner, with the magnificent view of the lights glittering above the Hudson River in front of him and his back to the sink.

Along with my alliance with Hermann Weigert, there was another alliance that was very important to me at the time. I do not know what passport my family used to enter the United States, most likely Austro-Hungarian. At the time we arrived, both of my parents were Hungarian, but Hungary had become a separate nation only after my mother and father had left there, and my father's birthplace had meanwhile become a part of the new nation of Czechoslovakia. Whatever nationality we had when we arrived, if we wished to remain, we would have to take up citizenship in the United States.

In my teens, I had applied for citizenship, which then resulted in my being summoned to the immigration center on Ellis Island, off Manhattan. I remember my feeling of uneasiness if the authorities were to find some reason why I shouldn't be allowed to remain in the country, but my fears were unfounded, because I met all the requirements, and my citizenship application was routinely processed. Five years later, in accordance with the legal regulations at the time, I became a citizen of the United States of America. The date was March 15, 1943, and I was welcomed into the family of Americans with an obligation I'd already been meeting for a couple of years, namely, paying taxes. In those days, March 15 was the final deadline for filing our federal income tax returns. Although he had been in the country a far shorter time, Hermann Weigert received his citizenship a couple of years before I did, in early December 1941, just a few days ahead of my début.

The smooth transition from one nationality to another was not always vouchsafed to all our artistic colleagues. Many failed to qualify and had to return to face an uncertain future back in Europe. Ezio Pinza was subjected to the anxiety and humiliation of imprisonment, based on a false charge of spying for the Italians, who were then fighting the United States on the side of the Germans. As Mr. Pinza relates in his autobiography, entitled simply *Ezio Pinza*, another bass at the Metropolitan thought he might fall heir to some of Pinza's roles by having this great artist put away on trumped-up accusations, but it did not work in this case, and the accuser met with a sad end.

Perhaps that barely averted disaster was the reason why Mr. Pinza's elderly cook was so eager to become an American citizen. She was a firm fixture in the household, as the preparation of delectable meals is one of the elemental keystones of domestic bliss in many an Italian home. The only problem in her case was that the citizenship procedure called for at least a working knowledge of the English language and some familiarity with American history and government. Until then, the lady had never needed to know anything other than the Italian language and the recipes for an abundance of savory dishes, which kept everyone happy at the dinner table, but which weren't going to stand her in very good stead before the citizenship judge.

Finally the Pinzas managed to teach her a smattering of both English and American lore, and a friend of theirs was able to arrange for her to appear before a judge whose family had also immigrated from Italy, and who was thus able to prompt her in her native tongue, if all else failed. The same friend also approached the judge and asked, in the interests of the Pinzas' gastronomical well-being, to be lenient with this candidate. The compliant judge said he would only ask her the essentials.

The day of the hearing arrived, and the cook, fortified by the good wishes of the entire Pinza family, nervously faced the judge. First he asked her name, *il suo nome*, and she of course answered the question with flying colors. Then the judge quizzed her a little about the United States government. Just as soon as she found out from His Honor that "chief executive" was basically the same thing as *capo del governo*, she was able to reply that the gentleman in question was *il Presidente* Roose-a-da-velt.

That was close enough. The judge then inquired about the legislature—*la legislatura* . . . "Ma, certo," the housekeeper replied, "at's-a de house of-a de representativi . . ." Again, right on the button. But America, the judge explained, has a bicameral legislative system, which provoked a look of total panic on her face. Gently, the judge went on to explain, if the House of Representatives is the Lower House of Congress, what is the Upper House? The housekeeper pondered this for a second. "De uppa house? De uppa house . . . ?" Then an incandescent smile of recognition illuminated her face. "Esatto—de uppa house, she's-a onna de Broadway anna de thoity-nint' street. At's-a where Mr. Pinza, he's-a sing onna de stage."

I'm not sure how true the foregoing yarn is, but it was just too good to leave out of this book. America being America, I would not be the least bit surprised if one of that lady's descendants was currently a distinguished member of either branch of Congress!

SCENE THREE

Dependent and Independent Women

THERE SEEMS TO BE an unwritten law that opera singers whose careers start off as well as mine are given a kind of two- to three-year grace period, during which they are mostly praised and accepted as a potential asset to the art. Then the critics begin to remove their gloves. Rather than take umbrage at what the reviewers were saying about my work, my mother, Maestro Weigert, and I all agreed that well-founded negative statements were worth serious consideration.

With more than a dozen New York City newspapers and periodicals covering the Metropolitan Opera simultaneously, and a wide scope of critical opinion being expressed, we had great difficulty assessing whom to believe. Each critic's knowledge, background, experience, and taste had to be screened. In our opinion, only a few were qualified to advise us. Foremost amongst them were Noël Strauss and Olin Downes of the *New York Times*, John Rosenfield of the *Dallas Morning Star*, Virgil Thomson of the *New York Herald Tribune*, and Harold Rosenthal of London's *Opera Magazine*, who paid frequent visits to the United States. A few others varied from uninformed to unscrupulous. As a matter of fact, one major critic doubled as a voice teacher, but his reviews applied a special yardstick to prominent divas who either took lessons from him or bought concert gowns from the excellent dress designer he lived with. It was worth it—the gowns were beautiful.

Obviously I was young, and both my body and voice were in a state of ongoing development. (No singer is ever perfect, and certainly not at the beginning of a career.) Even with the relatively easy schedule I was performing, the exclusivity of Wagnerian roles finally caught up with my immaturity, and I began to have some vocal imbalance. A crisis?

Everyone has one or two crises in the course of a singing career. Anyone who denies ever having had a crisis has either experienced a miracle or is telling a downright untruth. As a person's body changes throughout a lifetime, for whatever reasons, the singing apparatus is definitely affected. Beyond this, any emotional upheavals will also leave their mark. In short, the difference between singers and non-singers is that non-singers have a body with two vocal chords in the throat, whereas a singer has two vocal chords surrounded on all sides by a body, this is what makes us singers latent hypochondriacs!

Nowadays, the kind of soluble problems I was facing back in the early and mid-1940s would probably cost me my job or at least my reputation, but people had more time and more patience back then. Moreover, the Metropolitan management had invested a great deal of confidence in my abilities, and they were determined to see me through whatever difficulties might arise. When a particularly devastating review had severely shaken my composure, I asked for an appointment with Mr. Johnson to discuss the situation. He told me a story about his own career, a story I will always remember. He almost gave up singing, he told me, when one critic wrote a one-line review, to wit: "A tenor from Canada by the name of Edward Johnson was engaged to sing 'Dick Johnson' in Puccini's *La Fanciulla del West* . . . WHY?"

My negative write-up filled an entire paragraph, lauding my acting and interpretation, but deploring part of my singing. By pointing up this comparison to his own review, Mr. Johnson lifted my spirits. He then suggested I consult a second singing teacher, so as to leave no stone unturned. I might perhaps be able to add to my present knowledge and clear up the problem. The party he named was an excellent pianist who liked *talking* about singing, although he himself had never actually sung.

My initial reaction to the suggestion of taking lessons from this person was skepticism. Furthermore, I was extremely reluctant to place the responsibility for my singing in the hands of an unknown quantity, when my mother's tuition had brought me to the stage of the Metropolitan. My mother didn't agree. While she was firmly convinced that time would alleviate the situation of its own accord, she felt it would be diplomatic to take Mr. Johnson's advice and avail myself of further vocal coaching. However, she was adamant that I study with a teacher who was more than just a pianist: in other words, a person who loved and understood the human voice.

Mother then proposed that I take a course of study from a former Metropolitan tenor who had sung Wagnerian roles, and who had gone into vocal teaching following his retirement from stage activity in 1941, only a few months before my Metropolitan début. His name was Paul Althouse. His newly established studio would ultimately produce several major artists. In years to come, I often sang with two of the most celebrated ones: Eleanor Steber and Richard Tucker. When I reported this alternative to Edward Johnson, he spontaneously agreed.

Those lessons were quite an experience! Having recently retired from the stage, Mr. Althouse's voice was still in good shape, and he often taught by example, which is to say he would sing Siegmund to my Sieglinde. He felt this was a good way of teaching through hearing. I personally tend to favor an analytical approach, knowing exactly why and how something is being done.

It was in Mr. Althouse's studio that I first met a young musician who would become one of my dearest friends. Recently emigrated from Germany and eager to become a professional singer herself, Lys Bert would exchange a full day's accompanying for a single lesson from the parsimonious Mr. Althouse. Lys Bert finally applied her vocal knowledge and her pianistic brilliance to becoming one of the finest coaches on two continents and a trusted musical assistant to the prominent composer Kurt Weill.

A few years after our first encounter, Lys was playing rehearsals for a Weill opera called *Street Scene* and fell in love with one of the members of the company, whom she subsequently married. Her husband, Randolph Symonette, had a long and excellent career singing *Heldenbariton* roles in both the United States and Europe. When I was singing in Germany and points beyond, Lys and Randolph Symonette's apartment in Düsseldorf was for many years my "home away from home," and their friendship was one of the great supports of my personal well-being. Today, Lys is a board member and musical administrator of the Kurt Weill Foundation for Music in New York and tours the world promoting the master's music, which means we have an opportunity to get together and talk over old times every now and again.

While I was ironing out my vocal problems, I became aware of an unforeseen development. A kind of inner dynamic seemed to be propelling me away, slowly and gradually, from the Wagnerian ingénues. The golden opportunity arrived through the planning of the Metropolitan seasons in the late 1940s. I was being moved away from the dependent ladies like Elsa and Elisabeth, who were more acted upon than acting, and assigned to more independent

This picture was not planned. The American Airlines logo just happened to feature Brünn-hilde's wings. Still, it was a portent of things to come. This was the Met tour of 1940. *Metropolitan Opera Archives.*

characters such as Ortrud, Isolde, and Kundry, who take their destinies very much into their own hands.

Let me give you an example of the juxtaposition between two kinds of Wagnerian heroines: Elsa and Ortrud in *Lohengrin*. Elsa needs to be saved by someone and is not sufficiently independent to save herself. Her nemesis, Ortrud, on the other hand, is totally on her own, using her keen intelligence to dominate the situation. There is something almost mannish in Ortrud's single-minded devotion to her religious faith and territorial ambitions, but she certainly has more than enough feminine sex appeal to inveigle the basically decent Telramund into making common cause with her.

In my opinion, it is false to portray Ortrud solely as a sorceress. This interpretation couldn't be further from the character's *inner* truth. In essence, Ortrud is just as devout in her belief as is Lohengrin in his, and the *magic* she practices is an integral part of her religious faith. Ortrud is the last of an aristocratic dynasty, which had once ruled the land. She is determined to retrieve this territory in her own right and restore the religion that had dominated the region for centuries. I see her as a proud and independent woman, who, in the early Middle Ages, had very few inherent rights, nor was she allowed to assert her own claims or act as a combatant. This is the reason why she needed a physically strong man, over whom she could exert her superior intelligence and erotic appeal to impel his actions in the direction she wanted them to take, hoping ultimately to re-establish the pre-eminence of both her ancestral line and her traditional religion. Everything she does would be thoroughly defensible except for one fact: her attempted destruction of human life. This is where she sows the seeds of her own destruction. For me, the opera *Lohengrin* treats the confrontation between two creeds: Christianity (Lohengrin) versus paganism (Ortrud); and two attributes: dependence (Elsa) versus independence (also Ortrud). These conflicts must be played sincerely.

An interviewer once told me that my Ortrud in the first act left an indelible impression on the audience, despite the fact that she has very little to sing, though she is present throughout the action. He wanted to know what technique I used to create this impression. I answered him, "I simply listen to what the other protagonists are saying, as if I were hearing everything for the very first time, and then I react accordingly within the frame of reference of the character." Now, this may sound easy, but the level of concentration required can be just as demanding as singing. I was told I radiated a flow of energy, which carried over to the audience. This is what makes the difference between a singer and a singing actress.

Isolde has often been described as complex. I wonder why! I do not find her complex in the least. In fact, I see her as perfectly feminine, natural, and understandable. It has always been a source of amazement to me how well Richard Wagner understood and expressed the intricacies of the female psyche. One might almost say he was part woman. In our own day, the medical profession has ascertained that every human being has both male and female components. Genetically, Richard Wagner must have had both of them in sizable amounts.

Isolde is able to take the initiative in every situation, regardless of where her determination might leave her in the end. While she is profoundly in love with Tristan, she isn't dependent on him for anything. Their union is not based on dependency, but rather on the fact that their love for one another forms an imperative that holds valid, even if their relationship is outside the then-existent bounds of social mores.

Before I actually essayed the role, I followed my principles and did massive research on this archetypical mediaeval legend, which can be found in a number of different sources, the foremost among them being the courtly *epos* by Gottfried von Strassburg, based largely on the writing of the Anglo-Norman Thomas of Brittany. Throughout his compositions, however, Wagner always rearranged the core material to suit his own personal situation. Why, then, delve deeply into these courtly and folkloristic Celtic tales? Because a knowledge of the conventions in the period of the legends, coupled with an awareness of Wagner's changes, as he altered the legendary material to accommodate his own agenda, led me to understand and ultimately re-enact Wagner's "self-legend."

So much is made of the so-called love potion, which is extraneous to the core of the plot. If the two of them had merely taken a drink of water from the golden goblet, they would still have had to succumb to their inner compulsion to declare their love for one another, a love that had begun long before the curtain opens on the opera. In fact, it is the central theme of the prelude. At best, Brangäne's potion serves to intensify their feelings, and the feelings do the rest. So, once again, we see that Isolde is not the victim of some form of necromancy but rather very much the captain of her own fate.

Just before Isolde hands Tristan the goblet, she gives him an opportunity to account for himself. His reply is phrased so cryptically that only a few interpreters of this opera have ever taken the trouble to ponder it. His words are: "Des Schweigens Herrin heisst mich schweigen: fass' ich, was sie verschwieg, verschweig' ich, was sie nicht fasst" (The sovereign of silence bids me to be silent. While I comprehend what she once withheld [that is, that she loved me], I now withhold what she does not comprehend [that is, that I love her]). He is honor-bound not to reveal his feelings, because the situation is now beyond his control.

But Isolde is still in full control of *her* situation. Although she misinterprets this enigmatic statement, perhaps to mean he is trying to avoid the fateful drink, she still refuses to accept any hesitation on his part, and her determination seals their fate. This forcing of the issue is a telling illustration of Isolde's taking matters into her own hands, an attribute on which the entire opera hinges. A more independent woman would be impossible for me to imagine.

As I worked my way through the characters of Wagner's maturity, I found myself drawn to the intricate personality of his final female protagonist, Kundry in *Parsifal*, one I consider both dependent and independent, with the major emphasis on the independent side. The triune personality of Kundry, derived as it is from so many different legendary, mythical, and biblical sources, is far and away the most complex to define. In a single character, she embodies the biblical Herodias, the Celtic demon Gundryggia, the legendary Wandering Jew in female form, as well as the characteristics of St. Mary Magdalene (for example, Kundry washes Parsifal's feet and dries them with her hair).

Kundry and the Flying Dutchman have the same legendary origin—both derive from the story of the Wandering Jew. Both have committed a blasphemy, the Dutchman swearing by all the devils, and Kundry laughing at the Savior on the cross. Their guilt is their punishment, the Dutchman wandering endlessly across the seas, unable to find peace in death until he is redeemed by the selfless loyalty of a woman. Kundry is the sum total of a number of different reincarnations. We encounter her final manifestations in *Parsifal*.

Her sexuality, without love or even a modicum of affection, is like a narcotic. The more Kundry indulges, the more she desires. Parsifal's unexpected rejection drives her to frenzy, to the extent that her mental processes become incoherent. Finally she confuses feelings and remembrances, and even goes so far as to believe Parsifal is the One she had laughed at. She begs and pleads with him to "unite" with her for her salvation. Parsifal's denial drives her to a form of madness. The effect is like drug withdrawal. The person goes through hell until he or she is healed.

To make matters even more complicated, Kundry has become a kind of schizophrenic, unaware of one manifestation of her personality while she is locked in the other. In act 1, despite her not realizing she had been at fault in seducing Amfortas, she also has an inner compulsion to atone, like someone on a pilgrimage to a sacred shrine, moving up and down the stairs on her knees. And for all the services she renders, she insists on being spared any form of gratitude. "Ich helfe nie," is her response to the thanks of the others, "I never help." The reason for this is her belief that gratitude will nullify the validity of the help she has given, and this would mar the selflessness of her acts. It's a very life-negating attitude toward what are basically simple virtues.

The temptress Kundry who appears on Klingsor's summons reveals a seductive power against which few men have a viable defense: she dwells on Parsifal's mother. The reawakening of his yearnings for maternal affection, especially in the case of someone who has been deprived of mother love, invariably catches the victim off his guard. It has to be very subtly maneuvered. In Parsifal's case, she immobilizes him by intensifying his remorse at having abandoned his poor, suffering mother. By claiming she is only trying to protect him and offering him a replacement for his mother's love, she is actually scheming to annihilate Parsifal, just as she had once afflicted Amfortas. But the pseudo-maternal kiss she offers him is actually loaded with sensuous venom. I am reminded of the serpent in Genesis.

Why Richard Wagner used sexuality in this feminine form of the Wandering Jew may be an enigma. I can only surmise that men, in general, are always susceptible to seduction, because of the strong sexual side of their make-up. See the history of the downfall of many men knowingly destroyed by women, either by their own will or in the employ of others: Judith and Holofernes, Delila and Samson, to name just two instances.

Parsifal's reaction is certainly anything but what Kundry had bargained for. Amfortas's tragedy instantly dawns on him, and with that awareness comes wisdom. Kundry tries again and again to conquer him, but to no avail. Her passion being unrequited, she resorts to imprecations, while her inner fire rapidly extinguishes. Toward the conclusion of this act, the singer must go to the nth degree of physical acting. She must seem to be uncontrollably involved, while at the same time constantly holding herself in check, to maintain the musical-vocal sound intact. Quite a task! Kundry then falls into a deep sleep, somewhat like a coma, which lasts many years, to awaken again on Good Friday, the day when her redemption is at hand.

The thought occurs to me that I could have avoided all the trouble of digging into the history and essence of this character, and just sung the role, but this approach would have left me frustrated. These independent characters represented exactly the kind of challenge I was seeking. Understanding them involved a profound level of thinking and searching, but it gave me a thousand gratifications.

The Father of Twentieth-Century Opera

VE–DAY ON MAY 8, 1945, marked the end of the Second World War in Europe and with it the re-internationalization of the American opera scene. Once again, the Metropolitan Opera House had access to some of the most outstanding singers in the world, and I had the good fortune to sing with many of them—in particular, two heroic tenors who had come to New York to relieve Melchior of the Herculean task of handling virtually all the heavy Wagnerian repertoire single-handedly. Max Lorenz from Germany and his Swedish counterpart Set Svanholm also provided an added benefit to the Metropolitan. Both of them were experts in the music of Richard Strauss, whose operas Melchior never touched.

Performing Strauss brought with it many pitfalls none of us ever faced with Wagner. Because Wagner had been dead since 1883, beyond the memory of anyone in the music world in 1945, his works were subject to reinterpretation without interference. Richard Strauss, on the other hand, was still alive at the time, and several conductors and stage directors at the Met had actually known him in Europe. This led to a chain of very heated disputes on the subject of Strauss's musical interpretation, with a number of know-it-alls swearing to high heaven that their tempo or style was in full agreement with the composer's wishes, while the dissenting side was equally zealous in defense of *its* point of view. During one of these endless discussions, Hermann Weigert heaved a sigh of exasperation and made one of those remarks that maintained his reputation as the Metropolitan Opera's resident quipster: "Too bad Strauss isn't around to defend himself!"

Of course, Strauss was "around" in the literal sense of the word. Although in his eighties, he was still very much alive and active in musical life, but since 1939 he had been inaccessible to us on the other side of the battle lines. Many contemporary commentators actually felt it would be disgraceful to perform his works at all, because he had allegedly thrown in his lot with the Third Reich. It would not be within the scope of my memoirs to consider the whole case of Richard Strauss in full detail, but I do think it is fair to set the record straight. Much has been made by his detractors of Strauss's willingness to accept a position in 1933 as president of something called the *Reichsmusikkammer*, a national musical council, one of many such bodies set up by Goebbels in an attempt to institutionalize cultural life in Germany. The real reasons for his assumption of that office had more to do with the preservation of musical culture in general and the rights of composers to the legitimate copyright ownership of their works in particular. His connection to this organization was severed in the wake of a debacle over one of his operas.

The work was *Die schweigsame Frau*, with a libretto by the Austrian Jewish writer Stefan Zweig, whose name Strauss insisted on keeping on the program despite official disapproval. As a gesture of tribute to Strauss's eminence, the Führer himself had offered to come to the Dresden première, but when he found out Strauss had been adamant about the program, he begged off, claiming his flight from Hamburg had been canceled because of inclement weather. In a letter to Zweig written on June 17, 1935, Strauss summed up his attitude toward this kind of pseudo-nationalistic bias with characteristic Bavarian bluntness. "Why did I play the role of *Reichsmusikkammer* President? To do good and prevent greater misfortune. Simply from a consciousness of artistic obligation." He then went on to say: "As far as I'm concerned, the *people* begin to exist at the moment they become the audience. I couldn't care less whether they are Chinese, Upper Bavarians, New Zealanders or Berliners, just as long as they paid the full admission price at the box office." The letter was intercepted by the Gestapo and never reached Zweig, but official disapproval of the sentiments expressed therein eventually precipitated Strauss's "resignation," which was announced on July 14 of the same year.

Throughout the years of the Third Reich, the composer continued to concentrate on his music, doing his best to ignore the events happening all around him. Strauss's apolitical nature, bordering on naïveté, can probably be best illustrated in an incident that took place in the 1940s and was recounted by the composer's grandson, Dr. Christian Strauss. As Dr. Strauss told the story, his mother's Jewish grandmother, Mrs. Paula Neumann, had been deported to the concentration camp at Theresienstadt. Richard Strauss was so devoted to his daughter-in-law, Alice, née von Grab-Hermannswörth, his musical secretary and the mother of his two beloved grandsons, that he decided to take advantage of a trip from Vienna to Dresden to make a stop for the purpose of paying a visit to the camp to see to her grandmother's well-being. Arriving in his chauffeured car, he casually walked up to the gates and asked the SS guards to inform Mrs. Neumann that her granddaughter's father-in-law had come to see her. The guards gaped at him as if he had lost his mind, but Strauss persisted, claiming that he was a very important person in the artistic world and certainly entitled to pay a call on a close relative by marriage. Finally, the SS-men summarily escorted him out of the place. Mrs. Neumann wasn't the only relative to be murdered. Some twenty-six of Alice Strauss's relatives perished in concentration camps, but the composer stuck by her throughout his life.

As far as the authenticity of Strauss performances was concerned, all the debating on fine points of style at the Metropolitan would ultimately prove unnecessary. Strauss was a practical theatre professional who listed himself in the Garmisch telephone directory as *Kapellmeister*, a term for a conductor of serious music, but literally translatable as "bandmaster." As such, he was aware of the variety of feasible interpretations of his works and welcomed new ideas as a matter of course, especially if purism might have cost him a royalty check.

Strauss's attitude is perhaps best illustrated by something that happened to my colleague Hans Hotter, who had collaborated with him both in the opera house and on the recital platform. Once, Hotter was rehearsing an opera with the composer himself conducting. Suddenly Hans sang a disastrously wrong note. Hans is an excellent musician himself, and the minute the orchestra took a break, he respectfully apologized to the composer for his error. Unfazed, Strauss replied, "You sang that note with such conviction, I must have composed it wrong."

This open-minded liberal approach to the performances of his works may have suited Strauss, but Fritz Reiner, who conducted *Salome* at the Met, held the diametrically opposite attitude and insisted upon perfect adherence to the instructions in the score. Although Reiner had figured significantly in my past, having introduced my parents to one another back in Budapest, this did not entitle me to any favoritism. In fact, it took him seven years from the time of my début before he engaged me to sing in Pittsburgh, where he was the musi-

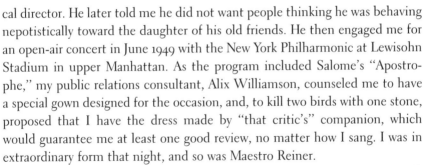

cal director. He later told me he did not want people thinking he was behaving nepotistically toward the daughter of his old friends. He then engaged me for an open-air concert in June 1949 with the New York Philharmonic at Lewisohn Stadium in upper Manhattan. As the program included Salome's "Apostrophe," my public relations consultant, Alix Williamson, counseled me to have a special gown designed for the occasion, and, to kill two birds with one stone, proposed that I have the dress made by "that critic's" companion, which would guarantee me at least one good review, no matter how I sang. I was in extraordinary form that night, and so was Maestro Reiner.

The reviews were ecstatic. Writing in the *New York Times*, Noël Strauss said, "There were cries of bravo for the singer at the close of this magisterial exhibition of superior artistry, with which she scored a signal triumph." Robert Bagar in the *World-Telegram* wrote, "Here is a voice of great power and beauty. It is a caressingly tender voice one moment and a viciously demanding one the next, just as you would want Salome's voice to be." Miles Kastendieck commented in the *Brooklyn Eagle*, "She triumphed in the final scene, winning the right to be considered among the very few who have sung this role with distinction." The *Post*'s usually acerbic Harriet Johnson noted, "The highlight of the evening was Miss Varnay's singing of the final scene, which combined vocal splendor with histrionic impressiveness." Douglas Watt commented in the *New York News*, "Withal Miss Varnay was superb." Jerome D. Bohm of the *New York Herald Tribune* joined the cheering throng, "The evening belonged to Miss Varnay. . . ." Once again, however, the inevitable Irving Kolodin checked in with the only lukewarm critique. The sea-green gown, by the way, with a silver lamé underskirt and a huge, provocative blood-red velvet bow on one side, fit perfectly with the role of Salome.

I was delighted that some of the write-ups also expressed the hope that the Metropolitan would cast me as Salome. Before that concert took place, however, I had already sung a staged production of the role twice at the Cincinnati Opera, in the summer of 1948, and was scheduled for two revival performances there only a week after the concert in 1949, with an additional two evenings planned for New Orleans the following November. Meanwhile, I had conquered my onetime adolescent revulsion at the plot of this opera as I became progressively intrigued with its striking musical and dramatic treatment of the original biblical sources.

At the time those Lewisohn Stadium concert reviews were published, the Strauss opera was already in the Metropolitan's repertoire, but not with me. Ljuba Welitsch had been engaged to bring her internationally celebrated Salome to the Metropolitan on February 4, 1949. Previous commitments in Vienna, however, prevented her from coming to do all the rehearsals with the company. I had been asked to assist the Met by doing her early rehearsals in January until she arrived. I thought the matter over and decided it would be a wise idea to be a good trouper. This afforded me an excellent chance to re-review the role and also gave the Metropolitan an idea of my interpretation.

Welitsch, with her incandescent red hair, her sensuous voice, and her innate histrionic flair, was known affectionately as the Bulgarian Bombshell, a designation that also carried over to her flamboyant offstage personality. One telling illustration of this was the story about her first trip to New York. Arriving at the airport, she was met by one of the Metropolitan's young production assistants, who had been assigned to escort her to her hotel. Without consulting anyone, he ordered the taxi to take a circuitous route so that he could give her an unsolicited guided tour of Manhattan. After about a half-hour of being lectured on the various landmarks—buildings, museums, statues, monuments, etc.—they were passing, she finally turned to him with a weary smile and exclaimed, "Young man, believe me, I come to New York for three things only—music, money, and men." The rest was silence. (Wow!)

To the role of Salome, Ljuba Welitsch brought one significant attribute, which at the time was often neglected. She actually performed the "Dance of the Seven Veils"! As amazing as this may seem to today's operagoers, who are used to seeing the same artist perform the role of Salome from start to finish, in those days, very few sopranos could or would handle that dance without embarrassing themselves. The general tradition was: the prima donna would sing the role, and then, when the time came for the dance, a solo ballerina, usually far less than half the soprano's live weight, would come floating out, do the dance, and retire to the wings while Madame Whoever finished singing the performance. It must have befuddled both Herod and the audience. This was certainly not the case with Ljuba Welitsch.

I had already tackled this problem before my first *Salome* in Cincinnati. One of Hermann's friends from his Berlin days, Kurt Adler, the chorus master at the Metropolitan, was married to Irene Hawthorne, our prima ballerina and a fine choreographer as well. Irene agreed to work with me. Starting in January 1948, I began learning the visual choreography. For all my confidence in Irene's impeccable taste, Hermann came up with the thought that I would have to make sure that, while the dance was sensuous and erotic, it didn't inadvertently go over the borderline to vulgarity. "We wouldn't want you performing like the girls in Minsky's," he said, referring to a chain of burlesque theatres

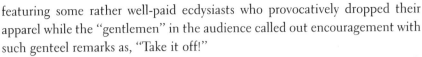

featuring some rather well-paid ecdysiasts who provocatively dropped their apparel while the "gentlemen" in the audience called out encouragement with such genteel remarks as, "Take it off!"

In those days, it wasn't easy for anyone living in New York to find out much about burlesque, as it had been banned from the city during the Second World War. Mayor Fiorello H. La Guardia felt that kind of entertainment might adversely affect the morale of young soldiers who passed through the city from all over the United States on their way to service in the European theatre of war. Our "Little Flower" felt this kind of show might give them a false picture of the city His Honor was so proud of.

So, on one of our concert tours, Hermann and I discovered a burlesque house in a city we were playing and decided to avail ourselves of a free evening to do a little *Salome* research. We slunk into the theatre, doing our best to look as inconspicuous as possible, slipped into the only two available seats—in the front row!—and began concentrating on what the dancers were doing. I noticed they tended to walk up and down the apron of the stage from one side of the proscenium arch to the other, tantalizing the public as they gyrated their way across the stage, many of them manipulating such props as oversized bubbles or ornate ostrich-plume fans. I made a definite mental note not to do *that* bit of choreography in the opera house.

A couple of weeks later, in San Francisco, both of us were involved in the autumn opera season, and we decided to take a busman's holiday and attend a performance of *La Traviata* featuring one of our favorite sopranos, Licia Albanese, in the leading role. When the time came for Violetta's first act bravura aria, "Sempre libera," Albanese began wandering back and forth on the apron of the Cinerama-sized San Francisco stage in the same pattern. To make the coincidence even more bizarre, she was brandishing an elaborate ostrich-plume fan. I slowly turned beet red trying to stifle my oncoming giggles, especially when Hermann decided to take advantage of the situation by leaning over and whispering mischievously into my ear, "Take it off!" I almost had to leave the theatre!

With Irene's tutelage, my performances in Cincinnati, and my field study at the burlesque house and the San Francisco Opera under my belt, I was superbly prepared to do Welitsch's *Salome* rehearsals at the Metropolitan. Things were going well until, about three weeks later, I explained to Maestro Reiner that I would have to take a few days off from rehearsing with the cast because I had an Isolde coming up. I don't know if this brief hiatus was the reason for his suddenly getting strangely and unnecessarily picky with me when I returned to the *Salome* rehearsals.

Reiner was an excellent pianist, and, when the mood struck him, he would take over the keyboard from the scheduled rehearsal accompanist. In one such session, he interpolated a few wrong notes, and these in a peculiar, non-composed rhythm. I had all I could do to sing the part correctly against his distorted accompaniment. At one point, he stopped, looked at me with an acerbic expression, and observed, "Hah, so you know your part?" At a loss for words, all I could sputter out was, "I'm supposed to know it, am I not?"

It dawned on me that Reiner was putting these false accents into the accompaniment as a kind of snare to see if I really knew the score as well as I was supposed to, and then lord it over me if I stumbled into his trap. I wondered if he was perhaps trying to hone me into recognizing his superior erudition, which I acknowledged anyway, or merely trying to hog the spotlight, as many conductors are wont to do. He had come to the wrong address with that ploy. I was just too well prepared for these backstage power games.

The new production was going into its final stages, and Ljuba Welitsch was still absent. This meant I would have to do the piano dress rehearsal as well. It was the first time any of us had taken this production onto the Metropolitan stage. I was thrilled to be singing this role here, even in rehearsal, but my enthusiasm was instantly squelched. Hardly had I opened my mouth and sung the first phrase, when Reiner stopped and bluntly corrected me. At the end of the rehearsal, Max Lorenz came over and told me he had just happened to be following the score backstage when Reiner made his remark. He assured me I had sung that passage correctly, and the conductor was talking through his hat.

Nevertheless, armed with the excellent response to the stadium concert and the staged performances in Cincinnati and New Orleans, I was all ready to tackle my first Salome at the Metropolitan on January 26, 1950, with Maestro Reiner in the pit. This came as a double honor for me, because *Salome* had also been selected as one of the operas to be presented at a public dress rehearsal for the members of the Metropolitan Opera Guild, a sort of rarefied operatic fan club, many of whose members were extremely knowledgeable.

Shortly before the day of the dress rehearsal, I was walking past Papa Senz's backstage lair and saw him chatting with someone. I said hello to Papa and was about to walk on, when I suddenly did a double-take. Could it be . . . ? It was my screen idol, Danny Kaye. Being familiar with his ingenious parodies of the classical music scene, I couldn't resist asking, "What brings you here, Mr.

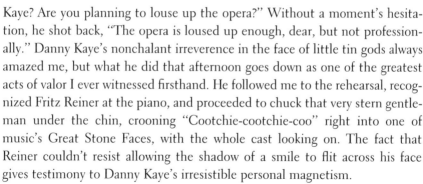

Kaye? Are you planning to louse up the opera?" Without a moment's hesitation, he shot back, "The opera is loused up enough, dear, but not professionally." Danny Kaye's nonchalant irreverence in the face of little tin gods always amazed me, but what he did that afternoon goes down as one of the greatest acts of valor I ever witnessed firsthand. He followed me to the rehearsal, recognized Fritz Reiner at the piano, and proceeded to chuck that very stern gentleman under the chin, crooning "Cootchie-cootchie-coo" right into one of music's Great Stone Faces, with the whole cast looking on. The fact that Reiner couldn't resist allowing the shadow of a smile to flit across his face gives testimony to Danny Kaye's irresistible personal magnetism.

Things went back to serious business as we ran through the opera time and time again, bringing our interpretation to the high polish that was invariably the benchmark of a Fritz Reiner performance. At one of the first stage rehearsals with orchestra, however, Reiner's pickiness backfired on him. It happened in the scene where the five Jews are debating hotly at the top of their lungs on theological fine points. The seeming confusion in the music is actually a stroke of genius on the part of the composer, who used a highly intricate musical and rhythmical setting to illustrate the way the Jews in Strauss's opera interrupt one another in the heat of their squabble. This scene is fiendishly difficult to learn and even harder to coordinate with the stage action. Experience has shown that it must be rehearsed again and again until it practically becomes second nature for the four tenors and one bass singing the parts. But even so, this scene is always brushed up right before each and every performance. Reiner did what any other conductor would have done in this situation. He rehearsed the scene with the Jews over and over again until he was satisfied with the musical accuracy. This unflagging repetition began getting on the nerves of the musicians in the orchestra, who had to keep playing the same passage over and over again to accommodate the singers. Although it wasn't their fault, the orchestra had been made part of the problem.

Reiner had a habit of using the orchestra's impatience as a weapon against the allegedly iniquitous vocalists. He would look ominously at the stage over what his pupil Leonard Bernstein once referred to as "his cruel little glasses" and remonstrate with them in his frog-like croak that he had a whole pit full of orchestra musicians to worry about, and he simply didn't have the time to spoon-feed the singers their parts. It should be noted that he did exactly the same thing with the orchestra when he wasn't satisfied with their work, claiming that he had a whole stage full of singers to worry about and insisting the people in the pit take more responsibility for their own work.

And so it went during the scene with the Jews. Reiner kept repeating it until he was finally satisfied that the singers knew what they were doing. Then he added one more repetition, just to make sure it hadn't been dumb luck the last time. When the final rendering was as simon-pure as the one before, he gave the singers one of his rare looks of approval, heaved a great sigh of relief, and said, "That was correct. The Jews can go home." Thereupon three-quarters of the orchestra rose to their feet and started packing up their instruments. In fairness to Reiner, it must be said that he was as amused as the rest of us at this little tension breaker.

There was no horsing around, however, on January 24, when the public dress rehearsal began. Shortly before going out onstage, I walked over to the stage manager's desk and rechecked the first passage I had to sing, the one Reiner had insisted I had sung incorrectly the previous year. I made my entrance and sang the first phrase, whereupon Reiner stopped the orchestra peremptorily and said, "you came in too late again!" Evidently he was laboring under the misapprehension that my alleged mistake had somehow become imprinted on my memory. In any event, it seemed like he had been waiting a whole year to pounce on it like a hungry hawk. As you can imagine, that public reprimand demoralized me! To this day, I do not know whether he did it on purpose to test my mettle or really thought he had heard a mistake. It took several pages of the score before I could pull myself together. Whatever Reiner had in mind, the end result was, for him anyway, counterproductive, because the irritation he induced had me so keyed up that I started giving that invited audience of aficionados the show of my life. Fortunately, both the rehearsal and the performance were enthusiastically received, and Reiner and I worked amicably together when the opera was repeated on the annual Metropolitan tour two years later. He never corrected me in public again.

What of the real Salome? I estimate her age at mid-teens, and in those hot climates, maturity and sensuousness develop very early. She is also a princess who is used to getting what she wants. She has witnessed the goings-on at the Tetrarch's court and wants none of its debauchery. However, she is fascinated by the sound of Jokanaan's voice, and when she sees him, she is overawed, because he is utterly different from anyone she has ever encountered. When the Baptist rejects her attentions, her petulance is like the stubbornness of a child who wants a piece of candy and will do anything to get it. This petulance slowly turns into vengefulness. Ljuba Welitsch certainly understood this factor in her characterization, and while her Salome was extremely tantalizing, it was never cheap or common. My voice, style, and demeanor were certainly very

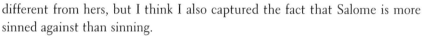

different from hers, but I think I also captured the fact that Salome is more sinned against than sinning.

If Strauss's Salome is sensuous and nubile, the title role in the composer's *Elektra* is the exact opposite. She is a grown woman: resolute, selfless, and virtually ritualistic in her single-minded quest for vindication. I had the good fortune to be able to learn this role for the first time with someone fully acquainted with original sources. In 1937, our friend Dimitri Mitropoulos had been invited to come to the United States to assume the musical directorship of the Minneapolis Symphony, beginning his contract in 1938. Between 1945 and 1947, I had the pleasure of appearing in concert with him on several occasions.

In 1948, prior to his assuming the directorship of the New York Philharmonic, he contacted me to elicit my interest in a concert version of *Elektra*, which he hoped to do with the orchestra the following year. He gave me the opportunity of first studying the role for a full year and then, if I felt I could do it, he would make a contract. If not, there would be no hard feelings. This gave me the peace and quiet to absorb a role of epic proportions at my own rate of speed.

After the allotted time had elapsed, I was pleased to be able to inform Maestro Mitropoulos that I would feel honored to sing the role under his direction in 1949. Mitropoulos, who had grown up only about an hour's drive from the rediscovered Peloponnesian fortress of Mycenae, where the events of *Elektra* are believed to have taken place, was familiar with the story in its many interpretations, all of which he had studied in the original Attic Greek. This put him in an optimum position to substantiate what Hermann had already taught me about the value systems of this antique period.

At the time he composed *Elektra*, Strauss was fresh from his triumph with *Salome* and still rejoicing in the reputation that opera had given him as the "bad boy of the lyric stage." Some of the liberties he and Hofmannsthal were accused of "mischievously" interpolating into the ancient sources may not have been authentic, but they certainly were enormously effective. In only a few years, after completing *Der Rosenkavalier*, which followed *Salome* and *Elektra*, the onetime "bad boy" came to be honored as "The Father of Twentieth-Century Opera," which, for me, he remains to this day.

Our success with the three Mitropoulos New York Philharmonic concerts on December 22, 23, and 25, 1949, may have led the Metropolitan management to consider venturing a stage production of the opera, knowing that they finally had a soprano who could handle the role. The concerts had taught me a valuable lesson, which figured significantly in contract negotiations. The three back-to-back Philharmonic concerts had been simply too close together for comfort, even without any stage business. A full-scale stage production of *Elektra* on a tight performance schedule would be out of the question. Despite the urgings of the Metropolitan management, I had to hold out for at least four days of rest between shows, not counting performance days. This meant if the first performance was on a Monday, the next one could not be scheduled until the following Saturday. Let this be an object lesson for young singers with avaricious managers.

The Metropolitan *Elektra* was planned for February 1952. The musical direction was entrusted to Fritz Reiner, and the cast included Walburga Wegner as Chrysothemis, Elisabeth Höngen as Klytämnestra, Set Svanholm as Ägisth, and Hans Hotter as Orest. The majority of the supporting roles were cast with artists of recognized merit. Alois Pernerstorfer, a fixture at the Vienna State Opera, was contracted to sing a number of principal roles, and also agreed to assume the one-line part of the old servant. Lucine Amara and Jean Madeira sang Klytämnestra's attendants. (Jean Madeira later became one of the best Klytämnestras in subsequent years in both the United States and Europe.)

The stage director was Dr. Herbert Graf, the son of the eminent Viennese music critic Dr. Max Graf. While Herbert Graf was raised in the Viennese musical tradition, I honestly felt that his rather straightforward approach did not come fully to terms with the profundities of the character I had learned from Hermann and Mitropoulos. This prompted me to continue my own research with such sources as Robert Graves, Edith Hamilton, and other experts on those times.

Our production of *Elektra* was the first time the Metropolitan had ventured that opera since the 1938 season, when the title role was sung by the Hungarian dramatic soprano Rosa Pauly. Shortly before our première, Mme Pauly wrote to *Opera News*, the Metropolitan Opera Guild weekly magazine, from her home in Jerusalem, with a very gracious message for me. "Please give my regards to Mme. Varnay," she said, "and good luck to *Elektra* by me, who has loved that strange part and found inspiration therein." Over the years, I have sung two leads in *Elektra*, first the title role and then Klytämnestra, and just like Mme Pauly, I too found much inspiration therein—in both roles.

During preparations for *Elektra*, I was reminded of the great Australian tragedienne Dame Judith Anderson, who had set Broadway on fire with her incisive performance of Euripides' *Medea* in 1947. Hermann and I had the great pleasure of seeing this performance later on in San Francisco. After the play,

Strauss's Elektra: one of the mainstays of my career. *Metropolitan Opera Archives.*

our mutual friend Francis Robinson took us backstage to meet and congratulate the star.

Dame Judith had opened the play with a breathtaking effect. Sitting stage center, the dejected heroine broods on Jason's desertion and the terrible revenge she wants to take on him for his betrayal, just as the heartbroken Elektra ponders what to do to avenge herself against her mother and her mother's paramour. One striking feature of this scene was the way Dame Judith used her long black wig. She leaned over so far forward in her despondency that her hair actually obscured her face. At a suitably dramatic moment, she catapulted herself into the drama by letting out an agonized moan and swinging her head violently around, which sent the hair dramatically flying out of her face as she began her part of the action.

This was a very effective bit of business, and I catalogued it in my mind in hopes of "borrowing" it someday. I believe, as any conscientious actress must, that there is more truth than poetry to the old saying that tells us, "Imitation is the sincerest form of flattery." Of course, I did not copy Dame Judith's gesture to the letter, because the sequence of action in *Elektra* is different from that in *Medea*.

When I first entered as Elektra, I had my back to the audience so that my face was invisible. I could have been anyone at that point. In my second entrance, I let my hair fall partially over my face, and just before I uttered the word "Allein!" which begins Elektra's monologue, I lifted my head in a silent moan, revealing Elektra's anguished expression. This borrowed gesture and a few more of my own making made a major contribution to the success of my Elektra interpretation, and soon I wasn't even thinking about the source, until I was abruptly reminded of it with the news that Dame Judith was sitting in the audience with Francis Robinson and would come back to my dressing room with him to say "hello" after the performance.

Dame Judith was perfectly charming when she arrived in my dressing room. Shaking my hand cordially, she paid me one compliment after another on my own understanding of the character and suggested I keep up the good work. As she was about to leave, she suddenly stopped, looked at the wig which was still on my head, and smiling over at me, she took a few strands of hair in her hand, twisted them pensively in her fingers and gently asked, "Medea?"

All I could do was smile back.

Perils and Problems

In THE COURSE OF MY LONG CAREER, I have pondered more than once what might have happened had the war not come to America the day after my début. The most likely scenario is that I would probably have wound up as one of the "stalwarts" of the Met, understudying in both the German and Italian repertoires and occasionally getting a performance of my own, finally to retire many years later without ever having seen much of the rest of the world. Then again, I might perhaps have ventured across the sea to Germany or Italy. Who knows?

As it happened, fate vouchsafed me a different road, but as extraordinary as my opportunities often were, there were some sacrifices I was forced to make. Possibly the most difficult of these was that I was so heavily involved in German opera, I seldom had a chance to sing as much of the Italian repertoire as I wished to at the beginning of my career. Later years would bring some Italian roles, but never quite enough to satisfy my love for them. To this day, I miss never having had a chance to do a Tosca, a Donna Anna, a Donna Elvira, or a Giorgetta in *Il Tabarro*. During my second career, I would have jumped at the opportunity to sing Azucena in *Trovatore* and Marcellina in *Le Nozze di Figaro*, but it was not meant to be.

At the Metropolitan, I did sing three Italian roles, one of them with three of the most illustrious artists of that repertoire. The opera was Giuseppe Verdi's *Simon Boccanegra*, in which I enjoyed singing Maria Boccanegra opposite tenor Richard Tucker, baritone Leonard Warren, and basso Mihály Székely.

The legendary Helen Keller visited my dressing room during intermission at a *Simon Boccanegra* performance to share my music with her sense of touch. Normally, I don't let anyone backstage between acts, but this was a very high honor. *Metropolitan Opera Archives.*

My second Italian role was Telea in Gian Carlo Menotti's *The Island God*. When I recall the magnificent love duet Raoul Jobin and I sang, and think of the cry of many theatres for works by living composers, I wish this opera could be restored to the repertoire. I also understudied the legendary Zinka Milanov as Santuzza in *Cavalleria Rusticana*.

Mme Milanov was legendary, first of all for her magnificent singing, and second for an outspoken personality which generated innumerable anecdotes. One formidable example of this was her total refusal to refer to Ljuba Welitsch by name. One afternoon, I was chatting with Winnie Short at the switchboard, taking time out to enjoy some of the high points of a *Don Giovanni* performance we could hear transmitted from the stage over the intercom system. Suddenly the door flew open, and in swept Zinka Milanov, returning to the theatre following an absence of two to three years from the roster. Without so much as a "hello," she imperiously demanded, "Vat is de opera? Who is singing?" Piqued at her failure to greet us, I slowly and wickedly enumerated all the male singers involved, inwardly rejoicing at her impatience. Finally, she irately cut in: "Var-*nay!* Who is singing? Is it *she*, the redhead?" I never found out what had passed between her and Welitsch, and frankly, it didn't really matter.

By contrast, my next encounter with Milanov ended more than amicably. It was standard procedure at the Metropolitan for artists in the same voice category to "cover" their colleagues' performances. That means we had to be ready to assume these roles should someone become indisposed. As soon as I was officially assigned to cover Milanov as Santuzza, I did what I always did with any new role. I saw as many performances as possible, both out front and backstage.

One evening, in the wings, I suddenly found myself confronted by an indignant prima donna. Fixing me with a gaze that would melt tungsten, Milanov inquired, "Var-*nay*, vat are you doing here?" Thank goodness, my wits were about me, and I humbly shot back, "Madame, I am learning." With that unexpected rejoinder, the steely Milanov suddenly turned to honey butter, having taken my simple answer for a tribute, and cooed, "Dot is good" as she stepped out onto the stage. When she exited after her duet with Alfio, she stopped and graciously pointed out a treacherous table in the middle of the stage, telling me to be careful not to stumble over it, "Jost in case you hev to take uvver for me!"

Regrettably, *Boccanegra*, *The Island God*, and *Cavalleria* were my only Italian assignments in New York, but things were different, if often a trifle harrowing, in other cities. Many smaller municipalities had so-called "opera companies," where performances were slapdash improvisations, and fate often played as significant a role as did the sopranos and tenors taking the leads. San Francisco, Cincinnati, and Chicago were three great exceptions. With much shorter seasons than the Metropolitan, they still mounted productions of excellent quality with many of the finest singers in the world, some of whom, for one reason or another, were not on the Metropolitan roster.

Chicago was the only opera company under the leadership of a woman, but what a woman! Carol Fox was a native Chicagoan with a great love for baseball. She knew as much about the batting averages and pitching records of the Cubs and the White Sox as she did about the intricacies of operatic production, which is to say her knowledge in both areas was encyclopedic! She was also not the kind of lady who could be shouted down by the toughest conductor or the most temperamental prima donna. She had a delightful way of saying very calmly, "Only one person can run an opera company, and in Chicago that one person happens to be *me*." That bearded many a lion or lioness in their den!

Carol Fox was indirectly responsible for one of the oddest things that ever happened to me on an opera stage, with a delightful postscript at the stage door. After hearing me sing Kundry in New York, she came backstage and asked if I might be interested in playing temporary hooky from the soprano repertoire to sing two performances of the mezzo role of Amneris in a Chicago *Aida* production. To make the idea more enticing, she claimed I had one of the few voices she could find to match the special vocal qualities of her Aida, Renata Tebaldi, and the dramatic intensity of the Amonasro, Tito Gobbi. I was reluctant at first, because I felt more at home with the title role, but Carol Fox was a very persuasive lady.

During the final *Aida* orchestra dress rehearsal, Renata Tebaldi, for some odd reason, took it into her pretty little head to do a "Kipnis job" on me, by constantly trying to upstage me. In the duet before the Triumphal Scene, she began departing from the staging by inching me into a corner to avail herself of the greater part of the stage for her own action. With the experience gained from a few high-powered scene stealers I'd had to contend with before, I extricated myself quite vehemently from the neutral corner into which I had been forced, much to the wide-eyed astonishment of Aida. At the end of the rehearsal, as we were taking our leave of one another, Renata Tebaldi smiled and said, "Tu sei una leonessa!" From then on, she was a real colleague.

The première, however, put my sense of dramatic improvisation to the acid test. We had just concluded the Nile Scene and retired for intermission. Apparently nobody had noticed that the intercom system that connects the stage area with the various other parts of the theatre had suddenly decided to withdraw from the fray. This had a catastrophic effect on act 4. As I started the Judgment Scene, I became aware of a lot of agitation backstage, with all kinds of people gesturing, in classic Italian style, with an unmistakable aura of disaster ahead. That disaster graphically manifested itself when Doro Antonioli as Radames failed to appear on stage. By this time, a kind of muffled pandemonium had broken out in the wings, while everybody tried to figure out the cause for the tenor's absence without leave.

Meanwhile, I found myself faced with an agonized look in the eyes of Maestro Tullio Serafin, who for some reason seemed to think that *I* could give him a few pantomimic hints as to how to continue the performance minus a rather significant cog in the operatic wheel. Without breaking character, I melodramatically looked longingly offstage "wondering when Radames would appear." Maestro Serafin somehow picked up my helpless indication and, with great presence of mind, gave the drummer a sign to keep playing a hushed roll in hopes the enigma might somehow unravel itself. I decided to use the ominous drum roll as a cue for pacing up and down, casting a frequent longing eye to what I hoped would be perceived as the Egyptian equivalent of cell block B.

During one of those offstage looks, I overheard someone saying in Italian, "Go upstairs and get him!" Obviously somebody had finally figured out what had happened to the intercom system, and the stage manager himself started bounding up the stairs to the tenor's dressing room. He brought Antonioli calmly downstairs, so as not to panic him, which might possibly have affected his performance, while the remainder of his colleagues continued to gesticulate frantically like the next of kin at a Sicilian mass interment. As soon as I saw Signor Antonioli in the wings, I strode toward the pit and glared histrionically at the Maestro, hoping he would get the message. He did, and when Antonioli came onstage, we were able to continue the opera.

By the following performance, the electricians had managed to locate the anomaly in the intercom system, and everything functioned smoothly. As I was leaving the theatre that night, relieved that my improvisatory services had not been required again, I was buttonholed by a charming Chicago society lady, one of those elderly darlings displaying an oversized orchid corsage grandly oscillating on her bodice. The lady proudly declared she had attended both performances and enjoyed my work very much, which pleased me, but she was a little perturbed, as she stated it, "that they cut that wonderful scene in act 4 when you pace up and down like a caged tigress." I didn't have the heart to tell her what had really happened. I also promptly went back to singing the role of Aida.

Many was the time, however, when I wished that "caged tigress" had been my sole encounter with the animal kingdom. There is an old theatrical adage about never working onstage with animals and children. While they wear you out with their unpredictability, they always steal the show away from any but the most adept performers. Ask any battle-scarred soprano who has had to share the stage with a winsome but recalcitrant tyke who starts to wander on- and offstage (and worse!) in the second and third acts of *Madama Butterfly*. Animals are even worse, but people still insist on putting them on the stage in operas.

I had my share of agony with horses in Wagner's *Ring*. On one occasion, Dr. Otto Erhard decided to enhance the verisimilitude by adding a careworn mare to the production to portray the redoubtable stallion Grane, claiming that the superannuated nag would remain calm under all circumstances. The poor creature went to that big corral in the sky before the dress rehearsal. The management then supplied a replacement in the form of a well-trained circus stallion. Hermann showed me how to approach the horse to make friends with him. As I led him out on the stage, he followed spiritedly, and looked so hand- some and appropriate I began wondering if my reluctance to perform with livestock was perhaps a bit unrealistic.

Then disaster struck. Dobbin checked the situation and found nothing un- anticipated about it. There was the audience, admiring him as usual. There was the orchestra, to accompany his capers with the appropriate music. Then he saw the conductor, and, confusing him for the ringmaster at the circus, he began turning his hindquarters to the Maestro, which I hope was not a value judgment. I had all I could do to prod him back into position by jabbing the hollow of my back against his flank while I sang. I have no idea how I made it musically through the last part of the Immolation Scene. Friends of mine told me I sang the longest high notes they had ever heard from me. No wonder.

Richard Tucker had it even worse, when he came riding in on a mighty charger in *Boris Godunov*. The minute his mount saw the conductor's upbeat, he rose up on his hind legs, threatening to send the tenor hurtling to the turf. While Tucker held on for dear life, the maestro figured out some way of giving instructions to the orchestra by conducting laterally, and things returned to something vaguely resembling normal. Perhaps Richard simply restored the horse to order by telling him he used to be a furrier.

A couple of years later, possibly the funniest operatic incident with an animal was visited on Nicola Moscona in a performance of *Faust* at the Cincinnati Opera. As aficionados are aware, the company performs in an open-air theatre situated in the middle of the city zoo, which leads to a whole litany of special problems. More than once, our furry and feathered friends were so moved by the music that they simply joined in with the singers, in their own keys, of course. Sometimes they even united with them onstage, whether or not their services were called for by the score. Nicola Moscona was strumming his prop mandolin under Marguerite's window as Méphistophélès in *Faust*, singing his mocking serenade, which ends with a rhythmic laugh, jumping from a "Ha-ha-ha-ha" on a top G to the same figure an octave lower, and finally a cascade of laughter yet another octave lower than that. Nicola had just started his final chuckle, when a duck waddled out to join him onstage, adding her "quack-quack-quack-quack" to his "ha-ha-ha-ha" in exactly the same rhythm. To this day, I can never hear the serenade without thinking of that duck.

Not all our road problems involved animals or children. The spontaneous nature of the situation often made for some pretty perilous doings onstage. Unlike the Met, which meticulously mounted its productions wherever we went, there was a company down in Texas that secured our services in an ad hoc production, staged as part of a package deal by the same man who had rented them the costumes. Since this gentleman was Italian and knew all the traditions, there were seldom any major snags in this arrangement—at least, as long as he stuck to the standard Italian repertoire—but on this occasion, the opera on the bill was *Lohengrin*, a work with which he was, at best, only sketchily familiar.

The problem arose during the dress rehearsal, when the tenor singing Lohengrin took exception to the fact that the bridal chorus was still onstage when he had to sing the passage about how he hears their dulcet tones fading in the distance. When the tenor failed to find a mutually compatible language in which to communicate with the perpetrator of this mise-en-scène, I intervened to explain to the *regista* in Italian that the chorus had to continue singing offstage at the end of the wedding march. The director was a bit nonplussed by that request. "How dey gonna see de maestro?" he wanted to know. We managed to convince him that they could stay in rhythm if he would just use standard operating procedure in any opera house and have the company pianist mount a ladder behind one of the flats to watch the conductor through a hole in the set and then transfer the beat to the departing choristers. On the night, I stood there ecstatically looking at my newly wedded husband, but my reveries were briefly stirred by the sound of the stage director whispering in a voice that could be heard in Oklahoma: "Get offa de stage, and take-a every-thin' wid-a you." One of the obedient choristers felt honor-bound to help himself to Lohengrin's sword, which the hero would later need to defend himself against the nefarious Telramund. I quickly stood in his way, keeping the weapon onstage for future use.

A sword also figured significantly in another near-mishap down in Mexico, where the irresistible force of a determined tenor found itself confronted with the immovable object of an adamant conductor. The tenor was Kurt Baum, possessor of some of the best high notes in the business, and the issue was the traditionally interpolated high C at the end of Manrico's bravura aria "Di quella pira" in *Il Trovatore*, which Baum always sang in the correct key of C major. It is also traditional for the tenor to hold the high C, assuming he has the note at all, as long as he can, invariably triggering a rousing ovation from the house. The conductor was the fastidious Jean-Paul Morel, who was willing to sanction the interpolation, but nevertheless expected the high note to be held no longer than indicated in Verdi's score. Baum insisted that audiences, especially in Latin countries, expected some vocal theatrics to get excited about. Opera for them, he explained, was kind of like a bull fight without the moo. After a fruitless argument on the subject, Maestro Morel decided to take matters into his own delicate hands and instructed the stage manager in no uncertain terms to close the curtain on Baum the minute the cutoff came in the score.

When the night of the performance arrived, Baum's upper register was in the very best of condition. The first top C rang out, and the audience audibly poised for the second, which has to cut through the sound of the full orchestra and male chorus. Just as Baum let fly with a final high C that might well have cut through the back wall of the auditorium, I noted with great alarm that the curtain was rapidly closing. While I stood in the wings, nervously anticipating a major scandal, Baum showed a resourcefulness not frequently evident in the practitioners of his voice range. Whipping his sword from its sheath, à la Errol Flynn, he rapidly plunged it between the two halves of the closing curtain, marched valiantly to the apron, and held onto that high note for dear life, bringing the audience to its feet in enthusiasm. The ovation almost put us into overtime. When Maestro Morel came out to conduct the next act, the house hissed him, proving that Latin audiences want to be taken at face value.

That "you-sing-'em-we-stage-'em" director, who had caused us so much inconvenience in the *Lohengrin* production, kept showing up at various points in my American career, and wherever his "Rent-an-Opera" enterprise went, some calamity was sure to follow. In Mexico City, I shared a dressing room with a wonderful colleague and first-rate mezzo named Winifred Heidt, who was singing Laura to my Gioconda in the opera of the same name. As we started to put on the costumes supplied, Winifred panicked to discover that the back of the dress, where the hooks and eyes hold the garment together, was gradually fraying into oblivion. I always took the precaution of having safety pins in my kit whenever I went on tour, just in case . . . I spent the greater part of the preperformance period pinning Winifred into her gown and then draping her cape to cover the pins. As she prepared to go out onstage in this makeshift outfit, she looked plaintively at me and said, "Please be careful not to step on the train," to which I replied, "Tell that to the tenor."

On February 19, 1950, in San Antonio, Texas, we had a performance of *Tristan und Isolde* for which the same redoubtable gentleman had supplied the entire production, including a rather outsized palm tree that lent a shopworn, sultry note to the "Liebesnacht" in act 2. Before you go running off to your geography books, let me assure you that the Cornish coast is warmed by the Gulf Stream, and palm trees *do* grow there, although I have a sneaking feeling this prop tree was left over from a very old production of *Thaïs*.

In any event, there we were, Max Lorenz as Tristan and myself as his Isolde, about to launch into the ecstasies of our act 2 duet. As Max began singing "O, sink hernieder" (Oh, descend upon us), the tree decided to take this invocation literally and promptly started gently breaking free of its moorings. What was there to do? Max and I simply made a quick arrangement that whoever wasn't singing would support the leaning tree with his or her back. This way we made it through the love duet without any precipitating timber. During most of King Marke's monologue, I was desperately trying to figure out how I would handle that moment when Tristan is mortally wounded by Melot, and I rush to his side. Fortunately for all of us, the Brangäne in that performance was the quick-witted Blanche Thebom, who had obviously watched our human buttress act from her perch in the watchtower. Shortly before I had to run over to Tristan, I gazed over at Blanche, who meanwhile had descended from the tower to assist me, and whispered, "The tree, grab the tree!" Luckily, she followed through.

Symphony dates and vocal recitals are a little more predictable and a lot less harrowing. The logistics are reduced to getting to the place appointed at the time appointed with the music in my head, my voice in good shape, and a gown that fits well. From there on in, it's strictly music-making. Well, not always. Early in my career, I followed the example of many of my colleagues and got enthusiastically involved in the war effort, performing at military installations and singing for Victory Bond rallies. With the vast financial outlay involved in the American participation in the war, benefit events continued to be held in the years following the Axis surrender in 1945. Of course, all of us were expected to contribute our services to these charitable events and also to cover whatever other costs were involved, such as the fee for the accompanist and the price of getting our hair done professionally before our appearance. We were also expected to appear in the most elegant gowns we had in our own wardrobes.

In view of all these out-of-pocket expenses and the modest weekly income I was earning at the Met, I felt it would be fiscally irresponsible to take the usual taxi to a Madison Square Garden benefit held on March 5, 1946, featuring the beloved Mrs. Eleanor Roosevelt as principal speaker. Arriving at the hall, I put on my evening gown for the occasion, then sat backstage with my accompanist, Wolfgang Martin, waiting for the summons to go on. Mrs. Roosevelt stepped up to the lectern and proceeded to hold forth for so long that the greater part of the program scheduled to follow her speech was summarily canceled—including my contribution. After changing back to my street clothes and riding home on the subway, I entered into my performance diary the terse note: "Never got to sing because of Mrs. Roosevelt's long talk—paid W. Martin $25.00 anyhow." Twenty-five dollars was a lot of money in those days. Charity or no charity, he took it. This was my only public appearance canceled because of long-windedness.

Some of my European associates tend to carp at the recital programs Hermann and I performed in the American provinces, but they fail to realize that this is the only direct encounter many of those provincial audiences have with a real live opera singer. The listeners want to hear some of the music the singers are most famous for, which means arias as well at art songs. While I personally prefer not to sing operatic selections in a song recital, I have nothing against a popular program in which the singer showcases many aspects of his or her musical personality, mixing arias with art songs, ballads, and even folk music. It is a definite *must* in the American provinces, and it's a real audience-pleaser. I'm not pandering to them, I'm just meeting them halfway.

Our American recitals were frequently followed by a reception at the home of a local society lady, where a lot of small talk was exchanged over the inevitable plate of standardized chicken à la king. The artists were expected to attend. This would have been a kind, hospitable gesture except that we often found ourselves confronted with a request to give the guests another couple of songs.

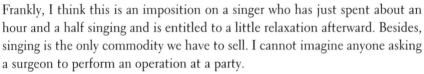

Frankly, I think this is an imposition on a singer who has just spent about an hour and a half singing and is entitled to a little relaxation afterward. Besides, singing is the only commodity we have to sell. I cannot imagine anyone asking a surgeon to perform an operation at a party.

There were, however, also beautiful and meaningful encounters. My heart still warms to the memory of a young girl who came backstage for an autograph after a recital I sang somewhere in the Kentucky mountains. She had heard me on the radio, she said, and saved her pennies to be able to hear one of her favorite singers in person. It was a special event for her, she went on to explain. Not only was this her first attendance at a live concert; it was also the first time in her life—she must have been about seventeen—that she had ever worn anything but sandals on her feet, and she added, touchingly, "I didn't feel my new shoes pinching when you sang."

It was the early 1950s, and life was good. My Metropolitan activities continued to be both challenging and rewarding. There was a full schedule of road appearances taking me to every part of the United States, and my international career was beginning to take shape. I had every reason to feel grateful for the course my life was taking. As far as I was concerned, there wasn't a dark cloud in the sky. Then, on one of our concert tours, on December 2, 1951, in Waco, Texas, tragedy struck.

Shoulda Gotta Horse

THE METROPOLITAN CAREER was firmly established, or so I thought, and our first successful European experiences were behind us. I had also joined Hermann as one of the regulars at the San Francisco Opera Company, where many Metropolitan artists went to fill in the autumn season between the summer festivals and the opening of the New York season in the early winter. Our management had offered us some concert and recital work on our way to and from San Francisco, and, both of us being enthusiastic drivers, we decided to take turns at the wheel. We first drove a rented car halfway to California, then flew the rest of the way out to the west coast and rented another car to enjoy the American countryside at our own speed on our way home. The San Francisco season in October included Kundry in *Parsifal* and Leonore in *Fidelio*, with some concerts in California interspersed between the performances, concluding with both operas in Los Angeles. When the curtain fell on our final *Parsifal* matinée on October 28, we began slowly wending our way back east, zigzagging back and forth across the United States as we went.

We met a most remarkable man in Albuquerque, New Mexico. He was a native American painter by the name of White Horse, and quite frankly, when first we met, I found it very hard to distinguish either his appearance or his manner from those of the average paleface. White Horse told us he was very fond of opera and enjoyed my performances. In gratitude, he asked to sing me an Indian song. The minute he picked up his guitar, the most incredible transformation came over him. He actually took on the appearance of the classic Indian brave of yesteryear. So, there were people in many walks of life, I told myself, who were able to transform themselves from one personality to another, just as I always strove to do on the stage. I will never forget that man's face.

It was the first of November. As our next appearance was not until November 7 in Iowa City, we made it a point to see as much as we could, not planning to leave the southwest until the fifth, in time to arrive in Iowa on the day before the concert. We were on the road somewhere in New Mexico on November 2, driving slowly around the picturesque countryside enjoying the view, when a state trooper suddenly drove up beside us and pulled our car over to the side of the road. The trooper explained that we hadn't been guilty of any traffic violation. He had been dispatched here by my management, which had given the San Antonio Symphony the name of the car rental agency, which in turn supplied the highway police with our license number so they could track us down, as they said, "somewhere between San Francisco and Iowa."

The officer went on to explain that Helen Traubel had been taken ill with a virus and would be unable to perform. The orchestra management said they would extend every courtesy to us if I was able to substitute for her. So, even in the wide-open plains of the Far West, I found myself having to save the bacon for some musical organization in despair. When the orchestra management said they would extend "every courtesy," they weren't kidding. One of the ladies on the committee, Mrs. Edgar Tobin, flew from San Antonio in her own private plane piloted by her son Robert to pick us up and fly us to Texas for the concert. It was easy to take over for Traubel because I knew her repertoire like the back of my hand. With the concert over, the gracious Mrs. Tobin arranged to have Hermann and me flown back to Albuquerque, where we picked up our car and continued our cross-country odyssey.

As we left Albuquerque, I have to confess I felt a certain smug satisfaction, thinking of the people back home in New York taking their winter woollies out of mothballs and jamming their feet into galoshes for the first time that season, while we drove blithely in the golden sunshine. Following Iowa City, we had another six concert dates, ending with a recital in Greensboro, North Carolina. Then we started back west toward Waco, Texas. The searing summer heat had subsided, which meant we had perfect weather all the way to our destination, stopping once again, whenever we felt like it, to take in the lush natural beauty and the charming towns and villages along the way. On December 2, on the final leg of our journey to Waco, we had scheduled ourselves, as usual, to arrive one day ahead of our concert there. I always insisted on being on-site at least a day early to get settled in the hotel, try the acoustics in the hall, and have a good night's rest before our performance.

As we approached the city, Hermann was driving. The central Texas weather was outstanding. I was relaxing on the front seat, when Hermann told me he wasn't feeling well, and that he didn't think he could continue driving. I took over the wheel, and Hermann fell silent. Through the silence, however, I could sense that he was very uncomfortable. When we arrived at our destination and checked into the hotel, he immediately lay down on the bed and asked me to call a doctor, complaining that his pulse was very slow.

A local physician arrived and diagnosed an unstable angina, which usually goes over into a threatening myocardial infarction. Apparently the fact that he had given in to his stoic impulse to stay quiet and made no pretense of being in a good mood when he was quite ill actually saved him from a more serious attack. Fortunately the attack had struck the posterior myocardial wall, which is not as life-threatening as many other forms of infarction.

Nevertheless, the doctor said he would have to be hospitalized immediately—and indefinitely. He arranged for him to be admitted to Providence Hospital in Waco. My first impulse was to cancel everything and remain there by my husband's side, but Hermann was adamant that I continue the tour. The doctor agreed, saying that by not interrupting my performance schedule I would be giving my husband tremendous moral support. He said if Hermann was aware of my continuing to work, he would more readily accept the doctor's reassurance that his affliction was not all that serious. On the other hand, were I to cancel everything, he explained, my husband would probably think the Black Angel of Death had taken up a position on his shoulder.

So I promised I would go on performing, which was all very well and good, but who was going to accompany me at the vocal recital the next day? When I presented my problem to the lady who chaired the local committee, she immediately sprang into action. She suggested I contact a professor at Southern Methodist University in Dallas by the name of Paul Velucci, the conductor of the symphony orchestra there. I was pleasantly surprised to discover Hermann and I had actually met Mr. Velucci before. With only one day to go before the concert, we would have to do some heavy-duty rehearsing, but at a quickly convened practice session, he proved himself more than equal to the musical challenges. As a matter of fact, he acquitted himself so beautifully at the concert that I asked him to accompany my last recital for the year a few days later in Corsicana, about halfway down the highway between Waco and Dallas.

When I returned to Waco, I was lucky to find a house across the street from the hospital with a sign on the door announcing that the lady who owned the place was offering rooms for rent. The idea of being here instead of at the hotel appealed to me geographically, and so I transferred my base of operations from the impersonal atmosphere of the hotel to a small room and bath in the lady's home. It was anything but the lap of luxury. On the infrequent occasions when heating was required, it was produced by a kind of pot-bellied stove, which reminded me of the garret in *La Bohème*. Nevertheless, it made my regular visits to the hospital as uncomplicated as possible, and the landlady was cooperative and supportive in my trying situation.

On December 14, I went up to Dallas to prepare for an afternoon Verdi concert on the sixteenth, singing arias from *Macbeth*, *Il Trovatore*, and *Un Ballo in Maschera* with the Dallas Symphony under the direction of Walter Hendl. At about the same time the concert was beginning in Texas, Helen Traubel's husband in New York called the Metropolitan front office to advise the management that Mme Traubel had not yet sufficently recovered from her virus infection and was still running a high temperature. Her doctor sincerely doubted, he said, that she would be able to sing the Brünnhilde in the following evening's *Götterdämmerung* performance. As I was the only other member of the company who had actually sung the role onstage, although never at the Met, the management contacted my agency, which advised them of my current situation down in Texas. Max Rudolf, the assistant manager of the theatre, telephoned Providence Hospital to ask Hermann about my availability, and Hermann advised Dr. Rudolf that I was staying at the Adolphus Hotel in Dallas; however, at that moment in time, I was just about to go onstage.

During the concert intermission, someone relayed the communication from the Metropolitan, asking me to come to New York at once to replace Traubel. My immediate reaction to this call for help was to hurry to the phone after the concert and ask the physician attending Hermann his opinion. The doctor spontaneously advised me: "Do it. You'll make Mr. Weigert very happy." He then put me through to Hermann, who enthusiastically seconded the motion.

Somehow I would have to get myself from Dallas to New York in the middle of the winter. This was before the onset of the jet age, but even then there were a few airline connections available to cover the 1,500 miles from Texas to New York. I called the airport and discovered there was a seat available on an American Airlines flight to New York, but the plane wouldn't be leaving Dallas until two o'clock the following morning.

Meanwhile, at the Metropolitan, things were rapidly getting hyperthyroid.

As my arrival had been cast in doubt, Margaret Harshaw was summoned to the theatre to run through the role of Brünnhilde with Maestro Fritz Stiedry, a role she had never sung anywhere before. At least I had done a half-dozen *Götterdämmerungs*, albeit not at the Met. As if that weren't risky enough, at the time, Margaret was in the process of switching over from mezzo-soprano to dramatic soprano. In fact, she was scheduled to do double duty in the *Götterdämmerung* performance, by singing the soprano part of the Third Norn and the mezzo role of Waltraute. A kind of strategic game of musical chairs began: if Margaret Harshaw had to take over as Brünnhilde, then Herta Glaz would have to be recruited to sing the role of Waltraute, but Mme Glaz was already cast in the role of Flosshilde, one of the Rhine Maidens in act 3. While they looked for somebody to take over Flosshilde, Thelma Votipka was put on standby to take over the Third Norn from Miss Harshaw, all just in case I didn't manage to get there.

The rest of the distinguished cast—Set Svanholm as Siegfried, Paul Schöffler as Gunther, Regina Resnik as Gutrune, Gerhard Pechner as Alberich, Dezső Ernster as Hagen, Jean Madeira and Margaret Roggero as the First and Second Norns, Paula Lenchner and Lucine Amara as the two soprano Rhine Maidens, Woglinde and Wellgunde, and Emery Darcy and Osie Hawkins as Gunther's two Vassals in act 3—were all on pins and needles wondering whom they would be working with that night. If *they* were nervous, Drs. Herbert Graf and Fritz Stiedry, the stage director and conductor of the performance, were near hysteria.

The only artist who kept his wits about him in the midst of all that chaos was Rusty, the black horse. He was reported by one newspaper as "relatively dispassionate at his scheduled appearance as Grane," which prompted the reporter to inquire why I was bothering with airlines at all, when the magic steed might have given me the lift I badly needed. In typical New-Yorkese, the paper suggested I "shoulda gotta horse."

I don't know what I did to pass the time from the end of the afternoon concert until flight time. I do remember that, as I got on the plane, I was so keyed up with the pressure of events that I took a tranquilizer to calm my nerves for the long flight ahead, as there would be no chance of getting a proper night's rest at home before I had to sing. I remember drifting off to sleep only to awaken an hour or so later to find the plane still holding on the Dallas airfield waiting to be cleared for takeoff. It seems the weather en route had turned stormy, and so we were forced to stay put until conditions cleared up.

Luckily, we were able to take off at some point during the night, but halfway to New York, the pilot, William Cherry, had to make an emergency landing in Memphis so he could check one of the engines to make sure the aircraft would be able to carry us the rest of the way. We spent the rest of the night and the greater part of the next morning cooling our heels in the plane on the Memphis airfield. Every once in a while, I mercifully dozed off. Finally, around noon, we flew on to La Guardia airport, where our plane landed at 3:40 P.M.

I took the airport bus into Manhattan and then hailed a cab at the Midtown Air Terminal to take me home. As I entered my apartment on West 110th Street, the telephone was ringing like mad in the living room. I had no time to pick it up. I was too busy boiling two eggs and packing up my perennial make-up, soap, tissues, and towel to hurry to the subway because it was rush hour in midtown Manhattan, and one was never sure about traffic jams at that time of day. I found out later that the telephone call was from the Met wanting to know if I had arrived safely.

They might have called the airline. They might also have sent someone out to Queens on that cold afternoon to meet my plane, but apparently they preferred to do their panicking in the comfort of their well-heated offices. They were apparently also very busy sending off press releases to get this irregular event as much newspaper coverage as they could. Had Edward Johnson still been the manager, chances are he might have come out to La Guardia to fetch me himself. He certainly would have delegated someone to make sure I got into the city safely, but Mr. Johnson had retired at the end of the 1949–50 season. His replacement, an austere Viennese martinet by the name of Rudolf Bing, apparently considered the well-being of the singers in the theatre incidental to the quality of the performances they gave.

For reasons best known to himself, Mr. Bing, who had certainly not cornered the market on the milk of human kindness, seemed to regard much of the German repertoire, particularly the operas of Richard Wagner and the people who sang them, as not worthy of the attention he accorded other areas of the theatre's activities. Within months of his arrival at the Metropolitan, his vacillation on the subject of contract negotiations with that mainstay of the Wagnerian repertoire, Lauritz Melchior, got Melchior and Kleinchen so annoyed that they handed him an ultimatum to come to terms with them by a specific deadline or risk Lauritz's precipitate retirement from the theatre. Perhaps the Melchiors' attitude was somewhat impolitic, but an artist of his calibre is entitled to be a little less than diplomatic from time to time. He was certainly worth much more to the theatre than the treatment he got, which was that Mr. Bing completely ignored his ultimatum and then proceeded to slander this great artist in print after he made good on his threat to quit the house.

Years later, the man who ghost-wrote Bing's memoirs, Martin Mayer, added insult to Bing's injury in a book of his own, suggesting that Melchior was a sloppy performer with a casual attitude toward rehearsals and a penchant for practical jokes that irritated more than they amused. Having collaborated with Lauritz Melchior in virtually every opera in his Metropolitan repertoire, I would like to go on record that I never once witnessed the kind of conduct Bing and Mayer claimed was so deplorable. On the contrary, no soprano could have asked for a more professional and caring tenor by her side on the stage.

Apparently Mr. Bing had similar problems with Helen Traubel, but, as he said in his memoirs, he resisted the urge to drop her from the company, because he was reluctant to dispose of a popular native-born American, even though he was incensed at her appearances on television and the way they reflected on the "dignity" of "his" theatre. Nowadays, it is a known fact that artists appearing in the media, especially in their own countries, illustrate that the people who make opera happen are anything but the remote aesthetes we so often see in caricatures. Mr. Bing seemed to have felt that Helen Traubel getting laughs on television with Jimmy Durante, and letting go with more than a few infectious guffaws of her own, was somehow damaging the cause of opera, when in fact she was drawing more patrons to the box office than all the artificial decorum the management could muster. In any case, Traubel and Melchior were "merely" Wagnerian singers and apparently unworthy of Bing's special consideration.

It was this atmosphere of neglect for the Wagnerian repertory that reigned at the theatre on that seventeenth day of December. I was so high-strung before the performance that I locked my dressing room door in order to steady myself, make up, run a few vocal scales, get into costume, and generally gather my mental and emotional resources for the task ahead. When Dr. Stiedry knocked on my door to discuss the role, I called out that I was unable to talk to him, whereupon he left in a huff, mumbling something about prima donnas. He evidently had no idea of what I had been going through.

When I came out onstage before curtain-up, Mr. Bing did have the decency to thank me for stepping in at such short notice, and Max Rudolf said he had spent much of the morning watching the sky wondering if the weather would be sufficiently clement for the plane to land. I had it on the tip of my tongue to ask Dr. Rudolf why nobody had arranged for my plane to be met, but I

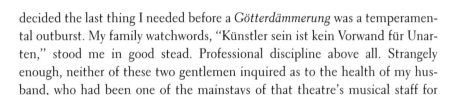

decided the last thing I needed before a *Götterdämmerung* was a temperamental outburst. My family watchwords, "Künstler sein ist kein Vorwand für Unarten," stood me in good stead. Professional discipline above all. Strangely enough, neither of these two gentlemen inquired as to the health of my husband, who had been one of the mainstays of that theatre's musical staff for almost two decades!

Sometimes being high on resentment can contribute a cutting edge to a performance one might not otherwise be able to muster. Friends who witnessed my Brünnhilde that night later said my voice had never had that degree of impact, so it really is an ill wind that bloweth no man (or prima donna) some good. When I had concluded the Immolation Scene, taken my curtain calls, and returned to my dressing room, I suddenly felt completely drained. Apart from the usual backstage people, my dresser, Jenny Cervini, and Papa Senz's assistant from the wig department, both of them warmhearted and concerned about Hermann and me, there was nobody in my dressing room other than myself and the little illuminated red EXIT sign above the door. This mood was broken a few minutes later by a soft knock on the door. Edward Johnson was paying a visit to New York from Toronto, where he now ran the opera school at the local conservatory, and he had been sitting in the audience. After the final curtain, he had the kindness to drop by to say hello. The first words he spoke when he embraced me were, "How's Hermann?"

Apart from that very thoughtful visit, there was not one single individual from the incumbent management to express gratitude to me for saving that show—or anything else, for that matter. Finally, I left the dressing room and found soprano Paula Lenchner, who had sung the Rhine Maiden Woglinde in act 3, and our mutual friend John Clark, patiently waiting to escort me home in a taxi. I'll never forget this kind gesture, which restored my belief in fundamental human decency.

Later on, as I lay in my bed wondering how Hermann's day had been, but unable to call Waco and inquire at that late hour, I have to admit that the cavalier attitude on the part of the new management had me wondering. After all, there was a sick man in Texas, and I wasn't certain whether I would find him alive or dead when I got back there. I kept ruminating on the many positive things that were happening for me professionally outside New York. The upshot of this contemplation was my firm decision to curtail my activities at the Metropolitan in the coming seasons. I remember saying to myself over and over again, "This is no way to treat a woman—this is no way to treat anyone!"

As if this were not enough, shortly after takeoff from La Guardia the following morning, the passengers were told there was a snowstorm raging en route to Texas, and the only way we could get there would be with a long stopover in Chicago, which did precious little to calm my nerves. When I finally got back to Waco and found Hermann smiling at me, the snowstorm was forgotten, and the sunshine returned to my heart.

Shortly afterward, I got in touch with our personal physician, Dr. Alfred Roseno, a European friend of Hermann's, and he arranged with his colleagues in Texas for Hermann to be transferred to a New York hospital. Although Hermann had partially recovered his health, Dr. Roseno still cautioned him to slow down. He would have to walk slower, eat slower, sleep longer, teach a bit less, and temporarily retire from his activities at the theatre.

While I was wondering how I could continue to perform as much as Hermann and I wanted me to and yet maintain a watchful eye on him through the various stages of his recuperation, the doorbell rang one day, and there, large as life, was Erna Janssen, the wife of the baritone, with a winning smile on her face, inquiring if there was anything she could do for us. Back in the old country, she explained, she had been a registered nurse, and she relished the opportunity to practice her old profession again while helping look after a dear friend. With typical Central European efficiency, she had inquired about the theatre schedule and then made a list, on which she had checked the times my services would be required. Erna told me in no uncertain terms to keep all these appointments, assuring me that Hermann would be in the very best of hands with her to look after him. In the coming weeks, she came sporadically to help, often with Herbert in tow to provide a little extra companionship and a lot of humor. The Janssens' generosity toward us turned an already good friendship to a bond for life.

By the end of that year, Hermann was starting to resume a somewhat truncated teaching schedule, while I returned to the theatre for my final performance that year, a blockbuster *Cavalleria Rusticana* in which I shared the stage with the handsome new mammoth-voiced Italian tenor, Mario del Monaco. Del Monaco was as great a gentleman as he was an artist. Just before curtain time, he dropped in to wish me well and then asked me if I had sufficient breath for long phrases. He explained that he liked extending the high notes at the end of the Santuzza-Turiddu duet, but he was not prepared to take those liberties unless he was sure the soprano beside him could keep pace. With a quizzical glance, I said, "Signor del Monaco, with me singing Wagner?" "*Ma certo! Naturalmente!*" he replied. We held onto those high notes indecently long—*all'Italiana*—which sent the Italians in the audience into spasms of joy. The following day, *Il Progresso Italo-Americano*, New York's Italian-language newspaper, kindly accorded me the high honor of saying no Italian soprano could have done it better.

As Hermann's willpower began to take the upper hand in his path toward recovery, I felt his old energy coming back. This energy would be a support to both of us as our musical road began taking us ever further afield.

Going International

Tʜᴇ ᴏᴘᴇɴɪɴɢ ᴜᴘ of Europe after the war soon became a two-way street. While America's few theatres were again able to engage artists from the "Old Country," the many theatres in Europe had begun welcoming talented American artists to their rosters. A few of these artists would spend their careers commuting back and forth across the ocean, while others, such as Theresa Stich-Randall in Vienna, Lawrence Winters in Hamburg, Grace Hoffman in Stuttgart, Jess Thomas and the husband-and-wife team of Claire Watson and David Thaw in Munich, and Jess Walters in London, would spend the greater part of their artistic lives in European theatres.

In the early 1950s, I was still one of the commuters. The first offer I received from outside the Western Hemisphere was from the Royal Opera House, Covent Garden, in London, where I made my début in November 1948. Of course, all of us in America had heard about the devastation the Luftwaffe had visited on the British capital, but nothing could have prepared me for the sight of the city that met my eyes when I first arrived there. The London government had erected a kind of Potemkin Corridor covering the route from the airport to the center of the city, by cleaning the rubble off this thoroughfare, so the initial impact was not all that great, but the minute I started moving around the city itself, I was heartbroken by the conditions everyone had to live in.

The theatre had reserved a room for Hermann and me at the old Waldorf Hotel. This location made it possible for us to walk to Covent Garden without having to cross the Strand, which could be perilous in time of fog.

Not only were many of the buildings barely habitable, but the necessities of life were in short supply, and food rationing was the order of the day, which we foreigners in our hotels had to participate in as well. Some exceptions could be made for hotel guests, but only under special circumstances. For example, if someone wanted a steak, it could be ordered from room service, but it was not on the menu. It would have meant having to stock too many steaks, and there was not that much meat available in England at that time. Needless to say, this bit of beef also had its price, and that price could be astronomical! On one occasion, I asked for some little sausages with my breakfast, but when they arrived they tasted like sawdust, because they were largely made of meat substitute. Now and then we would make a pilgrimage up to the Soho district, north of Piccadilly Circus, where some of the foreign restaurants were a bit more resourceful in coping with the scarcities than the standard English-fare places were.

Backstage at the theatre, many of the staff members were terribly embarrassed at the fact that they couldn't provide the singers with pianos in each dressing room or other facilities we had become used to in most places. One incident during a performance serves as a sad illustration of the desperate straits the Londoners were in at that time. I had a gossamer-thin silk scarf that I used in act 2 of *Tristan und Isolde* to signal Tristan the coast was clear. It was standard procedure in all productions that I would simply toss this scarf to the winds in my delight at seeing my beloved, and the wardrobe mistress would retrieve it for me after the curtain fell. In the London performance, the wardrobe mistress reported to me with great chagrin that my lovely scarf, which everyone backstage had admired so much, had somehow disappeared. I never saw it again, and I can only hope whoever took it really needed it.

For years after World War II, we could all still feel its effects in many little details of daily life, particularly when we had to step into the rest room, where we found the usual supply of that waxed toilet paper visitors often find so cumbersome. On top of that, the theatre paper bore the proud inscription, "Property of His Majesty the King," which had many of us wondering if we were committing larceny or lèse-majesté every time we made use of it. I couldn't resist the temptation to purloin a couple of sheets and send them to friends as an illustration of how the war had impoverished the populace, but their loyalty to their royal house was such that they found the money to place the monarch's crest on his "property."

The graciousness of the British extended even to citizens of the defeated Axis who had not been involved in the political activities of the Third Reich.

This eventuated my first encounter with Hans Hotter. He had remained apolitical throughout the Nazi era. Even though he was one of the most prominent musical figures in wartime Germany, he discovered after the war that his rapid denazification may have been the result of his sense of humor. At the outset of his career, Hans had been invited to participate in a kind of "talent night" introducing the company members to the audience at the German Theatre in Prague. Hans is a born mimic, and his imitations of just about everyone we ever worked with are legendary. On the occasion in question, his contribution to that talent night was a devastating imitation of Adolf Hitler, which had the audience laughing uproariously. A day or so later, he was summoned to the German Embassy and told that "that kind of unpatriotic behavior" would not be tolerated and could lead to stern disciplinary measures. The incident was also registered in his Gestapo file. When, after the war, the American CIC "liberated" the Gestapo records, they found the dishonorable mention of Hans's Hitler parody, and this evidence may have helped clear him for performances around the world.

The remainder of the Covent Garden *Walküre* cast was also fairly international: in addition to Hans Hotter as Wotan, Set Svanholm was the Siegmund and the Fricka was the Lincolnshire mezzo-soprano Edith Coates. Our conductor, Austrian-born Karl Rankl, another colleague of Hermann's from the Krolloper, enjoyed the profound respect of all and sundry. Like most conductors who started out in Central Europe, he commanded and received total obedience. On one occasion, however, I allowed myself the liberty of taking issue on a musical point with him. Hans Hotter and I were in an orchestra rehearsal, doing the third act of *Walküre*, and every now and then, one of those little Beckmesser-type assistant conductors would come out onstage with a piano score in his hand to indicate that this, that, or the other passage was to be cut, explaining each time that these were the passages Kirsten Flagstad, who was a regular guest here, in his words, "always eschewed."

Frankly, this way of going about things was a bit disconcerting, and I would have found it more practical for the little man to have sat down with me *prior* to the orchestra rehearsal to talk over the cuts, but the management apparently thought they would save time by skipping this conference. At one point we came to the wonderful phrase that starts with the words, "Der diese Liebe . . . ," and out came the little man again to tell me Mme Flagstad had eschewed this passage as well. I wanted very much to sing this phrase, so when he came at me with the cut, I stopped in my tracks at hearing yet another "eschewed" and said flatly, "This is impossible!"

Of course, my reaction communicated down to Maestro Rankl in the pit, and he promptly stopped the orchestra and asked me what was the matter. I courteously explained to him that I had been told Mme Flagstad had eschewed that phrase in the act, but I wanted very much to sing it. I must have expressed myself with a bit more emphasis than my English colleagues were used to, because Rankl suggested we discuss the matter privately after the rehearsal. I replied "certainly," and we continued.

A couple of days later, I ran across Constance Shacklock in the hall, and she immediately asked me, "What's this I hear about your having some kind of row with Rankl?" I explained that professionals frequently had differences, and their ability to resolve them is often a good measure of their professional approach. With that, the rumor was defused, and we went back to work with renewed zeal.

After my first London season, a couple of years passed before I was invited back, because most European theatres, even the largest and most prestigious ones, still had very tight budgets in those postwar days and were forced to pool the expense of bringing artists from overseas. When I received offers from the Maggio Musicale Fiorentino in Italy and the revived Bayreuth Festival in Germany, Covent Garden asked me to bridge the period between the Italian engagement and the start of the German season with performances of *Siegfried*, *Trovatore*, *Walküre*, *Aida*, and *Salome* in London.

The Florence engagement had come about by a rather circuitous route. After the concert performances of *Elektra* at Carnegie Hall in the Christmas season of 1949, Dimitri Mitropoulos wanted me to sing a staged production in Florence, but an emergency appendectomy intervened. When I had to cancel the Maggio Musicale, I did whatever I could to try to reschedule this production for a later date. That not being possible, they asked if I would accept a substitute engagement to sing Lady Macbeth in a production of the Verdi opera to be staged by Gustaf Gründgens, another colleague, a Krolloper stalwart, and a known factor to me from the German movies Hermann and I attended regularly at the Thalia Theatre down the street from our apartment in Manhattan. Many of these films had Gründgens in a starring role, others were directed by him, and quite a few had him doing double duty as director and leading actor. The fact that Maestro Vittorio Gui would be conducting the performances made it even more intriguing for me, and the icing on the cake was the date of the first performance—May 6, 1951. Ever since my Metropolitan début on the sixth of December, the number six has turned up often in my life, and even at that early stage, it had firmly established itself as my lucky number.

After the conventional productions at the Metropolitan and Covent Garden, plus some of the slapped-together affairs I had to endure in the smaller theatres of the Western Hemisphere, the thoroughly thought-out production in Florence was a true revelation—the kind of unity of drama and music I had been dreaming about for years but had been led to believe would probably never be totally feasible. In Florence it was all happening, and it was indeed worthy of the undisputed art capital of the world where it all took place.

We arrived in the evening, but were warned not to take any walks in the city during the late afternoon, because the mists rising from the Arno were not good for the voice, so we simply advised the theatre of our arrival and spent a quiet evening in our hotel. The following morning, after strolling through the magnificence of the Tuscan capital, we were treated to another artistic surprise when we entered the theatre. A rehearsal of Robert Schumann's rarely presented *Genoveva* was under way at the time. Just as we were sitting down in the auditorium to catch a bit of the rehearsal, a whirlwind of a woman charged out onstage and completely took the place over. The minute she started to sing, my ears perked up and my hair stood on end: this was a real operatic tragedienne of the first water. Her name was Martha Mödl. As she continued singing and acting, I remember saying to Hermann, "That's art!"

Shortly after this happy experience, Hermann introduced me to Gründgens. I extended my hand, but instead of shaking it, he made a ceremonious old-world bow and symbolically kissed it, muttering something in German. I replied, "Es ist mir eine Freude, Sie kennenzulernen," the courtly German equivalent of "Pleased to meet you." Gründgens's eyes lit up, and he expostulated, "Ein Weihnachtsgeschenk"—"a Christmas present." He then explained his overjoyed reaction. When he found out he would be working with me, he said, he actually flew to London to polish up his rusty English under the guidance of his actor friend, Anton Walbrook, so he would be able to communicate with what he described to Walbrook as "eine amerikanische Bestie" (an American beast). With the linguistic issue cleared up, we soon established a long-lasting artistic and personal friendship, but I never let him forget the "beast" remark. For the rest of his life, he received a telegram from me every opening night, signed, "Die amerikanische Bestie."

I had worked almost a decade with stage directors, most of whom more or less left it to us to act (or not), but Gründgens not only explained each motivation to us in all its aspects, but also physically performed everything for us, if necessary. This gave us a panoply of nuances to build on and prompted a lot of creative feedback from us. On top of that, he had a Weigertesque way of drawing us out. Once he was telling Ivan Petroff, who sang the title role, how he wanted him to react to the apparition of Banquo's ghost in the banquet scene, and then, in an instant, he suddenly turned into Macbeth, flew into a mad rage, overturned the table, and then, just as instantaneously, he was Gustaf Gründgens again, explaining intellectually what he had just done and inspiring us to become involved in that thought process.

Our collaboration was marked with great mutual respect, despite a small communication mishap right at the start. At her first entrance, Lady Macbeth is reading a letter from her husband, reporting his succession to the estate of the Thane of Cawdor, as the witches had predicted. When her servant interrupts to tell her that Macbeth will be arriving at the castle accompanied by King Duncan and his retinue, Gründgens wanted me to hurl myself into a chair and revel in the throne that would soon be mine.

I sang the whole aria and did the action as he had requested, and his response was a great big zero. I was so upset by his total silence, I went home near tears, explaining to Hermann that evidently I was either so bad that he took no cognizance of me, or . . . I don't know what. I was too overcome with emotion to think sensibly. As usual, Hermann decided to take the situation into his own hands and called Gründgens on the phone, calmly asking, "My wife is here dissolved in tears—what happened?" He answered that he was so totally satisfied with what I had done, there was nothing he wanted to change.

Gründgens also had a remarkable choreographic sense of stage geometry. In the sleepwalking scene, he wanted me to walk a single, direct diagonal line from one upstage corner to the opposite corner downstage. The set was completely empty, except for three enormous, rounded alcove windows upstage, with diaphanous cream-colored curtains. Behind the curtains stagehands knelt, waving them in rhythm, as if they were wafting in the breeze. As I glided along my somnambulistic path across the stage, dressed in a flowing white gown, I held a lighted candle in my hand. The doctor and Lady Macbeth's maid were at my side. At a certain point in the music, I would drop the candle, as if it were falling from my hand, and the maid would retrieve it. This was the start of my aria. We practiced the scene time and again in minute detail. Nevertheless, in order to get the sense of sleepwalking into my mind, I had to start my walk way backstage. Gründgens placed a guard at the spot where I started the walk, to make sure I wasn't disturbed as I worked myself gradually into my dreary, trance-like mood.

While he thought of the big picture in terms of stage geometry, he also paid plenty of attention to every little detail of hands and eyes. Needless to say, I was more at home with his kind of intensely thought-out, profoundly felt approach than I ever had been before. On top of this, Gründgens had even personally designed three costumes for the role. He left nothing to chance in this production, and that was also very much my way of doing things. Thank goodness, we were able to repeat this collaboration some ten years later in Düsseldorf. As we went into rehearsal of that production, I asked him if we would be doing the same staging on the sleepwalking scene, and he gave me a conspiratorial look and whispered, "Don't give away any trade secrets."

Apparently when Covent Garden found out I had been asked to sing an Italian opera in Italy, they felt they could ask me to sing some Italian opera for them as well. My second London season in 1951 came at a time when the theatre was switching over from the previous policy of doing all the operas in English, often in some pretty stilted, old-fashioned translations, and accommodating the new international nature of the company by singing opera in the original languages.

The majority of the German operas were all sung in German, but sometimes the Italian performances got a little more international than the composers had intended them to be. In the *Trovatore* production, Walter Midgely and Edith Coates sang Manrico and Azucena in English, I sang Leonora in Italian, and our American baritone, Jess Walters, accommodated all of us as Luna by switching back and forth from one language to the other, depending on whom he was singing with. In *Aida*, things got even more international, with Edith Coates singing Amneris in English, Hans Hopf doing Radames in German (my first appearance with him, by the way), myself singing the title role in Italian, and Jess Walters doing his switch-hitter act again as Amonasro to oblige whoever happened to be out there with him.

The London season dovetailed perfectly with the end of the Maggio Musicale and the beginning of one of the most productive associations of my life, my work at the Bayreuth Festival, which was about to rise like the phoenix from the ashes of the Second World War.

SCENE EIGHT

The Seeds of Slander

THE BAYREUTH FESTIVAL became aware of my work partly through the recommendation of Kirsten Flagstad, who at the time was just winding down her career. The 1951 London season marked her retirement from the Wagnerian operatic scene. It also included the second and last occasion she and I appeared onstage together. The date was May 31, and she had made two requests to the Covent Garden management: she wanted to sing her last *Ring* opera as Sieglinde, her only performance of this role in Covent Garden, and, as I found out several years later, she asked for me as her Brünnhilde.

Her reasons for selecting London, rather than New York or Oslo, for this performance were clear enough to anyone aware of the injustices this great artist had been forced to endure both in America and Norway over the preceding several years. The amazing part of it all was that these things happened to someone as fundamentally decent and totally apolitical as Flagstad, whose main desire in life, after home and family, was to be allowed to make music unencumbered. Coming from a country where performers are not lionized as they are in other places, she wanted no publicity of any kind regarding any aspect of her life other than the musical one. In other words, she wished to share none of her private life with the press or public, nor did she want to involve her family in any way in her career. As matters turned out, these desires were anything but respected.

When the war broke out in Europe in 1939, possibly no singer in the United States was more torn between two countries than Kirsten Flagstad. After her brief, unsuccessful marriage to Sigurd Hall, she fell in love with Henry Johansen, a kind of one-man Scandinavian multinational conglomerate with business interests in a number of areas, primarily lumber, hotel management, and the importation of wines and liquors. Johansen had always been enormously supportive of his wife's career, accompanying her on her musical tours whenever he could and sacrificing the companionship of a wife whom he adored when her career made it necessary for them to be separated for longer periods of time.

At the start of the 1940s, however, Flagstad found herself confronted with a series of very rough choices. While she was eager to return to Norway and be with her husband after her usual season at the Metropolitan Opera, her young daughter, Else Hall, just out of her teens, had become enamored of an American named Arthur Dusenberry and wanted to marry him and remain with him in the United States. While she liked her daughter's fiancé, she still nurtured hopes that the whole family could be together again in Norway. When it became clear that this was not in the cards, she began making plans for her own return to Scandinavia. At first, her husband wrote that she was free to make her own choices. If she wished to remain in New York until the political problems blew over he was willing to wait for her, but the political problems were not about to blow over for a very long time.

At the end of her penultimate prewar season, Kirsten was on the train to Cleveland to join the Metropolitan tour, already in progress. There, Lauritz and Kleinchen Melchior told her that the Germans were about to attack and occupy both Norway and Melchior's native Denmark. The Melchiors had decided to wait out the war in America and urged Flagstad to do the same. At the next station, Melchior hopped off to buy a newspaper. When he returned, his expression was grim: Norway and Denmark were now in a state of war with Germany. Arriving in Cleveland, they saw Kerstin Thorborg and her husband, Gustav Bergman, on the platform, weeping uncontrollably. Although their own native Sweden had been allowed to remain neutral, their feelings for their fellow Scandinavians were so strong that they were both reduced to tears.

For a while it was touch and go whether Flagstad would be able to get across the battle lines to return home, and the more perilous the situation became, the more urgently Henry Johansen pleaded with his wife to make every effort to get back before things got even worse. Almost everywhere she went throughout the following year, she found a cable from her husband waiting for her, begging her to return to her home before it was too late.

Booking passage and applying for the necessary visas to travel from the

United States to Norway was a long and difficult process, and so, to bridge the gap while she waited for all these clearances, Flagstad did a number of recitals and symphony dates, making several appearances in benefits for Norwegian war relief. On one of those occasions, in New York, she ran into problems with the local Norwegian committee. They felt she should use her influence to have the ticket prices reduced below the usual levels, so that as many Norwegians as possible would be able to attend. Kirsten disagreed. She felt the function of this concert was primarily to raise as much money as possible for her Norwegian homeland, and not just to entertain the Norwegians who happened to be safe in New York. While she and her management were seeking some kind of compromise on the ticket price issue, she received another message that the committee had demanded the right to approve or restructure her recital program. I can certainly appreciate her unwillingness to have her artistic freedom meddled with, and I can well understand her regretful decision, under those circumstances, to cancel the concert.

Time was running out, and so was Kirsten Flagstad's strength. A combination of overwork and worry about her home and family had taken its toll on her physical stamina, and she found herself suffering from a mild form of anemia, but this hardy Norsewoman went right on fulfilling her contractual obligations. At a concert in Washington, a peculiar protocol situation, over which she had absolutely no control, and about which, moreover, she knew absolutely nothing, sealed her fate. Shortly before the concert was about to start, the Norwegian Ambassador to the United States, Wilhelm Morgenstierne, took his seat in the audience and discovered the chargé d'affaires of the Third Reich seated in the adjoining box. For some odd reason, Morgenstierne decided the German diplomat had been planted there by Flagstad as a gesture of approval for what the Germans were doing to Norway. Nothing could have been farther from the truth.

The diplomat was still harboring a grudge against Flagstad for an imagined slight that had ruffled his hypersensitive feathers at a previous Washington recital back in 1938. Flagstad was singing the earlier concert despite a very bad cold. Reluctant to socialize with her audiences under any circumstances, she was even more adamant about staying away from casual conversations that might have affected her singing in her fragile state of health that evening. Just before stepping out onstage, she received a message that Morgenstierne and a bunch of dignitaries intended to pay a visit to her dressing room during intermission, something nobody who knows anything about musical performance would ever dream of doing. Apparently Flagstad's refusal to receive him at the

1938 concert, plus his resentment over the German diplomat at the later concert, injured his ego to the extent that he slowly began planting the seeds of slander that would have undermined a lesser woman, but Kirsten Flagstad was not about to fall victim to the whims of the small in spirit.

At last, her passage home was booked, and she set off on her journey. Halfway to her destination, she was forced to stop in Berlin, where she was put through an endless series of bureaucratic complications before being cleared to continue on to Oslo. She needed a visa to enter Germany, a visa to cross Sweden, and even a visa to re-enter her own country, although she held a perfectly valid Norwegian passport. Arriving home, she decided she would never leave Norway as long as the war raged on. All these hassles were just too much for her, and she simply wanted to remain in peace and quiet with her husband, her mother, her brothers and sister and their growing families!

During the war years, Kirsten Flagstad did accept two brief engagements to perform in Switzerland, but the rigors of having to cross German territory on her way to Zurich, plus the renewed bureaucratic indignities to which she was subjected, prompted her to cancel a proffered third engagement.

A few months after her return to Norway from the United States, one of her stepdaughters approached her with a request to urge Mr. Johansen to undo a naïve mistake he had made in hopes of preserving his financial interests. It seems he had joined the *Nasjonal Versamling,* a Fascist party under the chairmanship of Vidkun Quisling, who had started out as a normal if somewhat reactionary political leader, then appointed himself Prime Minister on April 9, 1940. When the freedom-loving Norwegians took exception to his ideology, he turned the entire nation over to German administration only six days later, on April 15.With Quisling's true seditious colors long since on display for all to see, Johansen's daughter felt it was high time for her father to get out of politics. She convinced Flagstad of her arguments and they discussed the matter at length with Johansen. He finally saw their point and promptly traveled from the family's country home in Kristiansand on the southern tip of Norway to the capital to tender his resignation.

In early February, 1945, only three months before the liberation of Norway, Henry Johansen was summoned to Gestapo headquarters and questioned about a number of things along with sixteen other men, who were subsequently executed. Johansen was as stupefied as anyone else when he was allowed to go free, particularly as one of his sons, Henry Jr., was a resistance fighter. In fact, Johansen had needed to use all his influence back in 1944 to get that son over the border to safe haven in Sweden.

On May 13, 1945, only five days after Norway was liberated, the Johansens were walking in their garden when a cordon of police suddenly arrived and took Henry Johansen into custody. As she later reflected, had her husband been married to a simple housewife, his arrest might well have turned into a routine check procedure, which would return him to his family in a matter of hours or days. As matters stood, this wealthy, influential man was the husband of arguably the most celebrated Norwegian in the world, and everybody wanted a piece of the headlines.

To make matters even worse, the case was assigned to a prosecutor named Ingolf Sundför, who had lost a civil suit to one of Johansen's companies many years previously and was yearning for revenge. His prosecution strategy was aided and abetted by reports on Flagstad's alleged conspiratorial activities, which Morgenstierne had been feeding the government from his perch in Washington, where he proceeded to make up one cock-and-bull story after another, claiming, for example, that Flagstad's difficult return to Norway had been undertaken on a German passport, and that she had met with, and performed for, a number of Nazi dignitaries. It was all made up out of whole cloth, but nobody wanted to believe the word of an opera singer against that of an allegedly distinguished diplomat.

The case against Henry Johansen never came to trial. He contracted lung cancer in prison and died in an Oslo hospital the following year, on June 23, 1946, without ever seeing his wife again. Although they had corresponded regularly, he asked her not to visit him in this situation.

In her bereavement, Flagstad realized that the satisfaction of giving the beauty of great music to others is one of the most comforting experiences an artist is privileged to know. And so she decided to go back on the road. She also longed to return to the United States to visit her daughter and son-in-law and to meet her grandson for the first time. When she applied to leave Norway, Sundför did all he could to throw obstacles in her path. He blocked access to her finances, suggesting churlishly that she pawn her jewelry, then allowed her only sufficient funds to transport herself to the Swedish border, where her former resistance-fighter stepson met her with his family and enabled her to continue onward. She was not immediately granted entry to the United States, because Morgenstierne was still doing his best to muddy the diplomatic waters, but finally this guiltless woman, *who had never even been openly accused of anything*, was permitted to re-enter the United States in March 1947.

After a reunion with her family and her accompanist and good friend, Edwin McArthur, she planned her return to the concert stage, but the lies and slan-

as, "What were her political associations?" "Was Flagstad anti-Semitic?" "Did she sing for Hitler?" the reporter got up and told Hermann he wasn't receiving the kind of information he had been told to bring back. In fact, he told Hermann bluntly that he had been of no use to him at all.

Obviously not everyone was as loyal to Flagstad as Hermann. Soon Winchell's attacks on her were not the only ones befouling the newspapers and the airwaves. Of course, she was doing whatever she could to rescue her reputation from all this character assassination, but while nobody in the United States seemed to want to publish her denials, the tide was turning in Norway.

On June 17, 1947, the Oslo *Aftenposten* newspaper printed an appeal signed by a group of distinguished Norwegian artists, deploring the fact that while those artists subjected to the longest quarantines because of their conduct during the occupation had long since returned to their work, the totally unfounded slanders against Kirsten Flagstad were still continuing unabated. The artists went on to appeal to all their fellow Norwegians to put a stop to these "attempts to undermine the name and reputation of Kirsten Flagstad."

If New York had been difficult, a concert two days later in Philadelphia, the "City of Brotherly Love," bordered on catastrophe. While the pickets had remained outside Carnegie Hall, somebody, allegedly a misguided Pennsylvania millionaire, had bought up large blocks of tickets for seats at various strategic points in Philadelphia's Academy of Music in order to plant groups of people there to boo and hiss the artist. When Flagstad arrived in Philadelphia, she was met by a concerned Edwin McArthur, who told her a contingent of police had been assigned to protect her from violence. The group of hired rowdies did all they could to disrupt Flagstad's concert, but apparently they had been instructed not to interfere with the music. Once she realized that she could sing undisturbed, Flagstad was able to weather the storm of boos and hisses, but the cries of "Na-zi!" from various parts of the hall hit her hard. Philadelphia was the last open display of hostility toward her in the United States, but the wounds cut deep. Although she finally did return to the Metropolitan, she understandably never felt comfortable in the United States again.

In Great Britain, with the nation's sense of decency and fair play, things were different. Flagstad had always been cordially welcome at Covent Garden and enthusiastically received in concerts all over the United Kingdom. In London, a group of independent Jewish philanthropists made a thorough, private investigation of her wartime activities. When they discovered that all the stories about her had been nothing more than petty slanders from headline-grabbing politicians, they invited her to sing at a gala concert for the aid of Jewish war orphans. Everybody who was anybody in the British Jewish community—dignitaries from the cultural and political world, rabbis, Jewish members of parliament—were present to welcome her with open arms and to accept with gratitude her special gift of music to further their worthy cause. With these many acts of cordiality, it was no surprise when she chose to conclude her Wagnerian career on the stage of the Royal Opera House.

At the end of act 2 of that *Walküre* performance on May 31, 1951, when I stood in line with her and the other principals bowing to the audience, she suddenly beckoned to me, then took my hand and escorted me downstage center to take a special bow with her. Suddenly she was no longer by my side, leaving me to remain alone in the place she had just vacated, and returning to join the others in the line. In a beautiful symbolic sense, she seemed to be telling me, "Take over!" To me, this sacred mandate from a great-hearted woman was like being knighted.

Her interest in my career, however, went far beyond symbolic gestures. As she told one of her biographers, Torstein Gunnarson, several years later: "Wieland Wagner came to me in Salzburg in 1950, and asked me if I would sing in Bayreuth. I said that I planned to retire, and that there were younger singers who ought to have a chance. On that occasion, I especially mentioned Astrid Varnay, whom I was very enthusiastic about, and she has sung there quite a lot." And so it was my operatic idol, Kirsten Flagstad, the friend of our family, who set in motion the wheels which ultimately brought me to the reopening of the Bayreuth Festival in 1951.

The aroma of slander slowly dissipated, and Flagstad was able to spend her final years in honor and respect back in her beloved Norway. Had it not been for the injustices perpetrated on a woman who gave so much to the international music world, her presence on this earth might have been lengthened considerably. Her physicians contended that the bone cancer that took her life had been induced and aggravated by the mental and emotional strain that had been inflicted upon her. On July 12, 1995, on the hundredth anniversary of her birth, the Norwegians held a mammoth celebration in honor of Kirsten Flagstad and subsequently adorned a postage stamp with her portrait.

SCENE NINE

Art Is What Matters Here

As our train chugged through the lush farmland north of Nuremberg, I found it hard to believe that this pleasant backwoods could house such an important and sophisticated festival, which had drawn artists and audiences from all over the world to the remarkable theatre on the hill. As a municipality, Bayreuth is one of the most underwhelming places in the world. A small town, nestled in the Franconian district of northern Bavaria, it is at best picturesque. There is none of the architectural grandeur of the other festival sites: Berlin, Edinburgh, Florence, Munich, Vienna; no grand cathedral and lavish palace like Salzburg; nor any natural splendor like Aix-en-Provence or Bregenz. Hermann and I likened Bayreuth to the Court of the Sleeping Beauty, insofar as it remains somnolent in the wintertime and then awakens to a thriving metropolis somewhere at the beginning of June.

Bayreuth would be little more than a dot on the map had Richard Wagner not built his festival theatre there. It opened its doors for the first time on August 13, 1876, for a première of *Das Rheingold*, inaugurating the very first full performance of the *Ring*. In more than a century since that momentous opening night, one generation after another has come to realize how ingenious Wagner's ideas on opera theatre construction were. The combination of an orchestra pit covered over with a hood made of solid wood, plywood, and corrugated metal, lined with a layer of cloth above it, and a spruce wood building structure with a raked auditorium floor has provided the theatre with an incredibly well-worked-out acoustical balance, which makes it possible for

167

singers and musicians to meet Wagner's vocal and musical demands more completely than in any other theatre. This is not to suggest that singers need not use the full volume of their voices when necessary. Instead, the great phenomenon lies in the fact that the very softest passages carry effortlessly throughout the auditorium, making it easier for audiences to follow the continuity of the drama. This way, Wagner used architecture to bring his lifelong dream of music-drama one step closer to reality.

Regrettably, Wagner's widow, Cosima, who held the operative strings of the festival in her iron grip from the time of the composer's death in 1883 until her own passing in 1930, almost fifty years later, wasted no time in disposing of her late husband's plea for constant re-evaluation and innovation in the approach to his works. For Cosima, Bayreuth was a sacred shrine and needed its precepts guarded with the zeal of religious fanaticism. Cosima's only son, Siegfried, survived his mother by just a few months. The succession then passed on to his widow, an Englishwoman by the name of Winifred Williams. It was her objective to turn Bayreuth into a temple of German culture and nationalistic philosophy, which made it an ideal staging area for the burgeoning National Socialist movement, which ultimately took over the nation.

The theatre gave performances right up to the 1944 season, with bombs falling all over Germany. During this period, it had become such a shrine of Naziism that once the war ended, there had been questions in the minds of the occupying forces as to whether they would allow the place to be returned to the family, or even reopened at all. There is a legend that the building had been saved from destruction by the quick thinking of a music-loving U.S. Air Corps officer, who allegedly removed the Bayreuth Festival Theatre from the list of targets for American bombing missions. I asked Wolfgang Wagner if there was any way of substantiating this story, and he assured me that not a word of it was true, but suggested I include it in these memoirs anyway because it's a good yarn.

Fortunately for the future of Wagnerian performance, the postwar authorities decided to entrust the management of the festival contractually to Siegfried and Winifred's two sons, Wieland and Wolfgang Wagner, simply because neither of them had been involved specifically with the previous festival administration. Little did they know that this rather arbitrary decision would make musical theatre history! Both grandsons were eager to follow their grandfather's injunction, "Kinder, schafft Neues!" (Create something new, children!), and were also determined to find ways of liberating his works from the bonds of antiquity and the political implications that the heroic approach had taken on during the past years. To underscore this new approach toward the performance of their grandfather's works, they also put an edict to everyone in the theatre on the bulletin board. Partly paraphrasing a quote from the *Meistersinger* libretto, the sign read: "Im Interesse einer reibungslosen Durch- führung der Festspiele, bitten wir von Gesprächen und Debatten politischer Art auf dem Festspielhügel freundlichst absehen zu wollen. 'Hier gilt's der Kunst.' " My reading of this is: "Art is what matters here. Kindly abstain from politics."

The Wagner brothers began looking for singers who would be amenable to their new way of approaching the operas. This was one of the reasons why they went to great trouble to find out as much as they could about many artists they had not known before, including myself. While the first recommendation for me had come from that 1950 conversation between Wieland and Kirsten Flagstad in Salzburg, the Wagner brothers still wanted to convince themselves. This is why they asked me to fly over to Germany in 1950 to audition for the 1951 inaugural season. I had to decline. I had a full calendar of engagements, and contracted performances must always take precedence. I suggested some- one might attend one of the *Macbeth* performances at the Maggio Musicale in Florence before the start of the Bayreuth season. Wieland Wagner planned to come himself, but he was unable to get away from his other responsibilities.

As their festival season was rapidly approaching, the Wagners decided to garner further information about me. Among the twenty-eight distinguished singers and conductors Wieland and Wolfgang consulted was a young Ameri- can baritone at the Vienna State Opera, whose work had impressed me im- mensely because I felt his attitude toward the symbiosis of singing and acting was on a par with my own. His name was George London. When the Wagners received positive reports from Flagstad, London, and the others, they decided to waive my audition and take a chance on me. This made me the only person in my generation to be contracted for the festival without an audition.

Neither Hermann nor I was the least bit apprehensive about what we would find when we got there. As far as we were concerned, the war was over, and we were artists with no political axes to grind. Moreover, we had both devoted a large part of our lives to the performance of Richard Wagner's works, and that was what had brought us to Bayreuth. When we arrived at the theatre and saw that sign urging the members of the company to avoid politics, we knew we had come to the right place. Obviously, the rest of the people there got the message as well, because, to my knowledge, nobody talked about the theatre's past. We were there to build the festival's new future.

We had traveled to Bayreuth on a real milk train. Shortly after we left Nuremberg, I took a little walk down the aisle and noticed that there was a lady seated in the adjoining compartment with a rather rotund gentleman. When I returned, I told Hermann I had played a little guessing game in my head during my walk and had surmised that the gentleman was one of the singers doing secondary roles, and the lady might be his wife. In fact, that gentleman was playing the same guessing game about us. He told his companion he had seen two people in the next compartment who might be husband and wife. He went on to comment, "Well, she looks like she might be one of the Valkyries."

After we disembarked from the train and settled ourselves in our rather modest hotel, we announced that we had arrived, and then decided to walk up the famous green hill for our first view of the *Festspielhaus*. When we arrived at the top, Hermann and I noticed two men disappear swiftly into the stage door as we approached. I later found out that they were the Wagner brothers. Knowing that I was coming, they both took up semi-concealed positions so they could get a good look at me. Later Wieland told me they heaved a sigh of relief when they discovered I wasn't the classic oversized dramatic soprano, advancing toward them like a dreadnought on combat maneuvers.

At my first stage rehearsal, I was introduced to the rotund gentleman from the train. It was Wilhelm Pitz, the definitive chorus master. He and his wife formed an enduring friendship with Hermann and me. Wilhelm later told me he was quite bowled over when he discovered the girl he guessed as "one of the Valkyries" was in fact singing the main Valkyrie, Brünnhilde.

To lead the *Ring* cycles, the Wagners had selected two of the most prominent conductors of the time, Hans Knappertsbusch and Herbert von Karajan. They were later joined by Joseph Keilberth, Rudolf Kempe, and Clemens Krauss, leading me to observe on one occasion that the prerogative for conducting in Bayreuth was having a surname that started with the letter K.

Some critics have accused Knappertsbusch of dragging Wagner's music. I think these criticisms are patently unfair. What Knappertsbusch was successfully trying to do was use broad, not slow, tempi, to bring out all the fascinating details of these complicated scores, to say nothing of the clear diction that was possible at that tempo. I was given some very good advice about Knappertsbusch by my tenor colleague Günther Treptow. He told me that you have to take very deep breaths, because you never know how wide he would spread those endless arms of his, which seemed to reach from one side of the orchestra to the other. He would start a crescendo while seated at the podium, and then, when you thought he had come to the crest of the musical wave, he would gradually rise to his full height, which was considerable, and the crescendo would continue even further until you found yourself going beyond what you thought were the boundaries of your own capability. I often had tender thoracic muscles after a Knappertsbusch performance. However, there was a bonus attached to this, because I soon found that my lung capacity was increasing.

Somebody once asked him why he didn't follow the contemporary trend and conduct from memory, to which he replied with classic Knappertsbusch bluntness, "Because I can read notes." This forthrightness notwithstanding, he felt it would have a comforting effect on the singers if they knew he always had the score to refer to in case we made errors. When real difficulties came along, he was always right there to assist everyone over the musical hurdles, giving all of us a smooth musical carpet to walk upon.

Karajan's carpet, on the other hand, was more modern in texture. While it was less velvety than Knappertsbusch's, it also seemed more like plush. Karajan's beat could sometimes be confusing. Although his upbeat and initial downbeat were always clear, so you at least knew where "one" was, he would then often start to form circles in the air with his eyes closed. He was enjoying and celebrating the music, sometimes very much for himself. That difficult beat and its effect on our performances ultimately got me into a conflict with him, which had unfortunate results on our relationship for quite a long time.

At Bayreuth, collegiality among the soloists was the order of the day. For example, Martha Mödl and I often shared roles. In *Walküre*, Martha would first sing Sieglinde, and I would sing Brünnhilde. Then we would switch back around in the next cycle. This principle also applied to Gutrune and the Third Norn. When somebody became ill, the other one would simply take over, no questions asked. "Hier gilt's der Kunst" not only prohibited the needless intrusion of politics into our work but also kept prima donna attitudes out of our fruitful collaboration.

The focal point of our activities in Bayreuth was formed by Wieland's revolutionary productions. In an era where everybody is trying to out-revolutionize everybody else, Christa Ludwig has claimed that Wieland Wagner was the most extreme of all the revolutionaries of this century, and certainly the most singer-friendly of the lot. The fundamental concept of all Wieland's productions involved using his vast knowledge of his grandfather's works, his visual-artistic sensitivity, his keen technical stage skills, and his profound sense of human communication to strip away the extraneous paraphernalia from the operas and get down to basics. "Basics," to his way of thinking, meant the human element.

His younger brother, Wolfgang, while graciously carrying out the arduous responsibility of managing all the day-to-day affairs of the festival, which he did in a very personal, hands-on way, also contributed his quiet dignity and huge knowledge to a number of productions. To me, the most significant of these was a *Ring* cycle for which he had developed a giant disc that split into a number of dual semicircular patterns to express the various scenes of the drama without any distracting superficialities of decoration.

It is only fair to add here that some of the decorative economies in both Wolfgang's and Wieland's productions were brought about by the strictures of the festival budget. In fact, most of us sang for far lower fees than we were able to command in other theatres, but the experience was more than worth it, and so was the international publicity! The resourcefulness of those two brilliant brothers more than made up for the financial strictures. I can remember my very first *Siegfried* Brünnhilde costume. It was made of the same material they use to sack potatoes, but the garment was formed so handsomely that it couldn't have been more appropriate to the production. When I sang my first Bayreuth *Siegfried* in that costume, I unwittingly broke with a long-standing tradition when I followed instructions by taking the first solo bow in Bayreuth history. As John Rosenfield told the story in the *Dallas Morning News*: "At the end of *Siegfried*, in which she had sung the tremendous music of the awakening Brünnhilde, the audience cheered for her by name. Wieland Wagner literally pushed her on stage to acknowledge the applause alone."

Not everybody cared for Wieland and Wolfgang's new, challenging interpretation. Mary Ellis Peltz, for many years the archivist of the Metropolitan Opera and a highly knowledgeable expert on operatic subjects, was not impressed. As she reported to a New York radio audience on her return from Bayreuth, "All Wieland Wagner does is turn out the lights." Of course, Wieland and Wolfgang used this interplay of the human factor and the frequent emptiness of the characters' surroundings, as well as the interaction of light and darkness, to suggest aspects far profounder than any literalism could have offered.

I realized that what had once only been a dream somewhere in the back of my imagination, a dream of an integration of music and drama, was becoming vibrantly true in the composer's house on the green hill. When asked to explain his philosophy of production, Wieland gave a meaningful reply to a cynical reporter, which also paid a handsome compliment to me: "Wozu brauche ich einen Baum auf der Bühne, wenn ich Astrid Varnay habe?" (Why do I need a tree on the stage, when I have Astrid Varnay?)

Commuting across the Atlantic

During the first Bayreuth season, Wieland and Wolfgang Wagner coincidentally acquired the services of a Wagnerian expert who had actually just come along for the ride. It was Hermann Weigert, and it all began with conversations between him and Wieland, in whichWieland soon recognized the depth of knowledge Hermann had of Richard Wagner's operas from an entirely different angle than his own. He saw this as an enhancement of his perceptions, and what had started as the give-and-take of two men discussing a subject they cared about soon began to have an impact on rehearsals. This led to Hermann's joining the staff that season as a general consultant, returning in 1952 with the title of *Musikalischer Assistent und Studienleiter*, which means head of musical preparation. This collaboration with the Wagner brothers was a winning combination right from the start. While the Wagners' knowledge was encyclopedic, Hermann's wisdom and taste on matters Wagnerian could certainly be described as Talmudic. The blend was unbeatable.

Hermann's input and sense of humor made a positive impression on Hans Knappertsbusch. When the maestro discovered that Hermann also played *Skat*, he suddenly became indispensable. The *Skat* players generally got together in the early afternoon or between rehearsals. Hermann would join them when invited, but only if I had something else to do. One day curiosity got the better of me, and I asked if I could sit in on a game. Knappertsbusch warned me that the language at the table sometimes got a little salty, but I was determined to acquire a better knowledge of this game that meant so much to my husband and his friends. Hardly had the game begun when I started to realize that "salty" was an understatement. Knappertsbusch brought the same passion to *Skat* that he took to the podium, and a reverse of his fortunes invariably brought forth spirited growls of obscenity from this otherwise courtly musician. After five minutes with these Knights of the Card Table, not only was my knowledge of the more vulgar aspects of the German language enhanced, my image of the larger-than-life Maestro Knappertsbusch was also rounded out.

Professor Hans Knappertsbusch was famous for his intense dislike of excessive rehearsal. His knowledge and experience held him in good stead, and he was used to working with competent professionals, so he restricted his rehearsal sessions to the problem areas, leaving the rest to the assistants. He had been engaged to conduct the opening *Ring* cycle, with Herbert von Karajan scheduled for the second. However, Mr. Karajan had been entrusted with the bulk of the rehearsals. This made it horrific for the singers, who had to keep switching back and forth from Karajan's accelerated rehearsal tempi to the broader approach of Knappertsbusch and then back to Karajan in the second cycle.

With a re-engagement in my pocket for the 1952 Bayreuth season, Hermann and I continued on to West Berlin, where I sang two performances for the Städtische Oper in its temporary quarters at the Theater des Westens prior to our return to the United States. It was my first appearance in a German repertory theatre. I had been obliged to wait until the conclusion of the first Bayreuth season in 1951, because I had an agreement with the Wagners that they would be allowed to inaugurate my career in Germany.

We approached the city where Hermann's musical education and early career had taken place with a fair degree of apprehension, an apprehension that turned to shock when we saw the condition the city was still in over six years after the end of the war. If London had been laid waste, Berlin was utterly devastated! With so many men killed in the war or still being held in Soviet prisoner-of-war camps, the women of the city had taken it upon themselves to clear the rubble from the sites where buildings had once stood, so that the job of reconstruction could get under way.

On our way to the theatre to rehearse, I happened to see two gentlemen in the distance and called Hermann's attention to them as they approached, saying they looked like artists, to which he replied, laughingly: "No wonder.

At the reception after the Bayreuth *Lohengrin* première. By then Hermann was a fixture on the Bayreuth musical staff. *Personal photo.*

They're Leo Blech and Peter Anders." The minute they recognized Hermann they fell into one another's arms as if it were old home week.

On September 6, I sang Isolde and on the eighth, Brünnhilde in *Die Wal-küre*, both conducted by Ferenc Fricsay in productions staged by Heinz Tiet-jen, who had been the director of the Staatsoper until 1943. The Sieglinde I held in my arms in the second and third acts of that *Walküre* performance on ders about her alleged wartime activities had preceded her. Her first encounter with pickets took place in early April of that year in Boston, but she received a warm welcome from the audience. When she and McArthur arrived at New York's Carnegie Hall for the next recital on April 20, 1947, she found the streets on all sides of the hall filled with pickets, protesting things that had never happened. Again, a lesser person would have turned back and canceled her appearance, but not Flagstad.

Hermann and I got to the hall early, saw the pickets, and, of course, were profoundly worried about her reaction to this demonstration. We were not aware that a similar event had already taken place in Boston. Mme Flagstad came out onstage, and the audience welcomed her with an extended standing ovation. Knowing that a sort of a rosy blush would appear on her chest as a sign of inner agitation, I noticed that the tumultuous applause had brought out this effect in her. My perception was substantiated when I heard the first two songs, which were rather shaky. Once she had composed herself, however, she outdid herself vocally, and the evening ended in a blaze of glory. We went backstage to greet, embrace, and congratulate her. Hermann and I were so upset by this experience that our discussion of the evening on our walk home lasted for several blocks.

Weeks passed, and then the calumny reached into our own lives. A former vaudeville hoofer, with no background or education in journalism, by the name of Walter Winchell, had taken it upon himself to become a news reporter in New York City. His journalistic zeal, however, was primarily geared toward selling papers and upping the ratings of his radio show, to which the tedious business of reporting the truth took a backseat. *Webster's New Biographical Dictionary*, copyrighted in 1983, described him as "known for slangy, gossipy, opinionated reporting." To make matters worse, he ultimately joined forces with the advocates of the House Un-American Activities Committee and a senator from Wisconsin by the name of Joseph R. McCarthy.

Winchell's office contacted Hermann and asked if one of his staff ferrets could do a little investigative reporting on the subject of Kirsten Flagstad with her former Metropolitan coach and good friend, Mr. Weigert. Being totally unaware of Mr. Winchell's intentions, Hermann agreed to a meeting. When Winchell's man arrived at our apartment, I happened to be in the kitchen adjoining the music room, where the question and answer session took place, and could distinctly hear the conversation. Very soon it became evident that the information he wanted from Hermann was the kind that would help destroy her reputation. After an hour of fruitlessly asking such loaded questions

September 8 was the same Maria Müller I had leaned over the edge of Pietro Yon's box to admire back in 1932 when I was only fourteen years old! At our performance together, Müller was fifty-three, but still as beautiful in appearance and voice as she had been nineteen years before.

The Berlin management offered me more performances for 1952, but, as my agents had already filled my schedule for that year, I could only promise them a single repeat Isolde the following September. We then returned to the States and resumed our musical activities with operatic performances in San Francisco and Los Angeles, followed by that fateful concert tour.

Hermann's heart attack on December 2, 1951, had placed the whole idea of returning as a couple to the 1952 Bayreuth Festival in question. Of course, I wanted to have him travel with me, and I knew how much he enjoyed his interaction with the élite collection of operatic colleagues there, but we were unsure whether he should risk the long journey. Finally I made up our minds. Explaining that there was no point in discussing something we both wanted to do, I made arrangements for us to get to Bayreuth as calmly and comfortably as possible. Dr. Roseno had told us that air travel was out of the question, because of the effects of air pressure changes during takeoff and landing, so I booked passage for both of us to sail long before the festival on a single-class Holland-America ship. The pleasant atmosphere aboard ship and the healthy sea air did both of us worlds of good, and we arrived in Europe relaxed and ready for new experiences. After paying a visit to some of the great art treasures of the Netherlands, we continued slowly by rail across the European countryside to Bayreuth. Hermann's work at the Bayreuth Festival gave him a new lease on life, and his good advice came in handy when an unfortunate crisis arose during the 1952 season.

I was contracted to perform two *Ring* cycles, under the baton of Joseph Keilberth, and sing Isolde opposite the handsome, dark-voiced Chilean tenor Ramón Vinay, in a new *Tristan* production to be conducted by Herbert von Karajan. If Karajan's beat had been somewhat confusing in the previous year's *Ring* production, it was downright irritating during the "Liebesnacht" in act 2 of *Tristan*. While Vinay and I sat upstage trying to decipher the tempo, Karajan was again down in the pit with his eyes partially closed, sketching clouds in the air with no clear rhythmic structure for us to follow. In an attempt to keep together, at least with one another, Vinay and I simply held hands, and whoever wasn't singing would beat time gently with the thumb on the back of the partner's hand, but even this sign language had its limitations.

At one rehearsal, all the mysticism at the podium got too much for Vinay's hot Latin blood, and he simply ran offstage in desperation. Hermann was delegated to smooth Vinay's ruffled feathers and convince him to return to the rehearsal. Hermann later reported he needed a full exercise of his none-too-modest diplomatic skills to accomplish the task. As for myself, after trying to make head or tail of what the maestro was doing, including a couple of vain efforts to discuss our problems with him directly, I completed the Karajan *Tristan* series as best I could.

Back in New York, I asked Hermann for advice on how to avoid having to face this predicament in the future. Hermann decided that I should write a letter to the Wagners, explaining my problem as tactfully as I could. I wrote that, in view of the circumstances, I felt that, with all respect to the conductor, I was unable to do justice to the opera with Mr. Karajan's occasionally enigmatic style of conducting, and thus requested to be left out of the cast of any operas entrusted to his care in Bayreuth. Apparently some other people had been having similar difficulties with Karajan, and so it was not surprising to me that the festival management severed relations with him. He never returned to Bayreuth. Whoever else may have had problems with him, Karajan took my own protest personally and refused to have anything to do with me for twelve years after the event.

Following the Bayreuth season and the single performance of *Tristan* on September 8 in Berlin, we moved on to Munich, where I sang eight performances at the Prinzregententheater. These included *Fidelio*, *Tristan*, *Tannhäuser*, and *Holländer*, plus two works by the Bavarian capital's most prominent composer, Richard Strauss: *Salome* and *Rosenkavalier*. The people in the theatre gave these performances the complimentary nickname of "The Varnay Guest Week."

Today I can safely reveal that I sang my first performance of the Marschallin in the composer's hometown as a result of a mild deception that I hope posterity will forgive. My previous experience with this opera had been only a few stage rehearsals for Lotte Lehmann, but when Munich asked if I wanted to do the opera, I was more than delighted to comply. At the time, I wasn't aware of the special connection between the city and the composer. My *Rosenkavalier* performance in Munich was a fortuitous event, because I was scheduled to sing a good dozen Marschallins, including seven in a row at the Metropolitan, following my return to the United States.

Hermann felt very much at home in the city of Munich and with the quality of work being done at the Bavarian State Opera. He liked both the musical-dramatic integrity and the grand tradition of a company that had performed

Chutzpah at work: not only did I sing my very first Marschallin in Strauss's hometown of Munich; the composer's son, Dr. Franz Strauss, was in the audience. In the background, Hermann feigned absence. *Sabine Toepffer.*

world premières of so many important pieces, including *Meistersinger* and *Tristan*. One day, he said, he hoped we would be able to settle in Munich and make it the home base for our artistic activities, a wish that I seconded.

Our European seasons shed a different light for us on operatic activity in the United States. While America was still enjoying the rather stodgy productions of yesteryear, great on singing and long on tradition but short on imagination, the European theatres were actively reassessing and restudying the old classics, while spawning a number of interesting new works to challenge the talents of their ensembles. On top of that, the rather tyrannical approach of Rudolf Bing to the business of operatic management was frankly not to many people's liking, including my own. Added to this was the fact that I was now beginning to get offers from all over for prime per-performance fees, while I continued to work at the Metropolitan on a weekly salary.

Another irksome circumstance of my Metropolitan relationship was the fact that, while I had been hired to do Italian opera in Italy, as well as various other places, such as San Francisco, Chicago, Canada, and Mexico, plus England and Germany, the Metropolitan management was still reluctant to use my services in anything but the Wagner and Strauss repertoire, apart from the *Boccanegra* and *Island God* productions, both of which had since been discontinued, and a handful of Santuzzas, where I had been initially an understudy for Mme Milanov. It became clear that career decisions were urgently pending. Perhaps an invitation to inaugurate the 1953 Philharmonic season as a guest soloist in a Carnegie Hall concert commemorating Tullio Serafin's fiftieth anniversary as a conductor would establish my bona fides as an Italian singer to the city of New York . . . ? Judge of my dismay when Maestro Serafin told me that he had always wanted to conduct Wagner, and would very much like to accompany me singing the "Liebestod"!!!

On May 31, 1953, I returned to Munich to sing Isolde at the Bavarian State Opera with August Seider as Tristan under Rudolf Kempe. Everything ran smoothly until the very end of the opera, as I began the "Liebestod" and discovered the muffled snore I thought I heard was, in fact . . . a muffled snore. Seider had obviously felt so comfortable in his recumbent position as the deceased Tristan that he simply fell asleep. In situations like this, it's hard to keep your wits about you and go on singing while your brain is ticking a mile a minute, trying to prevent disaster from striking. I knew I had to wake Seider up, but if I were to touch him too ungently, he might come to with a shock and let out a loud snort, which would ring through the house and get a huge laugh just before the solemn conclusion of this deeply serious opera. And that just would not do. As the orchestra and I started a forte passage, I leaned over and delicately prodded him, which kept the snort he emitted as he awoke gentle enough to remain, so to speak, within the family on this side of the footlights. Seider later told me this had been the third big role he had been obliged to sing that week, interspersed with a full schedule of rehearsals, and it was all just too much for him. He was so exhausted that, try as he might, he just couldn't stave off that short snooze.

The great joy for Mr. and Mrs. Weigert in 1953 was Hermann's return to the podium to conduct a series of radio recordings that marked our first conductor-soloist collaboration. On June 17, 1953, shortly before the start of the Bayreuth season, Hermann also conducted a German-language performance of *Trovatore* in Munich with me as Leonora. Following this, we recorded a complete radio production of *Salome* featuring two of the greatest interpreters of the other two leads, Berlin's Margarethe Klose as Herodias and Vienna's Julius Patzak as Herodes. Julius Patzak never lost the Austrian lilt to his German pronunciation, which he could make as ingratiating as a Vienna waltz or as menacing as the voice of his fellow Viennese Peter Lorre in a horror film. As Herodes, he had ample opportunity to do both.

On October 5, 1953, Hermann made a wonderful recording for the Bavarian Radio, featuring George London and myself in the third act Amonasro-Aida duet. The combination of George's towering performance and the Bavarian Radio Orchestra, which let Hermann whip it to a fever pitch, made for a real monument of operatic recording. Many years later, as George lay stricken with the terrible illness that ultimately took his life, the funds his family needed for his care had grown perilously sparse. I was amongst the artists approached to contribute the recording rights to a special release to raise money for his medical care. I was honored to be able to help in this way and pleased that, even under these harrowing circumstances, this glorious example of George London's artistry at its highest level was being made available to the general public.

The 1953 Bayreuth season made additional use of Hermann's talents when my Metropolitan colleague Eleanor Steber joined the singing ensemble to perform a radiant Elsa in Wolfgang Wagner's new production of *Lohengrin*, which opened the festival. Eleanor had been primarily active as a Mozart and Italian opera singer, and so Hermann was entrusted with the job of getting her interpretation of this German opera in line with the idiomatic approach of the others in the cast. The success of Eleanor's work with him and conductor Joseph Keilberth have been preserved on a commercial recording, which has been re-released on CD.

My pinch-hitting days were still not over, not even in Bayreuth. In keeping with festival tradition, I was sharing the role of Isolde that season with Martha Mödl. On August 5, Martha was taken ill on the day of the performance, and I came in at the last minute to substitute for her.

There were two *Ring* cycles in the 1953 season. The first was conducted by Joseph Keilberth and featured Martha Mödl as Brünnhilde. The second *Ring*, in which I sang the role, was under the baton of Clemens Krauss. This *Ring* and a *Parsifal* production that season marked his only appearance at the Bayreuth Festival.

During piano rehearsals with Maestro Krauss, I had a very strange experience with him. As we started work on *Siegfried*, Krauss decided to elucidate his concept before I actually began to sing. After a couple of minutes of his lecture, I felt the time had come for me to interject a statement, to wit: I would prefer to sing the role for him, and then elicit his comments on what I was doing. I will never forget the stupefaction on his face in response to my request. He kindly acquiesced, and I sang the role through for him. As I remember it, he then congratulated me on my interpretation, adding only a few tempo changes. I later heard from Hans Hotter that Krauss had told the accompanist he considered Miss Varnay rather cheeky, but he had to admit she certainly knew what she was doing.

If I had thought Leinsdorf and Karajan broke the speed records for Wagnerian interpretation, Krauss had both of them beaten—batons down. This rapidity was particularly evident in the beginning of the third act of *Walküre*. Krauss wanted to use a quick tempo to illustrate Brünnhilde's worried haste, trying to bring Sieglinde to safety before Wotan catches up with them. He urged the orchestra to a frenzy, which in turn had me delivering that scene breathlessly. On the day of the performance, I found a little parcel from one of my most enthusiastic fans waiting for me in my dressing room. Inside was a card reading: "To help you catch up with him." The box contained a toy fire engine!

The day after the *Götterdämmerung*, which ended the cycle on August 12, 1953, Hermann and I had been invited to join Mr. and Mrs. Hermann Uhde for a vegetarian lunch out in the country, which we hoped would give me a chance to relax from the *Ring*. While we were enjoying each others' company, three cars pulled up, and Wolfgang Wagner jumped out of one of them to tell me that Martha Mödl had collapsed after the first act of *Tristan*. Without hesitation, I simply said, "Let's go." They asked me which car I wanted to go to the theatre in, and I replied that Wolfgang's would be the safest, because he would have the most to lose if I didn't make it. When I arrived in the dressing room, I found Martha in very bad shape. Despite her illness, she was apologetic about my having to cut short my day of rest to take over for her on such brief notice. I calmed her down by telling her not to worry about me, but just regain her health. I then sang the second and third acts to a partial accompaniment of red peppers and green cucumbers. As the record shows, not only did Martha get better, her career continues to this day. Even well after her eightieth birthday, Martha Mödl remains synonymous with excellent performances in character roles all over Europe. More power to her!

Among my European performances in the autumn of 1953 was another series in Berlin, which included a *Rosenkavalier* performance. After the final curtain, I received a message that Walter Felsenstein had been in the house but had to return immediately after the final curtain to East Berlin. He nevertheless wanted me to know that he was overwhelmed with my reading of the Marschallin, because it was anything but the usual saccharine portrayal one so often sees and hears in this opera. For him it was a believable, vulnerable human characterization in act 1 with genuinely noble dignity in the final act. The message was clear: he was telling me in the kindest of terms that he wanted to work with me, but it never transpired. I would have loved to collaborate with Walter Felsenstein, whose ideas on music theatre matched my own on almost every level, but East-West politics regrettably got in the way.

Back in the States, I picked up a copy of the December 20, 1953, *New York (Sunday) Times Magazine* and discovered that I had been accorded the ultimate accolade. In the "Readers' Guide" by Sam Lake, there was a crossword puzzle in which the definition for 37 across was: "Miss Varnay of the Met." If that isn't distinction, I don't know what is.

When I returned to the Metropolitan at the end of 1953, my first performances were in the Dresden version of *Tannhäuser.* After the second performance, I was given the news that Rudolf Bing had treated himself to a bit of "creative casting" on an upcoming *Walküre,* scheduled for February 4, 1954. While he returned me to my début role of Sieglinde, he actually hired the world's foremost Wotan, baritone Hans Hotter, and then demoted him to the much smaller bass part of Hunding. On February 13, this performance was repeated at a Saturday matinée with the same cast in the same roles, which meant that Hotter would be featured on the radio as a supporting player in an opera where the rest of the world had acclaimed him in the leading role! Ten days later, on the twenty-third, Hotter sang Wotan to my Brünnhilde, returning to Hunding on March 17. I could not figure that out at all. I actually enjoyed an occasional excursion back to Sieglinde, which I had also sung in Bayreuth, but miscasting Hotter as Hunding was either an intentional slur or pure managerial incompetence.

This bizarre game of musical chairs has irked me from that day to this, but I was never quite sure of Bing's reasoning. This is why I placed a phone call to Hans Hotter on August 15, 1994, forty years after the event, and he told me the whole story. Hans had made his Metropolitan début on November 9, 1950, singing the title role of *Der fliegende Holländer,* in a performance in which I sang my very first Senta. In subsequent seasons up to 1954, Hotter sang a whole string of principal roles at his usual superb level of artistry. Shortly after the Hunding performances, when it came time to make a new contract for the coming season, Bing bluntly told Hotter he wanted him to sing only secondary parts at which he felt Hans excelled. In my opinion, Hans excelled at everything he touched, but he had a reputation to defend.

When his agent, Alfred Diez, didn't move a finger to clarify the issue in Hotter's favor, he decided to part company with the Metropolitan. Years later, Hotter came face to face with Bing on Maximilianstrasse in Munich, not far from the Nationaltheater. Bing offered to let bygones be bygones and suggested Hotter return to the Metropolitan. Hotter would happily have buried the hatchet, but he needed to know what roles Bing had to offer. When Bing spontaneously went into his Tibetan prayer wheel number to reiterate that Hotter should concentrate on "magnificent" secondary roles, Hans could only consider that suggestion as an insult. Now that I have been filled in on the details of that situation in 1954, I realize I was correct in the impression I gained of the new Metropolitan management when my breakneck return to rescue the *Götterdämmerung* performance had met with such great waves of apathy back in 1951. Thank goodness Europe was there.

As Hermann's health improved, he began taking on more and more conducting dates. In the early summer of 1954, in Munich, we made several radio recordings of my recital repertoire with Hermann back in his customary position at the keyboard. We stayed on in Munich to make an aria recording for Deutsche Grammophon, which was particularly interesting for the fact that we recorded a couple of the Italian arias twice, once in German for domestic sales and a second time in the original Italian for international distribution. With the current stress on original languages, this kind of project would be hard to imagine nowadays. Between the second and the fifth of June, we recorded Brünnhilde's Immolation Scene from *Götterdämmerung* with the Munich Radio Orchestra. This reading won the Grand Prix du Disque in Paris. Hermann next conducted two highly successful German-language *Trovatore* performances in Braunschweig on June 10 and 13. We then leisurely motored to Bayreuth.

On July 23, 1954, I sang Ortrud in Bayreuth with a new soprano from Stockholm as Elsa. Only a few weeks younger than myself, she had begun her international career a couple of years previously singing Mozart in Glyndebourne, and had joined the Bayreuth Festival for the first time the previous year for a single performance of Beethoven's Ninth Symphony under Paul Hindemith. Her name was Birgit Nilsson. In the *Walküre* performances that season, Birgit Nilsson was cast as one of my younger sisters, Ortlinde, in the third act. Assigning Birgit the role of Ortlinde did nothing to injure her ego or affect the subsequent self-confident business acumen with which she managed her career, and it added some ringing high tones to the ensemble.

Following some radio recording dates in Cologne and Munich, and a couple of *Tristan* performances in Hannover and Bielefeld, Hermann and I returned to the United States comfortably on the *Île de France*. In our branch of the theatre, almost every year we have a month or so off. In 1955, this pause came during the month of April. One day, while we were relaxing at home in New York, Hermann suddenly felt terribly unwell and collapsed in bed. He had clearly been stricken with another heart attack, this time a massive one. For a moment, I stood there helpless, wanting to call our doctor and yet not daring to leave Hermann's side. Then, providentially, the doorbell rang, and our maid arrived to bring back some laundry she had ironed. It was not her usual day with us. She recognized the emergency at once and ran to get a doctor who lived on the ground floor of our building. While the doctor was administering first aid to Hermann, I telephoned Dr. Roseno, who immediately made arrangements for Hermann to be hospitalized. He also ordered around-the-clock nursing care for him. Being aware that persons suffering from severe illnesses often have trouble communicating in languages acquired during their adulthood, I arranged for a group of German-speaking nurses to look after him. For a while it was touch and go. Then a week or so later, he lapsed into a coma. On the morning of April 12, 1955, the telephone rang at seven o'clock in the morning. The chief of the cardiac care unit at the hospital called personally and told me that Mr. Weigert had quietly passed away in his sleep. Dr. Roseno and other dear friends assisted me with the necessary arrangements.

It is strange what goes through a person's mind at such a moment. While settling things, I recalled a conversation we had when we were first married, in which I reminded Hermann that I still owed him $500 for payments deferred on lessons I took before the start of my career. He had told me to give it to someone who might need it. I quietly promised myself I would transfer his kindness one day in the form of lessons to deserving young singers. It's a debt I have since repaid with interest.

Hermann's urn was placed beside my father's in Fresh Pond Cemetery outside New York City. Both my father and my husband had hoped one day to return to Europe and resume their careers at the heart of the musical world. Bidding their earthly remains farewell, I promised myself I would achieve that goal, on both their behalf and my own.

As I began putting my life back together, I reflected on the words of the doctor in Texas when Hermann had been taken ill the first time. He told me the best thing I could do to keep Hermann's spirits up would be to keep right on singing. Now, with Hermann gone, I needed to continue working. As Karin Branzell told me at the time, "Work heals." I felt an added mission to take the wisdom that had been imparted to me by this loving counsellor, enhance it as best I could, and then share it further.

I closed the apartment for the time being, and, around the beginning of May, I flew to Germany for four opera performances and two concert appearances before rehearsals began in Bayreuth. My first date was *Elektra* in Wiesbaden on May 27, 1955.

Act III

BRANCHING OUT

"Allein? Nein!"

IN THE DEPTHS of my bereavement, fate had vouchsafed me a number of blessings to help me get across the chasm. Possibly the greatest of these was the fact that I almost immediately had engagements in Europe, starting with that *Elektra* performance on May 27 in Wiesbaden. The rehearsals with my colleagues in Wiesbaden and the guest conductor, George Sebastian, were going well, and I was frankly appreciating the perquisites of my status as a distinguished guest of both the city and the opera house. And yet, the first performance in this new phase of my life might have turned into a disaster had it not been for yet another blessing, and one that was no coincidence: the uncanny prescience of two of my dearest friends.

Valerie Wagner and I had been close since our standing room days, and she was one of my audience regulars since that day when she "lined up for Lehmann and got Varnay." When she married Si Glazer, she made an opera lover out of him in short order, and the two of them were members in good standing of my inner circle. A couple of days before the dress rehearsal I received a telegram from the United States. Pleased that somebody from over there had presumably taken the trouble to send me good wishes, I opened the envelope and read the message. The text was short, but it was one of the most important messages I ever received. It said: "Allein? Nein! We're with you. Valerie and Si."

Three thousand miles away, these compassionate friends had realized that my role begins with the word "Allein"—"alone," and felt that, after all that had happened to me in the past weeks, that single word at the start of a long and demanding opera might have sent me into an emotional tailspin. As it happened, by the time I went out onstage to start my role with Elektra's lament for her father, I was gratefully aware that friends like Valerie and Si would always be there, giving me the courage to go on. Si is no longer with us, but my friendship with Valerie continues to flourish well over fifty years after our first meeting.

The engagements I had in the weeks ahead were yet another sign of the careful way in which Hermann had lovingly shepherded my professional life right from the start. He had joined forces with the Felix Ballhausen Agency in Munich during the early part of my European career, and together, they took excellent care of me. Felix Ballhausen later revealed himself to be one of the most astute negotiators in the business, and I soon found myself learning from his example.

One summer, Ballhausen offered me a concert in a Belgian seaside resort. As I was eager to rest up from a busy season, I frankly didn't feel like another engagement. After a suitable amount of hemming and hawing on both sides, I finally decided to follow the old theatrical principle of asking more money than I thought they would be able to pay. If they refused, I would be off the hook. If they agreed, it would be worth the trouble to give up part of my summer vacation. Imagine my astonishment when the Belgians agreed to my demands, whereupon I told Ballhausen I would accept the concert, but only if they added travel and hotel expenses, etc. Once again, I hoped they would say no. When Felix called back to confirm that they had accepted all my conditions, I had no choice but to agree. In passing, Ballhausen couldn't help adding, "Astrid, darling, come work for me! You're just as big a crook as I am!"

On May 30, 1955, I sang Brünnhilde in *Walküre* in Braunschweig, then remained there to do my first German-language Lady Macbeth on the second of June. On to Bielefeld, where I sang Kundry in *Parsifal* on June 5, followed by an Isolde in Wuppertal on the tenth. Two orchestra concerts featuring Wagner followed, one on June 12 in Oberhausen, and the other on June 14 in Kaiserslautern. Then it was time to join the 1955 Bayreuth Festival ensemble.

Whenever I guested at smaller theatres, I always noticed the way many of the younger people in the company almost obsequiously treated those of us who did most of our work at larger houses. While this respectful deference was often flattering, it could make communication a bit awkward. I can recall one musical rehearsal of *Fidelio*, at which everybody was rather shy. They seemed somehow worried that their work would not meet with my approval, not that anyone had appointed me to judge them. To clear the air of the waves of trepidation I could feel during the beginning of our rehearsals together, I decided to make an intentional musical error, which startled the whole cast. After apologizing for having drawn a blank, I noticed that the atmosphere had undergone a complete change. This gave me a chance to ask the stage director to run through his concept with me, offering to fit in with what everybody else was used to. I added that if there were a few deviations from the staging I specifically wanted to add, I would voice my needs well in advance and discuss the matter. Once everyone realized that I, too, had feet of clay, they allowed me to descend from their pedestal, and we could get down to work in a spirit of camaraderie.

On July 22, 1955, I participated in the opening night of that year's Bayreuth Festival in a performance of the role I had once thought I couldn't learn: Senta in *Der fliegende Holländer*. As I worked on the staging with Wolfgang Wagner, I couldn't help reflecting on Hermann's determination to make me find my own way into the core of this figure without any easy road maps from him.

Singing with Hermann Uhde, with whom I had already been paired in *Lohengrin* as Ortrud and Telramund, was a welcome reunion. Unlike most of his baritone colleagues, who were majestic, massive gentlemen, Uhde was a tall but slender man, who represented an ideal combination of singing and acting. In addition to the solid, masculine burr of his voice, he was also a gifted musician, and he could be counted on to bring his dramatic intelligence incisively to bear on whatever role he portrayed. Beyond this, Uhde and I were able to communicate in two languages, German and English, both of which he spoke perfectly. This came in handy from time to time, especially as he had also acquired an up-to-date command of the American slang I have always enjoyed using, because it often helps me say a great deal with a very few well-chosen words.

Not a U.S. citizen himself, Hermann Uhde grew up in Northern Germany speaking English with his American mother, who had come there originally to study singing. He added the American slang during a brief period in the final years of World War II as a prisoner of war in a camp outside Chicago. What a pity that his career came to such an early end, when he succumbed to a heart attack onstage in Copenhagen, at the age of 51.

The Erik in that *Holländer* was Wolfgang Windgassen. Not a vocal colossus like Melchior, Windgassen made up for what he might have lacked in pure vocal force by what I considered vocal beauty, a healthy dramatic sense, and a high degree of musicianship, which were, as in my life, the hallmarks of a "family business." There were many parallels between Windgassen's biography and my own. Both of us were the children of a dramatic tenor and a coloratura soprano. His mother's name was Vally van Osten, and her sister, Wolfgang's aunt, was the famous Eva von der Osten, who had been the first Octavian in the world première of Strauss's *Der Rosenkavalier*. Wolfgang's maternal grandparents had been a well-known husband-and-wife team on the dramatic stage. Just as I had lost my father at a very early age, Windgassen was only nine years old when his mother died in 1923, one year before my father. I was my mother's vocal pupil, and Windgassen had learned his craft from his father, a well-known dramatic tenor from northern Germany, who served for many years, after his retirement from the stage, as a professor at the Music Academy in his adopted hometown of Stuttgart.

Professor Fritz Windgassen often visited Bayreuth, staying in the same Reichsadler Hotel where my husband and I had first resided. We would gather there for lunch or dinner, or after rehearsals, at a long table, which seated as many as twelve people. Papa Windgassen presided at the head of this table, which was always reserved for us. When the elder Windgassen passed away at the age of eighty in April 1963, we all felt a deep sense of loss. For a long time, Papa's chair was left empty. About a year later, Wolfgang was allowed to take his father's place at the head of the table without a word being said.

One day after lunch at the Reichsadler, I stuck around for a brainstorming session with Hans Hotter. He had been singing Wotan with other Brünnhildes in other theatres, while I had sung with other Wotans. We felt the time had come to compare notes on our interpretations and clarify who would do what, where, and when on the Bayreuth stage. We then asked for a session with Wieland to coordinate what we had been discussing, but Wieland was busy working on a new production and kept begging off, as he put it, "until some time later." As the first *Walküre* performance grew perilously closer, I felt the time had come to take extreme measures. The next time I saw Wieland Wagner in the theatre, I collared him and told him bluntly that if Bayreuth followed the tradition of lesser theatres and failed to rehearse performances adequately, it was likely to become reduced to an *Edelschmiere*, a German expression I had coined to force home my point. I suppose we could translate it loosely as a "high-class ham smokehouse." Without uttering a word, he gave me one of those Wieland Wagner side glances that indicated a rehearsal would be scheduled posthaste.

Rehearsing in those early years could sometimes be a chore, because there was no loudspeaker system between the director's desk in the auditorium and the stage. This meant the stage director often had to communicate with everybody by running back and forth. During the 1954 season, when Martha Mödl and I were sharing the roles of Sieglinde and Brünnhilde in *Walküre*, I was in the auditorium near Wieland Wagner watching him put Martha through her paces. Wieland was running back and forth as usual between the stage, where he worked with Martha, and around the twentieth row in the house, where I was sitting. He must have lost a lot of weight in those days. At one point, he leaned over to me and mumbled something to the effect of: "Why is Mödl moving in such slow motion?" I honestly couldn't answer him, because I didn't know at the moment, but I made it my business to find out as soon as possible, for my own benefit as well as his.

I went backstage and noticed Mödl had to make her entrance over a flight of six or seven uneven steps in the back of the set. Martha has always been very shortsighted, and, even in the light, she would probably have had difficulty negotiating those steps. In the dark, it was almost impossible for her. After thinking this problem over for a while and realizing that I might also find it troublesome to climb those steps in the semi-darkness, I sought out the chief stage carpenter and asked him if it was feasible to replace the steps with a ramp. He measured the area and said it would be no problem. I then asked him to give me a cost estimate on the job. Armed with the facts, I went to see the Wagner brothers with my proposal. Once Wolfgang approved the budget, Wieland promptly went up onstage and tried the steps out for himself. He must have agreed with my suggestion, because at the next rehearsal, the ramp was in place.

This was a typical case of Wieland being careful to see that, however visionary his productions were, the sets were always singer-friendly. It served his needs as well as ours. He wanted to see people's faces onstage and not have them forced to look at their feet. His thoughtfulness even went beyond the confines of the stage. During one of the early seasons, several of the men in the company were tall enough to qualify for the designation "giant." Unfortunately, the inside stage door was so low that they had to stoop to pass through it. After watching a few of these tall gentlemen practically genuflecting to get through the passage one day, Wieland Wagner exclaimed, "No singer in my company should have to bow his head except on stage!" and promptly had the top of the portal raised.

Wieland was so considerate of other people's needs and sensitivities that he once arranged a bit of stage business which was visible to only one person. But that one person was no less a personage than Professor Hans Knappertsbusch.

Wieland Wagner, the passionate revolutionary, and Hans Knappertsbusch, the avid traditionalist, were a study in contrasts, but their awareness of each other's expertise and their profound mutual respect often turned what might have been a head-on collision into a wonderful example of understanding and concern.

Wieland was a gifted painter with a keen interest in the effects of light and shadow on mood and atmosphere. He always designed his own sets, and he had a vast knowledge of lighting technology. In conjunction with his basic aesthetic of ridding his grandfather's operas of needless superficial rigmarole, he sometimes replaced such mythological apparitions as the dragon in *Siegfried* and the *Parsifal* dove with symbolic light effects. When it came to the sacred dove in *Parsifal*, Professor Knappertsbusch felt it was an indispensable part of the opera, while Wieland looked upon it as an inanimate stuffed bird. As the production began taking shape, Knappertsbusch kept badgering Wieland about the dove. It belonged there, he contended hotly, and there was nothing electrical that could ever take its place. Rather than incur the wrath of this often-irascible conductor, Wieland decided to effect a compromise, one that would suit both Knappertsbusch's needs and his own.

One afternoon, a large sign was placed outside the theatre, advising all and sundry that nobody not specifically on the stage crew would be admitted to the theatre section of the building. We were all aware of Wieland's fondness for doing technical stage preparations undisturbed, and so nobody wondered why he wanted to work behind closed doors that afternoon. Had we, however, known what was going on in there, I think many of us would have enjoyed watching something that no audience would ever see. In fact, Wieland and selected members of the crew were onstage hanging an artificial dove and determining a position to lower it to so that, at the moment indicated in the score, the bird would be well within Knappertsbusch's field of vision, but *nobody else's!* According to the grapevine, Wieland did this by assigning the tallest member of the crew to stand at the conductor's desk in the pit and placing another man in the front row of the audience. When the dove had been positioned in such a way that the tall stagehand, whose height matched the maestro's more or less, could see the bird, while the man in the front row couldn't, they knew they had it right.

In the actual performance, therefore, Professor Knappertsbusch smiled the smile of the victor when he saw the dove hovering above the Temple of the Grail, little suspecting that it had been placed there for the exclusive purpose of keeping him quiet on the subject. They say that when he later boasted to his wife about how he had forced Wieland to restore the dove to its rightful place, she told him she hadn't seen a dove anywhere, to which he snorted: "Ihr blöden Weiber seht sowieso nichts!" (You dizzy females never see anything anyway!). I wonder if anybody ever told him what really happened.

During that Bayreuth season of 1955, I was relaxing in the bathtub of the cottage I had rented for the season, when my housekeeper knocked on the door to announce that a gentleman was asking to see me. Quickly slipping into something appropriate, I went downstairs and welcomed Dr. Hermann Juch, the designated *Intendant* of the Düsseldorf Opera. Dr. Juch told me that the theatre in Düsseldorf was currently being restored and consigned to his directorship for the coming season, when its name would be changed to Deutsche Oper am Rhein. The ensemble would then serve audiences in both Düsseldorf and nearby Duisburg. He asked if I would be interested in opening the first season in the title role of *Elektra* and then remaining in that upmarket city as a regular member of the company. After my Metropolitan experiences, I was wary of attaching myself on a *permanent* basis to any opera company, but I told Dr. Juch I would certainly be more than happy to open the theatre and would also be available to him for a number of guest appearances there, provided I got plenty of advance notice.

When I returned to the United States, I realized the time had come to clear the air with the Metropolitan. While the European theatres were offering me handsome per evening fees, the Metropolitan was still interested in retaining me on a weekly salary, which would also make it possible for them to use my services as a cover for other artists. When I met with Mr. Bing, he was his usual courtly self, but he told me that, apart from a couple of *Parsifal* performances during Easter week, for which I was already scheduled, he was not prepared to make any further firm commitments for coming seasons. He then suggested I take a sabbatical year off from the Metropolitan to reassess my position. A truly pathetic offer after fourteen years with the company.

While he was handing me this line, a rapid series of thoughts went flashing through my mind. I thought of the doctor in Waco, who told me the best thing I could do for Hermann was to keep on singing. I recalled my breakneck midwinter journey through the snowstorms from Texas to New York to save the *Götterdämmerung* performance. I thought of the peculiar way Bing had treated Hans Hotter. Suddenly I awoke to the fact that Dr. Juch's Düsseldorf contract was available to me. I told Mr. Bing I would accept his offer of a sabbatical, which meant my name would be kept on the roster for an additional year. He agreed and asked me to keep the Metropolitan management informed of my activities. Deeply satisfied with my inner decision, I quietly replied, "You will be able to read about them in the papers."

It would be eighteen years after those two final Kundrys before I returned to the Metropolitan Opera.

The High Plateau

SHORTLY BEFORE those final Kundry performances in New York, I had an engagement in Chicago, singing Amneris to Tebaldi's Aida, as I mentioned before, and participating in the world première of a new opera by Raffaelo de Banfield, with a libretto by Tennessee Williams, based on one of the plays from Williams's *Twenty-Seven Wagons Full of Cotton* collection of one-acters: *Lord Byron's Love Letter*. We had hoped that Mr. Williams, whom I have always regarded as America's foremost dramatic poet, might be collaborating with us on this piece, the only opera at the time that had been based on one of his plays. If indeed he was around, we singers were not aware of it.

I did, however, enjoy working with the first-rate American soprano Gertrude Ribla, who sang the other principal role, that of my granddaughter, Ariadne, and a fine Italian-American conductor, Nicola Rescigno. *Lord Byron's Love Letter* offered me musical and dramatic challenges of the highest order, not the least of which was portraying an obdurate old woman in her eighties at the age of thirty-seven. Other sopranos might have been indignant at the idea of being asked to play a woman of that vintage, but I have never had ego problems with characters that have nothing to do with my own identity.

I have often wondered why a number of books and plays like this one, which could enrich the operatic stage, have failed to capture the attention of contemporary composers. Then again, I doubt if these great literary works would be enhanced by the cacophonic harmonic approach or the unsingable style of vocal writing in vogue these days. Pendulums, fortunately, have been known to swing back to where they started, and perhaps somewhere in the world there is a budding composer, with the soul of a Mozart, a Verdi, or a Gershwin, just waiting to add *singable, listenable* music to a great literary text. Several seasons ago there was a musical on Broadway based on Jean Giraudoux's *La Folle de Chaillot*. What a pity someone like Poulenc didn't make it into an opera! What a classic that might have been, and what a glorious opportunity for three inspired singing actresses to take a little time off from the heroines of Verdi. I would love to have sung the leading part!

From Chicago, I commuted quickly back to Europe for three Isoldes at the Gran Teatro del Liceo in Barcelona, which my New York agent, Marks Levine, had arranged for me, and for which some elaborate financial agreements had to be made before I left New York. Fifty percent of the fee for these January dates had to be deposited prior to September 30, 1955, in a New York bank, with the final half parceled out to us before each performance. This was a relatively civilized approach in contrast to experiences many singers used to have with ad hoc opera companies in the Americas. They often sat in their dressing rooms after act 1, refusing to come out for act 2 until their fees were paid. Before the founding of the American Guild of Musical Artists, the impresario might very well leave the city with the box-office proceeds before the final curtain fell. Sometimes, even when the fees were paid before the performance began, the money still wasn't safe in an unguarded dressing room.

In my childhood, I often functioned as "the bank" for my mother and some of her colleagues. Before the performance began, I would go into the dressing rooms to help the ladies get laced into their costumes and hook their high-button shoes. Once I finished that task, they would pin little cloth bags on the inside of my dress, so that their money was safeguarded while they were out onstage. Apparently the Catalonians didn't have the best reputation for fiscal reliability, and so Marks foresightedly organized that financial setup for us, so we wouldn't have to seek the services of little tykes to guard the take.

On March 16, 1956, I made good my decision to return to the title role of *Aida* in a performance with the Philadelphia Grand Opera Company. What the audience didn't know is that I also had to sing the role of the Priestess in the Temple Scene to help the Philadelphia management save money on a second soprano. This was standard practice in the smaller companies.

And then I sang those two final Kundrys at the Metropolitan. Not being fond of burning bridges, I made no ceremony of my departure from the theatre or the city. I simply closed up my apartment, which I continued to retain, made a few farewells, and quietly left New York to go back to Europe.

My return to the European continent took place at the same theatre in Wiesbaden where I had received the "Allein? Nein!" telegram the previous year. This time, I sang the role of Isolde. I continued on to the Grand Opéra of Paris, to make my French début with three Isoldes under the musical direction of Hans Knappertsbusch.

When the conductor's wife noticed that I was alone in Paris, she asked me what I was doing with my time between performances. I replied that I was sampling the delicacies of the local cuisine. She then begged me to join her and her husband for lunch. Perhaps my enthusiasm for French cooking might inspire Professor Knappertsbusch to forget his usually poor appetite and get some adequate nourishment for a change. One afternoon, I coaxed the maestro into ordering an *omelette aux fines herbes*. After consuming half of it, he suddenly looked over at me and asked me point blank what year I had been born. When I replied, "1918," I saw something happen to the look in his eye, and I suddenly realized that his daughter Anita had been only a year younger than myself. He had been inordinately fond of her, and when she passed away, still a young woman, he was so distraught by her death that he was unable to conduct for one whole year. I already knew that Knappertsbusch liked me for my musicianship and reliability. Now he and his wife also seemed to harbor parental feelings toward me. They more or less tacitly adopted me. From then on, he referred to me as "my prima ballerina."

In Switzerland I began a long and happy association with the Zurich Opera by singing two Kundrys there in the middle of June. A week later, an appearance in Mainz, singing Leonore in *Fidelio*, marked a momentous event in my life, one that only tangentially involved the performance. In act 2, when I drew my pistol and sang out defiantly to the evil Pizarro, "Töt erst sein Weib!" (First kill his wife!), I was looking daggers into the eyes of a man who would become one of my closest friends, Randolph Symonette.

Randolph was a former pupil of Paul Althouse and had also once auditioned for my husband. At the time, Hermann had praised his singing and suggested he work on the role of Kurwenal. I had lost track of Randolph since then. Now here he was again, married to my dear friend Lys Bert, and singing in Lys's hometown of Mainz. The massive figure of that heroic baritone, a stalwart Bahamian who had once been a sea captain, made quite a contrast to the petite Lys. They reminded me of Melchior and his Kleinchen, albeit a half-octave lower, in baritone form. Lys and Randy told me they had moved to Germany, where Randy was a regular member of the theatre in Mainz and slated to move on to the Deutsche Oper am Rhein in Düsseldorf. Imagine their surprise when I told them I would be coming to Düsseldorf as well. They later set up housekeeping with their little boy, Victor, at Bunsenstrasse 10, and offered me the freedom of their home whenever I came there. In future years, I would sing many performances in Düsseldorf, and while I always slept in a hotel, the apartment in the Bunsenstrasse became my home. My memories of the heartwarming and sometimes zany times with my friends the Symonettes number among my happiest recollections of days gone by.

In many ways, my sixth Bayreuth season in 1956 could be described as one of the highest plateaus of my career. This festival marked my first stage collaboration with George London, who sang the title role in *Holländer* to my Senta. For me, George London's reading of the tragic Dutchman represents one of the profoundest manifestations of the symbiotic unity of interpreter and role in Bayreuth history. With his heroic stature, his physical vigor, his dark, expressive voice, which he used with enormous flexibility, his depth of expression, and his seething inner fire, he stood on a pinnacle of his own. In short: George London was the Dutchman incarnate. All of these qualities evoked dramatic responses, which gave my interpretation of Senta a special incandescence.

My partners in that year's *Ring* production, commemorating the Eightieth Anniversary Festival season, were like a United Nations of operatic celebrities. Once again, Martha Mödl and I alternated in the roles of Brünnhilde and the Third Norn. At the final *Götterdämmerung* of the season, I found myself doing my one and only appearance as a quick-change artist on the Bayreuth stage, or anywhere else for that matter. Martha had become indisposed shortly before the performance in which she was scheduled to sing the Third Norn, and the management gingerly asked me if I would agree to deputize for her. They gave me a gauze veil to cover my head and face, plus a cape which snapped together in the back to conceal my Brünnhilde costume. After completing the Norn scene, I had to descend a flight of stairs rapidly in the semi-darkness for my quick change to Brünnhilde. While the hairdresser carefully removed the gauze veil and adjusted my wig, Wolfgang Windgassen (of all people!) ripped the snaps of the cape apart to help me get back onstage quickly. I then had to climb back up the stairs, with Windgassen in tow, so we could begin: "Zu neuen Thaten. . . ."

My performance came off without any problems, except for the last two or three minutes of the Immolation Scene, when I began to feel the effort of that extended performance. Still, I was able to pull myself together for the final phrases by taking very deep breaths and relaxing whatever nerves threatened to check in. The camouflage worked so well that only a few people noticed the change. I hoped I would never have to repeat this tour de force.

During that summer's Festival, I was approached by a young pianist named Heinrich Bender, who was working at the time as accompanist and conductor in the small theatre in the nearby city of Coburg. He told me he had heard a radio transmission of *Siegfried* from Bayreuth, in which I sang Brünnhilde, and was so impressed by it that he immediately applied for a possible opening on the musical staff. He was accepted for the 1955 season and remained in Bayreuth for the next four years. He said he thought it unfortunate that I had discontinued my activities as a recitalist since Hermann Weigert's passing, and I replied that I hadn't had the time to find as good an accompanist as my husband had been. He then informed me he had accompanied recitals for Hans Hotter and Josef Greindl, and asked if we could run through some song repertory together. The upshot of this encounter was that we ultimately did several seasons of concerts together, both recitals and symphony dates. Ramón Vinay's playful reaction to my selecting Bender to accompany my recitals was: "Varnay always grabs my best accompanists for herself."

Following the Bayreuth season at the end of August, I proceeded to Düsseldorf, where I was to begin preparations for the *Elektra* performances, which would officially inaugurate the first full season in the newly refurbished house on Heinrich-Heine-Allee. Lys Symonette had told the family she knew when I was arriving in Düsseldorf, but thought I would get inundated by this, that, and the other responsibility and would probably drop by to say hello in a couple of days. The minute I arrived, however, I quickly checked into the hotel; then, without removing my coat, I called the Symonettes and asked, "Hey, mind if I come over?" Without even unpacking, I hopped in a taxi and went over to their home.

It was during these first visits that little Victor began calling me "Tante Varnay," an honorary appellation he still uses almost forty years later as a grown man and a conductor in his own right. I was also delighted to learn that Randolph would be singing the role of my brother Orest in the Strauss performances. His gigantic, rich-hued voice and his impressive stage presence made him a valuable asset to the Deutsche Oper am Rhein for years to come, where he ran the gamut from high baritone to bass roles.

The Düsseldorf *Elektra* performances were directed, as in New York, by Dr. Herbert Graf and conducted by the exacting Prof. Dr. Karl Böhm, an often testy Austrian with a doctorate in law, who treated the musical score like a statute that had to be followed to the letter. Karl Böhm's vast knowledge particularly applied to the works of Richard Strauss, as he had known the composer well and had, in fact, conducted two of the master's world premières, *Daphne* and *Die schweigsame Frau*, under the composer's direct supervision during Böhm's tenure as general music director in Dresden.

Needless to say, Böhm had no patience whatsoever with people who had not prepared their work as assiduously as he. I happened to be one of the lucky people who did her homework on a regular basis, so I never fell victim to Dr. Böhm's ire. After all, I had studied this opera with three other Strauss experts. Hermann Weigert worked with me during the entire year I had been granted by a second expert, Dimitri Mitropoulos, to prepare the role for the concert performance. Then came the stage production with Fritz Reiner, who had been on the musical staff in Dresden when Böhm and Strauss prepared those premières. With this kind of groundwork behind me, you could call me up at three o'clock in the morning, and I would still know the role.

The Düsseldorf première was about to be my seventh *Elektra* performance, so Dr. Böhm's insights, as correct as they were, didn't come as any surprise to me. Nor was there any discussion about the traditional cuts in the opera Hermann had insisted that I make, because these excisions were always observed, even by Strauss himself, who was known to make whatever concessions were necessary to assure a smooth performance.

Karl Böhm must have respected my work as much as I did his, because this *Elektra* was the first of a long list of joint efforts, which concluded with his very last assignment at the age of eighty-five, shortly before his death. Just as it had begun, our work together also ended with *Elektra*, this time in a television recording with Leonie Rysanek in the title role and myself as her mother, Klytämnestra.

As the Düsseldorf rehearsals progressed, I witnessed Böhm's violent reaction to a number of things. He found it hard to endure the sight of singers in a position where they could not at least look peripherally at him, which often cut our acting options considerably. If anybody did move into such a position, he would promptly alter the tempo. I have no idea whether he did this out of petulance to prove a point, or quite unconsciously because of nervousness over not being looked at, but he could be counted on to do it nine times out of ten.

Years later, he finally expressed his admiration for my ability to stay in tempo regardless of what action I happened to be carrying out onstage, and he asked me point-blank if I had a secret. My answer was simply, "I count," which is true. If you don't count, and have to gawk directly at the conductor just to get the beat, you will invariably drop out of character, and that, to me, is anathema to any effective delineation.

Böhm was also a stickler for punctuality and could be downright lethal with anyone on the stage or in the pit who didn't show up on time. I witnessed this trait of his firsthand in the case of a young lady who was singing the short but significant role of the fifth serving maid. She had a perfectly gorgeous voice, but she showed up late for almost every rehearsal. Everybody was on their knees to her not to arouse any explosions from the easily ignited conductor and to try to do a little better on punctuality, but to no avail. She actually had the effrontery to wander in late to the penultimate orchestra dress rehearsal.

I was always in the theatre very early for these *Elektra* stage rehearsals, not exclusively for artistic reasons, but because bitter experience had taught me that stagehands can be very sloppy about nailing down floor cloths with carpet tacks. It goes without saying that a single loose tack can do terrible damage to a singer working either barefoot or, as I was doing in this production, wearing very thin-soled slippers. I had once told the theatre I wanted one Deutschmark for every loose tack I found, and they laughingly agreed, thinking I was exaggerating things. The next day, I actually found and removed over eighty nails from the set before the rehearsal began. When I walked into the theatre office brandishing my bag of tacks and demanding my money, the management knew I meant business. This eventuated the purchase of a magnet to get rid of loose tacks, but there were always a few that even evaded that device.

Having removed a few residual tacks before the *Hauptprobe*, I handed them to the stage manager and then settled down for a moment on the rock in front of the Atreides' castle and watched as the members of the orchestra slowly filtered into the pit, all of them on time. Böhm arrived, greeted me, and then went down to his place at the podium. As the curtain closed, I went offstage to prepare for my first entrance and discovered that only four serving maids and the overseer passed me on their way to start the opera. The fifth was still absent, and the stage manager's staff was starting to go haywire trying to locate her either by intercom or in person.

Böhm started the rehearsal. The curtain rose on the imposing "Agamemnon" theme that begins the opera. Then the conductor stopped the music, laid down his baton, and asked nobody in particular, "Well, where is the Fifth Maid this time?" He was answered by an extended, dead silence throughout the house. We could feel the air vibrating with nervous anticipation. When she finally came onstage, she got her comeuppance from both barrels. Böhm verbally laid into her in front of the entire cast, orchestra, stage crew, everybody, making her feel like a penny asking for change. In the course of this tirade, he remarked caustically, "If the protagonist can be onstage a half-hour beforehand, a minor light like yourself should certainly be on time." Then, without waiting for an answer, he had the curtain lowered and started the rehearsal from the top.

Somehow or other, the lady managed to get onstage in time for the grand opening performance to begin without delay. (Somebody must have fetched her.) Shortly afterward, however, she went back to her old habits, much to the annoyance of everybody else involved. Obviously Böhm's public denunciation had failed to leave any lasting effect on her, and it's unfortunate, because she really sang and acted beautifully.

The unreliable young lady notwithstanding, the grand opening of the Deutsche Oper am Rhein in its newly restored home on September 29, 1956, was a great success. This performance started a lasting tradition of operatic excellence in Düsseldorf, a tradition in which I was proud to play a part—many parts, as a matter of fact.

Keeping the Drama Alive

WHEN I STARTED freelancing in Europe, my year outside Bayreuth was a little like a roller-coaster ride up and down the quality scale. Some of the best theatres—Berlin, Milan, Düsseldorf, Hamburg, Munich, Vienna, and Covent Garden, for example—had large resident ensembles, and everyone spent weeks rehearsing. Although I appeared in these places as a guest artist, I could usually count on the solid foundation of a well-thought-out production plus a phalanx of colleagues who would hit the ball back and forth professionally like adept athletes, regardless of how much time we might have had to prepare our work together. I also, however, guested in smaller theatres, where the level of artistic preparation varied. Surprisingly, some of them did even better work than many of the larger houses, so that performing there was a real joy. In other smaller theatres, the quality often left much to be desired. This was due to either budget considerations or time strictures. It was then up to me to keep the ball in the air without sufficient rehearsal.

At the very beginning, it was the thoroughness of my preparation plus my instinct that kept my characters alive onstage, but while this may help launch a career, it will not sustain one for very long. For all the advance work you may do, you definitely need the interplay with the other people involved to create a character who functions like a normal human being. My rule of thumb has always been that a role starts to take on its own clear identity after you have sung it in at least six performances. The first half-dozen shows are the phase where you are still feeling your way into the work as a unit and yourself as a vital component of that unit. Once you have those first six performances under your belt, as long as your health and presence of mind remain with you, and you keep your nerves relatively under control, very little will be able to shake you as you move forward in your renewal and refinement of every characterization. Once the role "sits firmly," then you can start to experiment with it. If you are sure the perilous high note will come soaring out, no matter what, you can start varying some of the lower passages, or you can develop a better crescendo or diminuendo to underscore the musical moment.

The same principles applied to my acting approach. While always adhering to the basic blocking, I liked to indulge in little spontaneous, yet logical, changes in my acting to keep the character fresh. This is particularly important if you have a long string of performances of the same part over a very short period of time. This approach kept my friends in the audience guessing how I would perform a role on any given evening.

The copy-cat directing technique is always destructive. It takes as gifted an actor as Gustaf Gründgens to demonstrate an action in a way that conveys a sense not of "do what I do," but rather "make it your own." This meant that six different singers in a Gründgens production would do the same role six different, logical ways. The tangential aspects of a characterization never disconcerted me. As I went from theatre to theatre, changes in the sets, costumes, wigs, or other trappings, even the language, never altered the fact that every stage in the world has wooden boards beneath it, and once you've trodden on one stage, all the others are one and the same floor.

This musico-dramatic flexibility held me in good stead on one occasion at the Deutsche Oper am Rhein, in a German-language production of *Cavalleria Rusticana*, which, as usual with this company, was premièred both in Düsseldorf and nearby Duisburg. In the Düsseldorf performance, everyone sang in German. In Duisburg, on the other hand, an excellent Catalonian tenor by the name of Francisco Lázaro had been engaged for the role of Turiddu. Although he spoke German quite well, his diction when singing tended to get in the way of his vocal technique. After a couple of rehearsals, the management decided to let him sing Turiddu in the original Italian. I still had the role of Santuzza in my head in both languages, so when Lázaro entered and found me waiting on the village square, I simply shifted gears from German to Italian for our duet, much to the delight of the audience. As the baritone in that performance, Fabio Giongo, was a native Milanese, I presumed he would continue the opera in Italian. Judge then of my shocked amazement when he came out onstage and responded to my Italian phrase, "Ah, il signore vi manda, compar Alfio," with the words, "Sag, wie weit ist die Messe?" instead of singing, "A che punto è la messa?" which I had expected to hear from him. Slightly stuttering, I made another quick gearshift, and I was back on the other side of the Alps singing in German. At the end of the opera, I asked Fabio what happened to his Italian. He smiled sheepishly, admitting he had never sung Alfio in any other language. I couldn't believe it.

Tangentials can, however, play a significant role in the way we approach the visual delineation of a character. The kind of costumes the Wagners used to design for us in Bayreuth, surely the most beautiful stage garments I ever put on, invariably enhanced both my performance and my vanity. One of Wieland Wagner's brilliant touches was a sleeved undergarment beneath a sleeveless main garment. With this combination, you could lift one or both of your arms without causing the whole costume to ride lopsidedly up your body, as it would do on a sleeved costume. This served to emphasize my center of gravity further. Both Wagners also insisted that every costume be supplied with shoes and stockings that matched the basic costume's color perfectly. The shoes were especially made for us in the Bayreuth Festival cobbler shop, and once a production had run its course, I frequently bought a few pairs to wear on other stages, because they were so comfortable.

Of course, the greatest difficulty in moving from theatre to theatre is never the incidentals, but rather the variations in stage direction from one production to another. In those days, it was our good luck that about nine-tenths of the productions we were involved in made sense. In the case of the other tenth, if a director told me to carry out a certain action, I had no compunction about asking why. Either he would come up with a plausible reason for staging something the way he had, or else we would find a workable compromise. By the way, the same principle applies to the musical collaboration with conductors.

Once a production was set and repeated over and over in performance, many of my colleagues would settle comfortably into it like a familiar and reassuring ritual. *I needed more!* If I had to stay in the same city and repeat the same performance with the same people in the same setting for an extended period of time, it would soon reach a saturation point, which would make the role stale unless I could come up with those little experiments and variations I mentioned before.

The input of other colleagues on the same developmental quest often made a major contribution to my own variational possibilities. The late Gerhard Stolze, one of the definitive character tenors, was a good case in point. Somewhere along his path, he had contracted an illness similar to polio, which meant that, although a Stolze performance never went beneath its usual very high level, there were some days when he was simply not as strong as he was on others. On those days, Stolze was not comfortable singing long phrases and had to compensate for other factors of his performance he just couldn't manage that night, but his inventive mind was always working full tilt, which meant everybody on the stage and in the house could experience something new and different from every Stolze performance.

Singing Herodias to Stolze's Herodes, I could always sense his condition instantly. When he was in full possession of his vocal faculties, it was like a license for me to go full steam in our domestic squabbling, whereas, when he was indisposed, I would find plausible motivations for soft-pedaling my own characterization to match his. In the course of bonding with his indispositions, I discovered elements within my own performance that might never have come to the fore had Stolze always been in optimum condition. After all, acting always involves reacting.

An artist like Max Lorenz added yet a third ingredient to this equation—interacting. Acting with him engendered a kind of mutual feedback. Although he came from the old tradition, his thinking was never old-fashioned, and his interaction with my way of acting propelled him to surmount the border between his generation and mine. I attempted to use some of the insights gained from my experience with Max Lorenz with other tenors—but it didn't always work. However, much of what Lorenz brought out in me was perfectly usable with Wolfgang Windgassen, whose intelligence was on a par with his predecessor's, even if his theatrical approach was considerably different. I could always see from Wolfgang's eyes that he was taking in something new, and he invariably reacted in kind.

When Ramón Vinay alternated with Wolfgang Windgassen, the dynamic transfer required to accommodate these very different interpretations from two artists with diametrically opposite geographical and intellectual backgrounds was a source of great fascination to me. Ramón's Latin temperament would manifest itself in rapid reactions and movements, whereas Wolfgang's Teutonic heritage caused his body language to be more deliberate, regardless of how rapidly he might have moved. In short, while Ramón's trademark was instinctiveness, Wolfgang's intellect dominated his work. In the best of circumstances, instinct feeds feeling, and intellect guides that feeling.

Blending characterizations as we prepared a production for its première was a far easier task in those days because the concept our stage directors brought to their work was always a point of departure and not a fixed goal. As we worked together, creating this production jointly, everybody's contribution slowly evolved into something that totaled far more than the sum of its component elements. As long as our stage director could communicate his concept understandably and develop it in harmony with our artistic personalities, the result was a solid structure that supported limitless growth. This way we could easily follow Wagner's injunction: "Kinder, schafft Neues!"

Here are a few examples for the reader's consideration. In Düsseldorf, Jean-Pierre Ponnelle staged a very romantic *Tristan und Isolde*, in which he wanted the Isolde in the first act portrayed as a deeply loving woman, who is almost helplessly willing to walk the last mile in her attempt to understand Tristan's reasons for treating her as she feels he has. He underscored his idea by accoutering me in a Kelly green dress with long tresses in a warm Irish red color. This was a workable concept for me, even though it shifted the weight of the character toward a more womanly, tender creature than the first-act Isolde I had been used to playing in previous productions. In these stagings, she was a woman of stoic dignity, whose honor has been trampled in the dust, leaving her profoundly injured and resolutely determined to pay Tristan back in what she considers to be his own coin. Each of these conceptions, of course, changes the manner in which she goes about exacting her revenge.

There were even greater contrasts in my various portrayals of Ortrud. In the 1950s in Bayreuth, Ortrud was depicted as a woman with an ancient aristocratic background, whose presence in the first act was very powerful, and who in act 2 wasted no time in manifesting her superior intelligence and cunning in contrast to Telramund. This was vividly brought forth in her exterior trappings: a severe, long black wig and dark costume to underscore her stern manner. In a second Bayreuth interpretation, Ortrud wore a cultic, conical headdress, adorned with a kind of crown. This established her as a resolute pagan high priestess, prepared to go to any extreme to assert the primacy of her creed on its home turf. In Vienna, I wore a royal crown atop a shoulder-length black wig, which stressed her temporal power over the realm rather than her spiritual dominance. Professor Rudolf Hartmann in Munich chose a complete departure from the traditional view of Ortrud. In his staging, she is a tantalizing blonde with the emphasis on erotic appeal, which completely ensnares Telramund to subservience. I loved portraying Ortrud, for a change, as a seductive temptress! Kundry is *expected* to be sexy—but Ortrud? That's fun!

This interactive creativity is often stymied when a stage director decides to

Rudolf Hartmann's concept of Ortrud was based heavily on the erotic angle, making her a glamorous blonde. I don't know if Telramund enjoyed it, but I certainly did. *Sabine Toepffer*.

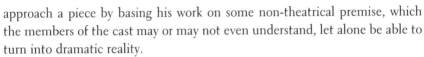

approach a piece by basing his work on some non-theatrical premise, which the members of the cast may or may not even understand, let alone be able to turn into dramatic reality.

A case in point: When Professor Kurt Horres came to Munich to stage Werner Egk's musical setting of Henrik Ibsen's poetic epic, *Peer Gynt*, he neither demonstrated what he wanted us to do, nor did he verbalize his directions, choosing rather to speak in parables and—I presume—expecting we would *understand* his intentions. The experienced actors among us somehow managed to take all this rhetoric and turn it into credible interpretations, but several of my colleagues just stood there with a lost look on their faces, as if his obtuse analogies were being conveyed to them in a far-out verbal language, after which they would be expected to deduce the meaning from the director's nonexistent body language. The whole experience taught me that, as complicated and multileveled as a work of art may be in its own right, and this certainly is the case with *Peer Gynt* with or without Egk's music, speaking about it in conundrums does nothing but becloud the issue.

The ultimate secret of making each performance come alive goes back several centuries to Aristotle and his theatrical precept of "the illusion of the first time." If you can make yourself really listen intently and hear the words as though you were hearing them for the very first time, you cannot fail to breathe ongoing life into your own performance. And you will also never commit the classic theatrical error of which some opera singers, especially beginners, are fond—reacting before the other singer's phrase is completed.

I never let audience response—positive, negative, or indifferent—influence the way I carried out my work. If the people were demonstrably in favor of what we were doing, that was just fine, but not decisive. On those evenings when they just sat on their hands, for whatever reason—they may have had a hard day at the office or an argument at home—all of us seemed to have an unspoken agreement that we would have to play the show for ourselves and derive the same satisfaction as if we had driven the audience to wild enthusiasm. As a matter of fact, I would make it my business to give a lukewarm audience an extra shot of adrenalin. Sometimes it works, sometimes not—but that's not our problem onstage. We're there to see to it that the show goes on, whatever the mood out front.

One of the reasons an audience takes the trouble to attend a performance in the house rather than listening to electronic perfection on a recording is that element of expectation of spontaneous moments. A recording remains the same, whereas a live performance is laden with possibilities. Sometimes an emergency, of which the audience has no awareness, serves to create an added dimension of artistry in the portrayal of a character. On one such occasion, I was the recipient of a level of wisdom that is born of considerable experience.

The performance was *Otello* in Mexico City, and I was singing Desdemona to the Moor of Ramón Vinay, certainly one of the top exponents of this role. And yet, every time he sang it, he was constantly adding, subtracting, refining, and responding *in character* to whatever stage situations might arise. This explained why many people would go back to hear him sing the role over and over, because there would always be some added profundity to his characterization. In the final act, after I had been well and truly suffocated by the hero, I happened to land in death heavily on one arm. As I had already shuffled off this mortal coil, to quote another Shakespearean source, I was in no position to retain my moribund verisimilitude and get comfortable at the same time. Somehow I managed to whisper to Vinay, "Ramón, my arm." His response was pure genius. Ever so gently, he drew my arm away from the edge of the bed and made it part of his acting, clutching it to his own grieving breast, studying it in motionless recumbency, and using it, so to speak, as a surrogate for the rest of me. It was an incredibly touching moment—even for me. It immediately recalled to mind Lothar Wallerstein's injunction to make full use of our presence of mind.

By bringing his accumulated experience to bear on an emergency, Vinay arrived by chance at a bit of business that added another layer of meaning to the rest of his already eloquent performance. It is the exercise of this kind of interactive wisdom between mind and heart in an impromptu situation that helps us along in keeping the drama alive.

Where, Oh Where Has My Winter Coat Gone?

AFTER I WAS WIDOWED and had terminated my fourteen years of binding contracts with the Metropolitan Opera, my interest in domestic bliss rapidly declined. Born and raised in the family business of making music, I always regarded being on the road as the essence of life. While many singers claim they seldom see much more of a city than a hotel room, an occasional short-term sublet, and the inside of the local opera house, I made it a point to add on a couple of days to my visits to many places. This way, once my performances had been completed, I could visit museums, tour historical sites, and, last but not least, see some interesting productions at dramatic theatres.

Being on the go also had certain benefits not available in a domestic situation. At the highest point of my career, I was more than happy to let the theatres collect my mail, let the restaurants of Europe (especially the Italian ones) prepare my meals, and let the hotel staff do my housekeeping. I needed the freedom to go where the action was, and this need is fundamentally inimical to being tied down either domestically or professionally. At no time—from the day I started out in Europe until this very minute—have I ever signed a binding yearly contract with any theatre.

In the early years, the center of my activities was the Deutsche Oper am Rhein in Düsseldorf, where Dr. Juch started me off with a guarantee of thirty-six evenings for the first year, with more or less the same amount in following seasons, depending on the repertoire. Somewhere along the way, a few enigmatic omens started to occur, and I soon found myself reorienting my priorities. The first of these portents came about simply enough. I was on the road, as usual, and one frigid day, I suddenly realized I was without my mink coat. Not only did I not have it with me, I could not for the life of me remember *where* I had left it. I began to think I would be better off if I had some place where my belongings would be readily accessible, but where?

Enter the second omen. Berlin was always a hassle. Getting to this "island city" by rail involved hours of waiting at one of the East German borders where some official would confront us with endless streams of red tape, becoming especially onerous when the transit passenger presented an American passport. So, from the very outset, I was advised to travel to Berlin by air. The snag in this arrangement, however, was that anyone was welcome to fly into West Berlin from West Germany without any documents, but you did have to show some kind of identification to leave the city by plane. Once, when I was about to go into the departures lounge, I had other things on my mind and just aimlessly meandered past the official's desk. When he stopped me and asked to see my passport, I inquired in a rather puzzled voice, "Isn't this Germany?" Said official responded with one of those looks that seemed to be asking if I had left several crucial brain cells in the hotel. My inner response to this event was to eliminate the fortressed city as a contender for subsequent settlement.

Throughout all my wanderings, the memory of Hermann's spontaneous reaction to Munich was always in the back of my mind. Even though it had been badly damaged by World War II when we first laid eyes on it together, we both saw the cultural life beneath the devastation. Beyond this, he felt that my success with the Munich audience indicated that my style of interpretation fitted well with the musical and theatrical style of the Bavarian State Opera. These two factors had prompted his suggestion that Munich would be the right place for us to maintain a second home, in addition to our then-permanent home in New York. With Hermann gone, of course, the whole idea of settling down anywhere took a back seat to what was happening to my life musically, and yet, each time I visited the city professionally, Munich continued to interest me.

Then, in another premonition of things to come, Professor Joseph Keilberth, under whose direction I had sung both in Bayreuth and Munich, assumed the coveted position of Bavarian *Generalmusikdirektor* starting with the 1959–60 season. Shortly thereafter, he asked me to sing in one of the first performances of his new régime, to take place on September 20, 1959. The role was Isolde, the same one that had marked my Munich début back in 1952, conducted at that time by Rudolf Kempe. This part continued to be my "visiting card" in a number of theatres on three continents for several years to come.

While I was delighted to help inaugurate Professor Keilberth's first GMD season in Munich, I was nonetheless disinclined to accept his offer until certain financial hurdles between the theatre and myself had been surmounted. Unlike many of my colleagues, who winsomely look the other way while contracts are being discussed, I have always taken a very down-to-earth attitude toward the issue of music and money, even though I let my agents do the actual negotiating. After all, I spend a large part of my life and plenty of my own hard-earned money acquiring the skills I have to sell, and I expect to receive the proper market value for my efforts. Besides which, my full participation in the business aspects of my career over the years has safeguarded me from being "managed" into oblivion by some avaricious agent. I see no conflict between this attitude and the integrity of the highest artistry of which I am capable.

To illustrate this point: Fritz Reiner once asked me to grant him a sizable discount on my usual fee. When I was reluctant to agree, he accusingly inquired, "Where are your ideals?" I responded that my ideals begin with the overture and end with the final curtain call; the rest is Business with a capital *B*.

My problem with the Bavarian State Opera was related to the fact that I had been absent from the Munich theatre for a couple of years because of previous engagements elsewhere. When we came to new negotiations, the theatre presumed I would accept the same fee I had received previously. Meanwhile, however, my price per performance had increased, as had the cost of living. Professor Keilberth intervened on my behalf, arguing that the government's obdurate attitude was impeding his artistic aspirations. He enjoyed such a high measure of respect that the Culture Ministry backed down, and the terms of the proffered contract were readjusted. Then the music-making began in earnest.

Somewhere along the line, Hermann's remark came back to me, and I figured a sufficient number of omens had occurred for me to know which way the geographical wind was blowing. I soon found an apartment in Munich and moved in before the start of the 1959–60 season. It was a move I never regretted. I never made any change, however, in my guest status. Over the years people often regarded me as a regular item on the theatre's inventory, which I am not. Nevertheless, they still keep me on the shelf and make regular use of my services both onstage and behind the scenes.

My work with Joseph Keilberth was a source of inspiration. I do not know whether this is a personal response or whether we can generalize about it, but I always have an instinctive reaction to any conductor. I can feel whether or not he has a sense of voice. Keilberth was a musician's musician, who both accompanied and led, which means he *knew singing*. Whether he knew it intellectually or intuitively is immaterial. The fact of the matter is: he loved voices. And when a person loves something, it becomes a part of him. Singing with him, I always had a feeling of being carried on the music. It was like having your father hold you, and in many ways we were all like his children, and his keen sense of humor made the exercise all the more enjoyable.

Wonder of wonders, Keilberth was also capable of self-criticism! A few seasons before he took over the general music directorship in Munich, he conducted a series of *Lohengrin* performances in Bayreuth. The festival had a contract to have the performances taped, with the best one to be released as an LP. After the first two performances, the engineers thought that something was not quite right with parts of Keilberth's conducting. They felt he was perhaps a bit too careful, because he was aware we were recording the piece. Whatever the problem, the performances lacked Keilberth's typical verve.

Hermann was asked to exercise his usual diplomacy on Keilberth, which he did by casually suggesting that the conductor listen to a few takes from the recording. After monitoring the tapes for a while, Keilberth silently rose from his seat, took his hat, put it on, and left the control room. The next *Lohengrin* performance really took wing. It wasn't particularly faster, just more intense and far more concentrated. In a general atmosphere of non-negotiable musical approaches, it takes a really big man to acknowledge the need for change and then go ahead and implement that change. Keilberth was just such a big man, and I genuinely felt the artistic give-and-take provided a firm basis for our collaboration.

Rudolf Hartmann, the Bavarian *Staatsintendant*, was a high-ranking stage director who created a goodly number of the productions himself and provided fatherly supervision to the other directors and their staffs. Professor Hartmann had known Richard Strauss well and had staged many of the master's operas, some of them in conjunction with the composer. Certainly no producer knew the Strauss repertoire better. In fact, he saw it as his mission to present as many Strauss operas as possible in Munich under optimum circumstances with full allegiance to the composer's musical idiom. He later wrote an authori-

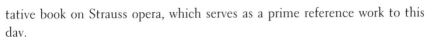

tative book on Strauss opera, which serves as a prime reference work to this day.

Hartmann brought far more than just tradition to his work. His frequent innovations and his pointed use of symbolism enhanced the audience's understanding of a work, without perverting the original concept by trying forcefully to shock everyone by superimposing some personal agenda or other upon the piece. I recall attending one production of *Don Carlo*, in which Helmut Jürgens's evocative setting for King Philip's monumental aria, "Ella giammai m'amò," was dominated by a huge crucifix hanging diagonally over the king's desk, and by extension over his thoughts. The message was clear: in the period of the Inquisition, the Christian religion was being used as a pretext to commit some of the most appalling atrocities mankind had ever known. In a sense, Hartmann and his designer took the suffering of the king and the agony of Christ on the cross to ask, "How often must I be crucified?" It was a typical Hartmann stroke of profundity. On top of attending to his own productions, he was available to all the members of the company virtually throughout the season. Leaving his home house to stage something somewhere else was a very rare event in his professional life, and his clear artistic vision gave unity and continuity to the theatre's work.

With the home-like atmosphere of the theatre, the artistic vision of Rudolf Hartmann, Joseph Keilberth, and their staffs, plus the extra added attraction of regular work with Hans Knappertsbusch at his base of activity, I felt I had acquired the kind of family a mature adult needs. For me, at this stage of my career, the Bavarian State Opera was not a child's home, caring for daily requirements, but rather a place I could return to, interconnect artistically with the "family members" for a while, and always feel welcome. I had finally found my geographic center.

Oh, by the way, I finally found that mink coat, too. It was in the Symonettes' front hall closet in Düsseldorf.

Three Brünnhildes, No Waiting

Back in the early 1950s, I was chatting with *Kammersänger* Fritz Windgassen over lunch in Bayreuth. I mentioned a *Tristan* rehearsal in Berlin, at which my partner and I went down to the canteen for a coffee break and were surprised to find a well-known Tristan playing *Skat* there with his friends. I thought this was very rare, but Mr. Windgassen said that in his time it was not unusual to find *two* Tristans playing cards in the canteen, while a third was singing the role on stage. They were not waiting to go on in case their colleague couldn't continue—they just happened to have a free evening and felt like spending it in the theatre.

Nowadays, if a good Tristan is indisposed, theatres often have to scramble hysterically all over the continent to find anyone else who can handle the same assignment, and they frequently have to settle for second-best or less, if indeed they can find anyone at all. I cannot recall ever singing Brünnhilde in a theatre with two other Brünnhildes relaxing in the canteen. I do, however, have pleasant memories of two top-quality contemporaries who fundamentally sang the same repertoire as mine.

To this day, Martha Mödl and Birgit Nilsson are still remembered amongst the most outstanding artists ever to sing the Wagnerian repertoire. As a matter of fact, for my generation, these two artists truly embody that hackneyed phrase "a legend in their own time." Any attempt to compare the three of us would be an exercise in futility; however, I think the time has come to record an appreciation of their artistry on the stage and some of the enjoyment we had together between performances. It might be worth noting that, apart from the "core curriculum" of Isolde, Brünnhilde, and one or two other heroines, there were very few Wagnerian parts all three of us sang.

Once I left the lighter roles—like Elsa, Eva, and Elisabeth—in the early 1950s, I never went back to them. Martha Mödl, who had switched from mezzo to dramatic soprano, never sang them in the first place. Birgit Nilsson, on the other hand, switched back and forth from the lighter to the heavier Wagnerian roles throughout her career, but never, to my knowledge, did she sing the part of Kundry, which Martha and I shared at Bayreuth, nor did either one of them make a specialty of Ortrud, which turned out to be my particular domain. This diversity of repertoires gave us an opportunity to sing with one another from time to time, especially at Bayreuth, where we spent several seasons together.

Birgit Nilsson retired from active performance several years ago and returned to Stockholm. Interestingly, we were born less than three weeks apart in the same year, 1918, and the same country, Sweden: I, as noted, on April 25 in Stockholm and Birgit on May 17 on a farm near Karup in the southwestern province of Skåne. Martha and I both live in Munich, which means we get to see a bit more of one another, but not all that much, because we both continue to maintain busy schedules.

Many operagoers look upon Wagnerian heroines as the province of austere ladies with no discernible sense of humor. The following story, I believe, proves otherwise. Martha and I were both in Bayreuth's small shopping center and happened to run into one another in front of a toy shop, which had tricycles on display out on the sidewalk. As we were both a little footsore from our shopping tour, we decided to take advantage of the tricycle seats to get a little rest. Soon we both developed an acute case of the sillies and began doing a kind of alternative ride of the Valkyries for the amused passersby. One spectator happened to be Siegfried Lauterwasser, the wonderful festival photographer, who recorded the event for posterity.

Naturally, there was much more to our relationship than peripheral monkeyshines. Our professional activity involved an enormous amount of intensive work, which both of us went at with a real vengeance. Martha has always been a great theatre person, with a kind of innate instinct for the dramatic moment. While I think of myself in that same context, our approaches to any given characterization couldn't have been more diverse. I build my characters layer by layer, tempering my natural instincts with the analytical blueprint I evolve. Martha, by contrast, seems to use her uncanny ability for putting the inex-

Martha Mödl and I practicing for act 3 of *Walküre*. *Siegfried Lauterwasser.*

haustible emotional intensity of her own personality directly into the passions of the characters she sings.

The result of her approach is an incorruptible authenticity of delineation and a profound sense of identification with the character's feelings, both intensified by a warm, rich voice featuring a lush lower register, like black velvet, which harkens back to her earlier career as a mezzo-soprano. The warmth of her voice, however, is also a clear manifestation of her warmhearted, outgoing private personality, which lends an effusive generosity to everything she sings. I always keep a certain percentage of my emotional energy in reserve, afraid I might otherwise lose control. This is a safety valve my mother insisted upon. Martha Mödl hurls herself totally into a role, never sparing herself for a moment in her theatrical zeal.

If Martha Mödl's delineation is the expression of her inner life-force, and my strategy may be described as based on a combination of instinct and analysis, Birgit Nilsson's approach to the same challenges was based almost exclusively on applying the radiance of her voice to full effect, especially those extraordinarily powerful high notes, which nobody in our generation ever matched. While fate had me singing leading roles at the Metropolitan in my early twenties, Birgit once told me her Wagnerian career began some eight years after my début, preceded by the usual European course of study at the Royal Conservatory in Stockholm and a series of non-Wagnerian appearances. Once she had gone beyond her native Sweden and burst onto the international scene, her career skyrocketed, crowned by her well-deserved success at the Vienna State Opera, where she dominated the scene for years.

Nilsson's pre-eminence in Vienna, incidentally, attests to both her undeniable vocal excellence and a negotiating skill that was even the equal of that consummate capitalist Herbert von Karajan, who was general director of the prestigious Austrian theatre at the time. In a *New Yorker* magazine profile published several years ago, Birgit told the story of one heavyweight bout in Karajan's office, where she, as usual, was handling her own salary discussions, not entrusting anything as fiscally crucial as her Wiener Staatsoper fee to the business acumen of "mere" agents. As the give-and-take between herself and Karajan progressed to something approaching verbal fisticuffs, the chain holding Birgit's necklace together suddenly snapped, sending pearls cascading all over the carpet. Karajan summoned several members of his entourage and ordered them to retrieve the pearls. While they were scrambling around, the maestro couldn't resist remarking sarcastically that they shouldn't miss a single one. After all, he said, these were doubtless the priceless natural pearls she purchased with her handsome fees from La Scala in Milan. Birgit instantly shot back that they were only cheap imitations she bought with the pittance she received from the Viennese. Obviously, they finally came to terms.

An encounter between the two of us in the Austrian capital points up the cordial nature of our relationship. I was in town to sing Ortrud in a couple of *Lohengrin* performances, while Birgit had come there to sing the title role in *Turandot*. One afternoon, we happened to meet on the Philharmonikergasse behind the theatre and, as both of us had time on our hands, we spontaneously decided to drop into the Sacher Hotel across the street for lunch. While we were enjoying our meal, she casually suggested we continue our conversation the following evening in her dressing room before the *Turandot* performance.

I couldn't believe anyone would want any backstage visitors before that onerous assignment, but she waved off my concern, saying it was just a few high C's, and once she had sent these clarion tones to the back of the house, the rest of the piece was clear sailing. Besides, she added, *Turandot* was far shorter than almost all of the Wagnerian roles she had to sing. After being solemnly assured that what other sopranos regard as the height of difficulty was a mere pushover for the special talents of Birgit Nilsson, I agreed to come by and keep her company for a few minutes on my way from rehearsal.

That evening, I discovered Birgit being helped to apply all the ornate appurtenances that traditionally go with the character of the Chinese princess. The elaborately adorned wig, the long fingernails, and so forth and so on, took up the greater part of an hour to put in place before her first brief, non-singing appearance in act 1. The conversation during this process revolved around one of Birgit's grandest passions: no, not opera—or concerts, for that matter—not even finance, but rather the Oriental carpet auctions she always enjoyed attending while she was in Vienna. As she was describing a particularly handsome rug she was coveting at the time, being careful to use her speaking voice as gently as possible, the door suddenly flew open, and Egon Hilpert, the director of the theatre, came striding in for his regular preperformance visit. Dr. Hilpert was so involved in exchanging the usual niceties with Mme Nilsson that at first he didn't noticed anyone else in the room. When he turned to go, he suddenly discovered me in the corner and emitted a shriek of amazement. While Birgit and I exchanged baffled looks, we heard Hilpert wandering down the hall, yelling: "Two *Hochdramatische* in one dressing room—in *my theatre!*" The story made the rounds, with everyone, in typical Viennese fashion, adding their own embellishments.

When I hear the often-bizarre tales of great operatic rivalries, most of them involving coloratura sopranos and tenors, I cannot help wondering why so few of them are ever told about our voice category. In the more than fifty years I have spent as a professional singer, I never found myself faced with the kind of underhanded competition that hounds the paths of so many singers in the lighter repertoire. Personally, I just like to think that big voices and big hearts go together.

It certainly attests to the sagacity of Wieland and Wolfgang Wagner that they had all three of us at the festival more or less simultaneously, each making her special contribution to their success and ours. Perhaps the best comparison of our separate qualities could be drawn from moments in a role all of us sang: Brünnhilde in *Götterdämmerung*. Birgit's phenomenal high notes, her dignity, and her deep sensitivity predominated in the scenes of romantic passion, such as the big act 1 duet and the final moments of the last act. One might say I held somewhat of an edge in the scenes of dramatic intensity, especially the fiery oath in act 2. But nobody could match the telling profundity of Martha's "Ruhe, du Gott!" toward the end of the Immolation Scene, majestically heralding the end of the epic tragedy and the dawn of a new era, to be dominated

The three Brünnhildes swap stories at a televised get-together in 1996. All of us are still going strong. *Bavarian Television Press Office.*

by a higher ethic. *Summa summarum:* all three of us created characterizations that were especially our own.

Neither Martha nor I would have touched Turandot, with which Birgit made operatic history. Martha Mödl's Kundry in Bayreuth had a personal identification with that many-faceted character which nobody else ever matched. As for myself, I think the part that best defined my contribution to the operatic stage was Ortrud. Or—was it Elektra?

Mending the Rift

On one of my rare lazy afternoons, the phone rang. Walter Legge, the ultimate recording impresario, a consummate entrepreneur with his finger in a vast array of musical pies, was on the other end of the line with a rather enigmatic query: would I, he wanted to know, be prepared to let bygones be bygones? When I asked him to be more specific, he advised me that Herbert von Karajan, with whom he maintained a highly profitable association, was planning to open the 1964 Salzburg Festival with a new production of Strauss's *Elektra*, adding that I was under serious consideration for the title role. The reason for his call was to ask if I would be willing to work with Maestro von Karajan again.

The question had me, quite candidly, baffled. Although I have never been the type to bear grudges, and certainly not on differences of artistic opinion, it was Karajan who had taken our problems at Bayreuth as a personal affront and had blacklisted me for years at the Vienna State Opera. If there was any-one to let bygones be bygones, it would have to be Karajan and not me. I had always had great respect for Walter Legge, who matched his commercial acu-men with an exhaustive knowledge of musical matters and the highest possible level of taste, and I was inclined to follow his advice on almost anything. But Karajan, of course, was another story.

This is why I first wanted to know if this casting was Mr. Legge's idea, as he seemed to be implying, or had Karajan merely delegated him to make the call? Legge assured me this was a decision they had thoroughly discussed with one another, and both of them were agreed, as he flatteringly put it, that I was the optimum casting for the role. There would be only one condition, he added before hanging up: Karajan was unwilling to discuss past differences. This seemed reasonable to me.

The offer of a Salzburg début in one of my best roles with the Vienna Philharmonic in the pit was tempting, both artistically and fiscally, and so I decided it would make sense to reassess the Karajan problem. Starting on the minus side, the spectre of having to beat my own rhythm in the palm of my hand while the maestro stood glowing in his own spotlight on the podium, communicating mystically and (for us mere mortals) incomprehensibly with the spheres, as he had during our work together on that Bayreuth *Tristan*, haunted my deliberations. On the plus side, a lot of water had passed under the bridge since the time when his strangely occult approach to the task of keeping a performance together had proven so frustrating to the cast.

His meditative posturing back then had been the cause of at least one possibly apocryphal anecdote, involving a performance he conducted for the no-nonsense audience at La Scala in Milan. As the story goes, Karajan emerged from the nether regions and gravely mounted the podium, where, after acknowledging the audience's tumultuous applause, he proceeded to sink into a deep and seemingly endless contemplation, his eyes tightly shut, and his head almost buried in his expressive hands. The great man was finally roused from his trance by the voice of a helpful patron in one of the upper balconies calling out, "Coraggio, Maestro, coraggio!"

At the time of the Salzburg offer, however, I hadn't heard any complaints about this kind of behavior recently, nor did any of the performances I listened to on the radio from Vienna sound disorganized. Karajan must have found what he was looking for in his trance and come out of it. As for myself, in the time since my first American Elektra, I had sung the role all over the European continent, including the opening performance of the final Munich Festival at the Prinzregententheater. The production was an enormous success and was carried over to the refurbished Nationaltheater when the company moved there the following winter. It was in the Nationaltheater where I was also accorded the honor of singing the title role in *Elektra* in a special performance on June 11, 1964, commemorating the one hundredth anniversary of the composer's birth. I thought to myself, were I to accept the Salzburg offer, the première would represent my fortieth Elektra onstage, not counting concert performances. If I had advanced to this degree, why shouldn't Karajan have undergone his own development?

There was another, more important consideration in favor of participating in the project. At the time we had first worked together, Karajan was an employee of the Bayreuth Festival, just as I was. This is a perfectly normal situation for any singer, but I have run across more than one conductor or stage director who feels impeded by having to take orders from anyone, yet functions perfectly well when in a position to give the orders. One example of this mindset was the General Manager of the Marseille Opera, Jacques Karpo, who staged one excellent production after another there, but hardly ever anywhere else. When I asked him why he seldom worked elsewhere, he claimed he simply could not function properly when his work was subject to the final approval of another theatre director. Perhaps the same jurisdictional factor was the case with Karajan, who now dominated both the Vienna State Opera and the Salzburg Festival, as well as holding control over a number of media ventures.

At the end of all this reflection, I decided I would accept Karajan's proposal in the spirit in which it had been offered and do my part to mend the rift that had kept us artistically segregated for over ten years, so I said yes to Mr. Legge and asked him for further procedural information. He told me the business people in his organization would first settle the financial side of things with my agent. Then Maestro von Karajan would like me to come to Vienna on a given date and wait in the anteroom of the director's office at the State Opera, where he would join me after completing a rehearsal. I presumed he wanted this meeting to run through the role with me, because he had a reputation, like many of his colleagues, for reviewing a part in an opera with any soloist, no matter how frequently that singer might have sung it, to make sure there were no insuperable conceptual differences. I can certainly understand that. No conductor wants to be faced with unpleasant surprises when rehearsals begin, nor does any singer.

I traveled from Munich to Vienna the day before our appointment and checked into the Sacher Hotel, picking up the tab for both the trip and the accommodation. I then spent a pleasant evening enjoying the excellent cuisine in the hotel and retired early to get a good night's sleep to bolster my fortitude for the encounter on the morrow. It was a beautiful, sunshiny day when I crossed the street and went up to the wing of the building where the members of the directorate have their offices. There I sat, reading theatre periodicals, while I waited for the maestro to arrive. Quite a while passed before he finally put in his appearance, wearing his usual turtleneck sweater, with his jacket slung casually over one shoulder. He didn't wear turtlenecks, incidentally, to create some kind of image, as popular opinion contended, but because he was afflicted with a chronic case of bursitis, not an atypical illness for conductors, and needed to keep his neck and shoulders warm.

For a moment, Karajan just stood at the far end of the corridor, making no move to come over to where I was sitting. Rather than wait on protocol, I decided to rise and meet him halfway between my seat and the door, which was where we shook hands and exchanged opening courtesies along with the usual questions as to one another's health and well-being. We both then went into a room and sat down. Karajan ran through the general details on rehearsals and performances, which I duly noted, and that was that. Then, without even mentioning the opera, Karajan excused himself and wended his way into the inner office, while I wended my own way back to the hotel to pack and return to Munich. And so a unilateral ten-year stalemate quietly came to an end.

Meanwhile, contract negotiations had begun. I had told my agent that I insisted upon receiving the highest fee payable to a solo singer in Salzburg at that time, which eventuated a lot of hemming and hawing from the management side of the negotiating process, but I stood firm. It was clear to me that this was likely to be the only opera I would ever perform in Salzburg, and I wanted to be adequately compensated for my services. Once the business details had been settled to my satisfaction, I began to look forward to my stay in Salzburg.

When I drove into the city in midsummer, I was greeted with a light drizzle, which, on the frequent occasions when it occurs, invariably casts somewhat of a pall over the enjoyment of an otherwise impressive locale.

Rehearsing with Karajan, who both staged and conducted the opera, clearly reluctant to share one iota of authority with anyone else, was an experience for all parties concerned. In addition to myself, the cast included Martha Mödl, returning to the mezzo repertoire after many years as a dramatic soprano, singing the part of my mother, Klytämnestra; Hildegard Hillebrecht as a young Chrysothemis; Eberhard Wächter as a handsome Orest; and James King as an attractive Ägisth. Salzburg being Salzburg, all the supporting roles were cast with first-rank singers.

Over the years since performing the role of Elektra with Dimitri Mitropoulos in concert, I had subjected my interpretation to an ongoing refinement process. I had also had an opportunity to visit the ruins of ancient Mycenae, where the story allegedly took place. There I intensely felt the atmosphere of the warm breezes, whispering through the sparse, dry vegetation above the eternal sands on the lonely plateau where the original lion gate of the royal palace still stands. As I listened to the sound of that lonely wind, I felt virtually transported back to the era of those tragic events. From that moment on, I knew that this sensation would be an inseparable part of my characterization. Whenever I interpreted her desolation, all I had to do, before I started singing, was to recall the emotion I had felt on that visit to Mycenae. In short, by the time I began the Salzburg rehearsals, I was already steeped in both the ancient Greek traditions and the Viennese fin-de-siècle background of the opera, but, as always, I was still willing and eager to continue to add new layers to my own image of Elektra.

As luck would have it, Karajan's once-autocratic attitude had mellowed to one of sharing the responsibility for artistic decision making, which made our discussions richly productive. For example, he drew an idea from *The Libation Bearers*, the second play in the *Oresteia* trilogy of Aeschylus, the oldest known source of the story of the House of Atreus and, in fact, one of the first plays ever written. In Aeschylus's version, Electra comes to her father's tomb regularly with the mourning *Choëphoroe*, bearing funeral libations, and lays a lock of her hair on the sepulchre as an offering, symbolizing a sacrifice of her female beauty to the memory of her murdered father.

Before we started rehearsing, Karajan asked if I would be amenable to doing a short-haired Elektra, basing his request on what I considered his thoroughly viable approach. We both agreed that Elektra's close-cropped hair emphasized her complete devotion to her mission, adding a poignant note when she speaks wistfully of having once had hair so lush, it had caused men to tremble. Now she has destroyed her beauty in order to keep the once-covetous eyes of men away from her.

The interplay between voices and instruments was an element Karajan passionately cultivated. He knew that I had such responsiveness to what he was doing that he could use my voice at times solely as an instrument. His fondness for refining the music and bringing out its delicate points (which became an obsession in his later years) led us at one juncture to a difference of opinion. There were one or two phrases I wanted to sing with sharp sarcasm, when I made reference to my mother, and when I taunt Chrysothemis for what I perceive as her egoistic self-preoccupation, to the detriment of the noble task that lies before us. This choice of intonation went against Karajan's grain, and he asked me to be less sarcastic, because he felt my sarcasm might verge on vulgarity.

Frankly, I didn't agree then, and I still don't. Elektra virtually cuts her mother's reputation to shreds when she hurls scorn at the degeneracy she attributes to the older woman's conduct, as well as that of Ägisth, the character she pejoratively refers to as her mother's paramour, almost constantly refusing even to utter his name. I see no point in holding back in those passages, and my own aesthetic would never allow me to overact the role to the extent of vulgarity. I felt Karajan was being oversensitive. Nevertheless, he was adamant, and so, rather than rock the boat, I decided I would seek a compromise to keep us both happy, while perhaps providing myself with one of those alternative approaches to a characterization that could prove useful under certain circumstances. I subdued the harsh sarcasm of my diction into something subtly, acerbically cynical, underplaying what Karajan looked upon as "vulgarity" in favor of pointing up muted contempt in such phrases as "Tochter meiner Mutter" (daughter of my mother).

Singing with that most elite of all orchestras, the Vienna Philharmonic, was an unforgettable experience. Those musicians can emit the kind of inner radiance that occurs when the sun rises over one of the crystalline lakes in the Salzkammergut region around Salzburg, setting the ever-changing colors dancing on the surface of the water. In short, every participant was a professional of the highest order. Yet, despite all this expertise, Karajan had an odd rehearsal practice, which was detrimental to my work. In order "to save our voices" during staging sessions, Karajan made us act to the sound of a commercial recording that had been made with other singers. The soprano singing my role on the recording made several musical errors, which would slowly have etched themselves into my memory, ultimately confusing me to the point where I might have carried over those mistakes into my own performance. Luckily, I was able to convince the maestro that I had sufficient routine in "marking" to handle the rehearsals without depleting my vocal resources in the process, and I managed to get him to drop using the recording when I was singing.

Finally it was time for the full dress rehearsal. When I entered my dressing room, I saw an enormous bouquet of magnificent long-stemmed red roses on the table. Attached to it was an envelope, which I was superstitiously hesitant to open until after the rehearsal had concluded, just as any good trouper keeps mail unopened until the final curtain has fallen, fearful of having a performance thrown by a preoccupation with unexpected news: good, bad, or indifferent. Noticing my reluctance to look at the message, my dresser said she thought it would be all right for me to open the envelope on this particular occasion, which I did, discovering a message from Karajan, thanking me for the wonderful rehearsal time we had shared, and adding that he wanted me to return for a revival of this *Elektra* production in the following year's festival. Considering we hadn't even premièred the production, I thought this was an unusually gracious gesture from the maestro. For me, it eradicated any vestige that might have remained of our previous difficulties.

When I returned to my hotel after a very satisfactory dress rehearsal, I received a telephone call from Munich. Herbert List, who did double duty as stage director and administrative manager of the Bavarian State Opera in Munich, was on the other end of the line. Mr. List charmingly wished me every possible success at my Salzburg première on August 11. Then, in the same breath, he suggested I save a bit of voice during the performance, because he needed me to replace an indisposed Inge Borkh as Elektra at the Nationaltheater on August 14, only three days after the Salzburg première, and another three days before the next Salzburg performance on August 17. I must confess, that request certainly took a bit of the bloom off his good wishes for my first-ever appearance at the Salzburg Festival. For a moment, envisioning the stresses and strains involved, I was tempted to invoke my guest status at the Munich Opera and refuse his summons, but being a member of a theatrical family, I took the injunction "the show must go on" with due seriousness. After all, Inge Borkh would have done the same for me. It goes without saying that I *did not* save my voice in Salzburg, nor did the cheering audience!

The following year, after the last curtain call for the closing performance of the revived production, I received evidence that Maestro von Karajan felt that this *Elektra* represented such an apex of quality in his artistic career, and exerted such a powerful emotional impact on him, that he did not wish to conduct the opera ever again. Certainly this was a flattering remark for all of us, but I must admit that, at the time, I took this declaration with a grain of salt. I presumed that, farther down the road, he might encounter an inspiring soprano whose excellence might tempt him to forget his decision. But he never conducted *Elektra* again.

In 1992, the Salzburg Festival released a commemorative Austrian Radio aircheck recording of the *Elektra* performance, for which they asked me to reduce my royalty claims, so that a portion of the proceeds could be used for the benefit of the Festival. This recording was one of several releases of Salzburg performances issued under the title "Festival Documents." While I was happy to do something for the institution, I cannot help hoping that, although some of the proceeds from this recording may be benefiting the current turn the Festival has taken, the recording itself may eventually act as a kind of example of what a great music festival can be when the essence of the score stands as the basis of the production.

It was a source of satisfaction to both of us that we had finally mended the rift that first came about in Bayreuth, but fate never brought Herbert von Karajan and me together again.

The Spice of Life

WHEN I WAS FIRST at the Metropolitan, principal sopranos and tenors like Traubel and Melchior hardly ever touched anything but Wagner, an attitude strongly supported by the management, which made a point of keeping the artists in the various wings separate. For me, not only was variety the spice of life, I also felt that every time I got away from Wagnerian music, I invariably returned to it with new insights. The most important non-Wagnerian role I performed was Leonore in Ludwig van Beethoven's *Fidelio*, which I sang fifty-seven times over a period of fifteen years, extending from my first performance on October 19, 1951, in San Francisco to my final Leonore in Munich on October 25, 1966.

The great Beethoven's only operatic work, with its profound commitment to humanity and justice and its straightforward dramatic style, devoid of most of the conventional vocal and theatrical adornments, ushered in a completely new form of operatic utterance. Today, there is a tendency to discredit the libretto of *Fidelio*, calling it hackneyed and unbelievable, particularly in the depiction of the leading character, whose disguise as a young man seems so convincing that the jailer's daughter, Marzelline, has actually become infatuated with "him," and her father, Rocco, who is all too eager to turn over his daughter to this enterprising "youth." Regarded in the framework of its time of creation, however, this element takes on telling plausibility.

The subordinate status accorded to women in pre-twentieth-century society was so firmly entrenched that they often had to masquerade as men to realize their personal visions. Consider the many Shakespearean female characters who needed to disguise themselves as men to be taken seriously. In the nineteenth century, great authors like George Sand and George Eliot hid behind masculine pen names to avoid rejection in the male-dominated literary world of the day. Fanny Mendelssohn-Hensel, strictly prohibited by her social-climbing father from "stepping out of line" by having her music printed, published several works under the name of her better-known younger brother, Felix Mendelssohn-Bartholdy. In the dramatic and operatic literature of the nineteenth century, the spectacle of a woman posing as a boy or man to avoid danger can be found in a fair number of works. Think of Gilda in act 4 of *Rigoletto* or the frightened Leonora in act 2 of *La Forza del Destino*, to mention only two of many examples.

Beyond its touching tribute to female ingenuity, however, the element of *Fidelio* that most appealed to me was the universality of the character's devotion to the cause of humanity. In act 2, Leonore descends to a subterranean dungeon, where innocent political prisoners are held captive by a totalitarian despot. Her mission is to rescue her husband, if indeed he is the mysterious prisoner kept isolated and near starvation there, but the light is so dim she cannot recognize his features. Yet she extends her feeling for her husband's plight to all persons in this predicament. It is in this moment of profound compassion that her fundamental sense of human decency in the face of arbitrary injustice comes to the fore, prompting her to state, in a steadily intensifying repetition: "Whoever you are, I shall rescue you." Whenever I sang that phrase, I always felt a very special identification with Leonore, going beyond her established objective toward the goal of making a selfless contribution to the redemption of all humanity from the shackles of oppression.

Just as the attribute of self-sacrifice, inherent in the roles of Fidelio, Elisabeth, and Senta, appealed to me, I must confess a certain attraction toward portraying ladies of a more sinister bent, because these portrayals called for an intense exercise of my imagination. Knowing that Wagner's "bad ladies" were limited to Ortrud in *Lohengrin* and Kundry in the second scene of act 2 of *Parsifal*, I had to turn to other composers to bring my operatic villainy to the fore. Lady Macbeth was one of my favorites. After the initial performances at the Florence Maggio Musicale in 1951, I continued to sing the role in regular seasons at other theatres, the Deutsche Oper am Rhein in particular.

One of my first departures from the traditional soprano repertoire was the conniving character of Herodias in *Salome*, which I sang for the first time at the Deutsche Oper Berlin on December 13, 1962, right in the middle of my

At the start of my career, Leonore was a role I kept away from. Later, I sang it so often, I had my own costume made. *Sabine Toepffer.*

dramatic soprano career. At the time, it was a somewhat daring piece of casting, as audiences associated me more with parts like Isolde and Brünnhilde, but, as the record would ultimately show, the circumstances justified the decision made by Wieland Wagner that I was the right person for his concept. Wieland had engaged a svelte young soprano by the name of Anja Silja on the basis of a youthful quality he felt would add new dimensions to the interpretation of certain Wagnerian roles. Anja was no stranger to me, as we had already joined forces at Bayreuth, where her portrayal of Elsa, somewhat reminiscent of my own ideas about the role, served as a viable counterpoint to my Ortrud. Wieland envisioned Herodias as the great, omnipresent mother figure who stands onstage as a dominant force in the action from the time of her entrance to the end of the opera. He needed a strong personality to help create a foreboding mood, like a dark shadow cast across the stage, even when she is not at the center of activity.

The whole idea of moving from the title role, which I had stopped singing in 1952, some ten years before Wieland's offer, to the part of Herodias intrigued me on a number of levels. First of all, two outstanding Salomes had come on the scene, both of whom possessed the prerequisites of looking child-like while being able to come to terms with the vocal difficulties of the score. Anja Silja was one of them. Felicia Weathers, with whom I later sang, was the other. On the other hand, ladies capable of portraying Herodias were few and far between, and the thought of trying a new kind of role, which might ultimately prove marketable, also interested me.

Many operatic productions are conceived to emphasize the talents of a certain singer. In Wieland Wagner's *Salome*, however, for all the stresses placed on the individual characters, it was the huge cistern in the middle of the stage that completely dominated the production. Everyone's attention was rooted on that cistern, and the impact—positive or negative—its prisoner, John the Baptist, had on all the others. The cistern was the fulcrum of all the action, the center of the earth. If we accept the original element of a Christian parable in the opera, which I certainly do, this was the logical placement of dramatic weight. My work on Herodias helped me discover an added aspect of my theatrical personality that still holds true to this day. Put the right artistic carrot in front of my nose, and I'll run for it.

By far the most fascinating excursions I made from the beaten path of Wagnerian music during this period involved new works. For an experimenter like myself, it was an exciting exploration into virgin territory to be able to première a brand-new work such as Carl Orff's version of the ancient Sophocles classic *Ödipus der Tyrann*, or participate in an early definition of a new composition, as I did with *Der Besuch der alten Dame*, Gottfried von Einem's setting of the twentieth-century classic by Friedrich Dürrenmatt.

When the world première of Orff's version, based on a German poetic translation by Friedrich Hölderlin, was being planned for December 11, 1959, at the State Theatre in Stuttgart, I was offered the role of Jokasta opposite Gerhard Stolze in the title role. Initially, I was quite uneasy as to whether I would be able to do justice to the part. This was one of the composer's later works, and in it he abandoned much of the melodic lyricism of earlier pieces like *Carmina Burana* for a severe, declamatory style that involved almost as much speaking as singing. Gerhard Stolze had been an actor on the legitimate stage before launching his career as a tenor, and German was, of course, his native tongue. While I had spoken German virtually all my life, and certainly had no pronunciation problems in my singing roles, the idea of having to declaim much of Hölderlin's classic text in spoken German, with a slight accent that isn't easy to pinpoint (although it is clearly not native German), and then switch over to singing an unusually precarious tessitura, with three high C's, and finally having to scream in excruciating pain preceding Jokasta's offstage suicide all made me a bit hesitant. That little bromide about God helping those who help themselves has always held me in good stead professionally, as was the case with this work. What ultimately convinced me to accept was Günther Rennert's remark that my accent would give an interesting hue to Jokasta's speaking voice.

The composer, with his refined but spicy sense of humor, was an enjoyable gentleman to have around. A true Bavarian, with a bucolic spirit and his feet firmly planted on the ground, Orff was anything but the ethereal figure that has become the cliché of creative artists. Apparently, he had great faith in both Rennert and conductor Ferdinand Leitner, because he never became heavily involved in our preparatory work. He once showed up in a rehearsal room, where we were hoping he would illustrate some of the tempi he wanted. When he sat down at the piano, however, he played the passages so rapidly, we thought he was trying to give us a demonstration of keyboard virtuosity. He didn't seem particularly distressed when we went back to rehearsing in the slower tempo we had become used to.

Possibly the highest tribute our production received came when the Stuttgart company was invited to perform this German version of a keystone of Hellenic dramatic literature in the Herode Attikou arena at the foot of the Acropolis in Athens. We were rather timorous about presenting this legend at its birthplace, so to speak, *and in German,* but the audience, which knew every word of the story in the original Greek, went wild over our rendition. Stolze and I later repeated our roles in a new production in the composer's native city of Munich, where we were received with the same enthusiasm.

Der Besuch der alten Dame ranks as one of the seminal plays of the twentieth century. This macabre tale of unrelenting vengeance and large-scale corruptibility has seen a number of important productions, featuring as wide a variety of actresses in the title role as Therese Giehse in Munich, Lynn Fontanne both on Broadway and in the London West End, and Ingrid Bergman in an unfortunately watered-down film version. Like the Munich *Ödipus* production, the launching of *Der Besuch der alten Dame* was also very much of a hometown affair, with two almost simultaneous productions, in deference to the two different native cities of the composer and the dramatist, who, incidentally, had been born only a few miles apart, von Einem in Bern, Switzerland, and Dürrenmatt in Konolfingen, a small village located a few miles to the southeast of the capital.

Von Einem, however, had been taken by his family to Austria while still a small child, and had come to be known as a native Austrian composer. The Vienna State Opera served as the cradle of this work, just as it had for his previous theatrical compositions, *Dantons Tod,* based on the Georg Büchner play, and his setting of the Franz Kafka story *Der Prozess.* The Vienna world première took place in May 1971, featuring Christa Ludwig in the title role, in a production directed by Otto Schenk.

Four months later, on September 5, 1971, the first performance in playwright Dürrenmatt's native Switzerland opened at the Zurich Opera, in a staging by Harry Buckwitz, an expert German director who frequently crossed over from drama to opera and back again. While Mr. Buckwitz had a keen sense of theatrical possibilities, our Zurich production had the additional benefit of the playwright's regular presence during rehearsals. Friedrich Dürrenmatt was a wise and witty man with a thoroughgoing knowledge of theatre, attested to by both his long catalogue of audience-provoking plays and his theoretical writings on theatrical subjects. His remarkable story, with its social and political allegories, lays bare the foibles of small-minded villagers, leaving the members of any audience to review their own moral priorities at the end.

For this multifaceted story, Einem selected an eclectic musical style, which earned him the wrath of certain critics, who accused him of plagiarism. This sort of thing happens to any composer who is not born, like Mozart, with a brand-new style of music writing in his brain, but even Mozart saw fit to help himself to the occasional musical theme from Johann Christian Bach or Carl Friedrich Abel or Franz Joseph Haydn, and it was what he did with that thematic material which made him the master he was. Long before rehearsals began in Zurich, I decided to visit Vienna to see how Mr. Schenk and Mme Ludwig were handling the character, and to see if I could use any of their ideas in my own interpretation.

Claire Zachanassian, the old lady of the title, suffers from a severe disability, eventuated by a partial amputation of one arm and one leg. In the Vienna production, that disability was so heavily stressed that, in my opinion, Claire's walking problems made her less dangerous than she is drawn in the text. For all my admiration of Christa Ludwig's work, I felt that here she had been somewhat misguided. Then again, perhaps I had missed something in my own preparations.

When I approached Mr. Dürrenmatt with my problem, he assured me that Claire, being one of the richest women in the world, would certainly have consulted the finest orthopedists she could find to reconstitute her lost limbs prosthetically. Beyond this, with a clear sense of personal dignity, she would exert every effort to hold herself as sedately as possible, with her disabilities coming visibly to the fore only in those moments when her thirst for revenge has excited her beyond her usual rigid self-control. Only this way, he felt, could I stress his point that, while her body may have been destroyed to some degree on the outside, the true destruction was housed within her in the form of her single-minded dedication to her sinister plan.

After both productions had been premièred, the protagonists from the two casts switched back and forth with one another, bringing Christa Ludwig to the Zurich staging and taking me to Vienna. Prior to my first Vienna performance, I asked for a rehearsal with Otto Schenk to clarify his concept. I was baffled at his reluctance to take time off from whatever else he was doing at the time to get together with me. When we finally met, he simply told me to jiggle my leg and arm a great deal to stress the disability and, apart from that, to be inscrutably stone-faced. This certainly didn't concur with Dürrenmatt's version.

The idea of creating an opera for the special talents of an unusually gifted singing actor or actress has almost faded into oblivion in favor of a greater occupation with academically oriented structures and combinations. I think this is unfortunate, and while I will certainly never have another chance to help bring an author's new work to life, as I did with Carl Orff's and Gottfried von Einem's pieces, it would please me to think that future generations of composers and librettists might take their inspirational cues from the talents of the collaborating artists on the stage.

SCENE EIGHT

Crossing the Rubicon

STARTING AT THE END of the 1950s, the late John Culshaw of Decca Records (London Records in the United States) began organizing a mammoth project to make the first studio recording of the *Ring* in its entirety, under the direction of Georg Solti. As the production neared its conclusion with preparations for *Götterdämmerung*, Mr. Culshaw recalls in his memoirs, *Ring Resounding*, that he approached me to sing the role of Waltraute, and, as he says, for reasons he never understood, I declined his kind offer. I think it is time to clarify the point.

At the time of the *Götterdämmerung* recording, I was at the apex of my soprano career, and I felt it would have been poor tactics to accept a mezzo-contralto role like Waltraute, especially on a medium as permanent as a recording, because managers and theatres might have drawn the wrong conclusions. After consultation with my own manager, who advised me not to venture into this repertoire prematurely, I felt honor-bound to say no to the Decca contract. Too bad the offer came too soon . . .

A short time before Wieland Wagner's tragic death in 1966, at the age of only forty-nine, he had proposed that I sing Fricka in a *Ring* cycle he was in the process of planning, but death intervened, and the production never happened. My faith in Wieland's judgment on my capabilities was so strong that I would have done the role for him, knowing I could have returned at will to anything else I might have been doing at the time. And so I went on singing my Brünnhildes and Elektras, et cetera.

As the 1970s began, I became aware of a gradual change affecting my vocal technique. While my voice had added lustre in the lower and middle registers, I was beginning to lose some of the ease with which I had formerly been able to negotiate the extreme top notes. This is a common phenomenon among professional singers, a natural development every one of us has to face sooner or later. The human voice has a certain similarity to wine. No wine ever gets lighter with time. On the contrary, it settles and becomes heavier and fuller-bodied, adding a richness it did not have when it was young. Just as the voice changes with age, so too, the flexibility of the throat and thorax muscles is affected by the passage of years.

Unfortunately, there are no hard-and-fast rules for dealing with this development. With some singers, changes come about early. With others, they come later. We may be able to postpone the inevitable for a while by first taking some time off from performing and then rebuilding our vocal technique. If two years fail to restore the previous vocal ability, then the change is irreversible, and it is imperative to think seriously about the future.

Several roads are open to singers in this situation. First, as hard as this may sound, it may be the wisest policy to consider retirement. Second, many singers have found their niche by passing on their knowledge to aspiring young performers. Third, a repertoire change to a lower register can be achieved if the voice and the acting personality lend themselves to the new roles. Finally, a singer may have the good fortune to be able to add a limited extension to his or her present career.

For example, sopranos and tenors specializing in the Italian and French repertoires have been known to attenuate their performing life by transposing the music containing their most exposed top notes a half to a full step down in pitch. In fact, there is a recording of forty tenors singing the stretta "Di quella pira" from *Trovatore*, and it is interesting to note how they move up and down the scale depending on the security of their high C. This tactic, however, is virtually impossible in Wagner's works (except perhaps for Brünnhilde's battle cry in the second act of *Walküre*). The complex musical continuity of Wagnerian compositional style simply does not allow for arbitrary transpositions to interrupt the harmonic flow.

When decision making in my career became imperative in the early 1970s I had already been commuting, so to speak, for several years between the standard dramatic soprano repertoire and some of the roles shared between heavier-voiced sopranos and mezzo-sopranos. The latter roles were beginning to become more and more appealing to me, however, largely because of their acting values. My first taste of this transition had come about in 1962, as I said before, with Herodias, which is one of those roles that can be sung with equal effectiveness by either a soprano or a mezzo. This also applies to Kundry and Ortrud.

On May 24, 1963, I was accorded the honor of being made a Bavarian *Kammersängerin*, a title once bestowed by the nobility on those singers whose service to the theatre and whose consistent quality of performance entitled them to the privilege of performing for the nobles in camera, that is to say, at official court ceremonies. Unfortunately, the title of *Kammersänger*, in some cases, has an ancillary significance of being inducted into the operatic senior citizens' community, a kind of first step to oblivion. With some of my most prestigious soprano performances still ahead of me (remember, the Salzburg *Elektra* was yet to come in 1964), oblivion was not something I had to consider.

Gradually, I began getting more and more offers to exert my interpretive approach on character parts—in other words, roles that demanded heavier stresses on delineating the *characters* of more mature individuals. One of these was the Kostelnička Buryjovka, the sextoness in Leoš Janáček's "scenes from Moravian country life," *Jenůfa*, a classic crossover role. The mother in Humperdinck's *Hänsel und Gretel* is another good case in point of a *Kammersängerin* part, usually accorded to an Isolde of yesteryear, who lends weight, often in more ways than one, to this maternal character. When I did my first *Hänsel und Gretel* mother in Munich on December 5, 1968, the same year as my first Kostelnička in London, I was fully able to take the exposed high B in this role with the same ease I had with the Brünnhilde I sang in Düsseldorf only two evenings later.

As I slowly moved into the character repertory, beginning to appreciate what a wonderful future lay before me with these roles, the thought of one day saying good-bye to my soprano career took on an almost enjoyable aspect. I had already taken my leave of Kundry on November 1, 1967. On July 12, 1969, I sang my final *Siegfried* Brünnhilde, bidding a reluctant farewell to Elektra on December 10 of the same year in Munich. The following year witnessed my final *Walküre* Brünnhilde on November 15 in Düsseldorf. My last *Götterdämmerung* Brünnhilde took place in Stuttgart on February 7, 1971.

The final move started innocuously enough. I just happened to be working in Vienna and found myself in the corridor on the executive office level waiting to see someone in the rehearsal department to get one of my rehearsals rescheduled. While I waited, the deputy director of the theatre, Dr. Egon Seefehlner, came down the corridor. He imparted to me the happy news that he had been appointed to assume the post of *Intendant* at the Deutsche Oper Berlin. He then went on to say he had been planning to contact me with an offer to inaugurate his first season at the Berlin theatre in the role of Klytemnästra in *Elektra* with Ursula Schröder-Feinen in the title role. My spontaneous response was, "I see no reason why not." That seemingly casual decision was, as always in my career, not the consequence of a momentary whim, but the result of some serious consideration. When I stopped performing the title role, I began studying Klytemnästra, just in case. When I reached the point where I was sure I could encompass the requirements of the part, I simply waited for what I hoped would be the inevitable invitation. Dr. Seefehlner's offer generated a move that had to come.

In accepting the role of Klytemnästra, I was crossing my own operatic Rubicon, making an irrevocable step which bore no comparison to the other character roles I had sung, roles that allowed me to enjoy so many years as a crossover artist. While Herodias, the Kostelnička Burjovka, and a few others were parts that were equally suitable to the talents of a mezzo and a soprano, Klytemnästra had been written for the contralto voice, in fact for the woman who defined contralto singing for her generation throughout one of the longest singing careers (fifty-nine years) in music history, Ernestine Schumann-Heink.

Having said "yes," I proceeded to seal the agreement by asking Dr. Seefehlner when he planned to première the production. He replied that the first performance would be taking place on September 12, 1972. For a moment he looked at me, and I looked at him. I then added that I was very poor at remembering specific dates, asking him if he would be kind enough to put the details down on a piece of paper. He took a piece of scrap paper and scribbled, "September 12, 1972, Klytemnästra," and then he automatically signed his name at the bottom of the paper. I thanked him most sincerely, assured him we would come to terms, and stuck the scrap of paper in my purse. Shortly afterward, I showed Dr. Seefehlner's note to my agent and asked him, "Is this tantamount to a contract?" He replied in the affirmative and proceeded to negotiate terms. And that's how it came about.

Right from the start of my association with the Berlin Opera on September 6, 1951, that company had often been a venue for my premières. Apart from Schröder-Feinen and myself, the 1972 cast of *Elektra* featured Caterina Ligendza as Chrysothemis and José van Dam as Orest in a production directed by the distinguished German stage, screen, and television actor Ernst Schröder, all under the baton of the Paris-born American conductor Lorin Maazel.

Throughout what I have come to regard as my "second career," I have never

Klytämnestra, in a magnificent production by Ernst Schröder in Berlin, was my first and loveliest version of the role. *Deutsche Oper Berlin.*

pretended to be a mezzo-soprano or a contralto, despite the fact that I sang parts generally assigned to those voice categories. While I moved the center of my vocal gravity down a few notes, I continued to sing in the same soprano voice I used for all my other roles, without any attempt to apply any artificial tricks to darken my voice beyond its own natural color, which had already been darker in tone than the average dramatic soprano, starting right from my first Sieglinde in 1941.

The switch from a strictly soprano repertoire to this second career had been an organic process running almost a decade, so that my voice was able to encompass every note Klytemnästra is called upon to sing with ease and confidence. A few days before the scheduled opening night of this production, I received an urgent message to call the head of the administration office, Mr. Siegfried Müssig, who asked me to come over to the theatre immediately. In his office, he informed me that Mme Schröder-Feinen had become indisposed, and that it was uncertain whether she would be able to sing the première. The hills, he added, had been scoured as usual. While a reasonable selection of Klytemnästras had been found, nobody who could do justice to the title role would be free that evening.

The request was clear: could I turn the mother's role over to another singer and assume the lead again after a three-year hiatus from the role, starting in 1969? I frankly couldn't answer the question straight off and asked for a couple of hours to think the matter over. I then returned to my hotel, lay down on the bed, and contemplated the pros and cons of the issue. After an hour or so, I called Mr. Müssig and thanked him for his kind offer. I then went on to explain to him that I had taken my leave of Elektra at the height of success, and I felt there was no point in trying to go backward. Therefore, I would regretfully have to decline.

Fortunately Mme Schröder-Feinen recovered her health and was able to join us on opening night. As for myself and my operatic future, the die was cast.

➲ *Act IV*

THE SECOND CAREER

There Is a Season

Probably the most exciting thing about my move from leading soprano to character roles was the fact that there was nothing all that exciting about it. I have always tried to set reasonable goals for myself along the way, and have then gone methodically about the business of implementing them. It's all a little reminiscent of the old joke about the Texan on his first trip to Manhattan, who approaches a venerable rabbi on Broadway and Fifty-seventh Street and asks him how to get to Carnegie Hall. "Practice," answers the wise man, "practice!" And I have been practicing my craft all my life.

The switch-over was basically as simple as the elementary but profound wisdom we find in the Book of Ecclesiastes: "For every thing there is season, and a time to every purpose under heaven." In my career, one season had simply come to a gradual end, and another was getting started. This principle held true for my vocal development as well. I had no need to go into an extended vocal retraining to sing my new roles. My voice simply moved into place, leaving me free to embark on my new repertoire. As I delved into this repertoire, however, rather than being appalled at the volume of work at an age when many sopranos are starting to wind down, I was more than grateful that these mature characterizations were giving me a second career, which would prove as full of fascination as the first. Moreover, the length of the second career almost matched that of the first one.

"Opera as theatre" had come a long way since my first Sieglinde in New York back in 1941. Innovative theatrical ideas were beginning to hold their own alongside musical values. Whereas in the past I had been occasionally hampered by diehard traditionalists, with little or no interest in the acting side of opera, I was now being *encouraged* to continue what I had always done: to rethink the characters in terms of their own inner dynamic and seek new ideas within myself, which both made sense to me as a performer and, more important, increased the tension within the drama itself.

Herodias and Klytämnestra were two intriguing cases in point. Historical and literary study, as always, provided excellent guidelines, especially now that I was playing one woman who had really lived and another who figures significantly in the most ancient mythology of the Western world and may very possibly also have lived. Both Herodias and Klytämnestra are princesses of royal blood. They have been thoroughly trained in the kind of demeanor that goes with that social stratum. This accounts for their noble bearing and self-control even in the extreme situations of the drama. The most important factor is: both of these women have legitimate grievances, which have to be taken at face value by the artist singing the roles.

The issue in Herodias's day was no different from the controversy raging throughout the world today under the general heading of "family values." In fact, I am firmly convinced that *nothing has changed since the beginning of recorded history except the clothing styles!* While average Judaeans, like common citizens of almost any other time and place, saw a dominant religion and a stable home life as the basis of all society and looked to their leaders to set a virtuous example, the Romans and their influential Judaean friends were worshiping a whole pantheon of gods, marrying incestuously, changing husbands and wives like clothing, and using their domestic situations as a vital tool in achieving their power ambitions.

Herodias was the granddaughter of King Herod the Great and the wife of one of her half-uncles, Herodes Philippos. On the death of King Herod the Great, his realm was divided by Caesar Augustus into four sections and distributed among his sons. Shortly after this division was made, a game of musical thrones took place, during which Herodes Antipas divorced his first wife, the daughter of the Arab King Aretas, and married Herodias, who didn't get around to divorcing Philippos until shortly after formalizing her union with Antipas. Whatever the reasons for Herodias's change of husband, there must clearly have been a great deal of affection and loyalty involved. How do we know this? Years later, when a number of intrigues and failed power plays had finally precipitated Herodes' downfall, he was exiled by Emperor Caligula to Gaul and replaced by Herodias's brother, Agrippa I, who immediately offered

Herodias, here with Gerhard Stolze as Herodes, was my own personal record—213 performances. *Sabine Toepffer.*

Herodias an opportunity to remain with him at the Galilean court or to establish herself in Rome. Herodias refused, preferring to follow her husband into
banishment.

At the time of the biblical *Salome* story, Herodes' dominion is imperiled by
adverse reaction to his claims to his brother Archelaos's royal throne in Judaea
and Samaria, in addition to reprisal threats from King Aretas, the father of his
first wife. In this precarious political situation, the "powers that be" cannot
afford to allow a clash of cultures, as manifested by the Baptist's condemna-
tion of Herodias, to unsettle the security of the realm. Beyond this, Oscar
Wilde's Herodias is keenly resentful of being castigated for marital behavior
that the dominant Roman society considers quite normal and proper. She
finds her husband's respect for the Baptist, whom he regards as a holy man,
incomprehensible. For her, the cistern is a symbol of needless compromise,

because, as she sees it, this self-styled prophet is being held captive when he should have been summarily executed like any other rabble-rouser. Herodes' squeamishness over Jokanaan's possible holiness, Herodias tells him, is meaningless in the face of the condemnations hurled at the Baptist by the high priests of Jokanaan's own religion. By investing this historical knowledge into the foundations of the operatic characterization, we have a good chance of achieving a three-dimensional, humanly credible personality.

There is a fascinating parallel between the conclusion of Wilde's *Salomé* and the beginning of the Klytämnestra legend. *Salomé* ends with a mother losing her daughter, whereas it is the sacrifice of Klytämnestra's eldest daughter, Iphigeneia, long before the beginning of the *Elektra* opera, which sets off the chain of fateful events reaching far beyond the final curtain. A number of plays and operas have treated the events on the island of Aulis, where Agamemnon and his fleet have been stranded by the absence of favorable winds on their way to participate in the war against Troy. When Calchas, the high priest, tells the Mycenaean king he must make a sacrifice to Artemis, goddess of the winds, Agamemnon sends for Klytämnestra and Iphigeneia under the pretext that the daughter is to be betrothed to Achilles on Aulis. When the two women reach the island, Klytämnestra is horrified to discover that Iphigeneia is to be sacrificed to the gods. Even before this sacrifice was made, Klytämnestra had small cause to love Agamemnon, who had murdered not only her first husband, Tantalos, but also their newborn child. After that, he forced a loveless marriage on her, resulting in four children, and finally abandoned both family and realm to depart for the seemingly endless Trojan War.

To add insult to injury, once Troy had been defeated, Agamemnon claimed Cassandra, daughter of the Trojan King Priam, as part of the spoils of war, and returned to Mycenae in triumph with both Cassandra and the twin sons he had begotten on her. All these blows to her dignity are more than Klytämnestra can endure. After all, her station is just as high as her husband's, if not indeed even higher. When Agamemnon, whom Klytämnestra regards as the murderer of their daughter, returns home with a royal concubine whose offspring might threaten the claim she and her regal line have to the throne of Mycenae, she sees no recourse but to conspire with her paramour, Aegisthos, to destroy Agamemnon, Cassandra, and their twins. While Elektra may think of her mother as the foulest of the foul, in Klytämnestra's own eyes the queen was driven to her drastic act by the unrelenting injury to her motherhood, her dignity, and the ongoing threat to her exalted position, not to mention the possible threat to her life, should Agamemnon decide to supplant her on the throne with Cassandra.

When I first sang the role of Klytämnestra in Berlin, the respected German actor and director Ernst Schröder, who staged the opera, relied on the historical accounts of the queen as being a woman of enormous beauty and stateliness. This gave me an opportunity to interpret the duality of the queen, who is outwardly an attractive, mature woman, while inwardly racked with anxieties about the retribution she knows she is likely to receive for the acts of vengeance in which she has participated, however justified the vengeance might have appeared to her at the time.

The standoff between mother and daughter is an archetypical one for Hellenic drama. In an ultimate moral sense, every character is in the right, and every character is in the wrong. This multidimensional Greek approach to the issues of morality bears an intriguing resemblance to the plastic art of sculpture, which reached one of its highest periods of creativity in ancient Greece. Like the sculptures, the characters in Greek drama are totally human, and, as such, visible from many different perspectives.

Our job as singing actors is always to preserve this multidimensionality of perception for the audience, and thus retain the spectators' privilege of reaching their own ethical conclusions about the characters, if they are so inclined. Placing subjective value judgments on the individual characters is the exclusive province of the spectator, not the performer. And so, as long as I sang the title role, Elektra was one hundred percent right, and her mother equally wrong. From now on, my reading of Klytämnestra's attitudes and anxieties would have to be totally justified, and Elektra's scorn completely wrong.

My first Klytämnestra performances in Berlin completed the task of laying the groundwork for the start of my second career, just as my first Herodias performances had started the transition. These two roles would soon be joined by a third principal character role from the Richard Strauss repertoire, the Amme (Nurse) in his fourth major operatic collaboration with Hofmannsthal after *Elektra*, *Rosenkavalier*, and *Ariadne auf Naxos: Die Frau ohne Schatten*.

When a friend recently asked me if I could sum up the inner meaning of *Frau ohne Schatten* in just a few words, I replied, "Your guess is as good as mine." In actual fact, a profound analysis of the many elements that come together in this enormous opera would burst the bounds of this volume of recollections. One would probably need a separate book to discuss this opera and its many sources in the detail it deserves.

In the course of my own research, I came to the realization that one very significant element makes *Die Frau ohne Schatten* more European than Asian. In most Asian cultures, the attainment of a state of spirituality is the highest goal of life, and this goal can be achieved only by a concentrated effort to liberate the soul transcendentally from the earthly fetters of the body and its physical exigencies. In *Frau ohne Schatten*, on the other hand, the watchmen in the night entreat the people in the houses to hold one another closely, and the unborn children of the dyer and his wife implore their parents to bring them into this world. The adversary in the piece is surely the nurse, who has nothing but unbridled contempt for humans and their ways. Obliged to accompany her mistress, the Empress, on her earthly journeys, she spits out her loathing of this earthly race, saying she cannot abide the very smell of humans.

In my characterization of the Nurse, I would have to portray a number of conflicting emotions. Her contempt for humanity is only one element in her character. There are also positive attributes, such as her loyalty and concern for the noblewoman placed in her charge. While she uses every bit of the magic power at her disposal to make her mistress happy by trying to secure the shadow of the dyer's wife, and with it the promise of fertility, she continues hoping their mission might go awry. She is convinced the only way for the Empress to be free is to liberate herself from her affection for a "mere" human by precipitating that human's petrification and returning to the spheres of pure spirituality. This is why she avails herself of every means at her disposal, much like Ortrud, to support a cause she believes to be utterly justifiable—and by her terms, it is.

While the discussion of the profounder meanings of this piece will doubtless continue forever, there is no gainsaying the magnificence of Strauss's music, which is clearly the key to the opera's enduring success. But what a grueling task it was to learn that music! The role calls for a complete command of the intricate chord progressions that form the musical fabric. Because of this factor, I knew I had to concentrate on those harmonic structures when doing my homework. In a long career of difficult roles, this one numbered amongst the most complicated.

Fortunately, the assignment came to me at the end of the opera season, prior to the start of the annual theatre vacation in the summer of 1971, which meant I would not be distracted by the necessity of performing anywhere. Luckily, I was able to adhere to my standard principle of always starting to learn a major role at least six months before the first rehearsal. I decided to take advantage of that liberty by going into total isolation. After a quick trip to the supermarket to load up my refrigerator with necessary provisions, I locked the door to my apartment, turned off the doorbell, ignored the ring of the telephone, sat down at the piano, and pounded the role into my head for a full nine days, taking time out, literally, only for the basic necessities.

When that preparatory work was done, I contacted Dr. Günther von Noé, an excellent pianist and coach. I needed his help at the keyboard to get me away from the piano and confirm that I had truly memorized the score. At my first session with him, we were both satisfied, that, apart from one or two insecure passages, the role was firmly anchored in my memory. By the way, Dr. von Noé refused to believe I had done all the memorization myself in a mere nine days. It was the one and only time I had ever done this kind of a total immersion on any musical material, but it wound up paying off.

The première of the new production was scheduled for February 13, 1972, during Günther Rennert's directorate of the Bavarian State Opera. It was in keeping with the company's grand tradition of putting on optimum perform-ances of the operas of the city's local musical hero, Richard Strauss. Oskar Fritz Schuh was slated to direct the production, with Wolfgang Sawallisch conducting. James King and Ingrid Bjoner were cast as the Emperor and Em-press, with Dietrich Fischer-Dieskau and Hildegard Hillebrecht as Barak the dyer and his wife.

In one review of the production, published on February 15, 1972, in the Mu-nich *Abendzeitung*, critic Antonio Mingotti mentioned that my interpretation of the role, which he referred to as "magnificent," seemed to abandon the staging. If it did, it was a case of virtue being the mother of necessity, because our distinguished producer, Dr. Schuh, was inclined to snooze off in his seat on the aisle of the seventh or eighth row of the orchestra during stage rehears-als, particularly in my scenes, which I took as a tribute to my theatrical re-sourcefulness. Rather than disturb the tranquility of his slumbers, I more or less took it upon myself to fill in the gaps in his staging, which apparently provoked the comment in Mr. Mingotti's review. At one rehearsal, Dr. Rennert dropped in to see how things were going and inquired, "Is he asleep again?" With great concern, he then assigned somebody to keep an eye on the rather frail Dr. Schuh, so that when he woke up he wouldn't fall off the seat and hurt himself.

While his staging work in the rehearsal rooms was impeccable, I looked upon Dr. Schuh's somewhat tranquil approach to the task of putting on the finishing touches as a grand paradigm of the Somnolent School of Operatic Production, and I couldn't help wondering if he hadn't perhaps once joined forces with that past master of narcoleptic music-making, Herbert von Karajan. By contrast, Maestro Sawallisch's Strauss interpretation certainly more than made up for whatever might have been skipped in the physical production, and following the première, Karl-Heinz Ruppel in the *Süddeutsche Zeitung* described the enthusiastic reception of our audience as a kind of tidal wave, going on to describe my own performance as "grandiose."

Following this initial success, I was invited to sing the Nurse at the Nuremberg Municipal Theatre, in a production that took place a year and a half later, in September 1973. One review of that performance reminded me a little of my standing room days back at the Met, when I wondered about that missing dramatic quality and speculated on what one might do to add life and meaning to the theatrical side of opera. The reviewer, Fritz Schleicher, writing in the *Nürnberger Nachrichten,* confirmed my success at practicing what I had always preached by suggesting I had demonstrated "what musical theatre can be, the fascination of the human element, supported by music, a unity of emotion and reflection."

The Munich production was on the boards of the Nationaltheater from 1972 to 1978, including performances at the 1972, 1973, and 1977 Munich Opera Festivals. All in all, I sang a total of twenty-two performances of *Die Frau ohne Schatten* and was gratified by the enthusiastic reception of the press and public. However, the highest accolade I received, although somewhat extravagantly delivered, was from a pre-eminent colleague with whom I never had the privilege of collaborating, although I think the two of us could have set the woods on fire.

It happened like this: I was just coming offstage from taking my final bow, when a small, grey-haired figure genuflected before me, ullulating loud and extravagant praises. There, at my feet, knelt one of this century's most influential figures in music—musical theatre in particular—paying unrestrained homage to what I had just done. Well, what does one do when one finds oneself confronted with an immortal? I don't know what anyone else would have done, but in the face of all this adulation, the best I could come up with was: "Thank you very, very much. Now, would you please get up, Lennie!"

Out of the Dust

A̤ᴛ ᴛʜɪs ᴊᴜɴᴄᴛᴜʀᴇ in my story, I would like to beg the reader's indulgence for an occasional jump backward and forward in my memoirs. The reason for this is that I prefer to present a chronology of subject, rather than a mere sequence of dates. This is why I first established the fact of my second career before going into detail on a role I started singing in the middle of my soprano years, and which ultimately became a mainstay of the phase that followed— the Kostelnička Burjovka in Leoš Janáček's opera *Jenůfa*.

When we see the name of the Moravian master Janáček writ large on the posters outside today's opera houses and music festivals, it seems hard to imagine that he was once considered a minor master at best, whose works "justifiably" gathered dust on the shelves of a few music libraries. I do not know who the first person was to retrieve a Janáček score from the shelves, blow the dust off the covers, and begin rediscovering a series of major works that have assumed their merited place amongst the great masterworks of operatic history. Whoever it was, I am very much indebted to that person.

In the years of the Janáček revival, which started in the late 1940s and entered my professional life in 1968, I have performed three of his operas, including his great masterpiece, *Jenůfa*. I might have sung the role of the Kostelnička Burjovka back in the mid-fifties, when an agent offered it to me. At that time, however, I was so shocked at the idea of anyone being able to destroy the life of an innocent infant that I adamantly refused even to consider doing the part. Oddly enough, I had no problem instigating a few murders as Lady Macbeth, and Ortrud almost manages to do away with a child in the person of the boy-prince Gottfried of Brabant. For me, the role of the Kostelnička was different. Perhaps it was the immediacy of Janáček's musical utterance that made the character so real, and thus so overwhelmingly gruesome.

In 1967, after completing the season in Bayreuth, the first one following Wieland Wagner's death on October 17, 1966, I decided my ninetieth *Götterdämmerung* Brünnhilde on August 23 would be my swan song at that festival, where I had been a regular member of the ensemble for seventeen consecutive years. I did, however, continue singing the *Götterdämmerung* Brünnhilde in other theatres, finally putting her to bed after my ninety-ninth performance of the role on February 7, 1971. At the time, I was almost fifty-three years old and had been singing soprano heroines for a scant thirty years. I began shopping around for other worlds to conquer.

It was at this juncture that the management of the Royal Opera House, Covent Garden, in London contacted me to ask if I would be interested in appearing in a series of English-language performances of *Jenůfa*, a revival of a production first performed at that theatre in 1956, conducted by Rafael Kubelík. Arguably, no musician ever understood the special problems of Janáček's music better than he. He was also intimately acquainted with Moravia, having served as a conductor at the Brno Opera, following his first of two periods as musical director of the Czech Philharmonic, a post Janáček had previously held.

When Maestro Kubelík became musical director of the Royal Opera in 1955, he wasted no time in adding *Jenůfa* to the repertoire. It was premièred in December of the following year, much to the distress of the Covent Garden management, who watched in glum horror as box office receipts dwindled down to almost a record flop. The production was finally discontinued in 1958. Apparently, Janáček's time had not yet come, despite the presence of a major conductor in the pit and two of the most popular sopranos in the house, Amy Shuard and Sylvia Fisher, onstage. Although Kubelík left the post of musical director at Covent Garden in 1958, he continued on with the company as a regular guest conductor. Throughout the coming decade, he persisted in his advocacy of the Janáček work and finally succeeded in pushing through a revival, scheduled to be premièred in 1968, with Ande Anderson staging Christopher West's original 1956 production and sets and costumes by Jan Brazda, a Czech artist living in Sweden, and featuring the Australian soprano Marie Collier in the title role.

Between my initial refusal of the role back in the fifties and the London invitation in the mid-sixties, a fortuitous occurrence had somewhat mystically released me from my squeamishness about the role. On April 30, 1964, my godchild, Matthias, the elder son of my friend and accompanist, Heinrich Bender, was born. Holding this infant in my arms, I was made forcibly aware of the necessity to reassess the difference between my involvement with a real live baby and the baby in the opera. Matthias's birth had brought me back to earth, so to speak, and this served as a kind of propitious danger signal, showing me how immersed I had become in some of the characters I was playing. That made it a double blessing for me.

I was able to perceive the essence of the Kostelnička's character by the set of needs that regulate the lives of country people, so different from the rules that guide us urbanites. For us, the mysteries of life and death usually take place behind the closed doors of hospitals and are then objectively reported in the newspapers. Out in the country, life and death, and all the tribulations that go with them, are tightly interwoven with daily existence. In my understanding of the sexton's widow, the woman was driven to despondency by the things that happened to her foster daughter. However, once having made up her mind to take drastic action, the actual "disposal" of the child, who has been the guiltless cause of it all, becomes almost as routine an affair as a farmer's wife drowning a litter of unwanted kittens or slaughtering her children's pet piglet or lamb for dinner. This forms part of the harsh reality of country life as I have witnessed it in the farmlands around Munich and in parts of the Swiss Alps, where a hard-drinking, resilient populace face the elements head-on every moment of the day. And yet, these same rugged people can tear your heart out with the simple music they make on their instruments or with the singing and chanting of their pure voices.

The Kostelnička began taking shape from the *outside in:* a woman in black, who not only makes regular visits to the church but practically lives there, and who fully accepts the severe aspects of country life without any taste for some of the frivolity which serves to relieve that austerity. In an odd sense, she destroys the child's life to spare it what she, with her exaggerated sense of right and wrong, regards as a fate far worse than death for both mother and child. She does this, however, only after exhausting all the other avenues of escape, including humiliating her own proud character by literally getting down on her knees to the child's father, Števa, and imploring him to sanctify the birth by marrying Jenůfa. Števa, however, has lost all interest in Jenůfa ever since his half-brother Laca, in a fit of jealousy prompted by a profound and genuine love for Jenůfa, inflicted a wound on her cheek. The resulting scar is so revolting to Števa that he wants nothing further to do with his former love. The response of this hayseed Lothario proves his superficiality and his egocentric indifference to any but the outward aspects of the people in his life.

Števa's rejection of Jenůfa, despite an act of humiliation usually reserved exclusively for the Kostelnička's relationship with the Lord God, causes her world to come crashing down. By the time the stolid, earthbound Laca intrudes upon her misery, she is almost mentally absent. Half here, half there, she reveals the truth of Jenůfa's plight to him. He replies that, while still perfectly willing to enter into a union with his beloved Jenůfa, the thought of taking on his brother's "soiled goods," in the person of the innocent baby, fills him with horror. This reaction inflicts another heavy blow on the older woman's reason. Ultimately, she becomes so distraught over her predicament that her sense of sinfulness and retribution ("Born of sin, let it die in sin!" she says) takes precedence over her sense of human decency, precipitating her tragic act, even at the cost of her immortal soul. When her crime is finally revealed with the melting of the ice, in an eloquent parable of the winter and springtime of the human soul, she is just a shell of her former self, as she asks Jenůfa for understanding and forgiveness.

I had the good luck to find able assistance in learning the role from an excellent Czech pianist and opera coach at the Bavarian State Opera by the name of Gerhard Poppe, who had grown up, both physically and musically, in the only part of the world where Janáček's operas were still enthusiastically received. As we got into our preparatory work, Mr. Poppe told me that, as a small child in the mid-1920s, he was walking through Prague with his father, and they saw an elderly gentleman with a leonine mane taking his constitutional stroll. Pointing him out to young Gerhard, his father told him, "That's the great Janáček!" For someone as fond of augurs and omens as myself, this little anecdote from the man teaching me the master's music represented a kind of apostolic succession—from Janáček to Mr. Poppe to myself to the audience, all in an unbroken chain of tradition.

Mr. Poppe explained how Janáček used to go out to the country to listen to people's speech patterns, and then use their rhythmic utterance and intonation in his setting of their words to be sung. With such a symbiotic bond of the music to the original Czech words, I honestly wondered how much of its forcefulness would carry over into another language. The English translation I would be singing in London had been written with great loyalty to the original text by the English conductor Sir Edward Downes, Covent Garden's resident musicologist and polyglot, working in conjunction with the Czech baritone Otakar Kraus, who had been a mainstay of the London company since the war years.

In the intervening years since my first visits to London in the late forties, the city had risen from the ashes like the proverbial phoenix, and the wonderful shops and department stores were doing a land-office business, to which I made several contributions in between rehearsals and performances. Many of the pleasanter things in London had fortunately remained the same. The atmosphere in the Covent Garden dressing rooms had not changed, and if there had been a particularly agreeable pub on a corner near the theatre, I was pleased to note that it was still in the same place. The man behind the bar might have added a few grey hairs—but, then again, so had I. For an old romantic like myself, this resistance to *needless* change in London always made me feel right at home.

However, the mustier operatic traditions were now yielding to a healthy renewal and revival—yet another sign of a good sense of proportion. Rehearsals went very smoothly, until an event occurred that shocked all of us and shattered Maestro Kubelík's composure to its foundations.

We were working with the orchestra. As they were about to start on Jenůfa's prayer, the orchestra's union shop steward rose to his feet and announced that his aggregation had a job somewhere else—a radio or recording date—and they would have to leave a little early. Maestro Kubelík readily acquiesced, and Marie Collier began singing her prayer. Right in the middle of the prayer, which Marie was singing beautifully—right in the middle of a phrase, for that matter—most of the orchestra got up and walked out. The stunned conductor looked off after the departing musicians, then muttered to nobody in particular: "Times have changed. They could have waited for the last ten bars." This shocked me particularly, because it was anything but the kind of English good manners I had been used to. They simply ruined a beautiful musical moment by beating a hasty retreat. Kubelík became livid—he was really seething with rage—which was not his style at all. The concept of musical idealism had dissipated in favor of doctrinaire trade unionism.

Don't get me wrong. We are all working musicians, and we all have to see where our next dollar, mark, or pound is coming from. In a larger sense, however, one of the most important commodities we have to sell is our artistic sensitivity. Lose that, and we lose the core of our craft and the source of our income! If they had simply told us they would need to leave in fifteen or twenty minutes, Maestro Kubelík would not have even started rehearsing the prayer. Fortunately, we were able to reunite our forces and move on to a successful première.

I was very proud when Andrew Porter wrote of our performance: "Astrid Varnay, last heard here as Brünnhilde in *Götterdämmerung* in 1958, and *Jenůfa* returned to Covent Garden after an absence of nine and ten years respectively—*in English!*" Mr. Porter went on to praise my English diction, suggesting that some English singers could take a page out of my elocution book. I hate to burst any British linguistic balloons, but I do think it should be stated unequivocally at this point, for once and for all, that we *do* speak English in the United States—especially in New York City!

Loved Her ... Hated Her!

Having taken this brief excursion to my native language, I began developing a genuine affinity for the Kostelnička. News got around, and soon I found myself receiving and accepting an offer to sing *Jenůfa* at the Deutsche Oper am Rhein. The production was staged by the Czech director Bohumil Herlischka, and conducted by Arnold Quennet. It made its bow at the theatre in Duisburg on November 19, 1969, with a subsequent première in Düsseldorf on December 11 of the same year. Of course, for the Deutsche Oper am Rhein performances, I had to relearn the part in German. Again I was supplied with an idiomatically flawless translation by Max Brod, a Czech author and philosopher, who had been a member of the literary circle in Prague, which gave the world such great writers as Franz Werfel, Jaroslav Hašek, and Karel Čapek. Franz Kafka's works found their way into publication and achieved their international recognition largely thanks to Max Brod's passionate advocacy.

Bohumil Herlischka was an ideal producer for *Jenůfa*, because he knew exactly what he was talking about when it came to staging people's behavior in the Moravian countryside. There was something of the emotional peasant in our stage director himself, specifically in the things he loved and hated. One of his pet peeves was climbing to the rehearsal room on the top floor of the Düsseldorf Opera House. He preferred to work exclusively on the main stage, but this was not feasible because other productions were going on at the same time. To assuage his irritation, he laid in a generous supply of wine, which helped him retain his composure during his banishment to the upstairs region.

Another of Herlischka's quirks was a fixation on sequence. It was so intense that any "interference," such as a question on the staging, would send him right back to the beginning of the scene, until we could perform it uninterrupted from one end to the other, while he continued to imbibe and direct, more or less in that order. I have absolutely no idea what wine he drank, but I fervently wish the same vintage could be made available to a few other producers, because he gave brilliant directions.

In fact, Herlischka was so keenly (and justifiably) aware of his own brilliance that he would brook no tampering with any of his concepts. Once, when he was trudging up the stairs beside me in a fairly good mood because of the sunshiny weather, I grasped the opportunity to ask him if there was anything I could offer him from my own impressions of the role to give him some feedback for his own work, to which he bluntly replied, "Why do you want to change things?" I assured him that major alterations of the staging were the farthest thing from my mind. I merely wanted to add to what we had already developed. "Isn't it enough what I'm giving to you?" he persisted. "Look, you and I, we feel the same thing. We *must* feel the same thing." When I asked him what he meant by that arcane statement, he answered, "Because you and I, we are born on the same day." (I could barely resist the temptation to say, "But not the same year!") "If we are born on the same day," he went on to expostulate, "then we must have the same feelings," which, as he said, would naturally substantiate my "willingness" to do whatever he wanted.

Herlischka's explanation was a little mystical, but in this case it worked, at least as far as my stage comportment was concerned. From the neck up, however, to the delight of some directors and the anguish of others, nobody can stop me! This means my words and the way I deliver them are always a very personal matter. The director is welcome to direct my physical movements, but I can always interpolate my own ideas through my vocal interpretation.

While I frankly resented Herlischka's spasms of authoritarianism, I couldn't help marveling at the rightness of his visual sense. One of the most effective aspects of Herlischka's production was a scene in which he filled one side of the stage with a multitude of lighted candles, such as you'll find inside a Roman Catholic church during one of the high festival days, when everybody invokes the intercession of his favorite saint, setting the whole sanctuary aglow. Images as telling as this made the task of circumventing their creator's intransigence worth the effort.

If Bohumil Herlischka's approach was a firm demand for the uncompromising observation of his directions, Günther Rennert was a master of interaction between cast and director. This is not for one moment to suggest that Dr. Rennert didn't do his preparatory homework. In fact, you could build a skyscraper on the sturdy framework of his preparation. His stagings made so much sense that they could be temporarily removed from the theatre's repertoire for a period of years, and when they returned, I would be able to find my way around as if I had rehearsed them just the day before.

Günther Rennert's Munich *Jenůfa* production premièred in 1970, two and a half years after he had assumed the directorship of the company on Rudolf Hartmann's retirement. The opera was again conducted by Rafael Kubelík, with settings by Alfred Sierke and costumes by Lieselotte Erler. This production was captured in all its magnificence on television, with the network selecting the best acts from three different performances for the final cut. Some people may look down with scorn at the "naturalism" of this staging, but I defy its detractors to come up with a reading of this very real opera that will prompt audiences to forget that people are singing, or even that they are in a theatre at all. In Rennert's staging, people reacted to the characters in the drama as if they had known them all their lives, because they were all human!

Rennert's obsession with thoroughness, which, of course, we all valued, once led to an unfortunate controversy between the two of us. The event in question took place during the preparatory work on a *Salome* production, in which I was cast as Herodias. One morning I arrived for one of the final rehearsals and was told that my services would be needed a couple of days later, because the baritone singing Jokanaan would be available to rehearse with us *only* on that day. I reminded Dr. Rennert that I had a performance of the title role in *Elektra* the evening of that rehearsal day and would therefore be unable to attend. He stood there nonplussed, finally reiterating that all he needed of me at that rehearsal was my physical presence—I wouldn't need to sing a note. I countered that I always kept to myself on performance days, especially before as demanding a role as Elektra. He stood firm. When he was rehearsing, everything else took second place, and he was not about to make any exceptions. Not wishing to take time off from the rehearsal in progress, he suggested I go home and think it over.

The product of this suggestion was a sleepless night, in which I kept asking myself why *I* should have to be the one to make these decisions, when *he* was the head of the theatre, in addition to being the director of the *Salome* production. It was just unfair. The following day, I decided to pass the buck back where it belonged—decision making was his job, not mine. He promptly announced that he would engage another soprano to sing the *Elektra*, so he could have me for the rehearsal that morning. Evidently, rehearsals meant more to him than performances.

When it was announced that I would be replaced that evening by my colleague—an excellent Elektra, incidentally—they tell me a voluble groan emerged from several members of the audience who were particularly fond of my work. This was a shame, because it passed prejudgment on an artist who had had nothing to do with my being replaced. Gladys Kuchta, a fine professional, took it in her stride and gave a first-rate performance. Sad to say, nothing was done to compensate my bank account for the loss of the healthy fee I always earned for singing Elektra! It was my good luck that there were no performance conflicts during the *Jenůfa* rehearsals, and the minute work on every aspect of characterization and coherence proceeded unperturbed.

One of Dr. Rennert's tactics was to cast singers who really knew how to think—not everyone does—and induce them to set their thought processes in motion. This insistence on constant awareness often led to emotional outbursts on everybody's part, as we sought for coherent bridges between the individual fragments of the drama, but it inevitably took us to far higher levels of operatic immediacy. While we struggled to interpret our own contribution to the event, Dr. Rennert never lost his overview of the big picture, enabling him to indulge in a constant spate of fine-tuning, adding a little here, filing down a little there, dovetailing everything so that it made sense. The resultant production, as televiewers attest to this day, is operatic staging at its highest level, which audiences acknowledged at the Nationaltheater première on March 17, 1970, with a tumultuous ovation and with the cast brought out for forty-four curtain calls! The press notices were so positive they sounded like we had bribed the reviewers.

During the first run of the Munich *Jenůfa*, I woke up one morning on a performance day with a horrible backache, so bad, in fact, that something had to be done about it if I expected to make it through the evening. Thank goodness, I was able to avail myself of the services of Dr. Hanns Galli, a prominent Munich orthopedist, who also took excellent care of Munich's "1860 Lions," one of the local soccer teams, named for the year it was founded. He gave me sufficient medication to allow me to sing the Kostelnička with a minimum of discomfort. The following morning the phone rang several times, each call from a colleague or a fan telling me how impressed they had been with the previous evening's performance, in particular what they described as my "sliding, lateral gait." It took me a moment or two to realize what they were talking about. Needless to say, I had sufficient sense memory to recall what I had

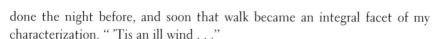

done the night before, and soon that walk became an integral facet of my characterization. " 'Tis an ill wind . . ."

After singing the part of Kostelnička in three different productions—in London, Düsseldorf, and Munich—the character had begun to assume a very warm spot in my heart. In a sense, I had come to love this confused, almost demented creature, who does the most horrible things for the most lofty reasons. I looked forward to the same experience with her "counterpart," the Kabanicha in Janáček's later work *Káťa Kabanová*, based on a play called *The Thunderstorm*, written by Alexander Nikolayevitch Ostrovsky, one of those gloom-steeped mid-nineteenth-century Muscovite dramatists whose works must have inspired Ira Gershwin to describe the fruitless quest for love as having "more clouds of gray than any Russian play could guarantee." I sang this opera for the first time on April 14, 1974, at the Opera House in Zurich.

For all my affinity for the Kostelnička, however, no matter how many times I sang the Kabanicha, starting in Zurich and later in two other productions in Düsseldorf and Vienna, did I ever develop anything but antipathy for this self-willed woman. Here, I found myself faced with the first character I genuinely despised, so that playing the part became more obligation than satisfaction. Thank heaven, the piece was not given often, and I made a firm decision that, should anyone else want me for this part, I would arrange to be conveniently unavailable.

Between *Káťa* performances there were other roles, some of them strictly "filler" material, which served to help me regain my equilibrium. One of these enjoyable "filler" operas, staged for the purpose of treading operatic water in the Munich theatre schedule, so to speak, between *Tristan* and *Aida* productions, was Sergei Prokofiev's early opera, *Igrok (The Gambler)*. The fun of playing a gambling woman made *Igrok* pure pleasure to act in, and in the final performance, I was able to follow through on an old Central European theatrical tradition and change something to crack up my colleagues onstage.

The scene in question involves a confrontation between me and my destitute grandson, who has just depleted his fortune at the gambling table and demands more money from the grandmother to go on betting. In this sequence, I, as his grandmother, have also lost a sizable amount and am about to be transported out of the casino in a sedan chair, carried by about eight or ten hardy extras. As a parting shot, I tell my grandson—from that great height—that he will never get any of my money. At the time of the closing performance, on November 26, 1973, Europe was locked in a petroleum crisis, and everybody was trying to come up with ways to cope with it. I took advantage of the situation by looking scornfully down at my grandson and changing the line slightly, so that I said, "You'll never get any of my oil," following which I was conveyed offstage. As I planned, the cast cracked up, and nobody in the audience caught on—which is one of the fundamental rules of the game.

In the Düsseldorf production, there was a very fine Káťa named Stella Axarlis, whose origins were every bit as multinational as my own, and whose career paralleled mine in several ways. Born in Alexandria, Egypt, of Greek parents, Stella grew up in a suburb of Melbourne, where she later taught mathematics at local schools, just as I had worked as a secretary. Stella ultimately benefited from the precedent I had set with the establishment of my second career. In the course of performing *Káťa*, Stella and I became close friends. Yet, for all the friendships this opera might have engendered, the piece itself always left us with a bad taste in our mouths, not because it is a poor work, but because its effect on all of us, participants and audience alike, is so unrelentingly dark that it plunged us into a profoundly negative mood for quite a while. The hypocrisy both Ostrovsky and Janáček so tellingly perceived, manifested in the determination of Kabanicha not to sanction anyone else's happiness unless she was calling the tune, was probably so distressing for all of us because of the presence of the same harsh reality all around us.

Káťa Kabanová, for all its severity, points up one very significant maxim: no matter what excuses are made for dominating us, when faced with this form of unjust authority in our adult lives, we have recourse to only two choices—to give in or to get out. With the circumstances surrounding her, Janáček's Káťa has no escape but a watery grave. In my case, when a dictatorial theatre manager tried to run my life, I simply cut my losses and got out—in this case, out of the theatre and out of the country. Providentially, I was able to get out on my own terms, and because of that, I was also able to come back.

You *Can* Go Home Again

THE VOICE ON THE TELEPHONE from New York was that of Paul Jaretzki, assistant artistic administrator, second in command to Charles Riecker at the Metropolitan during the era of Schuyler Chapin following both the retirement of Rudolf Bing in 1972 and the tragic death of his designated successor, Göran Gentele. There was a note of affable irony in Mr. Jaretzki's voice as he asked me, "How come we haven't heard much from you here lately, Mme Varnay?" Without naming any names, I couldn't resist the temptation to reply, "I wasn't asked." Thereupon, Mr. Jaretzki, doubtless acting on Mr. Chapin's behalf, extended a cordial invitation to me to return to the Metropolitan—on a guest contract!—in the early winter of 1974 to sing the Kostelnička in *Jenůfa*.

Suddenly a remark Günther Schneider-Siemssen had made at Kloten Airport in Zurich began to make sense. It was one of those chance encounters between two professionals on their way from one theatre to another. Obviously the first question we asked each other as we waited for our respective flights was where the other one was headed. Schneider-Siemssen replied that he was on his way to New York to design a production of *Jenůfa* at the Metropolitan. At that point, his flight to New York was called. On his way to the gate, he said matter-of-factly, "Looks like we will be seeing each other soon." I didn't give this remark a second thought, which is why Mr. Jaretzki's offer came out of a clear blue sky. When I ran into Schneider-Siemssen in New York a few weeks later, I asked him when he had found out about my engagement, and he solemnly swore that he never had. He simply took it for granted I would be doing the part. That's how associated a singer can become with a role.

It had been eighteen years since I last stood on the stage of the Met, despite the fact that I had made several visits to the United States during the intervening years, where I sang opera performances in San Francisco and Chicago, among other places. I also sang three consecutive concert performances in the title role of *Elektra* with William Steinberg and the New York Philharmonic at Lincoln Center in 1964. The Klytämnestra in these concerts was Regina Resnik, who had been making headlines in her new career as a mezzo. It was a double pleasure to be appearing with a good friend and a fine artist. As an added touch of artistry, I appeared in those concerts in a Hellenically draped, terra-cotta-colored gown, created by, of all people, the dramatic tenor Jess Thomas, who moonlighted as a designer of special-purpose evening wear for his close friends. Ten years later, in Severance Hall in Cleveland and Carnegie Hall in New York, with the Cleveland Orchestra under the baton of Lorin Maazel, I was the Klytämnestra.

Returning to the Met after so many years defied all the ominous predictions one hears. In the boxing world, there is a saying, "They never come back." And one of Thomas Wolfe's most famous novels is entitled *You Can't Go Home Again*. Well, I *would* be back at the Metropolitan, but, poignantly, I wouldn't really be coming home. There was no more home and family in that city for me to return to.

After his postwar service in the marines, my brother, Lucky, had met one of an attractive set of identical twins in California, and, as I quipped at the time, once he had learned which one was his beloved and which one her sister, he decided to ask her to marry him. Lucky and his new bride honeymooned in Honolulu and were so taken by the beauty of the place, they decided to settle in Hawaii, where my new sister-in-law got a secretarial position, and Lucky became an executive with another company. Their reports of life in the Hawaiian Islands were so glowing that Mother was delighted when they invited her to join them there, after first securing my assurance that my feelings would not be hurt if she settled so far away from me. I explained that, while I would have loved to have her with me, my brother could offer her more domestic stability than I could in Germany, where she would unfortunately have to face the fact that I was on the road most of the time. Mother really enjoyed Hawaii, and the climate did a world of good for her health. I have a photograph of her in her later years in Hawaii, still glowingly attractive and straight as the trees behind her, some seventy years after her little ditty in the cherry tree in Rákosli-get set a whole sequence of events in motion.

Unfortunately, Mother's family idyll was short-lived; Lucky suddenly became afflicted with cancer. In the depths of her concern over her son's condition, our mother, now in her early eighties, remained the consummate theatrical professional, insisting that the illness be kept secret from me, because she felt this news might trouble me so much it could affect my performances, and that was absolutely out of the question *in the family business!* Besides which, she rightfully argued, cancer patients have been known to go into remission, and should Lucky get well, I would have been unnecessarily distressed. The others complied, and the secret of my brother's illness was kept assiduously from me for almost three years, until the beginning of 1973. Sadly, Lucky's luck didn't hold, and he passed away on February 6, 1973, only one month short of his forty-sixth birthday, and a year and a half before I returned to the Met. The tragedy affected my sister-in-law to such a degree that she left Hawaii and returned to California; our contact gradually broke off. We never actually met face-to-face.

Mother, on the other hand, was thriving in Hawaii and decided to stay on, moving into a retirement home, where she instantly made very good friends. There was a group of ladies who came to the home on a regular basis to take people shopping or to medical appointments and so forth. With a resourcefulness reminiscent of my father, Mother approached one or two of these volunteers and arranged for them to escort her and her friends on little excursions, either to the natural wonders of the island or to the theatres and concert halls of the capital. Being still a teacher at heart, she also could not resist the urge to give little lectures preparatory to the musical events. These talks were very well received, as they added greater substance to both her listeners' lives and her own. Having to take her child to his final resting place, however, depleted her energies to such a degree that it would have been too strenuous for her to embark on a long journey to New York to attend my *Jenůfa* performances.

The New York production was staged by Günther Rennert with settings and costumes by Günther Schneider-Siemssen in cooperation with associate designer David Reppa. The title role was cast with an excellent young Polish soprano named Teresa Kubiak, and the two tenors were William Lewis as Števa and Jon Vickers as Laca. Jean Kraft appeared as Grandmother Buryja, Alma Jean Smith as Karolka, John Reardon as the foreman of the mill, and Richard T. Gill as the mayor. Fortunately, we were able to use the same Otakar Kraus/Edward Downes English translation I had sung in London. As an interesting sidelight, our conductor, John Nelson, had been born on December 6, 1941, the day of my Metropolitan début. When I joined the company, I was a junior, and now I found myself in the opposite position.

Opera at the Metropolitan had undergone many changes since the traffic-management style of the early forties. It is only fair to give credit here where it is due—to many of the fine directors brought from the legitimate theatre to the Metropolitan over the years at the behest of Rudolf Bing. He also engaged some of the world's finest singing actors, such as Jon Vickers.

I had shared the stage with Vickers only once before, during the *Todesverkün-digung* scene in the second act of *Die Walküre* at a Bayreuth Festival performance conducted by Hans Knappertsbusch on July 28, 1958. Meanwhile I had heard stories of his reputation for being difficult, but decided to take a "wait and see" attitude toward him, and, after several weeks of rehearsal with this precise artist, I realized that the gossip about his being difficult was nothing more than that—just gossip. (In one of these rumors, he once allegedly stopped singing during a *Tristan* orchestra rehearsal, walked over to the pit, and called the conductor's attention to the fact that Richard Wagner had marked the passage they were rehearsing "piano," quietly and courteously asking him to observe that dynamic marking, so he would be able to sing the passage softly, as intended by the composer.)

Rehearsing with Jon Vickers was enriching. An absolute stickler for perfection, his devotion to the work at hand blended perfectly with mine. In the course of rehearsals, the three of us—Rennert, Vickers, and I—once admitted to each other that we were having such a good time, we wished the preparatory phase could go on forever and never have to end at the première.

Regrettably, Dr. Rennert had to leave the city right after the final dress rehearsal to return to his responsibilities in Munich, which meant he wouldn't be around for opening night on November 15, 1974. Expectations for our première had been sparked by an interview by Richard Dyer, music correspondent of the *Boston Globe*, which appeared in the Sunday edition of the *New York Times* on November 10, 1974. In his article, Mr. Dyer said, "One of the greatest singing actresses ever to honor the Metropolitan stage will return to the company where she made her début nearly 33 years ago, and where she has not sung since 1956."

Reporting later on our première, several reviewers noted with pleasure that Dr. Rennert had eschewed the usual practice of using the ballet to perform the folk dance in act 1. Instead, the countryfolk, made up of the soloists and chorus members, did the dance with all the awkwardness one might expect of peasants on the village square. When I appeared onstage to put the quietus on all this raucous merriment, somebody out there in the audience shouted, "Welcome back, Astrid!" and all hell broke loose. In contrast to European manners, American audiences almost always "greet" a well-known artist on his or her first appearance with a round of applause before the singer even starts to sing, much to the distress of many conductors, who see the musical continuity needlessly interrupted. Remembering this, I expected some audience response on my first entrance, but nothing on God's green earth could have prepared me for what happened after that spontaneous greeting. People were on their feet, clapping, cheering, yelling "bravo"—it went on and on. I looked down into the orchestra pit and saw Maestro Nelson just standing there with his baton in both hands, waiting patiently with a broad smile for the ovation to abate so he could continue the performance. While it was gradually ebbing, I pulled myself together and began singing. It was a stroke of luck that the Kostelnička sings only a few lines in the first act, because I was so choked up by this acclamation, I doubt if I could have done much creditable long-term singing at that point in the performance. In the intermission, I was able to calm down.

Before the curtain rose on act 2, there was another ovation. Somehow, news must have gotten out that Maria Jeritza was in the audience. Mme Jeritza had been the first Jenůfa in Vienna back in 1918, and had also introduced the work to the Metropolitan in 1924. When the eighty-seven-year-old prima donna resumed her seat in the box for act 2, her appearance triggered a spontaneous and well-deserved tribute to a distinguished artist, who had once lent the considerable influence of her name and reputation to the cause of new, *good* opera.

When she first appeared in the role at the Met, the distinguished English critic Ernest Newman, writing as a guest reviewer for the *New York Evening Post*, referred to the work as "crude" and its composer "only a cut above the amateur." Writing in *Musical America* at the time, under the somewhat misleading headline "*Jenůfa* Achieves Successful Première at the Metropolitan," reviewer Oscar Thompson stated, "Musically, it cannot be described as important," going on to comment, "It lacks the musical substance for any very long career outside of Central Europe." Mr. Thompson did, however, reserve some faint praise for Mme Jeritza, saying, "Emotionally and vocally, she met every demand made upon her." Now the opera had finally achieved the glory it deserved, and the first American Jenůfa, Maria Jeritza, was there to share it with us. At the end of the opera, we were all greeted with deafening applause, and I could finally step out of character and show my deep appreciation for this wonderful welcome.

In contrast to Ernest Newman's review of the earlier presentation, Harold C. Schonberg, writing in the *New York Times*, said, "One would have to look back to Boris Godunov to find a parallel in opera," going on to add, "One leaves a performance of *Jenůfa* by Leoš Janáček convinced that mankind still has some good in it." Commenting on my own performance, he said, "The veteran of the cast, Miss Varnay, gave a powerfully characterized performance of Kostelnicka."

Max de Schauensee commented, "Astrid Varnay, making a return to the Metropolitan after many seasons, was immense as the sexton's wife." In the *New York Post*, Harriett Johnson claimed, "Miss Varnay makes Kostelnicka ugly and domineering, and it is a convincing portrait. . . . She carries the part with conviction." Writing in New York's German-language paper *Aufbau*, critic Robert Breuer stated: "The great tragédienne of today's opera world, Astrid Varnay, experienced a fully deserved triumph. Both her outstanding acting performance and her heroic vocal achievement were unforgettable." Egon Stadelmann, critic of the other German newspaper, *Herold*, said: "Seeing Astrid Varnay again, after a much too long absence from the Metropolitan stage, was a true delight. This unique artist presented an unforgettable portrait of the foster mother."

Finally, my "old friend" Irving Kolodin gave me one of his usual qualified raves, claiming my performance was truly spellbinding and then giving most of the credit for the characterization to Wieland Wagner's instructions. In Mr. Kolodin's words: "Certainly her performance of Kostelnicka emanates from her own richness of spirit and fertility of mind: But the craftsmanship to convey them through such details as a palsied hand, a wandering glance, a catatonic gait, has stamped on it: 'Made in Bayreuth.'" This review left me wondering how Dr. Rennert had figured in this production!

A few days after the première, I came down from my room at the Barbizon-Plaza Hotel on West Fifty-seventh Street to have a bite of lunch at the small coffee shop. Because I was unaccompanied, the waiter asked me to take a seat at the counter, where I sat, munching on a large salad, thinking to myself about everything and nothing, while my eye scanned the room, looking casually at the others having their meals. People's faces have always interested me, and this had become an unconscious habit of mine. Suddenly, I noticed an elegant-looking gentleman, sitting with what looked like a group of secretaries in one of the corner booths. It was Rudolf Bing.

For a moment, I debated with myself as to whether I should walk over and say hello, but finally a pixie must have prodded me, because I stopped by Mr. Bing's table on my way out. I smiled and said, "Good day, Mr. Bing. I hope you're feeling well." With his usual genteel good manners, he acknowledged my greeting, but I could see in his eyes that he had not the faintest idea of who was talking to him. I then took my leave of him and his party and started toward the cash register.

While I was waiting in line to pay my check, I suddenly noticed he was standing beside me. "I beg your pardon," he started to say, "but I just can't place you at the moment." "Mr. Bing, I'm the Astrid Varnay who was once in your Metropolitan ensemble." To which he responded, "Oh, my God!" For the first time in my association with this very smooth gentleman, I actually witnessed him at a loss for words.

When he finally asked what had brought me to New York, I had all I could do to keep from telling him to read it in the papers. I recall him stuttering something or other, and as we parted company, I felt a very deep sense of quiet contentment, reflecting on his discomfiture at our encounter and thinking about all the people he had ousted or humiliated. There was no smug satisfaction in this feeling. It was as though all these colleagues, whom he had often treated more like commodities than humans, were gathered around me.

There was Lauritz Melchior, casually tossed aside. Helen Traubel, eased out of the ensemble. Hans Hotter, subjected to the ups and downs of arbitrary casting based on the contention that he needed to be "disciplined" for having sung at Bayreuth. James McCracken, stuck in comprimario parts at the Met until he left to become a renowned Otello. Robert Merrill, suspended from the company for the "unpardonable sin" of making a motion picture. Maria Callas, whose only offense was to protect her voice from untoward exploitation, a voice that, as everyone knows, is the only commodity any of us has to sell. Regina Resnik, whose Carmen was the toast of Paris, but who was forced to introduce that stellar characterization to her hometown at the City Opera, while languishing in secondary parts at the Met.

I thought of all the audiences in New York who were temporarily or permanently robbed of the opportunity of hearing these and other fine artists, many of them native Americans, because of the whims of one martinet. And so they sought their fortunes elsewhere—and succeeded. For my own part, I was "just visiting," and able to go back home. And "home" to me is where my friends, my work, and my comfort are—*wherever* that may be. In a way, by taking away my operatic home, Rudolf Bing gave me an opportunity to gain a larger home throughout the world, which once again included the place I started out. The feeling in my heart was a quiet one, not the least bit vengeful. There I was, fresh from a new triumph—and that at the Metropolitan. And there he was, having lunch with the secretaries.

My visit to New York was one of several in the course of my professional journey. A year or so after my return to the Metropolitan, another long journey, far distant from my new home in Munich, was slowly winding to its end. My mother had been contending for some time with a mild form of leukemia, which her physicians had somehow managed to keep under control. Then, on June 6, she sent me a letter from the hospital, advising me that she had suffered some internal bleeding, and that she was undergoing diagnostic tests. I will let her tell the rest of the story in her own words.

> There are too many white cells, and they have to be diminished. I have already had six batches of blood transfusions, and in one way, they have to get the bleeding stopped. In case it doesn't stop, they will put a tube in the vein and directly place medicine against the bleeding. The doctor said at the present it is not serious, but nobody can say for the future.
>
> I know, dearest Astrid, you are outstanding, intelligent, and I beg you to be strong. Don't worry. Nobody can live in this life forever. We all do our best, but knowing my strong faith, I hope that in a short while, I will be able to go home, and the moment the bleeding stops, that is the promise of the doctor. I had a good life, a happy life, and my dearest, adorable child, and you know how much I love you and admire you. Please don't let it destroy your career. Mother is 86 years old, and she will be 87 with God's blessing, but if our Superior Lord calls me home, I will be ready to go. Please calm down, don't speak about it to nobody, it don't help, it irritates only.
>
> I will keep you posted for further developments, and I hope the good Lord blesses me that I should be able to go home again and write a letter with my own blessings, with God's blessings.
>
> I love you, I adore you, I admire you. You are an outstanding child. The goodness, the generosity from you and Lucky is unique in the world for which I can't thank you enough with my love and gratitude. Kisses, love and admiration forever. Your eternally loving mother.

After the typewritten section she had dictated to a friend in the hospital, she added these words in her own handwriting, recalling the name I had given myself in my earliest childhood when I had trouble pronouncing Ibolyka. "Dearest Bonx," she wrote, "All my love and adoration! Amen!! Your ever-loving Mom,—!" So like her—telling *me* to be strong!

She didn't make it to her eighty-seventh birthday in October, nor did she get to go home from the hospital. She died peacefully there on July 9, 1976, and now reposes near Lucky on the island that had meant so much to her in her later years.

God rest her soul.

Near the end of her long life, she had been vouchsafed the pleasure of hearing the December 21, 1974, matinée of our last *Jenůfa* in a rebroadcast two weeks later on station KAIM in Honolulu. Strange that this fifty-sixth performance of the role also happened to be the final Kostelnička of my career!

However, I had no time to ruminate about the seven *Jenůfa* performances at the Met or my encounter with Mr. Bing. On the afternoon of December 22, I had to fly back to Munich, where, on December 23, I sang the Mother in the regular Christmas series of *Hänsel und Gretel* performances. After a good first act, where the mother does the bulk of her singing, I spent the rest of the evening trying to outwit the jetlag and remain alert to sing my phrases toward the end of the opera. During the Christmas holidays, while scanning some of my New York *Jenůfa* reviews, the whole experience seemed somewhat dream-like.

A Tray Full of Tradition

THE PART OF MAMMA LUCIA in Mascagni's *Cavalleria Rusticana* is, in my humble opinion, generally treated like a kind of operatic stepchild. Because the character does not have that much to sing, she is often casually cast and hardly dealt with in the staging, abandoned to one corner of the stage, where she alternately wipes the tables in her *trattoria* and nervously wrings her hands as events take place. I have a feeling that few stage directors have ever really understood the function of this supporting part in the progress of this powerful operatic drama. In my eyes, she stands as a symbol of that "rustic chivalry," which, as the title implies, forms the very core of a story that has continued to hold audiences in its spell from the time of its creation to the present day.

I had always enjoyed this opera while I was still singing Santuzza because it gave me a chance to sing with some wonderful tenor and baritone colleagues who hardly ever ventured into the Wagnerian repertoire. They included such tenors as Mario del Monaco and Richard Tucker and baritones like Francesco Valentino at the Metropolitan. It was also a gratification to be able to work for the same fee in an opera that lowers its final curtain at the very point in the evening when Brünnhilde and Isolde are just getting warmed up. More significantly, so much of *Cavalleria* reminded me of some of the happiest moments of my childhood, in the Italian communities of New York's Greenwich Village and Jersey City, where I first encountered the fascinating admixture of unyielding adherence to set rules on the one hand and total devotion to friends and family on the other.

One particular incident, which happened when I was a young girl, kept returning to mind whenever I thought of *Cavalleria*. My stepfather had asked me to take a written message to a local Sicilian family. When I arrived, there was a steaming pot of something savory on the stove, and I was graciously (and unconditionally) invited to join the family in sampling the fare. It was a pleasantly warm summer evening, with all the windows open, and the sun was still high in the sky. While I sat at the table, being showered with the same affection accorded family members—in the form of spaghetti, a magnificent tomato sauce, and a healthy portion of grated parmigiano—the door opened, and one of the grown sons walked in. Grown? He was well over six feet and looked like he could take any champion heavyweight on the circuit for fifteen rounds or more without ever sustaining so much as a scratch. His father, on the other hand, looked like a strong wind would blow him away. Just as I was trying to figure how these two could be related, the father exploded, demanding to know where his son had been, and why he wasn't at home promptly at dinner time! Dissatisfied with the excuse his son was stammering, he simply jumped up in the air about a yard beyond his own height and gave his oversized descendant a resounding slap on the face. Nobody intervened, nor did the son, whom he had really hurt, make any effort to defend himself. In that community, rules were rules, and parents were to be obeyed unquestioningly!

When I finally put Santuzza out of my repertoire, with my thirty-third performance on June 8, 1970, I began thinking of the way Mamma Lucia should be played: as a driving force and a reference point in the community, just as the Sicilian parents had been in America. My first Mamma Lucia was a production *in German*, of all things, presented at the Deutsche Oper am Rhein, premièring on June 29, 1977, in Duisburg and on the following July 13 in Düsseldorf.

Meanwhile, when I found out the Bavarian State Opera was planning to present an *Italian*-language *Cavalleria-Pagliacci* evening, premièring on Christmas Day 1978, with *Cavalleria* to feature Leonie Rysanek and Plácido Domingo as singers and Gian-Carlo del Monaco, son of one of my favorite Turiddus, as stage director, I definitely wanted to be a part of that cast. This is why I "casually visited" Otto Herbst, who handled the administrative chores for August Everding, who had just succeeded Günther Rennert as director of the Munich theatre. In the course of conversation, I mentioned the upcoming *Cavalleria* production and dropped a gentle hint (about as gentle as a sledge hammer), inquiring if Mamma Lucia had already been cast, to which Mr. Herbst asked, with equal subtlety, if I would be interested in the part. I, of course, answered in the affirmative. Mr. Herbst grinned and said he would give the "matter very serious consideration."

On my way out of the theatre, I started walking down Maximilianstrasse to the nearest taxi stand, to go out to the airport for a Düsseldorf flight. I saw August Everding on the other side of the street, looking nervously off in all directions. We waved to one another, then met in the middle of the street. Professor Everding seemed so perturbed, I asked him if there was anything wrong, and he told me he was waiting for the car that had been ordered to take him to the airport. I told him I was going there anyway and offered to share my cab with him. He politely declined; his car was certainly on the way. Then he asked me what I would be doing in Düsseldorf. "The mother in *Cavalleria*," I replied, and a light bulb seemed to start glowing above his head. As we wandered back to the safety of the sidewalk, he asked, "Would you consider doing the part here for us?" I replied, "Why not? If I can do it in German in Düsseldorf, I should certainly be able to do it in Italian in Munich." It was the only contract in my career formalized while dodging traffic.

Oddly enough, the role of Mamma Lucia, which a lot of singers will do anything to avoid, became one of my favorites, and I was more than happy to fish for it whenever I saw the chance of performing it with such select colleagues. When Gian-Carlo del Monaco found out I would be in the cast, he was equally happy. His late father—whose memory he ardently reveres—had mentioned our collaboration and those industrial-strength high notes we shared in *Cavalleria* so many years ago. Of all the stage directors I have worked with, many of them past masters of their craft, I have seldom come across anyone with such an all-around knowledge of the work at hand as Gian-Carlo del Monaco. While some directors try to produce an opera referring exclusively to the libretto, or worse yet, using a translation of the libretto, Gian-Carlo knows every note of every vocal and orchestral score he directs, having had it fed to him since babyhood. He also understands the dramatic reasons why the composer wrote this passage, for example, for the bass clarinet, and the recapitulation for the bassoon, in addition to which he has a good working knowledge of most operatic languages and an alert sense of the essence of any drama.

Gian-Carlo saw the key to *Cavalleria* in the heritage of the ancient Greek influence on Sicily, where, in Syracuse in 734 B.C., Corinth had founded one of the oldest Hellenic colonies in Italy. With that in mind, he viewed the inevitability of events (Greek), the commenting chorus (Greek), the unyielding regulations of society, and the submission of all the characters to the surging tide of fate (Greek) as the salient elements of Giovanni Verga's drama, on which Pietro Mascagni's opera was based. Gian-Carlo's Mamma Lucia was to loom much larger in the telling of the tale than is usually the case in other productions. As Gian-Carlo decided to add visual dimension to the overture, Mamma Lucia appears very early in the action, not as a jolly innkeeper but as an almost black eminence in her widow's weeds, ramrod straight, an earth mother, one of the focal elements of the village community, whose age and position have made her a magnet for affection and deference. Mamma Lucia, as I played her, is vaguely aware that all is not well on this Easter morning. When Santuzza mentions her connection with Turiddu, deploring the renewed affair he is indulging in with Lola, my Mamma Lucia does not beg and plead to be filled in on the details. She grabs Santuzza by the hair, roughly pulls her head back, and demands in no uncertain terms to be told the whole truth.

In Gian-Carlo's production, Mamma Lucia's participation in the tragedy is driven home more forcibly, thanks to a set of circumstances that sparked a flash of inspiration nobody could have planned. As we all know, Turiddu and Alfio go off at the end of the opera to a fight to the death, accompanied by the village men. One of the peasant women behind the scenes has inadvertently witnessed what has happened and suddenly starts screaming, "Hanno ammazzato compare Turiddu!" Singers have a terrible time switching from singing to letting out that excruciating scream. This is why they usually assign the scream to an extra, preferably one with stage experience. At the Met, there was no problem finding women with Italian backgrounds, and they just let go with that scream as a matter of course. This was not the case in Munich.

After several failed attempts to get the right sound from chorus members and extras, I told Gian-Carlo I would know how to do it, but unfortunately I was onstage at the time, reacting to the tragedy as I watched the duel from my position at the parapet, and Mamma Lucia certainly wouldn't refer to her own son as "compare Turiddu"—neighbor Turiddu. Gian-Carlo said that if we simply dropped the word "compare," there would be no need to do it backstage, so we hit upon the idea of my twisting around from my position, after watching my son brutally knifed to death, as if I had been stabbed by the same knife, and grabbing that part of my body where I would have felt the labor pains when I bore Turiddu. In this subconscious recollection of my prepartum pain, a deep groan would issue from my very insides: "Hanno ammazzato Turiddu!" Santuzza would then echo the same words in a cry of vengeful triumph with a glow of joy on her face, only to recoil in horror at the catastrophe she herself has precipitated.

While preparing this production, we were faced with a new "guest" phenomenon in the operatic arena: the arrival of one of our star singers, more or less at the last minute, because of other commitments. It was Plácido Domingo, who arrived in Munich during the final rehearsal phase to prepare both tenor leads for the double bill. I am sure he expected to be doing what he usually did, walking into a fairly standard mise-en-scène, to which he could adapt readily by making use of his highly developed sense of routine. This is something all of us have to go through when time is of the essence. Some artists are rather naïve in thinking things are going to remain the same from one theatre to another, but this certainly does not apply to Plácido, whose musical and dramatic sensitivity far exceeds mere routine. When he realized that new ideas were going to be affecting his character, he did not pull a fit of temperament but simply thought it over, then commented, "Hmmm . . . I like this," and proceeded to make it his own, a feat which he accomplished in a short but intense three days.

Our Alfio, a native-born Sicilian baritone by the name of Benito di Bella, had a richly timbred voice, which he showed off to magnificent effect with the interpolated high notes in the Prologue to the companion piece, *Pagliacci*. During the initial *Cavalleria* rehearsals, Mr. di Bella was a very taciturn colleague, to the point where I almost feared that we might have done something to bring about his reserve. By communicating with him as often as possible and asking him questions about his career, I was finally able to mellow him out. This made for a cordial atmosphere in the ensemble and gave me a chance to find out more about his Sicilian background. I needed some corroboration from him, as a genuine Sicilian, to add dimension to my own characterization. After several conversations, I began to realize that while he had been away from his native island for many years, his Sicilian upbringing was still very much with him. He confirmed that Sicilians are still extremely rigid on the subject of male-female relations in any form. This even includes the contact between a younger man and an older woman, whom the former always treats with deference and appropriate distance. This relationship is even pointed up in the grammatical structure of the libretto, in which both Santuzza and Turiddu use the respectful form of address, "voi," when speaking to Mamma Lucia, while she replies with the more familiar "tu."

Benito di Bella's information helped generate a number of significant points of my characterization, one of which I had to defend after Benito's departure

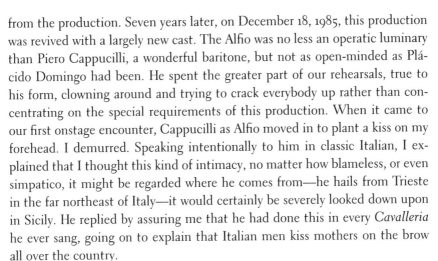

from the production. Seven years later, on December 18, 1985, this production was revived with a largely new cast. The Alfio was no less an operatic luminary than Piero Cappucilli, a wonderful baritone, but not as open-minded as Plácido Domingo had been. He spent the greater part of our rehearsals, true to his form, clowning around and trying to crack everybody up rather than concentrating on the special requirements of this production. When it came to our first onstage encounter, Cappucilli as Alfio moved in to plant a kiss on my forehead. I demurred. Speaking intentionally to him in classic Italian, I explained that I thought this kind of intimacy, no matter how blameless, or even simpatico, it might be regarded where he comes from—he hails from Trieste in the far northeast of Italy—it would certainly be severely looked down upon in Sicily. He replied by assuring me that he had done this in every *Cavalleria* he ever sang, going on to explain that Italian men kiss mothers on the brow all over the country.

Without revealing anything of my own background or my research with Cappucilli's Sicilian predecessor, I took it upon myself to confirm my point at the Bella Roma Restaurant, near my home in Munich, where I frequently go for meals because of the excellent food cooked up by Chef Salvatore Pagano, but also because I love the home-like atmosphere, in which I have a chance to use my Italian. One afternoon, I corralled Adriano Debole, one of several Sicilians in the place, and asked him for some data on Sicilian customs. I explained the kiss on the forehead and asked whether something like that would be sanctioned even today. Adriano instantly replied, "Oh, no!" and went on to add that any man of any age in Sicily who tried to get that familiar with any woman, for any reason, is liable to be given a stern reprimand, or even a thrashing, by the men in her family—or else knives might come out. In the case of an older woman, he went on to explain, the place for the kiss is on the back of her hand, as a sign of respect—but only if she extends it. Otherwise, simply saying "bacio la mano" would be in order, just as in Vienna a gentleman will take his leave of a lady with the words "Küss die Hand." Anything else would just be asking for trouble.

Armed with this intelligence, I went back for a rehearsal with Mr. Cappucilli and clarified the issue with him, explaining that a kiss on the brow from Cappucilli would be an honor and a pleasure, but not for Mamma Lucia when he was singing Alfio. He was very gracious, readily confessing he thought this gesture was a sign of respect throughout Italy, and he reluctantly agreed to defer to my wishes and leave the kiss out. The evening of our performance, I went out to take my solo bow and received the usual ovation accorded me from an audience that regards me as a good friend and remembers me from former triumphs, besides having been impressed by my performance of Mamma Lucia. When I returned to the wings, Cappucilli just stood there gaping open-mouthed in stupefaction. He then said, without wishing to seem impertinent, that he had never in his whole life witnessed applause like that for a Mamma Lucia! I couldn't help playing my trump card with him, and, switching into an Italian dialect, which he didn't realize I knew, explained amiably that a good Mamma Lucia is like a good tenor—a rarity in any theatre—whereas "baritoni ci sono a bizzeffe!" which can be translated into American English as "baritones are a dime a dozen!"

Fortunately, Piero had the good humor to take my joke in the same spirit as the clowning he always parlays. Laughing his head off, he put his arms around me and gave me a playful little offstage "Cappucilli" kiss on the forehead. It sealed a fast friendship.

Life among the Electrons

At the time of my début, the only studio recordings generally available for home use were 78 rpm discs pressed on shellac, with running times of only a few minutes on each side. This is why the recording companies in those days contracted the majority of opera stars almost exclusively for solos or short ensembles. In 1948, the first 33⅓ rpm LP records came on the market. It was at this stage of technological development that companies began bringing out larger editions of short complete opera recordings, such as *La Bohème* and *Rigoletto*. They also started seriously considering making studio recordings of full-length Wagner and Strauss operas. There are a number of records of my earlier performances available on CD, most of them pirated "air checks," illicit recordings of radio broadcasts, but these were not recordings I had anything contractually to do with. I just sang the performances, and somebody put them on whatever was being used at the time to preserve sound.

In 1951, the first year of postwar Bayreuth, the third act of *Walküre* was recorded live from the stage for Columbia Graphophone under the aegis of Walter Legge, with Herbert von Karajan conducting the festival orchestra. Sigurd Björling and I teamed up as Wotan and Brünnhilde respectively, with Leonie Rysanek as Sieglinde. At the time, Karajan had hoped this would serve to test the waters on market response to a long-term scheme to record the entire *Ring* cycle. His problems with the festival management, however, culminating with his departure from Bayreuth, prematurely truncated that project, leaving me and several other colleagues tied to a seven-year exclusive contract, which prevented me from recording *Walküre* anywhere else. Of course, I could have recorded *Siegfried* and *Götterdämmerung*, but no self-respecting recording company, then or now, would think of releasing those two operas other than as part of a complete cycle, which meant my mature Brünnhilde was lost to the studio, except in one instance. During that same 1951 season, Decca's John Culshaw was recording the Bayreuth *Götterdämmerung* performance under Hans Knappertsbusch, but the Columbia-EMI forces managed to block its release until 1999, when it was brought out in a superbly re-engineered CD edition by TESTAMENT, to whom I am eternally grateful both for releasing the recording and for coming to a financial agreement with the artists involved or their heirs.

At a point in time when I might have done a few complete studio performances, Birgit Nilsson burst upon the scene as a huge star with her generous voice and her magnificent top notes and proceeded to record her Wagnerian repertoire. These studio discs virtually exhausted the limited budget available under prevailing market conditions, precluding complete Wagnerian recordings by any other company. While I certainly do not begrudge Birgit this pride of place, I do regret that these events hadn't happened a few years later, when recording companies began to take pleasure in issuing alternative versions of virtually every standard opera in the repertoire, giving collectors an excellent chance to compare notes on different readings. Occasionally new operas are recorded for posterity, regrettably predicated on the assumption that the first presentations of a new piece may very well be the last. I am afraid this was the case in 1966 with Carl Orff's *Ödipus der Tyrann*, in which I recorded the part of Jokasta for Deutsche Grammophon with Gerhard Stolze in the title role and the Bavarian Radio Orchestra and Chorus under Rafael Kubelík. The work has not achieved the kind of recognition accorded some of Orff's other compositions, but I think it is a good policy to have a permanent record of a lesser-known piece by a major contemporary composer, recorded in optimum conditions under Professor Orff's direct supervision. In the mid-1970s and early 1980s, I went back to the recording studio for three character roles and also filmed the two best-known Strauss interpretations of my second career, Herodias and Klytämnestra, for television, following which both telecasts were made available for video release.

A recording of *Cavalleria Rusticana*, made in London in August 1979, gave me an opportunity to put at least an audio version of my Mamma Lucia interpretation on record for posterity. The conductor was the excellent Maestro Riccardo Muti, and the cast featured Montserrat Caballé as Santuzza, with her fellow Catalonian José Carreras as Turiddu, and the Tunisian-born French baritone Matteo Manuguerra in the role of Alfio. As the sessions progressed, I had an opportunity to observe the way both Catalonians brought a sincere Mediterranean quality to their artistry as well as to their personal relationships, particularly their deep affection for home and family. I witnessed two very different but equally touching examples of this kind of familial devotion. Caballé and I were staying at the same London hotel, and we often ran into one another in the lobby. On several of these encounters, she would arrive, laden with mountains of purchases she had made in the splendid London shops for her children. From the quantity of merchandise she kept hauling into that hotel, I often got the impression she was planning to open up a children's clothing store in Barcelona. She adored her family and wasted no time manifesting that profound affection in the palpable form of wearing apparel.

The second example of Mediterranean family loyalty I experienced in London actually came about in the studio. José Carreras and I were at the microphones at the beginning of the scene in which Turiddu says his final farewell to his mother toward the end of the opera. When Carreras started singing the first words of his aria, "Mamma, Mamma . . . ," he suddenly burst into tears and was so overwhelmed by sorrow, he had to stop. Montserrat waited a second, then proceeded to calm him down by speaking gently to him in their native language. At that point, the producer in the control room suggested we take a break.

During the pause, Montserrat Caballé drew me aside and explained that, when he was eighteen, José Carreras had lost a mother to whom he was deeply devoted. She was only fifty-one at the time of her death. The thought of evoking a final parting from a profoundly beloved parent shattered his composure for the moment. This episode serves to illustrate how the set of nerves an artist has to deal with in the recording studio differs from the nerves that plague us onstage. Why is this?

When we make a recording, every sniffle, every loud breath, every raspiness is likely to go onto the tape, and so we must be doubly careful to keep our singing as clean and free of extraneous sound as possible. The kind of perfection required in the studio has everyone sort of treading on raw eggs, so to speak, as a result of which a slight impulse may unsettle us, as it did in the case of José Carreras, whose relationship with his mother formed a cornerstone of his life, and yet, on the positive side of the ledger, the studio also provides us with the flexibility to repeat anything that didn't go right the first time. At our *Cavalleria* session, the producers wisely postponed recording Turiddu's farewell until a few days later. With his composure regained, his continuing closeness to his emotion inspired José Carreras to give a heartrending interpretation of the aria, which might perhaps not have happened at that level of profundity onstage.

The next recording came about when the Decca Record Company discovered that I was singing the cameo role of Madame de Coigny in Giordano's *Andrea Chénier* in Düsseldorf, and asked me to return to London in August 1982 to repeat the role in front of the microphone at sessions held in Walthamstow Town Hall. Studio work being the piecemeal business that it often is, some of the cast actually came back to Walthamstow two years later to complete the opera. The performance, under the direction of the amiable and ultraprofessional Maestro Riccardo Chailly, featured three pre-eminent stars of the Italian repertoire at the time: once again Montserrat Caballé, this time as Maddalena, joined by Luciano Pavarotti in the title role and Leo Nucci as Carlo Gérard.

Returning to London in July 1983, almost a full year after the *Chénier* recording, to join forces again with Maestro Chailly to sing the role of "Mother Goose," the bawdy lady in Igor Stravinsky's *The Rake's Progress* (a role I never sang onstage), was a welcome prospect for a traditionalist like myself, who can spend hours just looking at the beautiful old houses in this regal city, which by then had its war-damaged buildings restored to their prewar splendor. The only other singer in the cast—besides myself—from an American background was the fabulous Samuel Ramey, singing the role of the Devil's disciple, Nick Shadow, to perfection. This was the first time I had ever heard him, and I was totally bowled over by his artistry. It was fascinating to hear his interpretation of this essentially British role. Ramey, who hails from Colby, Kansas, sounded every bit as authentically British as the remainder of the soloists, most of whom were local London singers, such as Cathryn Pope, Sarah Walker, Stafford Dean, and Philip Langridge. It should be added here that Samuel Ramey, with his chameleon-like sense of diction, brings the same authenticity to every role he sings, whether it's in French, Italian, or any kind of English called for in the score.

Almost ten years before I did the aforementioned London sound recordings, I also began registering the complete performances, sound and visual, of my two Strauss character roles for the motion picture camera. I don't envy anyone who has to make movies. The day is long and often grindingly wearisome. The artists have to report for work between five and six in the morning, so they can be on the set in full make-up and costume by the time the sun comes up. In the course of the day, you may actually get a few seconds, or, if you're lucky, even minutes, of film in the can. Or you may find yourself sitting in the studio from morning to evening without being called to perform at all! This idle waiting leaves you even more exhausted than a full day's shooting.

Both *Salome* and *Elektra* were directed by Götz Friedrich and conducted by Karl Böhm. The *Elektra* film, in fact, was the last opera Professor Böhm conducted prior to his death in 1981 at the age of eighty-six. At the end of his life, Professor Böhm had a remarkably dual personality. He had grown extremely frail, and, in private situations, his wandering mind was the cause of several hilarious anecdotes. Possibly the funniest of these took place on the occasion of his final performance in London. As the likelihood of his ever returning to the city was virtually nil, Sir John Tooley, the director of the theatre, decided to give a little speech, paying homage to the venerable conductor for his many years of service to the theatre. When Dr. Böhm joined the singers onstage at Covent Garden, Sir John stepped out from the wings and proceeded to address the audience. And they, in good old English tradition, punctuated his homage with cries of "Hear! Hear!" One of the younger members of the cast was not familiar with this custom and asked nobody in particular what the audience was saying. With the aspect of a wise old owl, Professor Böhm looked over at the young singer and explained to her: "Sie sagen, dass sie hier sind" (They're saying that they're here). But for all his occasional irrationality outside the theatre and the concert hall, Professor Böhm was in full possession of his faculties in the recording studio, and the tiniest gesture from his baton could make the music virtually incandescent.

As in the composer's chronology, *Salome* was the first work to be filmed—in August 1974. It was later televised on February 23, 1975. The soloists included Teresa Stratas as Salome, Hans Beirer, a former Siegfried and Tristan partner from my dramatic soprano days, as Herodes, Bernd Weikl as the Baptist, Hanna Schwarz as the young page, and Wiesław Ochmann as Narraboth. One of the unusual things for a stage performer is the way a film director will take many shots of reactions, to be checked out at the daily screening of material and set aside, perhaps, for further use at the director's discretion. One example of this was the scene where the five Jews are squabbling. I had asked that we try to do each take as if it were the last, just in case we got lucky with at least one. Götz Friedrich did a setup with the Jews on the side and me in various close shots. As they started their scene, with me just listening, Friedrich called out from behind the camera, "Act! Act!" I did, and he cut the shot and sent it down to be printed. The silence that followed was broken by a voice saying,

Wishing Herodes (Hans Beirer) a happy birthday in Götz Friedrich's telefilm version of *Salome*. UNITEL.

"That's art!" It was Götz Friedrich. I wasn't quite sure what he was talking about. I had felt that the stage movement had caused me to come in a little too soon, lip-synching a high note, to which he replied, "I don't care." I felt a sense of discontinuity with that kind of operation, but I must admit, when it was all put together, it made complete dramatic sense.

Teresa Stratas is a fabulous soprano. Her Salome is a true document of what an intelligent singing actress can do in the full possession of remarkable gifts. In that *Salome* film, our brilliant director of photography, Wolfgang Treu, captured one extraordinary take that is very near to my heart—it shows Teresa

Stratas and myself in a joint profile as mother and daughter. In the course of that shot, which reminded me of two rare, antique coins meeting, I briefly eclipsed her profile and then moved on to the other side of her face. Götz Friedrich perceived it as an allegory for our single-minded intent, two women united in the desire for the Baptist's head, albeit for two totally different reasons. In many ways, that shot symbolizes my feelings toward Teresa, with whom I have shared the same wavelength from the first day we worked together.

During the musical preparations for the *Salome* film, Teresa Stratas accomplished one of the most remarkable feats I ever heard of. Because she could not secure a release from singing Zerlina in a series of *Don Giovanni* performances at the Metropolitan, she was unavailable to sing at the musical recording sessions for *Salome* with Professor Böhm and the orchestra. Necessity then became the mother of invention. The orchestral accompaniment was first recorded by Professor Böhm without her voice. At a later date, then, Teresa went into the studio and first just listened to this orchestral recording. After a while, she put one of a pair of headphones over one of her ears, leaving the other ear free to hear her own voice. She then overdubbed that recording in the sound studio in a single session—several hours of concentrated singing, and this with no conductor! I personally would have been far too nervous even to have attempted this feat.

The film production was a onetime affair for Teresa, because she didn't feel she had sufficient vocal power to carry over the enormous orchestra in a stage performance of this opera, but her television *Salome* is downright definitive. Frankly, I see no reason to condemn this kind of electronic wizardry, if it gives audiences an opportunity to witness a rendition as splendid as Teresa's. After all, the stage and the electronic media are ultimately two entirely different art forms, and they have to be taken at face value.

There was one old film tradition observed to the letter on both telecasts, and it rankles me to this day. While *singers* recording an opera are always invited into the control room, where they listen intently to the music they just taped, *film performers* are seldom if ever admitted to the screening room to look at the rushes of the previous day's shooting. The contention is that seeing our performances on-screen will make us self-conscious about our acting and take some of our freedom away. I do not think any true professional needs that kind of coddling, and I am sure being able to see my dailies could only have been beneficial to my interpretation of the role. When I later saw the complete *Salome* film, I found my performance in spots a bit too operatic for

Life among the Electrons 289

the screen, but Götz Friedrich assured me that was the way he wanted it. He said his concept involved Salome and Jokanaan being interpreted naturalistically, as in today's motion picture style, with the other two principal characters, Herodes and Herodias, theatrically exaggerated in an operatic manner. Was he trying to show a generation gap?

The film studio also gave us the benefit of witnessing Leonie Rysanek's Elektra. Like Teresa Stratas, Leonie knew this was a role she would never sing onstage, but Professor Böhm had asked her to perform it for the screen, and she agreed. Looking at that film today, one is amazed that Leonie survived to sing anything again after what she was put through in the studio during the summer of 1981. Götz Friedrich had come up with the rather far-out idea of having the opera begin and end with rain pouring down from the heavens. He intended this as a symbol for the never-ending futility of trying to cleanse the house of Atreus. This was further pointed up with a quote from Maurice Maeterlinck flashed on the screen at the beginning of the introduction. The quote read: "Pour out water, pour out all the water of the Great Flood—even then, ye shall never come to the end." As the opera starts, we see the five serving women and the overseer working under the pouring rain. Elektra even starts her monologue in the rain. At the end of the opera, she dances and sings in whirlpools of blood emanating from the palace and mixing with the torrents of falling rain. Several members of the cast began snidely suggesting that Elektra had not died of a heart attack (or a broken heart—depending how melodramatic the beholder may be), but rather from overexposure. Or perhaps she just drowned.

While I felt Götz Friedrich's concept of Klytämnestra had been more justifiable than his approach to Herodias, I still think it varied radically from my own conception of the role. When I later saw the complete film, it reminded me of silent movies, in which the actors had to exaggerate their characterizations to make up for the absence of sound. I found myself too monstrous, somewhat like a bird of prey. I felt this negated the fact that the woman had once possessed great beauty and dignity. The bloom of youth may have faded from her countenance, but she still retains traces of it along with her regal bearing. Left to my own devices, I certainly would have transposed the brutality of the character to other facets of the dramatic and vocal interpretation. I began by toning down parts of this interpretation, as I had with Herodias, because I felt it would bring out the high points with more potent effect, but Mr. Friedrich was adamant and simply "outvoted" me. If I had been able to see my rushes, I believe I could have provided some significant input on the final document.

There is a trendy theory that motion picture directors are the "authors" of their films, and fully accountable for everything that comes on the screen. I find this theory absurd on the face of it. While the vision of any competent director is the driving force of the film experience, the final product is invariably the sum total of all the artistry involved: cinematography, art direction, editing, and all the individual interpretations of the performing artists. These views notwithstanding, both of those thought-provoking opera films continue to hold the screen to this day, especially the *Salome*, which has the cinematic impact of a good mystery.

After seeing these films, which serve to capture what might be called the crest of my second career, many people have asked me whether I had ever been tempted to quit the opera stage and begin a stint as a motion picture actress, but at the time, I was just too involved in opera. After all, the operatic stage was giving me everything that I wanted in the way of a dramatic outlet, so I never really missed not having made more motion pictures.

Off My Beaten Track

W HEN, AT THE HEIGHT of my Wagnerian career, I would sit in the Symonette living room on Bunsenstrasse in Düsseldorf, listening to Lys, who had been Kurt Weill's trusted musical assistant and rehearsal accompanist, and Randy, who had a featured part in *Street Scene*, telling the stories of their work with Weill, it never entered my mind that one day I would be singing the role of Leokadja Begbick in one of the composer's most important works, *Der Aufstieg und Fall der Stadt Mahagonny*, a piece I would later help introduce to New York at the Metropolitan Opera. However, my first *Mahagonny* was not at the Met, but in Düsseldorf in 1970. The production ran for two more years, until 1973, with a total number of twenty-three performances.

The problems discussed in *Mahagonny*, in my opinion, have affected the world from time immemorial. These problems will continue to assail humanity unless a workable solution to them can be found, a development I am sorry to say I consider highly unlikely. Kurt Weill was not a man for causes. When asked about the impact of his works on later generations, he once replied, "The hell with posterity. I write for now." His librettist collaborator, Bertolt Brecht, on the other hand, had a missionary zeal that made him a kind of Billy Graham of the theatre. It had been Brecht's hope that his writings would shake up society toward a greater awareness of the inequalities of the times, thus leading all of us to rethink the idea of capitalism and realign our social and economic structures to eliminate the profit motive. However, he didn't even manage to *alienate* the capitalists—much less change their minds. To illustrate this point: I sang Begbick to packed houses in three financial capitals: Düsseldorf, Zurich, and New York. The well-heeled audiences listened attentively to the performances and applauded us generously, but the next day, the ladies and gentlemen went back to their boardrooms and garden parties, seemingly unaffected by the passionate entreaty of the piece. None of the above, however, invalidates the impact of *Der Aufstieg und Fall der Stadt Mahagonny* as a provocative evening in the musical theatre.

My own initial confrontation with *Mahagonny* began, as did many of my other professional experiences, with a phone call. The gentleman on the line was the peripatetic agent Robert Schulz, who had just returned from a visit to Düsseldorf, where he had conferred with Dr. Hermann Juch's successor as *Intendant* of the theatre, Dr. Grischa Barfuss, on casting the coming season's repertoire. Dr. Barfuss had told Mr. Schulz he was planning a production of *Mahagonny*, an opera that takes place in a kind of mythical America, and was eager to have Astrid Varnay, with her American background, to lend a note of authenticity to the part of Leokadja Begbick alongside Joan Caroll, a fine soprano from Philadelphia, who had been cast as Jenny.

Mr. Schulz explained that Dr. Barfuss had felt a little reluctant to approach one of the Düsseldorf theatre's resident Brünnhildes and Isoldes personally, to ask her to do this frankly grotesque character role, which offer he felt she might take amiss, so he delegated a trusted agent to make the contact. I replied that, as long as I continued to sing my regular repertoire at the theatre, I would be very happy to take a little excursion "off my beaten track" by adding *Mahagonny* to the list. I commented that I had met Lotte Lenya personally and had learned a great deal about Kurt Weill and his music in conversation with both her and Lys Symonette. When Mr. Schulz pointedly added that Bohumil Herlischka was slated for the director's job, that was all I needed to know. From experience I knew that Herlischka was definitely the man to stage this piece.

Following the *Mahagonny* première on December 8, 1970, the members of the press commented on the authenticity of my Brechtian style, displaying amazement that someone as steeped in another kind of theatre as myself could pick up the elements of that very special kind of playacting so readily. In the *Rheinische Post*, critic Heinrich von Lüttwitz said, "As a sharp satirist, Astrid Varnay was the one and only one who really went at it with a will. She sang and played the harridan, Leokadja Begbick, as domineeringly evil, vulgar and violent, as one might expect of her, unless we regard it as a miracle that such an accomplished musical tragédienne moved so smoothly into these theatrical waters." Writing in Munich's *Abendzeitung*, Helmut Lesch said, "Nobody could be anywhere near as convincing as Astrid Varnay as the frighteningly evil Begbick."

So much has been written and spoken about Brechtian style, this is probably the point in the narrative where I should also discourse on its fine points, but I'm afraid I'll have to disappoint my readers. I made no particular effort to do anything different from what I have always done with my portrayals: feel the style of the verbal and musical writing and then play the character from the inside out. I certainly never tried to play Begbick with the kind of intellectual distance some academics have attributed to Mr. Brecht's *Verfremdung* (alienation) theory, but rather relied on the same interiorization approach I would have used for Isolde or Elektra. The fact that informed critics found my portrayal "authentic" in a Brechtian sense is both a compliment to my work onstage and a commendation of Bertolt Brecht.

The same was the case when I did *Mahagonny* five years later in the production at the Zurich Opera House. Zurich is a strange city, very moralistic in the old Calvinist tradition on the outside, but the activity beneath the surface can get pretty heavy—or so I've been told. Finance, in all its legitimate and illegitimate manifestations, is at the center of everybody's attention, Zurich being the "Bank of Europe," which would have made it absolutely the wrong place for a play condemning avarice, but the Zürchers loved it. In the prestigious *Neue Zürcher Zeitung*, the critic commented, "Astrid Varnay, the famous dramatic soprano, has started a new life with this role, and was rewarded by enthusiastic applause." And the *Tagesanzeiger* added, "At no point did Astrid Varnay, the acclaimed Wagner heroine of the postwar years, sink to cheap *Grand Guignol*. Her presence alone exuded menace—she needed no additional hammy tricks." Eugene V. Epstein, writing in the English-language *Zürich*, commented, "Astrid Varnay, as the cold, calculating Leokadja Begbick, was the hit of the evening. She has a marvelously rich voice, a marked affinity for Weill/Brecht and is a great actress to boot." Shortly after the success in Zurich, I was invited to do the part at the Metropolitan.

New York, however, was not the only American city where I sang my second-career roles. In September 1968, the *Salome* production at the Chicago Lyric Opera was staged by Virginio Puecher and conducted by Bruno Bartoletti, with sets and costumes by Rudolf Heinrich. It featured Felicia Weathers in the title role, with Gerd Nienstedt as Jokanaan and Hans Hopf and myself as Mr. and Mrs. Herod.

In the Lyric Opera *Salome*, there was real fruit in the silver salver that would later hold the head of the Baptist. Puecher staged Hans Hopf to try and tempt Salome by holding up the salver and grinning over the fresh fruit, which she then refuses, after which he disappointedly sets the silver tray back down on the table. In the opening night performance, Mr. Hopf slammed the tray down on the table, sending a green cascade of grapes plopping down on the stage, where they proceeded to bounce almost in time with the music before coming to rest right at the area where Felicia was going to perform her "Dance of the Seven Veils." The minute I saw where the grapes had landed, I sensed how urgent it was to get them out of the way, but *how?* When Herod asks Salome to dance for him, it suddenly came to me. I rose to my full height, expostulating that I didn't want her to dance, using that anger to kick the grapes out of the way. As Felicia later told me, she was trying to figure out what I was doing so far away from the throne. When she saw me kick the grapes, she realized I had cleared the route for her dance and was more than grateful for the removal of that hazard.

After a magnificent première and an equally gala opening-night party, I returned to my Chicago hotel and left my salary check and the jewelry I had worn at the party in the safe, retiring with satisfaction for a good night's sleep. Judge of my stupefaction the following morning, when I asked for my safe deposit box, and a desk clerk, pale as a ghost from embarrassment, stammered the news that the hotel safe had been burglarized during the wee, small hours of the morning, and I had been one of the victims. Everything was gone, including my travelers' cheques and my passport, along with a costly Florentine ring and a Bavarian brooch, both of inestimable sentimental value because they had been gifts from Hermann.

Despite my shock at this crime, I was grateful that it had not been perpetrated directly before we were scheduled to return to Europe. I had made careful note of my cheque numbers, and the cheques were immediately replaced for me at the nearest American Express office. At my next stop, the passport bureau, I was promptly sent around the corner for a new photograph, while the official behind the counter checked the passport number I had written down, by telephoning, at my expense, the State Department in Washington. When I returned from the photographer, the clerk had a new document ready for me and pasted my photo into it, but said Washington insisted on further identification before I could be given the passport. I suggested he call the theatre, and while the telephone was still ringing there, a lady stepped in, carrying a stack of papers and books, and recognized me from the previous evening's performance. She was more than profuse with her compliments, addressing me by name. I turned to her colleague and asked if this was sufficient identification for him. He promptly set down the receiver and handed me my new passport. That's America for you!

Arriving back at the hotel more than a little frazzled by this experience, I decided to have a look at the write-ups, and what I read restored my good humor. Critic Bernard Jacobson paid lavish compliments to the musical and dramatic interpretation, taking issue with one small detail. In his words, "What is the point of Herod's asking Salome to bite on some fruit with her little white teeth and then offering her grapes?" The difference between cultures is sometimes overwhelming: while a German reviewer would be holding forth over the philosophical significance of this or that symbolic element, an American discusses the prop fruit!

Another series of U.S. performances featured *Salome* in San Francisco and Los Angeles, this time with Leonie Rysanek, William Neill, and Siegmund Nimsgern, with Hans Hopf and myself again paired as the terrible twosome. This production was based on Wieland Wagner's concept, carried out by Nikolaus Lehnhoff and conducted by Ottmar Suitner. In California, the fresh fruit was left at the supermarket. Then came *Jenůfa* in 1974, followed by five Klytämnestras the following year and three more in 1976, including a broadcast performance on the afternoon of January 10, 1976. In 1977, I presented my Herodias for the first time at the Metropolitan, premièring on February 2 with two subsequent performances, including a broadcast on February 12. Then finally *Mahagonny* in 1979.

The new Metropolitan Opera House at Lincoln Center was not as comfortable as the old one had been. The old building had a number of windows to let in the air, and we practiced in what one might call "natural circumstances." In the new house, many of the practice rooms are subterranean, like the locker room area of an urban athletic club, with the "artificial" air issuing from a ventilation system. All of this gave me the feeling we were doing our work in the realms of the Nibelungen. I disliked this area intensely. They told me there were practice areas on upper floors, but if indeed they exist, I never saw them.

The major change in the atmosphere of the theatre was not architectural, however, but human. Where once the place had been dominated by courtly continental gentlemen in ties and jackets, addressed by titles like Maestro or Herr Professor, the Met had become a more casual place, with most of the people on a first-name basis, in tune with the prevalent American atmosphere. Much of this informality was a pleasant change from Europe, but one aspect of it frankly irked me, and that was the frequent use of obscene language,

My farewell to the Metropolitan (unless something else comes up) was as Leokadja Begbick in *Der Aufstieg und Fall der Stadt Mahagonny*, seen here with Cornell McNeill as Trinity Moses and Ragnar Ulfung as Fatty. *Metropolitan Opera Archives.*

apparently predicated on the misconception that nobody's feathers would be ruffled by the unrelenting vulgarity. I am anything but a prude myself, but when I work, I want to concentrate fully on the matter at hand. While a little good humor, even of the spicy variety, can serve as an excellent tension-breaker at rehearsals, I definitely think there are limits that should be tacitly observed by everyone in the simple interest of getting the job done. Certainly, there is no place in any theatre for an attitude of trying to "curse" people into giving their best, which was the unfortunate style of our *Mahagonny* stage director, whose vocabulary was painfully rife with four-letter words.

This approach to directing was certainly counterproductive in my case. The blatant use of pornographic language, ostensibly to evoke some kind of reaction from me, stymied me more than it spurred me on. Beyond this, I honestly think it insults the intelligence of anyone whose skills need only be called on in a civilized fashion for them to go into action. And our cast certainly consisted of highly intelligent singers: Teresa Stratas as Jenny, Richard Cassilly as Jimmy Mahoney, the magnificent Norwegian dramatic tenor Ragnar Ulfung as Fatty, and the great Verdi baritone Cornell McNeill on a busman's holiday in the smallish role of Trinity Moses. This ingathering of musical and dramatic intelligence had little impact on our stage director, who continued to address all of us as if we were untutored stevedores with whom he could communicate only on the most primitive level. The scene became so redolent with coarseness, some of the soloists felt they had to get into the linguistic hog trough along with that man, which downgraded everybody. After enduring this onslaught of verbal compost to the breaking point, I knew I had to take the initiative. I told the "gentleman": "I don't enjoy working this way. Just tell me what you want—unembellished—and I'll do my best to give it to you." From the baleful look in his eye, I got the impression he thought of me as a prude of the old school, but I couldn't have cared less.

If our stage director was a source of annoyance, our conductor, James Levine, more than compensated with his ultra-professional music-making. He and I hit it off instantly, partly because of his professorial knowledge of music and his philosophical comprehension of its depth, and also because he had what I like to call a gypsy heart. Unfortunately, not everything we were doing was to the liking of the composer's widow, who visited several rehearsals along with Lys Symonette. As Lys later told me, Lotte Lenya was not at all happy with David Drew and Michael Geliot's English translation, which I found singable, nor did she care for Mr. Foulmouth's staging or approve of Maestro Levine's tempi. At one point, when the loose ladies were singing that wonderfully languid melody Weill used to set Brecht's rather inane attempt to write in English, "Oh, show us the way to the next little dollar . . . ," Mme Lenya rose from her seat and strode over to the pit to tell Maestro Levine to pick up the beat. Jimmy looked nonchalantly up at the stage and quietly said, "Those hookers are *very* tired." The tempo stayed just exactly as it was.

Our ten performances, starting with the première on November 16, 1979, included a live telecast on November 27, which was enthusiastically received, with many people writing to the Metropolitan to express their approval. Our reviews were what one might call mixed. Harriet Johnson in the *New York Post* said, "Astrid Varnay makes a formidable, sinister Leokadja Begbick, but she would benefit immeasurably by forgetting she ever was a Wagnerian soprano." Harold C. Schonberg, writing in the *New York Times*, said of the piece, "It is a pretty dated example of dialectical materialism, and to these ears much of the music is dated also," going on to praise me in the following words, "She has always been a marvelous actress."

In the course of preparing the *Mahagonny* production, I suddenly found myself having difficulty perambulating with what was turning into an insecure, faltering step. To be on the safe side, I used a cane or umbrella to enhance my interpretation of the role. This marked the beginning of the first phase of my life in which my physical condition was a factor. I got a premonition that I might at some future time be confronted with further difficulties, which could ultimately cut down my performing.

As it turned out, the *Mahagonny* production at the Metropolitan was my final appearance at that theatre. From 1941 to 1979 is quite a time span in any career. I may have walked into the Met that first day to audition for Mr. John-son as an innocent mademoiselle, but I can assure the reader I walked out of that theatre a full-fledged madame!

Medals and Cameos

Anyone confronted with a disability knows what inroads it makes in every phase of our lives, forcing us to evaluate each situation very carefully before we say "yes" to anything. The obvious decision for me, many might have said, would simply have been to call it a day, as far as my career was concerned, and spend my remaining years resting on my laurels. I had certainly amassed a number of gracious tokens of recognition for my artistic activities, and these honors kept right on coming in. The award dearest to my heart was presented to me on December 9, 1981.

The *Maximiliansorden* for Scholarship and Art had been instituted in a royal directive issued on November 22, 1853, by King Maximilian II of Bavaria to grant an encomium for exceptional accomplishment in the arts and scholarship, and confer upon the honorees the attribute of *Hoffähigkeit*, the worthiness to attend court occasions, much like the granting of royal honors and knighthoods in Great Britain. In fact, the first recipients of this award were known as the Knights of the Maximilian Order and appeared at their regular get-togethers in the official uniform of the society.

The list of knights was not strictly limited to citizens of Bavaria. The pantheon was made up of meritorious artists and scholars from many parts of the world. The very first list included such luminaries as the mathematician-physicist Georg Simon Ohm, the philologist Jacob Grimm (one of the fairy-tale brothers), the chemist Justus Liebig, the poets Franz Grillparzer and Joseph von Eichendorff, and the composers Heinrich Marschner, Louis Spohr,

Pardonable pride as Bavaria's Governor Franz-Josef Strauss made me the first woman to be inducted into the prestigious *Maximiliansorden*. Seated in the front row is my fellow honoree, the composer Werner Egk. *Rudolf Brauner.*

and Giacomo Meyerbeer. While this became a collection of Europe's most intelligent men, by a kind of tacit agreement the order was restricted exclusively to males. Occasionally an attempt was made to include distinguished women in the assemblage, only to be roundly voted down by the other members. In fact, membership was even refused to one of the most distinguished scientists of the age, Marie Skłodowska Curie, the co-discoverer of radium!

With the Nazi takeover in 1933, new laws were enacted regulating the awarding of medals and honors throughout Germany. As the *Maximilansorden* was not included in that legislation, it was decided to discontinue it. Forty-seven years later, on March 18, 1980, a law was enacted by the State Legislature, based on a suggestion from Professor Hans Maier, Bavarian Minister of Culture at the time, to the newly elected Governor, Franz-Josef Strauss, reconstituting the Order and establishing a new set of bylaws. To begin the new era, a list of nineteen members was prepared to form a core group. The list included the conductor Eugen Jochum, the composers Carl Orff and Werner Egk, the historian Golo Mann, and the actor Heinz Rühmann. The final name on the list, in strict alphabetical order, was Astrid Varnay, incidentally the first opera singer and the very first woman ever to be included in this august company.

The year 1988 added another great honor to my collection, when I received the Wilhelm Pitz Award, commemorating the great Bayreuth chorus master. It was presented to me for meritorious contributions to the German musical theatre by Germany's Union of Choral Singers and Professional Dancers on the express recommendation of the Bayreuth Festival Chorus, which, thanks to Maestro Pitz's initiative, continues to be, beyond any doubt, the greatest operatic chorus in the world. At the ceremony, after receiving a touching tribute from Götz Friedrich, I gave a short address of thanks in which I paid homage to the chorus, recalling to mind my very first *Götterdämmerung* with them in Bayreuth. In the second act, Gunther's vassals boisterously responded to Hagen's horn call in the most primitive, rough-hewn of tones, only to become as lyrical as a cathedral choir when they welcomed Brünnhilde to their midst an instant later. This transformation of musical mood was one of many virtuosic acts with which the highly professional members of this chorus excite the spirits of listeners year after year. It was sublime.

For all these honors and awards, however, I still saw no reason to hang up my career on the nearest hook and proceed to sail off into the dull waters of retirement. Besides, you can't put a medal on a sandwich. While I knew I would be limited in my locomotion, I felt I had a contribution to make to opera, and, as I still had contracts to fulfill, I slowly began moving into what Hollywood has come to refer to as "cameo roles": short, featured appearances. At the time, I was continuing quite a few of my principal characterizations, particularly Herodias and Klytämnestra, but the smaller roles supplemented both my enjoyment and my income.

Hänsel und Gretel was particularly enjoyable for me because of a few very close personal friends who were featured in the cast. These included Helena Jungwirth and Marianne Seibel in the title roles and David Thaw, a happily married man, uncharacteristically cross-dressing as one of the craftiest of witches, all under the musical supervision of Heinrich Bender. Herbert List's staging was one hundred percent child-friendly and remains unaltered in the repertoire from its first performance in 1965 to this day. One of the big disappointments of my artistic career was that I never sang the part of the witch. I had been offered the role in a magical, Disneyesque production I saw at the Metropolitan in New York, but I would not have been able to do all the dancing and prancing that character was called upon to perform, so I had to turn the flying broom over to more agile colleagues.

In the opening performance of the 1975 Munich Festival, in commemoration of the composer's eightieth birthday, I appeared as Euridike in Carl Orff's *Antigone*—an extremely difficult, yet gratifying, musical challenge because of the high vocal register. In the Wagnerian repertoire, I graduated from Norn no. 3, which I had sung in Bayreuth, to Norn no. 1 in the Munich production, at the request of Wolfgang Sawallisch, who meanwhile had become general music director in Munich. The *Ring* was staged by our boss, Günther Rennert, and ran from 1976 to 1983. I wonder why I never made it to Norn no. 2.

Although I have never been anywhere near Russia, I have developed a great affinity for Russian culture in general, and Russian music in particular, which made it keenly satisfying to perform the role of the governess, Filippyevna, in a German-language production of Tchaikovsky's *Eugene Onegin*, which ran in Munich between 1977 and 1979. The cast featured Hermann Prey in the title role, Julia Varady as Tatiana, and Clæs-Håkon Ahnsjö as Lensky. As much of the satisfaction of performing opera has to do with the quality of our partners, it was a special pleasure to portray Dame Marthe Schwerdtlein in the Bavarian State Opera production of Gounod's *Faust* in 1980, 1981, and 1982, because my partner in the Garden Scene was that buoyant Bolognese bass-baritone Ruggero Raimondi as a charming Devil. The Marguerite was Mirella Freni, who sounds as beautiful as she looks.

In 1981, I returned to *Holländer*, this time as Mary, who was the only "normal" figure, in my estimation, in an otherwise far-out production by a young set designer, at the time on the threshold of his directorial career. Shortly before rehearsals began, we were advised that the new director wished to convene a meeting with the cast to present his concept of the opera. As I was going to be guesting out of town on the date of this get-together, I suggested meeting with him later, and a date was set. At the time and place appointed, I arrived at the stage door to meet the gentleman and was amazed to find out that he was in the canteen. Not wishing to discuss serious artistic matters down there, I asked the stage doorman to advise him that I would be upstairs in one of the ladies' dressing rooms, where he was welcome to join me. He finally put in his appearance, accompanied by a lineup of about a half-dozen people, who, I presumed, assisted him. He asked if it would bother me to have his associates present, and, as we clearly had nothing to hide, I told him they were free to remain.

The director then began indoctrinating me into his concept of the opera.

He saw *Holländer* as a social allegory, the conflict of a brave new world striving against the restrictions of the established bourgeois system. My character, Mary, was to represent the repressive old era, while Senta stood for the modern generation, struggling to break free from the prevalent strictures. The Dutchman, on the other hand, was just as eager to "plop" back into the bourgeois civilization from which he had been banned for so long.

All very trendy.

As he went on to expound on this off-the-wall theory (as I saw it), my mind wandered back to all the years I had studied and sung the principal soprano role, starting with those hot summer sessions, sometimes lasting well past midnight, with Mother and the pitchers of lemonade on the fire escape in Greenwich Village. I recalled how I struggled to cram the score into my cranium preparatory to Maestro Weigert's fateful return from the West Coast. Then the many performances of Senta at the Metropolitan, Bayreuth, and points beyond. Why, I wondered, had the aspect of the work revealed by the director completely evaded me until this very moment?

While I was immersed in these reminiscences, our director shook me back into the present by detailing the set he had planned for the production, which would follow Wagner's original intention of staging the piece in a single, uninterrupted act. The first scene, at the storm-tossed seaport, would be suggested by a number of tarpaulins stretched over chairs and tables in the bourgeois living room of the second act, standing for the sandy beach, with steam rising to indicate the mists, which invariably appear after a squall at sea. At the end of that scene, the tarpaulins would be swiftly removed, revealing the confining middle-class drawing-room atmosphere from which Senta was determined to break out.

Frankly, by the end of his hour-long presentation, I found myself thinking this was a very interesting new approach, at least as far as the settings were concerned. Moreover, he talked a good game as he enumerated the various possibilities of staging the piece. That evening, at home, it entered my mind: Does he have the consummate stagecraft and skill to make this concept come alive? The answer, as the première brought out, was, regrettably: no.

In act 1, the audience was first treated to a rather believable illusion of a beach covered with drifting sands, with the mooring hawsers the only indication of the presence of seagoing vessels. This illusion was painfully shattered when the young steersman sat down on one of the alleged sand dunes, causing the tarpaulin to ride up, revealing the legs of the chair he was sitting on, giving the set the aspect of a furniture warehouse with dustcloths over the

Mary in *Der fliegende Holländer*, looking askance at a wall-to-wall flop production by Herbert Wernicke. *Sabine Toepffer.*

merchandise. Then the steam decided to do its own thing. Instead of wafting up from the nether regions to cloak the scene in mist, it casually wafted off the stage onto Wolfgang Sawallisch in the pit, much to the maestro's shocked annoyance.

When bourgeois morality, in the form of Daland's living room, finally put in its ominous appearance in act 2, the hawser lines continued to dangle into the scene behind a huge window. At the end of the opera, during a homecoming feast for the seafarers, for some odd reason held in the same living room as in act 2, Senta accommodatingly, and—to my mind implausibly—commits suicide by stabbing herself with a knife taken from one of the place settings, thus escaping from her confining, bourgeois surroundings, while simultaneously liberating the Dutchman from the curse he brought upon himself. Instead of sharing Wagner's apotheosis of redemption, the audience watched in bewilderment as the Dutchman, ignoring Senta's corpse, casually returned to middle-class society by dropping himself into the nearest easy chair!

Perhaps our director's reading of the opera was less romantic and had more relevance to contemporary society than the composer's original intention. On the other hand, however, the salvation of a tormented man through the selfless sacrifice of the woman who compassionately loves him is a central theme that runs throughout Richard Wagner's entire oeuvre, one which continues to possess pivotal significance for all time. By distorting this key image, the director deliberately swapped an eternal truth for a bit of maladroitly articulated social significance. Moreover, as a result of his obvious unfamiliarity with the technicalities of his own production, the whole concept, whatever its merits, went completely by the boards, leaving the public to wander home in total bafflement, while Wolfgang Sawallisch's wife probably rushed to the dry cleaners to get the steam damage expunged from her husband's dress suit.

The members of the audience were not the only ones confused by this production. The critics joined in their dismay. Writing in *Die Welt*, Reinhard Beuth suggested the audience should "simply close their eyes to it and forget this awful jumble," while Beate Kayser wrote in the Munich *tz*, after detailing some of the director's departures from the story, "The whole piece was swarming with such half-baked inspirations." The distinguished scholar Professor Joachim Kaiser said of our director in the *Süddeutsche Zeitung*, "If [Herbert] Wernicke doesn't like the essential elements of this piece, he should stage something else." To add to the controversy, a group of music lovers stood outside the theatre on opening night, presenting the arriving public with handbills reading, "Unfortunately, the administration of this theatre has been unable to unearth a work to fit Mr. Wernicke's staging." As Dante Alighieri once put it, "Abandon all hope, ye who enter here."

During the curtain calls, I was embarrassed to note that the thunder of disapproval directed at Mr. Wernicke's solo bows seemed to elevate his spirits, indicating that the scandal he had provoked, and which ultimately launched his career, was apparently more important to him than anything else. As for myself, I doggedly went on singing my "old-fashioned" Mary for the next five years with all the Wagnerian verve at my command, until this production mercifully wafted off with the mists.

On December 17, 1982, we brought out a double-bill of *Il Tabarro* and *Gianni Schicchi*, excellently conducted by Maestro Sawallisch, who has a great love for the Italian language. The productions were brilliantly staged by Tito Gobbi, one of the great Michele/Schicchi interpreters of the *Trittico*'s history. In his biography, *Tito Gobbi on His World of Italian Opera*, he mentioned our production in Munich with these words: "For *Gianni Schicchi*, I had the authentically Tuscan Rolando Panerai for Schicchi himself, the enchanting Lucia Popp for his daughter, while Zita was none other than the superb Astrid Varnay."

About a year later, on December 18, 1983, I performed the part of Juno in a German-language production of Offenbach's *Orphée aux Enfers*, staged by Götz Friedrich and conducted by Jesús Lopez-Cobos at the Deutsche Oper Berlin. My husband, Jupiter, in that production was Hans Beirer, my partner both from Wagnerian days and from the two television productions of *Salome* and *Elektra*, in which he sang Herodes and Ägisth respectively. Regrettably, Mr. Beirer had a lot of trouble remembering spoken dialogue, and, as we had been staged at an enormous distance from the prompter's box, everyone on-stage, particularly myself as the great god's scold of a wife, had to take turns "guessing what might be going on in Jupiter's mind," as a kind of informal prompting service. To add to our chagrin, the operetta was televised throughout the German-speaking world on Christmas Day of that year. A number of my friends, watching the telecast back home in Munich, later told me they marveled at my resourcefulness at combining the functions of singer, actress, and promptress in a single characterization.

On July 6, 1985, I made my first appearance as the wardrobe mistress in Alban Berg's *Lulu*, in Jean-Pierre Ponnelle's production. It proved a small part that seemed to take an eternity to learn, but once I had mastered its intricacies, I very much enjoyed my work. Jean-Pierre Ponnelle was a fine set designer who had become a brilliant stage director, and his wealth of scenic and directorial ideas lent a golden patina to every production he touched. In fact, the man's work has taken on the status of operatic legend. I profoundly regret that his *Tristan und Isolde* staging at the Deutsche Oper am Rhein and the Munich *Lulu* were the only opportunities I had to work with the late Mr. Ponnelle. In most productions of *Lulu*, the wardrobe mistress either sits there until she has to sing or comes racing out onstage to announce that Miss Lulu has just fainted, following which she sings the short ensemble and then walks off. In Jean-Pierre's production, the two of us came up with a completely three-dimensional character who exudes presence throughout the entire dressing-room scene. I was busy from start to finish: taking care of Lulu's costumes, hanging one of them up over the screen, brushing spots off the diva's hat with my elbow, reacting to everything the other characters were saying . . . and, to fill in the few breaks left over, I crocheted. Ponnelle initially wanted me to knit, but I don't know how, so he agreed to my crocheting.

At the première party, a lady walked over to the table I was sharing with some friends and inquired if she might ask me something in private. She said that she and her husband had made a wager as to whether or not I was crocheting in time with the music. Remember, this opera was written by Alban Berg! When I discovered she was sure my crochet hook had been whizzing in tempo with the complicated score, while her husband was equally convinced my handiwork was strictly free-form rhythmically, I decided to give her a little thrill and assured her she was perfectly right, sending her off on a cloud of joy over her acute perceptiveness. When I returned home from the theatre that evening, I checked the mirror to see if the tip of my nose had grown longer!

As the series of performances continued, all the members of our cast were grateful that our stage director had not just taken care of the production, but had also looked after us. Much of the stage rehearsal period was filled with pure anxiety, partially toward the intricacies of the score, but also because the stage had been covered with a slick surface that had us slipping and sliding, until Ponnelle came up with the idea of roughing the floor to give it a better hold and having as much of the footwear as possible rubber-soled, a necessary safety measure with all the acrobatics he had choreographed. The moral of the story: if you have a grand concept, it's a pretty good idea to carry it through all the way to the shoe soles, or you might just find yourself communicating your towering world vision exclusively to yourself and your devotees.

Silencing the Heavy Artillery

As THE EIGHTIES started moving toward the nineties, I continued interspersing my two Strauss monarchs with an increasing number of cameo performances. I then added one final principal character role, the Countess in Tchaikovsky's *Pique Dame*, which I sang in Russian at the Opéra in Marseille and almost sang in the same language at the Nationaltheater in Munich. The reason I only *almost* sang the part in Munich is one of the most bizarre happenings in my career.

My knowledge of Russian when I received the Marseille offer in late 1984 was virtually nil, but my fondness for Tchaikovsky's music and my fascination with the character prompted me to pick up the gauntlet and learn at least a smattering of the language plus the correct pronunciation I would need for the role. I secured the assistance of an expert on Russian music by the name of Alexander von Schlippe, a senior program presenter on the Bavarian Radio music staff, who, although German-born, had grown up in Russia. Shortly after starting work on the role, I became aware that the Bavarian State Opera was preparing the piece for a brand-new production. Apart from the Lisa, Julia Varady, who had learned Russian at school in her native Transylvania, the principal roles were cast entirely with singers from what was then the Soviet Union, with the conductor, stage director, and set designer also from that nation.

One afternoon, I ran into Otto Herbst, and he asked me to join him in his office—just for a chat. Under the general heading of "What's New?" I told him about the *Pique Dame* I was preparing for Marseille, to which he responded that this was good to know, whatever that meant. Shortly thereafter, the reason for his somewhat puzzling response was revealed. It seemed the lady scheduled to do the Countess had prior commitments at another theatre, which in no way clashed with the rehearsal or performance dates in Munich. However, only a few days after the start of rehearsals at the Nationaltheater, the dates at the other theatre were precipitously changed, and the lady discovered she would not be free to attend all the sessions with the Munich cast. Thereupon Mr. Herbst summoned me posthaste back to his office, where, on discovering I had the role ready in Russian, asked if I would be willing to help the theatre by substituting at a few rehearsals for the lady in question until she was free. So we struck a kind of informal horse trade: While I would not be remunerated for these rehearsals, my role would be firmly anchored in my memory when I got to France.

Time passed, and, as the rehearsal period was drawing to an end, I was again approached by Mr. Herbst, who had just been informed that our theatre would not have a Countess for the first dress rehearsal. Would I be willing to do that one as well? The preliminary rehearsals were one thing, I answered, but if I were to do a pre–dress rehearsal, I would expect to be compensated. After all, this is a performance-like situation, complete with costume and make-up. The theatre agreed to a full performance fee. Judge of everyone's amazement when Madame communicated that she would also be unavailable for the *final full dress rehearsal!* While the previous absences had been perhaps forgivable, in my opinion asking someone else to do a final dress rehearsal, open to an invited audience, in a brand-new, intricately staged production, was totally unprofessional, except in case of illness.

To cite one example of the difficult staging: I had to climb a narrow flight of rickety stairs from the cellar beneath the stage, to give the illusion we had come into the apartments from a lower floor. I couldn't help wondering to myself if the Russian lady would be able to manage that tricky entrance without practice. I was reassured that she was highly reliable, had performed the role many times before, and should have no trouble at all dealing with any part of the production.

It has always been standard theatre practice that whoever sings the final dress rehearsal also sings the role on opening night. When the chorus members saw me onstage for the final dress rehearsal, several of the ladies took it for granted I would be singing the first performance as well, and expressed their pleasure. I regretfully had to tell them I would not. They all regarded this as an affront toward a respected senior member of the company and said so in so many words. I calmed them down by reassuring them that I was being paid for services rendered at the rehearsal, and they replied that that was not the issue. Insult was then added to injury, when a photographer came over to take a couple of production shots for the posters outside the building and asked me to turn my head slightly, so the people looking at the poster wouldn't recognize my face. This kind of gratuitous treatment, quite frankly, I could happily have lived without.

Even though Mr. Herbst and I never discussed the possibility of my doing any performance of this role, he still felt honor-bound to tell me that the lady had "influential friends in high places" in the Soviet government. Were she to consider herself slighted, she might very possibly be in a position to have the services of all the other Russians in the cast withheld, thus effectively sabotaging future performances. For the first time in my life, I found myself locked in a political vise, and I was frankly upset over this, but I did appreciate our theatre's situation. Later on, I discovered that Alexander von Schlippe had spoken to the lady directly, suggesting she might release one of her performances in recognition both of my status in the theatre and the courtesy of rehearsing for her. There was no dealing with her. In language that would make a dockworker blush, he said, she claimed she owned the role and, although she had not attended one single rehearsal, she obdurately insisted on doing all the performances.

Munich's loss turned out to be Marseille's gain. The production, which opened on February 20, 1985, running for four performances, was an unqualified success. I assume I had done my homework well, because, after the opening performance, a charming older couple greeted me at the stage door, enthusiastically chatting with me in Russian, to which I had to reply in French that I didn't speak the language that well. They looked at me wide-eyed and exclaimed, "But that's not possible! You just sang it perfectly."

When I returned to Munich, I was approached by two members of the ladies' chorus, who expressed their regret that I hadn't sung their première, and proceeded to inform me that the Russian diva had handled the ascent on the shaky steps by adamantly ignoring the staging and simply entering from the wings. She also chose to play the ancient Countess as a much younger woman, for reasons she neglected to divulge to anyone. There's *no* business like show business!

In 1987, I added what sounded for all the world like a bass role to the repertoire, in Carl Orff's *Ludus de Nato Infante Mirificus* for ZDF Television, in which I sang Mother Earth. I studied the music, written in what I presumed was the mezzo-soprano range, but the conductor asked me if I might be able to sing the whole role an octave lower, as printed in the orchestral score. Although I was completely taken aback by this request, I said I'd give it a try. It worked, and the result was telecast. For the record, that's not technical wizardry, that's really my own voice!

I still had several *Elektra* performances contracted, both in Munich and other theatres, and, as Klytämnestra was the last of my leading roles, I was determined to keep going on with it as long as possible. To give the reader an idea of that determination: one event occurred on one of the coldest November days in recorded history, which might perhaps have fazed a less resolute performer. When I arose that morning, the radio reported that such freezing temperatures had not been recorded in Munich for the past thirty years. Early that afternoon, the cold let up just enough to allow a heavy rainstorm to flood the streets; then the temperature plunged back below freezing immediately afterward, which turned the whole city into an enormous labyrinthine ice rink, with all the roadways as slick as glass. I immediately called Mr. Herbst to apprise him of the situation. He told me to sit tight at home, and he would arrange for somebody to come pick me up. The car never arrived. I later found out that the driver had stepped out to check the street sign, promptly slipped on the ice, injured his knee, and had to be hospitalized. But Mr. Herbst was still sanguine I would be able to make the performance, although I must admit I thought he had taken leave of his senses when he casually announced he was sending me a fire engine, but he was as good as his word. In actual fact, I wasn't picked up by a mammoth hook-and-ladder truck, but rather by one of the especially equipped red cars that can negotiate just about any terrain on their way to a conflagration. When we finally got to the stage door, the driver actually took the vehicle right up onto the sidewalk, so I would have the barest minimum of ground to cover in order to get into the building. I just had time to thank him with a generous tip.

As I rushed into my dressing room, Hilde Bauer, my wardrobe mistress, was telling the ladies in the cast to keep calm, because the clock had already reached 7:40 P.M., with the curtain due to rise at 8:10 P.M., and I would need to get ready for the performance as quickly as possible. I elected to forget my make-up entirely and just concentrate on getting the elaborate costume, wig, and crown on, following which I took an eyebrow pencil, accentuated my eyelids and eyebrows, applied a heavy coat of lipstick, and then went straight to the backstage area to wait for my entrance. My adrenalin level was so high at that point, I felt that being near the stage was the only way I would ever

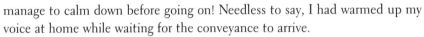

manage to calm down before going on! Needless to say, I had warmed up my voice at home while waiting for the conveyance to arrive.

The whole orchestra had made it to the theatre, although many of its members are dyed-in-the-wool suburbanites, and the chorus was present in almost full complement. The theatre has a seating capacity of 2,100, but on that evening only about a third of the audience had managed to brave the elements to get to their seats in the auditorium. If they had made it to the opera house, every member of the cast was determined to see to it that our patrons would get the best performance of which we were capable, and they certainly made up in enthusiasm what they lacked in numbers.

When we returned from taking our final bow, one of the wardrobe women greeted me with the words, "But you can't go home!" She was right. The fire department may have brought me there, but no provision had been made for home delivery, so the wardrobe staff suggested I simply stretch out on one of the dressing-room couches. They would then find some blankets to cover me up for the night in the unheated theatre. In the midst of all this confusion, someone looked out the window and discovered that the ice had completely disappeared. Apparently, there had been either a weather inversion, or else the fervid heat of our performance had somehow made short work of the ice. The following morning, all the papers featured my arrival with the fire department vehicle, so at least I got a good headline to reward me for my determination.

If this experience was scary, events that happened during a performance of the same opera at the Paris Grand Opéra back in 1975 had been downright traumatic. I was engaged to sing at the Palais Garnier with a real king-size cast: Birgit Nilsson and Leonie Rysanek were my daughters, with Hans Sotin and Richard Lewis as Orest and Ägisth respectively, in a production staged by August Everding under the musical direction of Karl Böhm. It premièred on April 11, 1975.

A subsequent performance of this series was selected as the high point for one of those grand ceremonial events the French do with such panache. The occasion was the state visit of German President Walter Scheel to his French counterpart, Valéry Giscard-d'Estaing. The event took place on April 21, with an international radio hookup over the European Broadcasting Union service to many parts of Europe. Normally, auditoriums are so dark that the singers onstage notice only vague silhouettes in the audience, but there was no way of fading out all the glitter of *that* audience, as the stage lights reflected off a profusion of opulent jewelry on the ladies and medals on the chests of the gentlemen. In short, *le tout Paris* was out in force. My scene with Birgit went

Three blockbuster voices: Leonie Rysanek, Birgit Nilsson, and myself. It was not our singing, though, that put the lights out in Paris. *Personal photo.*

magnificently. I then retired offstage to wait for the cue for the screams I have to emit in extremis when Orest assassinates me. Sotin made his entrance as Orest, and he and Birgit sang the short exchange in which she tries to ascertain who this mysterious bearer of bad tidings could be. The action reached its climax when Elektra realizes her brother has returned, and, in a spasm of ecstasy, sings: "Orest!" Then all the lights went out.

I had been relaxing in my dressing room, chatting with one of the assistant directors, when suddenly the bulbs on my dressing table dimmed and then went completely out, plunging the room into glum darkness. Only the red emergency exit lights remained on, enabling us to find our way around gingerly backstage. It is a tribute to everybody in the theatre that evening, on both sides of the curtain, that a panic did not break out. The orchestra stopped playing and waited for the lights to come back on, while Dr. Böhm stared in stupefaction at the blacked-out stage.

Meanwhile, what happened on the radio was a fascinating contrast between French and German attitudes toward broadcasting. Listening in Munich, one of my friends heard a loud cracking sound as the electricity in the theatre failed, followed by the frenzied voice of the French announcer, telling the radio audience that something unexpected had occurred, then going on to describe in detail everything he could perceive from his perch in the darkened auditorium. Back in Germany, his agitated voice was slowly faded out, and a German announcer, with all the emotion of somebody announcing the latest prices of soybean futures, apathetically stated that the performance in Paris had been interrupted and would resume in due time. Incidentally, that casual disclosure of the interruption was the only information provided on German radio about the power failure. Then seemingly endless minutes of dead air, followed by a recording of Strauss's *Death and Transfiguration*, apparently hastily rushed down from the music library, leading my friend to surmise that perhaps an assassination had taken place. Another friend, hearing the music selected, feared that Professor Böhm might have keeled over on the podium. Almost a half-hour later, the lights came back on, the German station took the *Transfiguration* off the turntable and switched back to the Paris remote, and the opera continued right where it had left off, except that Birgit had to repeat the cry of "Orest" to get back into the scene.

At the end of this distressing evening, we were assured that the power failure had been caused merely by overvoltage on the line blowing one of the main fuses. I didn't believe it then, and even now I suspect that sabotage was somehow involved. But I guess nobody will ever know what really happened. In any case, while we were slowly leaving the house, still highly upset, Birgit, in her inimitable Scandinavian lilt, relieved our tension with one of her classic quips, most of which were fiscal in nature: "You know, they should pay me a little more. I had to sing the word 'Orest' one more time than it is written in the score!" The final performance of this Paris series took place on my birthday, April 25, and I was the grateful recipient of a wonderful gift in the form of an entire performance without mishap.

Twelve years later, toward the end of 1987, I began having trouble with my knees. I started getting more and more worried about having to negotiate the steps leading down from the portal of the palace to the place where Klytämnestra confronts Elektra. Once, I stumbled and almost fell on the stage. I had to think quick as a flash how to make the tumble a part of the performance, but I managed to regain my balance and finished the evening with no further problems. But how much longer would I be able to handle the physical hazards of this role with the condition in my knee joints deteriorating? Then a management decision at the Munich Opera came to my rescue. Major renovations were about to be made to the Munich *Elektra*, which had been on the boards since 1972. At first, the theatre wanted to present a completely new production, but when this proved financially unfeasible, it was decided to give the opera a short rest, restore parts of the set and some of the costumes, and then return it on April 5, 1988, with other singers in the leading roles. After much deliberation, I decided I would take advantage of this development, and use my 121st and final performance of Klytämnestra on January 20, 1988, to put the role to bed, silence the heavy artillery, and continue my stage career in cameos.

About the same time, a gentleman by the name of Manfred Kreckel asked if he might do a television portrait of me. I was frankly delighted with the idea, and doubly pleased when the Bavarian State Opera granted permission to tape portions of the January 20 performance. Unfortunately, the news of my final *Elektra* performance led to some embarrassingly false reporting on the part of the network. Watching the telecast, I was at first baffled that the network had chosen to transmit the portrait in the middle of a program called *Mosaik*, a series largely devoted to issues concerning senior citizens—pension and insurance plans, medical problems, and the like—and usually viewed only by the older generation. I have never seen any reason to make a secret of my age, but I still couldn't understand what my vintage had to do with a telecast about my operatic career. I got the answer when the moderator of the program, a Ms. Ingrid Thomé, whom I have never met before or since, solemnly announced that I had come to the end of my theatrical activities, concluding with the incomprehensible statement that a long and renowned career had entered the history books. I was tempted to re-check my calendar to make sure my future performance dates were really there.

As if this weren't bad enough, at one point during the interview with Mr. Kreckel, I commented that I had been blessed with a number of wonderful conductors and stage directors, who were always ready to make our collaboration in the theatre a truly cooperative effort. I then went on to say, "With one exception," and proceeded to describe an intransigent authoritarian, who obstinately insisted on always having things his way. In an unpardonable spasm of second-guessing, the *Mosaik* staff flashed a subtitle on the screen, saying they were sure I was talking about Herbert von Karajan. I wasn't. Had I wanted to reveal the name, I would have done so.

On May 21, 1988, I added another Janáček characterization in the guise of the chambermaid in the third act of the composer's *Věc Makropulos*. This cameo role consisted largely of musical gossiping with Hildegard Behrens as Emilia Marty, while I combed her hair.

As time went on, my walking difficulty became more and more pronounced, and Dr. Galli finally suggested the best way to deal with the situation would be through surgery. This would, of course, involve convalescent and rehabilitation periods, following which there was no guarantee I could return to active performance. As I had joined the teaching staff of the Opera Studio on September 15, 1987, I knew I would at least be able to make a meaningful contribution, whatever the results of the surgery. I sang my twelfth and final *Makropulos* performance at the Munich Opera Festival on June 18, 1989, taught until the end of that festival season, following which I was admitted to Munich's Bogenhausen Hospital, where Professor Werner Keyl first did an exploratory arthroscopy on my left knee on July 20, going on to perform a major operation on July 24. For a while, after this first operation, it looked like I really might be calling it quits as far as my stage career was concerned.

I still had a contract for a total of twelve performances of Mamma Lucia and the *Makropulos* chambermaid in 1990, but I had to cancel them all because of my physical deficit. The walking was, at the time, still too strenuous, and there was no way we could eliminate the stair climbing Mamma Lucia has to do without distorting the production, nor would it have done for the chambermaid to comb her mistress's hair while simultaneously leaning on a cane, so I had to pass.

I continued teaching at the studio, adding August Everding's *Singschul'*, a one-month summer master class to provide continuing education to young singers. On January 16, 1991, Professor Keyl operated on my right knee, and I went through another rehabilitation period. To all intents and purposes, it looked like I was gradually putting myself out to pasture, but again, Dame Fortune had other plans.

Act V

LOOKING AHEAD

Nursing the Tsar

AFTER ALMOST FIVE DECADES ONSTAGE, there is something very gratifying about the time of reflection that follows all that activity. Gone are the worries of getting from one place to another on a tight schedule. One's own home takes on a newer meaning, as the owner wakes up every morning not wondering what city or country one may happen to be in. A person can enjoy a book without having to be 33,000 feet up in the air. The problems of staying fit for the next performance relax somewhat, and an extra helping of pasta can be consumed with delight—and without any pangs of conscience. Even better than that: I was actually able to fulfill my desire to attend performances at the opera more often without having to worry about an early rehearsal the following morning. And—wonder of wonders—it all happened so uneventfully.

They tell the story at the Met about Rudolf Bing asking the illustrious Zinka Milanov, after almost thirty years of service, what opera she wanted for her farewell performance, to which Mme Milanov is alleged to have replied, "Nyothink." She thereupon promptly and inconspicuously retired from the theatre without any further formalities. I, too, had managed to slip into the middle distance without the usual rituals of "retirement." There had been no mawkish ceremonies at farewell performances, no final tours, no sentimental tears of parting, nor did I wish to face the dubious pleasure of having to listen to a series of eulogies.

While not wishing to belittle honest and sincere regret over the departure of a revered artist from the active scene, it is almost impossible to ritualize this event without a smattering of affectation. As a case in point, I remember the times that we standees at the Metropolitan were distraught to learn that every *Rosenkavalier* performance Mme Lotte Lehmann sang would be her last public appearance. This distress lasted for some five years before she finally took her leave in a Town Hall recital. I had made up my mind even then that I would never inflict this kind of oppression on my audience—presuming, of course, that I would ever have an audience! My mood following my last Klytämnestra verged on euphoria . . . and yet, somewhere in the back of my head, there was still a little itch quietly but insistently waiting to be scratched. This time, for a change, the phone did *not* ring!

Gerd Uecker, Otto Herbst's successor as head of the administration office, had been deputized by Johannes Schaaf, who was preparing a new production of Mussorgsky's *Boris Godunov*, to sound me out as to whether I would accept the role of the "Mamka," the governess in Tsar Boris's palace. I liked the idea, but, I explained I would have to decline Mr. Schaaf's kind invitation, as I was still recovering from my recent knee operation and would certainly be hors de combat for the foreseeable future. He replied that Mr. Schaaf was aware of that, but he was absolutely adamant about wanting me in his production, going so far as to suggest that he would personally carry me on- and offstage on a sedan chair, if he could only have the power of my presence in his staging. Power of my presence? That did appeal to me, but I still wasn't quite sure what it meant in straight terms. After all, I had seen the opera a few times, and there is a little scene in which the governess dances with the Tsar's children. How, I wanted to know, did a practical man of the theatre like Mr. Schaaf propose staging that dance with a performer approaching the three-quarter-century mark sitting in a sedan chair?

Mr. Uecker clarified that issue by explaining that Mr. Schaaf and the conductor, Valery Gergiev, Director of the prestigious Kirov Theatre in St. Petersburg, had decided to opt out of all the various revisions generally performed in favor of Mussorgsky's original score. Both Schaaf and Gergiev maintained that modern ears, especially those of scholarly German audiences, would doubtless be more than willing to give the composer's original intentions a chance, and so they had determined to grant the original score a kind of belated world première. While this production would be taking the opera back to its musical roots, Mr. Schaaf had several totally plausible new ideas for the staging, ideas with which I concurred wholeheartedly. One of these was the inspiration of making the governess an old family retainer, who may once have been the Tsar's own nursemaid. As such, she had remained his confidante over the years, the mirror of his emotions, and when he pours his heart out in the famous monologue, he uses the governess as the addressee for his innermost thoughts and feelings.

Getting back to stage work after a forced two-year absence, especially in the company I was keeping, was pure delight. The exchange between Paata Burchuladze as Boris and Kenneth Riegel in the role of Shuisky began to bristle with tension. Even though I had very little music to sing, the concentration involved always had me emotionally depleted at the end of that scene. The reviews of the May 20, 1991, première were very flattering to me, calling attention to my contribution with a number of compliments. In Munich's *Abendzeitung*, Marianne Reissinger stated, "Astrid Varnay is the very incarnation of knowledge of the political realities," and Wolfgang Schreiber in the *Süddeutsche Zeitung* went so far as to suggest, "She transforms a mere turn of the body into an earth-shaking event." Reviewing a performance of the production during the 1991 Munich Opera Festival, Karl-Robert Danler in the *tz* echoed one of my very first write-ups back in 1941 when he wrote, "She is capable of filling the stage even when she just sits there in silence." Incidentally, Mr. Schaaf didn't need the sedan chair.

Boris Godunov continued for six performances in 1992, then took a long rest during the aforementioned obligatory theatre hiatus. In May 1995, *Boris* returned to the repertoire with yours truly in tow. While rehearsing for the final performances of the 1995 series in the autumn of that year, Kenneth Riegel asked if I would mind trying out a new idea, which he had effectively introduced in another theatre, also under Johannes Schaaf's direction. My reply was somehow evocative of the spirit that has guided my entire career: "Ken, I'll try anything, if you can tell me why." We worked out a bit of business in which he makes a supercilious remark to Boris, prompting me to raise my cane threateningly at him with a glare of loathing. To manifest his contempt, Ken as Shuisky simply snatched the cane out of my hand, leaving the governess virtually stranded on her chair without any form of physical support. Then, after a moment, he returned it to me with a sardonically elegant flourish. This added a touch of menace to an already highly charged scene.

About a week after the final performance, Gerd Uecker called to inform me that *Boris* had not been shelved. He wanted to know if I would be available for a new series. I assured him that he was welcome to ask me again when the time came, and, health permitting, I would be favorably inclined. I mentioned this to Paata, who, adorable Georgian bear that he is, expostulated, "If you don't sing, I don't come!"

And so, retirement, whatever that is, would be indefinitely postponed. While I welcomed the thought of some time off from stage work for the coming months, it wasn't as though I didn't have anything theatrical to do.

Growing Pains

I WAS OFTEN ASKED for voice lessons, and I invariably—politely but firmly—refused. Building the voice of a young artist is a touchy business and rightly belongs in the hands of someone who can give the student regular supervision. Besides, to be perfectly honest, I was never tempted to open a vocal studio, with all the administrative headaches that involves. Nevertheless, I had no objection to the idea of helping young singers overcome their growing pains under the aegis of an established institution. The opportunity finally came in 1970—in the twenty-ninth year of my profession, to be specific—in the form of a suggestion from an influential friend in Düsseldorf. City Commissioner Gerd Högener suggested that I should impart some of my operatic knowledge to vocal students by conducting a master class at Düsseldorf's Robert Schumann Conservatory of Music—today's Robert Schumann Music Academy. The idea, frankly, appealed to me, but could I really teach? I didn't know. Being able to do something—anything—does not necessarily mean we can teach it to others.

Gerd was sure that a singer as "famous" as myself surely had a great deal to give younger artists, but I insisted that fame had nothing to do with the case. He urged me to talk things over with the director of the conservatory. The result of that meeting was that I agreed to give it a go, but strictly on a trial basis! I made a proviso that if, after a period of six months or so, I felt I was not transmitting what I felt was necessary, or should the administration feel I was not adept at teaching, we would suspend the master class and part company amicably. With this understanding, I agreed to begin instruction there starting in May.

The lessons took place whenever I could spare time from the rest of my professional schedule. This generally averaged anywhere from six to eight full days a month. It would be nice to report here that all the members of that class are now glowing stars on the operatic horizon, but this is not the case. It is enormously difficult to get into our business, and even harder to stay in it. I was, nevertheless, happy to discover that I had the ability to ferret out whether students with the requisite vocal talent also had the requisite inner where-withal to make the grade.

Of the wide variety of cases I encountered, by far the oddest was a tenor who had a terrible time singing anything that dealt with romantic love. When I finally quizzed him on this, he told me he felt it was such a private matter, he couldn't sing about it in public. I decided to approach this dilemma by a circuitous route, and asked him if he had a favorite food. He immediately responded in the affirmative, going on to admit he had a passion for steak. I then suggested he try to imagine a juicy sirloin steak, grilled to perfection on an open charcoal fire and served with his favorite relish, along with a plate of crispy French-fried potatoes, glistening with freshly strewn salt. And perhaps a colorful vegetable salad with just a soupçon of garlic to add that perfect touch of zest to the dressing. By the time I got to the ruby-red vintage St. Émilion, exuding its heady aroma from a sparkling crystal goblet, he was virtually slaver-ing with delight. Thereupon I told him, "Now, sing the song again, but think about that steak dinner." Suddenly his voice took on an eroticism I never dreamed he had—nor had he, for that matter. He passed his course at the conservatory with flying colors, and he frequently sang with such ardor, he left me and the lady at the piano wishing we were both filet mignons instead of women.

The master class proved a meaningful supplement to my stage activities and lasted for several years, until my absences from Düsseldorf were becoming so frequent, I could not give the students the continuity they required. The conservatory was reluctant to let me go and even proposed keeping my name on the faculty list for the following year, hoping I would find time to rejoin the teaching staff. This was then repeated for a total of three years. During those three years, however, I was busily pursuing my second career, with as many engagements here, there, and everywhere as I had sung at the crest of my principal soprano activities. Therefore, at the end of the three-year wait, I regretfully decided to terminate the teaching contract and open the position for somebody else. My stint at the Robert Schumann Conservatory did prove one important fact to me: I really had a natural teaching ability, and this aptitude continued to hold me in good stead eleven years later when I took on my second pedagogic assignment.

Time was when talented young singers in Central Europe generally proceeded from their music schools to an engagement in a small theatre somewhere in the provinces. In the intervening years, this activity in the hinterlands dwindled to the point where the smaller theatres no longer provided sufficent training ground for these beginners. To ameliorate the situation, some of the larger houses initiated a kind of apprenticeship program. These studios offered gifted music school graduates threefold benefits. First, in some houses they were given a minimum living wage; second, their generally inadequate theatrical training was brought up to a professional level; and third, they received the excellent opportunity of rubbing elbows with top-flight soloists by singing small roles in regular productions. The members of the Opera Studio of the Bavarian State Opera received the additional benefit of singing roles in separate studio productions, which then toured the surrounding areas accompanied by a full complement of musicians from the regular theatre orchestra.

The first Munich study program, known as the "Young Opera," was founded during the administration of Rudolf Hartmann. Günther Rennert continued the institution, which went through several name changes, finally taking on its present title. Heinrich Bender was later asked to supplement his position as *Staatskapellmeister*, the Bavarian State Opera's resident conductor, by also becoming the administrative director of the studio and musical director of all studio performances.

My own involvement came about during a meeting with Wolfgang Sawallisch, who was director of the Bavarian State Opera at that time. Somewhere in the course of conversation, he broached the subject of young people in our business, to which I replied that the current climate in the trade was anything but salubrious for our younger colleagues. Where once budding singers were carefully nurtured, I commented, today many agents and theatres take promising talents and wring them out like a washrag, only to throw them away when they are worn out. This diatribe provoked Professor Sawallisch to raise one eyebrow, a rare flash of emotion on his part, followed by an inquiry whether I would do something about this situation if I had the chance. My reply was, if the opportunity were to present itself, I would definitely be agreeable. Before I knew it, I found myself teaching at the studio, starting on September 15, 1987.

My work as a teacher of vocal interpretation involved contributing to the preparation of the studio's full-scale productions of such standards as Mozart's *Don Giovanni*, *Così fan tutte*, and *Le Nozze di Figaro*, plus contemporary works by the well-known twentieth-century Bavarian duo, Carl Orff and Werner Egk. We presented Orff's fairy-tale opera, *Die Kluge*, and Egk's version of the riotous Gogol farce comedy *Der Revisor*, the same play that had audiences in stitches when Danny Kaye played the lead in a motion picture version entitled *The Inspector General*. All of this repertoire was rehearsed and performed in German. My work concentrated on *meanings*, helping the students find the subtexts of what they are saying on the surface. In this effort, I also encouraged them to work consciously at discovering and using their innate wealth of imagination toward the goal of developing their individuality.

At the conclusion of the two-year studio contract, many of our young colleagues were ready to move on to full-fledged professional lives. Many studio members were chosen to move directly into positions on the roster of the Bavarian State Opera, such as Colombian tenor Juan-José Lopera, who made his leading-role début in the Nationaltheater as Ernesto in *Don Pasquale*, continuing on to bel canto roles in Vienna. Mezzo-soprano Petra Lang was featured as Fenena in *Nabucco* at the Bregenz Festival and appeared as Brangäne in a concert performance of *Tristan und Isolde* in New York's Carnegie Hall. Basso Alfred Reiter has sung in the current *Meistersinger* production in the past three Bayreuth Festivals and is now slated for major roles in Salzburg and Berlin, while tenor Roland Wagenführer has really hit the big time with leading roles in Vienna, Dresden, and Munich. After a first engagement as Erik in a Bayreuth production of *Der fliegende Holländer*, Roland opened the subsequent festival season in the title role of *Lohengrin*. Another student with a fabulous voice is a good-natured Texan named James Taylor, who is now making a name for himself as a concert artist, appearing in recitals and oratorios internationally.

In one very special instance, we stretched a point, and the result was the privilege of putting the finishing touches on the work of an artist who is well on her way to major operatic eminence on a worldwide scale. It started simply enough when Gintaras Vysniauskas, a tenor in our chorus, heard a mezzo-soprano from his native Lithuania and was so impressed by the magnificence of her voice, he felt he had to do something to introduce her to a larger audience. When I later asked him why he was going all out to help his countrywoman, he replied that there are so few Lithuanians in this part of the world, all of them feel honor-bound to be supportive of one another. In fact, we *did* happen to be looking for a mezzo to take the place of a studio member who had moved on to an engagement.

It was the late afternoon of a long working day, and we had already heard a sizable collection of applicants, two of whom had sung very creditably, and I was frankly eager to call it a day. But Heinrich Bender said there was one more mezzo, and so I sighed lethargically and settled back to listen to yet another voice. The minute the woman started to sing, I sat up straight, instantly realizing that her timbre, her expression, her personality, her appearance, and her musicality were evocative of a major talent in the making, one of those exquisite voices that come along maybe once in a hundred years. Of course, there was room for improvement. Her extreme top tones were not completely free, but the rest of her voice, and everything that went with it, were so commendable, we decided we absolutely had to have her in the studio.

At the time she auditioned, she was living in a student dormitory, eking out the bare essentials of her existence with severely limited financial resources. To complicate matters, her permit to remain in Germany was slowly running out, and, unless something happened quickly, she would have been forced to return to Vilnius. Lithuania at this point in history was still very much under the thumb of the Soviet Union, and the likelihood of her getting out again was, at best, scant. Were she to return bearing a contract with a large opera house, however, they might just let her go back to the West. It meant moving as swiftly as possible, and that is exactly what Heinrich did. He immediately took the young lady to the upper echelons at the theatre and made it quite clear to them that the only thing that would rescue this singular talent from getting locked into eastern Europe indefinitely would be a studio contract from the Bavarian State Opera.

A brief audition convinced Gerd Uecker, who had to make the decision, that we had stumbled on just what we said we had, and the lady was promptly contracted to join the studio, despite the fact that she was a few months beyond our usual upper age limit. In the case of this artist, bearing in mind that she still needed some polish to help her realize her impressive potential, we felt that this was one rule that would be observed in spirit by violating it in the letter. With the contract in her pocket, the lady returned to her native country, leaving all of us trembling over whether or not, even with the promise of this engagement, the officialdom there would allow her out again. To our great relief, they did. In one of those remarkable historical ironies, the day after she arrived back in Munich, Lithuania became an independent, democratic country, and she would have been welcome to come and go as she pleased. But none of us had the foreknowledge to predict that event.

I will never forget the quality of her work at the studio. She had an infallible musical ear and an intelligence that would have been the envy of many an established artist. Moreover, she made up for what she may have lacked in background with an unerring instinct for the essential nature of everything she sang. Her high tones finally became so secure, we felt the time had come to present her to the public. At this point, fate took a hand, as August Everding's *Singschul'* was just in the process of formation. I suggested she enroll in my master class, to get a full month's lessons free of charge, and to give me the further opportunity to prepare her for the concert. Heinrich decided she would appear in the quartet from the king's Chamber Scene in act 3 of Verdi's *Don Carlo*, which concludes with the bravura aria "O, don fatale!"

She brought the house down!

Immediately after she completed her studio contract, she was engaged to sing in several places, including the 1994 Bayreuth Festival, where she sang the difficult role of the Second Norn in *Götterdämmerung*. She was unable to return there the following year, because by that time she was already contracted for the leading role of Fricka in *Die Walküre* under Riccardo Muti at La Scala. Her career is now firmly established on the highest international level, and as she moves from one triumph to another, the optimum quality of her performances continues to reflect glory on the people who had the excellent fortune to discover her and figure in her professional training.

Although the studio has now been discontinued by the current theatre administration, it still made it possible for music lovers throughout the world to thrill to the singing of Violeta Urmana. What a joy to recall that we heard her first!

SCENE THREE

On the Home Front

Is there intelligent life for singers beyond the opera house? The answer is: yes, but only occasionally.

In December 1994, I was interviewed by *Madame*, a women's magazine, talking about my life, both public and private, as it is today, and the quote that reporter Kit Raeder selected as the headline was "Opera singers must be able to endure solitude." In the more active years, we have to get used to being alone in airline terminals and hotel rooms and, even more important, regularly seeking the isolation we need to learn new music and refamiliarize ourselves with the material we already know. After a while, solitude becomes habit-forming, and even past the pinnacle of my career, I find myself wanting to spend the greater part of my life alone, "with a little help from my friends."

First of all, let me dispel all the grand illusions my readers may be harboring about an opera singer's glamorous life, complete with a huge entourage of obsequious servants carrying a veritable arsenal of luggage and hatboxes while looking after our every imaginable need. I must admit, however, that when I first arrived in Bayreuth, I did bring along a hatbox, but I immediately discarded it when I discovered that almost nobody was wearing hats anymore.

To some people, my private life may seem as unglamorous as an empty hatbox, but to me, it provides the balance I need to rekindle my inner flame. The few hours of leisure time I have are spent taking care of my mail, meeting with friends, burning up the phone lines, attending plays, watching TV, and—only occasionally—listening to music, seldom operatic. Oddly enough, having

331

been surrounded on all sides by opera, literally from birth, I am not an avid listener in my spare time.

I seriously believe that were I to be cast adrift on a tropical island, like the guests on that BBC Desert Island Discs series, and offered the opportunity to take along just one record, the music I would most like to hear would be by George Gershwin. Gershwin evokes an era I enormously enjoyed, and, in my considered opinion, he is as wonderful a composer as many of the classical titans. When I listen to his music, it conjures up a nostalgic vision of New York the way it was in my time.

I do wish I had more time to read. Back in my traveling days, I invariably took along a good paperback, which I would read in trains and planes, tearing off the pages I had read to lighten my hand luggage as I went along. If the book really held my interest, I would replace the defaced copy with a hardcover volume, which then became a permanent constituent of my small library. I enjoy the classic pursuit of matching wits with fictional detectives toward the goal of pinpointing the culprit before the author reveals the solution, and I am extremely fond of Agatha Christie's Miss Marple novels, both in book form and in the cinema and television versions featuring Margaret Rutherford and her worthy successor in the role, Angela Lansbury, a real actress's actress.

Friendship is a touchy subject with me. I am by nature a reticent person, reluctant to enter into close contacts and not particularly happy with casual acquaintanceships. Granted, the long years of travel have made it almost impossible to form fast friendships. As we know, a rolling stone gathers no moss. Under these circumstances, the few friends I have welcomed behind the wall of my own self-protection have grown very close, a source of comfort in distress, as all true friends are, with the extra added attraction that every one of them is a wellspring of fun and entertainment, two attributes I can never get enough of in this life.

All in all, my private life in Munich has been very pleasant, with one exception that crops up every now and then: the obsession of certain Germans with the inflexible observance of meaningless rules and regulations. This was unmistakably brought home to me in August 1994, when I attempted to wish Wolfgang Wagner many happy returns on his seventy-fifth birthday. Had it not been for my unbending Ortrudian persistence, I sincerely doubt if my greetings would ever have made it past the bureaucratic barrier. It began innocently enough, when I dialed the Munich telegram operator, and a young man answered the phone, exuding all the human warmth of a steel beam. When I told him I wanted to send a telegram to Wolfgang Wagner at the Festival

Theatre in Bayreuth, he asked for the street address. When I told him I was never aware there *was* a street address, he proceeded to inform me in the most authoritative of tones that "Festival Theatre" was not an officially registered street address, for which reason my telegram order was unacceptable. I assured him that I had spent a fair amount of time in the city, where virtually the entire populace is more than familiar with the house on the hill. In fact, that promontory is so elevated, there is hardly any point for miles around from which it *isn't* visible, unless, of course, you are facing the opposite direction, but he remained adamant. No street address, no telegram, and he hung up.

Perhaps the average citizen would have given up by that time, but I was determined to get all the required information relayed into official channels. So I phoned the Bayreuth theatre, where a pleasant stage doorman, whom I had known for years, was totally baffled by my request. When I explained the situation, he assured me that nobody who was anybody in Bayreuth—certainly not anyone associated with the local post office—was unaware of the location of the sprawling building that dominated the local landscape. He even added that, although he had been guarding the stage door for ages, he wasn't aware of any street address himself. After calling one office after another, he finally managed to locate somebody who actually knew the address: Festspielhügel Number 1! Armed to the teeth with this essential intelligence, I prepared to mount my attack on the telegraph office. This time a charming young lady answered the phone, and, after hearing my name and the precise destination of my telegram, assured me, "But Mme Varnay, certainly everybody in Bayreuth knows where the festival theatre is." She then proceeded to process my birthday message, *without* the street address, leaving me flabbergasted at my end of the line.

The following day, I happened to see Hans Hotter at a party and related this bizarre tale to him. He responded with one of his majestic expressions, shaking his head in stoically endured exasperation, and commented touchingly from his great height, "Astrid dear, to understand some things in this country, you just have to be *born* here."

Why?

Nᴏᴛ ᴇᴠᴇʀʏ ᴛᴇʟᴇᴘʜᴏɴᴇ ᴄᴀʟʟ I receive leads to a new engagement. In one case, a call precipitated an extended period of soul-searching, which has continued long after the situation was resolved. The gentleman on the phone was one of my favorite agents in one of my favorite cities, offering me an exorbitant fee to participate in the opening production of the season there. The prospect sounded more than enticing until the essential facts were revealed: the opera was a contemporary work I had seen elsewhere and disliked on the spot. Three further hearings in two different theatres did nothing to alter my initial reaction. To add to the problem, the stage director was someone who had recently come into vogue for a series of far-out productions, which, to my mind, had obfuscated rather than clarified the operas. And yet this individual counted as a veritable paragon of a new school of staging that has taken much of the institutionalized intellectual world by storm, while, at the same time, bewildering and alienating some of the most educated and receptive audiences throughout the operatic world.

While my reaction to both the work and the director was decidedly negative, I still wanted to be fair, and so I asked the agent to grant me more time to think over the matter and reassess my attitude toward his proposition. He apparently thought I was holding out for more money, because every couple of days he would get back to me with a new offer, but I was still locked on the horns of a dilemma.

The reason for my indecision was a complicated one. I have always regarded myself as someone who wants to sail uncharted waters, finding new truths in old operas and helping bring new, meaningful works to the attention of the audience, but try as I might, I felt that this work was no more than an exercise in premeditated cacophony, void of mood, drive, or characterization, while the director impressed me as being vapid, posing as profound by virtue of a perverse tendency toward overloading every production with needless superficialities.

I finally reached the conclusion that the people planning this venture might be hoping to use my services in a very small cameo so they could say to a few holdouts: "Varnay, with her decades of operatic experience, has signed on. What are *you* waiting for?" In short, they probably wanted me to legitimize the project with a kind of "Good Housekeeping Seal of Approval," which, in my considered opinion, it did *not* deserve. I realized that this imprimatur was not really something I wanted to foist, even indirectly, on my defenseless colleagues, who would be less able to refuse this offer, and so I followed my initial inner instinct and politely but firmly declined. I soon discovered the production had finally been scrapped but never learned why. I cannot help surmising that many of the other singers approached may have shared my misgivings.

The whole episode set an intense thought process in motion, in which I found myself questioning and re-questioning some of the basic issues of the family business I have now been practicing for well over a half-century. For whom are we doing this and why? Is our activity directed toward everyone in the audience, or are we addressing a charmed circle, perhaps hoping that the others may follow suit and start acquiring the background the initiated bring with them to the theatre? In all honesty, I lean toward the general public, realizing that we have something significant to give even those with neither the time nor the overwhelming inclination to do major research before approaching an operatic performance.

As I advanced professionally, I had the opportunity to sing operas that, at the time, were called "modern": de Banfield, Barber, Berg, Egk, von Einem, Honegger, Janáček, Menotti, Orff, Prokofiev, Schönberg, Stravinsky, and Weill, including four world premières of works by living composers and the American première of *Mahagonny!* With these credentials, I can hardly be called a musical prude with a militantly traditionalistic attitude when it comes to works by contemporaries. By the same token, from the very beginning of my interest in opera, I have always been fascinated by new ideas in staging, as witness my work with a variety of innovators: Wallerstein, Gründgens, Rennert, Buckwitz,

Ponnelle, Schröder, del Monaco, Friedrich, Herlischka, Schaaf, and—first and foremost—Wieland and Wolfgang Wagner. Each of these artists, like Alexander Várnay in his day, sailed boldly into uncharted waters.

Nevertheless, my adventures in music and staging have invariably been infused with an awareness of valid tradition, the realization that opera, as an art form, is a grand edifice, masterful in its construction and yet, like every antique building, in need of ongoing refurbishment. This important restorative work, however, must never reach the point of destroying the substance of the building for the sake of those who dwell within—and the generations of descendants still to come.

Now, what is it that I look for in an operatic performance on those occasions when I find myself in the audience? In my opinion, if the performance in all its elements moves me to the degree that I become so immersed in hearing and seeing the progress of the human drama that I forget myself and my surroundings, then I have experienced an outstanding evening in the opera house. This complete immersion in the opera happens very seldom to someone as familiar with the craft as myself—*but it does happen!*

Taking this as a basic objective, what are the fundamental ingredients required to reach this level of audience involvement? First and foremost: an opera must have Sound. The singing and music-making must be on an optimum level. Then, I want the staging to emphasize the human element, so that, by the end of the performance, I feel I have encountered authentic, flesh-and-blood individuals with genuine emotions, despite the fact that everybody on stage is singing. From these points on, individualistic approaches are not only permissible, they are heartily welcome. It is a source of infinite fascination to me to watch other singers doing the roles I had once made my own and noting the new and exciting values they have drawn from the verbal and musical texts. All of us deal with the same material and still come up with highly varied approaches. This response proves that there is limitless room for individuality, providing nothing happens to the basic core.

Despite several offers, I have never been tempted to direct opera myself, because that larger vision has never been my specialty. My imagination focuses on my function as a "detail person." For this reason and more, I have nothing but admiration for the authentic geniuses who can take a group of incredibly disparate individuals, with cultural backgrounds ranging from the American Far West to the Asiatic Far East, and focus them in the noble cause of a dramatic unity. It is this master plan that gives each performance its raison d'être and joins together the operatic dialectic of action, reaction, and interaction.

I may not be able to conceive the Grand Idea, but I certainly can appreciate it when it is well carried out, and I can spontaneously recognize its absence when the execution of it is inadequate. Many of the newer directors seem to have trouble distinguishing a period piece, locked in the time and atmosphere of its setting, and works that will allow for a greater variety of location and chronology. Any attempt to "modernize" a period comedy of manners like *Rosenkavalier* is always an exercise in futility. This opera is so totally affixed to early eighteenth-century Vienna in the codes of behavior, court rituals, laws, customs, and mores of that era, that to digress from it leaves the piece foundering like a ship without sails or anchor. This does not for one minute invalidate the universality of the emotions in the opera, but it is the restrictive quality of the rococo environment, with its whalebone corsets, its powdered wigs, its arranged marriages, and its fixed rituals for every human activity, which brings out elements in those emotions that do not have the same relevance in a different time and place.

Die Meistersinger is yet another opera locked in its time and place, with its conflicts between the established aristocracy (Walther) and the emerging bourgeoisie (the Master Singers), between rules of form and freedom of expression, with Hans Sachs as the catalyst in both cases. But beyond all this, *Meistersinger* is a celebration of learned skills and the inseparability of craftsmanship and art. The masters construct their songs with the same meticulousness they apply to their handcrafted shoes and metalwork. Put this opera in any era later than the time of the industrial revolution, when factories started making shoes and soap, and all the analogies that bring the opera to life will go flying out the nearest window.

Similarly, all three Mozart–da Ponte collaborations (*Figaro, Giovanni*, and *Così*) are largely inspired by the master-servant conflict, or, in a deeper sense, the confrontation between nobility of birth and nobility of spirit. Of course, the same rules applied on many levels to Edwardian England, which I believe would be a perfectly legitimate setting for all three operas, but to transpose these works to a period without an inherited aristocracy is to invalidate their message. And yet, some stage directors insist upon taking every single opera and moving it, as a point of style, to any time or place other than its own. Others think the only way to convey the essence of an operatic work is to place it in the "immediacy" of our own time. They seem to think that an audience that studied history in school and watched period plays and movies from early childhood will be unable to react to any other time and place but its own. Why?

Wagner's mythological operas, the *Ring* in particular, are, as the composer's grandsons have proven, virtually unrelated to time and place. They even benefit from a kind of abstract never-never-land situation, which gives the audience far more opportunity for the healthy use of their imaginations than all the pathetic attempts to superimpose contemporary references on them. And yet, some producers are really convinced that they get closer to the meaning by having Wotan and Fricka carry matched luggage or directing Mime to read the local newspaper. Why?

There are, however, operas that offer producers an excellent opportunity to take an established work and use it to drive home a contemporary theme. *Fidelio*, the greatest example, with its passionate devotion to all-embracing freedom and human decency as manifested in Leonore's determination to rescue the unjustly imprisoned man, *whoever he may be*, is appropriate to almost any time or place. The setting "near Seville" is incidental. This means the interpretation of the opera is limited only by the imaginations of the director and the members of his or her cast.

A goodly number of the new stage directors come from non-theatrical backgrounds, having started professional life as easel riders and desk jockeys. As a result, they often have an inadequate familiarity with the possibilities of sharing their ideas with the members of the cast. They seem to feel that the only way they can use the singers to the best effect is by treating them with the same respect they would show to the paint they squeeze out of a tube or the keyboard on which they type their essays. What a pity they seem so unaware of the creative possibilities of co-artistry!

Now it is time for me to take up the cudgels for my colleagues. While jokes about singers of limited mental capacity are almost as old as the profession itself (and generally about as funny as *Werther*), I ask the reader to consider for a moment the brain power and level of education required just to *learn* a role like Fidelio or Semiramide, Wotan or Pélléas, often in a language first acquired by the singer long after the onset of adulthood. This intelligence, this learning process, this intense involvement with the countless facets of a character's personality, all constitute contributory factors a stage director ignores or overlooks at his or her own peril. If the producer of an operatic performance regards the singers merely as pieces in a pattern of his own exclusive design, if he sees his production as a mosaic to which they contribute merely their vocal and physical presence and their obedience to his whims—then all he offers the audience is a marionette show. Furthermore, those whims can be quite repulsive.

To put it bluntly, I have seen so much naked flesh, so much needless carnal and post-digestive activity, so much gratuitous violence, vulgarity, and mayhem on the operatic stage, all totally unrelated to the work at hand, it might almost come as a relief to go back to the old-fashioned productions where everybody just stood there in a fancy costume and warbled! But Peter Sellars was absolutely right when he addressed the opening night audience of a recent Salzburg Festival, likening the developments on the theatrical scene to the earthquake that almost devastated Los Angeles. In the aftermath of both these phenomena, he rightly said, *there is no turning back*, but is the present course necessarily moving forward? In some cases, yes. But those cases are still too few and far between! Why?

No doubt about it, no art form can survive by standing still. Like Lewis Carroll's Red Queen, it must keep moving, but where? If, as is so often proclaimed, the object of contemporary art is to deal with hidden meanings, let the producers delve into the works, bring out the manifold meanings placed there by the original creators, and interpret those meanings in a way that points up their musical and verbal truths. Unearthing the many levels of significance in a work as complicated as a forceful opera score, I admit, is an arduous exploratory effort. By contrast, overloading an opera production with a superfluous agenda that has nothing whatsoever to do with the original concept is the simplest thing in the world. For all the gravity of the program notes, this tactic has about as much intellectual integrity as the proverbial moustache on the *Mona Lisa*. In short, you never improve the seaworthiness of an ocean liner by attaching barnacles to the hull.

In recent years, some producers have introduced the so-called "principle of production" predicated on *taking issue* with both the work and the audience. Questioning the work should never be the function of the producer. He or she must believe in the composition and not take issue with it. This is the only way they can possibly do it justice, inspire the singers, and give the audience their spiritual and fiscal money's worth. This style of production also dwells on the "obligation" of the performing arts to make a contemporary political or socio-political statement, in a sense, taking issue with the audience. If producers really want to make a statement about the socio-political situation of our day, or anything else that occupies their attention, let them join forces with a gifted poet and an inspired composer and create a brand-new work, specifically designed to bring home that message as convincingly as possible. In my view, this is a far more inspiring challenge than merely pasting slogans over old masters.

In a very real sense, this whole "taking issue" virus is little more than an egregious manifestation of small-mindedness. The current dominance of this dead-end philosophy in the theatres of the world evokes Karl Kraus's telling epigram: "When culture has reached the end of the day, even midgets cast long shadows." Fortunately, my career eclipsed only the outer perimeters of the Inane School of Production, vouchsafing me very positive feelings about both the past and the future. Nevertheless, apart from the peculiar *Holländer* in Munich, I did have a brief encounter with one of those paragons of the "nothing succeeds like excess" theory, and I dealt with it in what my friends have come to refer to as "classic Varnayesque style."

I had been invited to sing Klytämnestra in two festival *Elektra* performances, using the production then running at the theatre in question. When I arrived two days prior to the first performance, the staff and I ran through all the usual rituals, such as checking the set, rehearsing with my colleagues, and coordinating the musical portion of the performance with the conductor. In the wardrobe department, I was presented with an elaborate regal costume, festooned with an artificial blue arm, dangling from the left sleeve. The assistant stage director elucidated that this arm symbolized the queen's guilt for the murder of her husband, in the form of atrophy in the limb that had struck the fatal blow. Reluctant as I was to disabuse the resident maven of his illusions, I felt obligated to inform his assistant that the mortal blow, as anyone might have deduced from most versions of the legend, had been struck not by Klytämnestra but by her paramour Ägisth. As my readers will recall, Klytämnestra only cast the net over Agamemnon. In a deeper sense, I further explained that, in my opinion, the use of inanimate elements of the production to *pass judgment* on one of the characters in this remarkably even-handed ancient drama (remember, Klytämnestra had valid *reasons* for wanting Agamemnon put out of the way!) replaces the moral ambiguity of the plot with arbitrary verdicts that have nothing whatsoever to do with it. Moreover, the unsightly artificial arm would constantly draw attention to itself and away from my performance. I could act myself into a lather, but there was still no way I could contend fairly with that appurtenance.

At the evening rehearsal, the stage director himself attended and tried to convince me that eliminating that arm would impair one of the crucial allegories of his concept. Not wanting to stand in the way of that concept, I delicately suggested that I could bow out of the production altogether and let the blue arm do the role. Result: the following evening, I did sing, and the odd appendage was retired to the costume department, where it hung on a hook like the Picture of Dorian Gray.

SCENE FIVE

Some Practical Precepts
in Parting

O NE OF THE MORE frustrating experiences of being in the opera business as
long as I have is being forced to say no to the great number of young people
and their families who approach me in quest of aid and counsel on establishing
a foothold in this profession. Even if time were to permit, however, there is
precious little I can do for them, because like everything else worthwhile in
this life, an operatic career can be acquired only by dint of immense dedication, single-minded devotion, and countless hours of hard work, not connections with established singers. Nevertheless, I would like to conclude this book
of memoirs with a few simple precepts as a parting present to my loyal readers.
Doubtless, a sizable majority of my readers are not the least bit interested in
a singing career, but regard opera solely as a spectator sport. Even so, I would
like to beg their indulgence for this brief chapter of shop talk. Perhaps some
foreknowledge of the obstacle course every singer has to run before the curtain
can rise may grant them a deeper appreciation of what they are experiencing
as they enjoy an operatic performance.

While preparing this pocket primer of pragmatic precepts, practical principles, and pre-eminent propositions, it precipitously dawned on me that the
primary proportion of these profitable postulates start with the same letter. It
was not previously planned, nor is this seemingly precious pattern a premedi-

341

tated power play, a perpetual prototype, or a practiced procedure on my part. In point of fact, it probably would get pretty pathetic, if not potently pitiful, were it to persist permanently, but before perpetrating such pandemonium on my potentially plagued perusers that they petition the provincial police precinct, I promise to pull this program back to a permissible level. (Come to think of it, this alliterative approach may somehow be subconscious. Well, once a Wagnerian, always a Wagnerian.)

Let us start this consideration with the first P-word on my list: *prerequisites*. The one absolute *conditio sine qua non* for this entire consideration is *potential*: a clean bill of health, especially in the *pulmonary* region, and clear vocal cords, plus a serviceable singing voice. Beyond vocal *prowess* and musical and theatrical *proficiency*, the next unconditional *precondition* for an operatic career is a burning *passion* for the art of singing. The issue is not success or fame—these either happen or they don't. The decisive factor here is an absolute determination on the part of the would-be singer to vault every hurdle toward the goal of a career at whatever level, and, take my word for it, there are plenty of hurdles to vault.

The potential singer should not be devastated if the experts have their doubts about a future career. In the long run, this admittedly disappointing negative appraisal will save him or her a never-ending road of heartache, sacrifice, and astronomical expense toward an uncertain, if not indeed a nonexistent, destination. Please listen to that advice carefully, though. Sometimes a negative evaluation may turn out to be a blessing in disguise.

This was what happened to me back in my late teens when I decided to use a few of the vocal skills I had learned from my mother to earn a little extra Christmas money. I recalled an advertisement for semi-professional singers to participate in a Protestant church choir, so I decided to apply. I sang for the organist. He shook his head apologetically and said that, although he liked my voice, he could not use my services, as it was simply too big. "But I can take my volume down," I countered. The organist was adamant. His choir, he explained, was truly semi-professional, nothing more. A resonant voice like mine, he said, would simply cut through all the other sounds, no matter how much I might tone it down, and ruin the choral balance. As I started home, my mood was bittersweet. On the one hand, I was sorry to lose the Christmas money, which, in my mind, I had already spent. On the other hand, the idea of having such a big voice that it would cut through any chorus appealed to me—please note, I left the word "semi-professional" out of my reveries. When I arrived home, I announced to my mother that I had sung for an expert and been pronounced large of voice. Perhaps, I asked her, I might therefore be all ready for a big career? Mother smiled her most knowing smile and just indicated my usual place at the piano.

Should the young would-be singers amongst my readers have the unusual good fortune of receiving a positive evaluation (that is, better than semi-professional) on their vocal material from the experts I mentioned before, that *still* isn't enough. They should also make certain they have personality, a theatrical flair, a reasonably pleasant appearance, plus an active imagination and reliable work habits. This may sound like a tall order, but aren't these the very attributes we look for in a singer when we attend a performance? Why should theatre managers be any less discriminating than we are?

If we can evoke a definite "yes" from our soul's mirror on all these *prerequisites*, then we may decide to begin a serious program of vocal study. Before implementing this decision, however, I strongly recommend that every young singer equip him- or herself, well in advance, with a *practical* occupation to fall back on in case the career ambitions, for one reason or another, should not pan out. Remember, I studied to be a commercial secretary.

Having taken out this form of occupational insurance, the next thing to do is select a competent professional voice teacher. So much of this phase is a question of compatibility. The best voice teacher in the neighborhood is worthless to a young singer if they have a clash of aesthetics, or if their inter-personal wavelength somehow fails to harmonize. Preparation is a joint effort, and young singers need a pedagogue they can trust when the going gets rough—and it *does* get rough! There are no hard-and-fast rules when it comes to the gender of a vocal teacher. Kirsten Flagstad studied voice with a man, and Fritz Wunderlich learned his craft from a woman.

No operatic career is feasible in this day and age without a working knowl-edge of the languages in which the artist will be singing. Even though many of the smaller theatres may concentrate on opera in the local language, no singer is likely to get anywhere without a reasonable command of the five *basic* operatic languages: Italian, French, Italian, German, and, last but not least, *Italian!* I am often shocked at people who think they can learn an operatic text like a parrot repeating syllables without the vaguest awareness of each word they are singing. They assure me that they are singing the "sense of it," but that is inadequate.

While the voice is developing and taking on its artistic identity, it is impera-tive for its owner to work on his or her theatrical and musical identity by attending as many performances as possible, not just in the opera house but also in the concert hall, the ballet, and the cinema, as well as the legitimate stage, including musicals and variety shows. While comparing these experiences helps build your taste, it also adds immeasurably to your *perceptiveness* and your options.

When it comes to repertoire, it is worthless simply to learn one aria after another. When you start having a career, you will need to know the scores from start to finish, with all their challenges and pitfalls. It is certainly not a must to be able to read an orchestral score, but a thoroughgoing knowledge of the accompaniment and the orchestral sounds that will be cueing and supporting your performance is absolutely imperative. A good set of implements is indispensable for your *preparation*: these include a *piano score*, a *piano* to play the accompaniment, a *pitch pipe* to keep your intonation under control, and the two most important *props* for any operatic career: a *pencil* and a *piece of paper*.

Once you have reached a sufficient command of mind, voice, and body to begin considering a professional career, you should start looking around for a reliable agent. The subject of legal stipulations binding the activities of theatrical agencies is so complicated, and so widely varied from country to country, there would be little point trying to deal with it in detail here. These are things to inquire about in advance before signing any contracts. The most important thing at this early phase is to write to as many agents as possible, giving them a short description of your age, your height and weight, your academic background, your vocal range, your full repertoire, your languages, and so forth, and requesting an audition. While contacting the theatres directly may represent both a shortcut and an economy, many theatres will not even consider an application without the recommendation of an agent.

Once a theatre offer comes along, you must always bear in mind that the voice continues to be your *property*. Even early in the game, you must insist on remaining the owner of your repertoire and make sure your *Fach* (voice range) is listed in the contract. If this *Fach* is not specifically stated, the theatre may be entitled to insist on your peforming an unsuitable repertoire, which could leave your vocal equipment hanging in tatters. The theatre will then have no further use for your services on any level. When questionable propositions come along, unless you are dead certain you would be totally miscast in the part, it is always wise to consult whomever you trust on your career decisions, but you must also develop more than a nodding acquaintanceship with your own capabilities.

Punctuality is a must, as is *preparation* and a diplomatic *pleasantness* in your *private* relations within the ensemble, and, first and foremost, *professionalism*, which is nothing more or less than knowing what is expected of you, by the task at hand, by your employer, by your colleagues, and, most important, by the terms and conditions of your own professional integrity, and delivering the goods unreservedly. As my mother was fond of saying: "Do not yearn for words of praise. This is a student attitude. You are fulfilling a signed contract. If praise comes, be happy about it and say 'thank you'! You will *always* receive criticism." A little harmless gossip is part of any profession, but do not spread unfounded hearsay or use it as a tool to get ahead. You will just be wasting your energy, while at the same time alienating your colleagues. A certain respect for *privacy* is called for if you have a problem with the director or another member of the cast. Seek a private setting to discuss your differences. Don't get involved in controversies with the conductor in front of his orchestra. Wait until the rehearsal is over and then ask him for an appointment, at his first convenience, to deal one-on-one with the issue at hand.

It is virtually impossible to have an answer for everything in the theatre. Nevertheless, you cannot possibly go wrong if you always bear in mind the incandescent wisdom that definitive dramatist, William Shakespeare, placed in Polonius's advice to his son, Laërtes, in act 1, scene 3, of *Hamlet*. This maxim has guided my professional and private life from the first exercise I sang in my mother's studio to this very moment. I would like to recall it to my readers' memories as I take my leave of this volume of recollections:

> *This above all; to thine owne selfe be true;*
> *And it must follow, as the Night the Day,*
> *Thou canst not then be false to any man.*
> *Farewell: my Blessing season this in thee.*

Repertoire

Composer	Opera	Role	Number of Performances
Raffaelo de Banfield	Lord Byron's Love Letter	The Old Woman	2
Ludwig van Beethoven	Fidelio	Leonore	57
Alban Berg	Lulu	Die Garderobiere	12
Eugen D'Albert	Tiefland	Martha	12
Werner Egk	Peer Gynt	Åse	19
Gottfried von Einem	Der Besuch der alten Dame	Claire Zachanassian	14
Umberto Giordano	Andrea Chénier	Contessa di Coigny	16
Charles Gounod	Faust	Dame Marthe Schwerdtlein	17
Arthur Honegger	Jeanne d'Arc au Bûcher	La Mère aux Tonneaux	31
Engelbert Humperdinck	Hänsel und Gretel	Die Mutter	51
Leoš Janáček	Jenůfa	Kostelnička Burjovka	56
	Káťa Kabanová	Kabanicha	31
	Věc Makropulos	Komorná	12
Pietro Mascagni	Cavalleria Rusticana	Santuzza	33
		Mamma Lucia	43
Giancarlo Menotti	The Island God	Telea	4
Modest Mussorgsky	Boris Godunov	Mamka	19
Jacques Offenbach	Orphée aux Enfers	Juno	18

continued

Composer	Opera	Role	Number of Performances
Carl Orff	Ödipus der Tyrann	Jokaste	31
	Antigone	Eurydike	4
	Ludus de nato infante mirificus	Erdmutter	1
Amilcare Ponchielli	La Gioconda	Gioconda	4
Giacomo Puccini	Gianni Schicchi	Zita	19
Sergey Prokofiev	Igrok (The Gambler)	Babushka	8
Richard Strauss	Elektra	Elektra	81
		Klytemnästra	121
	Die Frau ohne Schatten	Die Amme	22
	Der Rosenkavalier	Die Marschallin	32
	Salome	Salome	13
		Herodias	213
Peter Ilyitch Tchaikovsky	Eugene Onegin	Filippyevna	11
	Pique Dame	Grafinya	4
Giuseppe Verdi	Aida	Aida	5
		Amneris	2
		Sacerdota	1
	Il Trovatore	Leonora	19
		Inez	1
	Macbeth	Lady Macbeth	22
	Otello	Desdemona	4
	Simon Boccanegra	Maria Boccanegra	5

Composer / Opera	Character	
Richard Wagner		
Der fliegende Holländer	Senta	40
	Mary	25
Lohengrin	Elsa	30
	Ortrud	114
Die Meistersinger von Nürnberg	Eva	14
Parsifal	Kundry	74
Der Ring des Nibelungen		
Das Rheingold	Freia	1
Die Walküre	Sieglinde	28
	Brünnhilde	137
Siegfried	Brünnhilde	93
Götterdämmerung	Brünnhilde	99
	First Norn	14
	Third Norn	5
	Gutrune	9
Tannhäuser	Elisabeth	22
	Venus	10
Tristan und Isolde	Isolde	105
Kurt Weill		
Der Aufstieg und Fall der Stadt Mahagonny	Leokadja Begbick	45

Discography

Complete Opera Recordings

Year	Work	Role	Composer	Conductor	Available on
1941	Die Walküre	Sieglinde	Richard Wagner	Erich Leinsdorf	CD
1943	Lohengrin	Elsa	Richard Wagner	Erich Leinsdorf	CD
1948	Tannhäuser	Venus	Richard Wagner	Fritz Stiedry	CD
1949	Elektra	Elektra	Richard Strauss	Dimitri Mitropoulos	CD
1950	Der fliegende Holländer	Senta	Richard Wagner	Fritz Reiner	CD
1950	Lohengrin	Ortrud	Richard Wagner	Fritz Stiedry	CD LP
1950	Simon Boccanegra	Maria Boccanegra	Giuseppe Verdi	Fritz Stiedry	CD
1951	Siegfried	Brünnhilde	Richard Wagner	Fritz Stiedry	CD
1951	Götterdämerung	Brünnhilde	Richard Wagner	Hans Knappertsbusch	CD
1951	Die Walküre (act 3)	Brünnhilde	Richard Wagner	Herbert von Karajan	CD
1952	Elektra	Elektra	Richard Strauss	Fritz Reiner	CD
1952	Götterdämmerung	Brünnhilde	Richard Wagner	Joseph Keilberth	CD
1952	Siegfried	Brünnhilde	Richard Wagner	Joseph Keilberth	CD
1952	Die Walküre	Brünnhilde	Richard Wagner	Joseph Keilberth	CD
1953	Götterdämmerung	Brünnhilde	Richard Wagner	Clemens Krauss	CD
1953	Siegfried	Brünnhilde	Richard Wagner	Clemens Krauss	CD
1953	Die Walküre	Brünnhilde	Richard Wagner	Clemens Krauss	CD
1953	Elektra	Elektra	Richard Strauss	Richard Kraus	CD
1953	Lohengrin	Ortrud	Richard Wagner	Joseph Keilberth	CD LP
1953	Der Rosenkavalier	Die Marschallin	Richard Strauss	Fritz Reiner	LP
1953	Tristan und Isolde	Isolde	Richard Wagner	Eugen Jochum	CD

Year	Title	Role	Composer	Conductor	Format
1953	*Salome*	Salome	Richard Strauss	Hermann Weigert	CD LP
1954	*Lohengrin*	Ortrud	Richard Wagner	Eugen Jochum	CD
1954	*Macbeth*	Lady Macbeth	Giuseppe Verdi	Vittorio Gui	CD
1954	*Parsifal*	Kundry	Richard Wagner	Fritz Stiedry	CD LP
1954	*Die Walküre*	Brünnhilde	Richard Wagner	Joseph Keilberth	CD
1954	*Cavalleria Rusticana*	Santuzza	Pietro Mascagni	Wolfgang Sawallisch	LP
1955	*Der fliegende Holländer*	Senta	Richard Wagner	Hans Knappertsbusch	CD LP
1955	*Götterdämmerung*	Brünnhilde	Richard Wagner	Joseph Keilberth	CD
1956	*Der fliegende Holländer*	Senta	Richard Wagner	Joseph Keilberth	CD
1957	*Der Ring des Nibelungen*	Brünnhilde	Richard Wagner	Hans Knappertsbusch	CD
1957	*Die Walküre*	Brünnhilde	Richard Wagner	Hans Knappertsbusch	CD LP
1958	*Lohengrin*	Ortrud	Richard Wagner	André Cluytens	CD
1960	*Der Ring des Nibelungen*	Brünnhilde	Richard Wagner	Rudolf Kempe	CD
1960	*Lohengrin*	Ortrud	Richard Wagner	Lorin Maazel	CD LP
1962	*Lohengrin*	Ortrud	Richard Wagner	Wolfgang Sawallisch	CD MC
1964	*Elektra*	Elektra	Richard Strauss	Herbert von Karajan	CD LP
1966	*Ödipus der Tyrann*	Jokaste	Carl Orff	Ferdinand Leitner	CD
1970	*Jenůfa*	Kostelnička Burjovka	Leoš Janáček	Rafael Kubelík	CD VID
1974	*Salome*	Herodias	Richard Strauss	Karl Böhm	VID
1978	*Cavalleria Rusticana*	Mamma Lucia	Pietro Mascagni	Wolfgang Sawallisch	CD
1979	*Cavalleria Rusticana*	Mamma Lucia	Pietro Mascagni	Riccardo Muti	CD MC
1982	*Elektra*	Klytämnestra	Richard Strauss	Karl Böhm	VID LD
1984	*Andrea Chénier*	Contessa di Coigny	Umberto Giordano	Riccardo Chailly	CD LP
1984	*The Rake's Progress*	Mother Goose	Igor Stravinsky	Riccardo Chailly	CD LP

continued

Year	Work	Role	Composer	Conductor	Available on
Recitals					
1956	Wesendonck Lieder		Richard Wagner		CD
1961	Deità Silvane		Ottorino Respighi		CD
1961	Lieder		Richard Wagner		CD
1961	Zigeunermelodien		Antonín Dvořák		CD
Portraits					
1951	Astrid Varnay Sings Halévy, Verdi, Ponchielli, etc.				CD
1954	Astrid Varnay (Munich, 1954/1961)				CD
1994	Great Voices: Astrid Varnay				CD
1994	A 1940's Radio Hour—Volume I				CD
1995	Opera Stars Sing on Radio—Volume II				CD

da Ponte, Lorenzo, 337
d'Albert, Eugen, 38
Dallas Symphony, 145
Damrosch, Walter, 10
Danler, Karl-Robert, 323
Dantons Tod, 237
Daphne, 202
Darcy, Emery, 91, 146
De Angelis, Fortunato, 46, 52, 53, 58, 104
De Angelis, Fortunato "Lucky," Jr., 12, 52,
    53, 268, 269
de Banfield, Raffaelo, 197, 335
de Paolis, Alessio, 65–66
de Reszke, Jean, 21
Dean, Stafford, 286
Death and Transfiguration, 315
Debole, Adriano, 281
Defrère, Désiré, 7
Del Monaco, Gian Carlo, 277, 278–79, 336
Del Monaco, Mario, 150, 276
Delius, Elisabeth, 73
Deutsche Oper am Rhein, 199, 206, 213,
    233, 261, 277, 307
Deutsche Oper Berlin, 233, 242, 307
di Bella, Benito, 280
Diez, Alfred, 183
Doe, Doris, 11
Domingo, Plácido, 87, 277, 280, 281
Don Carlo, 217, 330
Don Giovanni, 2, 133, 289, 328, 337
Don Pasquale, 328
Downes, Edward, 258, 269
Downes, Olin, 110
Downing Stadium, 51
Drew, David, 298
Durante, Jimmy, 10, 148
Dürrenmatt, Friedrich, 236, 237, 238
Dusenberry, Arthur, 160
Dux, Claire, 40
Dyer, Richard, 270

Easton, Florence, 47
Egk, Werner, 211, 301, 302, 328, 335
Eichendorff, Josef von, 300
Einem, Gottfried von, 236, 237, 238, 335
Elektra, 127–28, 129, 130, 155, 185, 189, 195,
    201–2, 203, 224, 225, 230, 241, 243, 242,
    250–51, 263, 268, 287, 307, 312, 316, 340
Eliot, George, 233
Epstein, Eugene V., 294
Erhard, Otto, 136
Erler, Lieselotte, 263
Ernster, Dezső, 146
Erpekum Sem, Arne van, 35
Eugene Onegin, 303
Evangelimann, Der, 39
Everding, August, 277, 278, 313, 317, 330

Fanciulla del West, La, 35
Farrell, Eileen, 92
Faust, 21, 137, 303
Fellner, Siegmund, 15,
Felsenstein, Walter, 181–82
Fidelio, 92, 94, 142, 177, 190, 199, 232, 233,
    234, 338
Fischer-Dieskau, Dietrich, 253
Fisher, Sylvia, 256
Flagstad, Karen Marie, 38
Flagstad, Kirsten, 6, 12, 37–38, 39, 43, 44,
    68–69, 74, 75, 80, 87, 98, 104, 154–55,
    159, 161–62, 164–66, 169, 343
Flagstad, Lasse, 38
Flagstad, Marie Nielsen Johnsrud, 38, 39,
    44
Flagstad, Michael, 38
Flagstad, Ole, 38
fliegende Holländer, Der, 79, 80, 83, 177,
    182, 191, 200, 303–4, 305, 328, 340
Flynn, Errol, 138
Folle de Chaillot, La, 198
Fontanne, Lynne, 237
Forza del destino, La, 84, 233

Fox, Carol, 134
Franz Liszt Academy of Music, 22, 23
Frau ohne Schatten, Die, 251, 252, 254
Freni, Mirella, 303
Fricsay, Ferenc, 175
Friedrich, Götz, 287–88, 289–90, 302, 336
Furtwängler, Wilhelm, 91

Galli, Hanns, 264, 317
Galli, Rosina, 74
Galli-Curci, Amelita, 47
Gambler, The (Igrok), 265
Ganci, Ralph, 56, 61, 78
Garbo, Greta, 56
Gärtner, Eduard, 21
Gatti-Casazza, Giulio, 73, 74
Geliot, Michael, 298
Genoveva, 156
Gentele, Göran, 267
George V, king of England, 37
Gergiev, Valéry, 322
Gershwin, George, 198, 332
Gershwin, Ira, 265
Gianni Schicchi, 307
Giehse, Therese, 237
Gill, Richard T., 269
Gioconda, La, 139
Gioielli della Madonna, I, 25
Giongo, Fabio, 206–7
Giordano, Umberto, 286
Giraudoux, Jean, 198
Giscard-d'Estaing, Valéry, 313
Glaz, Hertha, 146
Glazer, Si, 11, 189, 190
Glazer (Wagner), Valerie, 11, 189–90
Gobbi, Tito, 134, 307
Goebbels, Josef, 91, 119
Gogol, Nikolay Vasilyevitch, 328
Goldmark, Karl, 20
Götterdämmerung, 45, 81, 84, 85, 101, 145,
146, 149, 181, 183, 195, 200, 222, 239, 241,
256, 260, 284, 302, 330
Gounod, Charles, 303
Graf, Herbert, 2, 128, 146, 201
Graf, Max, 128
Gran Teatro del Liceo, 198
Grand Opéra de Paris, 199, 313
Grand Prix du Disque, 183
Graves, Robert, 128
Greindl, Josef, 201
Grillparzer, Franz, 300
Grimm, Jakob, 300
Gründgens, Gustaf, 155, 156–58, 206, 335
Grundheber, Jürgen, 43
Gui, Vittorio, 155
Gunnarsson, Torstein, 166
Gustav V, king of Sweden, 30, 36

Haböck, Franz, 20
Hagen, Holger, 40
Håkon VII, king of Norway, 36
Hall, Else, 160
Hall, Sigurd, 39, 160
Halvorsen, Leif, 34, 44
Hamilton, Edith, 128
Hamlet, 345
Hannevig, Christoffer, 35, 42
Hänsel und Gretel, 241, 275, 302
Harshaw, Margaret, 91, 146
Hartmann, Rudolf, 209, 210, 216,–17, 327
Hašek, Jaroslav, 261
Hawkins, Osie, 146
Hawthorne, Irene, 122, 123
Haydn, Franz Joseph, 238
Heidt, Winifred, 139
Heinrich, Rudolf, 294
Hendl, Walter, 145
Herbst, Otto, 277–78, 309–10, 311, 312, 322
Herlischka, Bohumil, 261–62, 293, 336
Hiemstra, Dr. Siegfried, 47
Hillebrecht, Hildegard, 227, 253

Maud, queen of Norway, 37
Maximilian II, king of Bavaria, 300
Maximiliansorden, 300–301
Mayer, Martin, 148
McArthur, Edwin, 163, 164, 165
McCarthy, Joseph R., 164
McCracken, James, 273
McNeill, Cornell, 297, 298
Medea, 130
Meistersinger von Nürnberg, Die, 68, 83,
    102, 169, 178, 328, 337
Melchior, Anna Hacker ("Kleinchen"),
    96, 97–98, 147, 160, 199
Melchior, Lauritz, 7–9, 10, 13, 34, 87, 91,
    95–98, 118, 147–48, 160, 191, 199, 232, 273
Mendelssohn-Bartholdy, Felix, 233
Mendelssohn-Hensel, Fanny, 233
Menotti, Gian Carlo, 133, 335
Merola, Gaetano, 54
Merrill, Robert, 273
Mertens, André, 86
Metropolitan Opera, 1–2, 13, 47, 48, 55, 56,
    67, 73, 74, 75, 83, 86–87, 91, 92–94, 95,
    96, 98, 104, 105, 108, 110, 111, 118, 119, 120,
    121, 122, 124, 127–28, 131, 137, 142, 145, 147,
    155, 156, 160, 172, 178–79, 180, 182–83,
    195–96, 198, 213, 221, 232, 254, 267–68,
    270, 271, 272, 273, 274, 276, 289, 292, 296,
    299, 302, 304, 322
Meyerbeer, Giacomo, 301
Midgely, Walter, 158
Mignon, 24
Milanov, Zinka, 133, 179, 321
Mingotti, Antonio, 253
Mitropoulos, Dimitri, 71, 107, 127–28, 155,
    202, 227
Mödl, Martha, 87, 156, 171, 180, 181, 193,
    200, 218–20, 220, 22,–23, 223, 227
Morel, Jean-Paul, 138
Morgenstierne, Wilhelm, 161, 163
Moscona, Nicola, 107, 137

Mozart, Wolfgang Amadeus, 180, 183, 198,
    237, 328, 337
Müller, Maria, 56, 176
Müssig, Siegfried, 244
Mussorgsky, Modest Petrovitch, 322
Muti, Riccardo, 284, 330

Nabucco, 328
Nationaltheater (Munich), 225, 254, 309
Neill, William, 296
Nelson, John, 270, 271
Népopera, 19
Neumann, Paula, 120
New York Philharmonic, 92, 121, 127, 268
Newman, Ernest, 271, 272
Nienstedt, Gerd, 294
Nikisch, Artur, 41, 71
Nilsson, Birgit, 87, 183, 218–19, 220–22, 223,
    284, 313–14, 315
Nimsgern, Siegmund, 296
Nougués, Jean, 19
Novotná, Jarmila, 2, 13, 65
Nozze di Figaro, Le, 11, 131, 328, 337
Nucci, Leo, 286

Ochmann, Wiecław, 287
Ödipus der Tyrann, 236, 237, 284
Offenbach, Jacques, 307
O'Gorman, Edward, 13
Ohm, Georg Simon, 300
Olheim, Helen, 11
Opéra Comique (Kristiania), 33, 38, 40,
    42, 43–44, 68, 72
Oresteia, 228
Orff, Carl, 235–36, 238, 284, 302, 303, 311,
    328, 335
Orphée aux Enfers, 307
Ostrovsky, Alexander, 265, 266
Otello, 24, 43, 46, 84, 212

Pagano, Salvatore, 282
Pagliacci, 21, 39, 277, 280